THE HANDOVER

The Handover

How Bigwigs and Bureaucrats Transferred
Canada's Best Publisher and the Best Part of Our
Literary Heritage to a Foreign Multinational

Elaine Dewar

BIBLIOASIS
WINDSOR, ONTARIO

FIRST EDITION

Library and Archives Canada Cataloguing in Publication

Dewar, Elaine, author
     The handover : how bigwigs and bureaucrats transferred Canada's best publisher and the best part of our literary heritage to a foreign multinational / Elaine Dewar.

Issued in print and electronic formats.
ISBN 978-1-77196-111-0 (hardcover).--ISBN 978-1-77196-112-7 (ebook)

     1. Publishers and publishing--Canada. 2. McClelland and Stewart Limited. 3. Consolidation and merger of corporations--Canada.
4. Consolidation and merger of corporations--Law and legislation--Canada.
5. Investments, Foreign--Law and legislation--Canada. 6. Canada. Canada Investment Act. 7. Book industries and trade--Canada. 8. Press law--Canada. I. Title.

Z483.M33D48 2017   070.509713'541   C2016-907946-5
                                                  C2016-907947-3

Edited by Daniel Wells
Copy-edited by Allana Amlin
Typeset by Chris Andrechek
Cover designed by Michel Vrana

Canada Council for the Arts   Conseil des Arts du Canada   ONTARIO ARTS COUNCIL / CONSEIL DES ARTS DE L'ONTARIO   50 YEARS OF ONTARIO GOVERNMENT SUPPORT OF THE ARTS / 50 ANS DE SOUTIEN DU GOUVERNEMENT DE L'ONTARIO AUX ARTS

Canadian Heritage   Patrimoine canadien

Published with the generous assistance of the Canada Council for the Arts and the Ontario Arts Council. Biblioasis also acknowledges the support of the Government of Canada through the Canada Book Fund and the Government of Ontario through the Ontario Book Publishing Tax Credit.

PRINTED AND BOUND IN CANADA

"For my friends, anything, for my enemies, the law."[1]

In Memoriam
For friends, colleagues, and ideas
on the other side of the grass

Contents

Beginnings and Endings

This is a story about the slow, secret murder of Canada's nationalist publishing policy.

After telling you that in the first sentence, I should probably just say Kaddish for this book before I write another word. In fact, one famous former Canadian publisher, Avie Bennett, said as much.

"It's a book no one will read," he said.

"I'm not writing one, Avie," I replied, which was true at the time.

I only planned to publish a blog post about how he'd managed to hand over McClelland & Stewart Ltd., Canada's longest-lived and best independent publisher, to a foreign entity, in spite of the *Investment Canada Act* which forbids same without government approval. It was a curious transaction that involved the sale of shares to Random House of Canada along with the apparent gift of control of the company to the University of Toronto. At the press conference Bennett gave at that time—late June, 2000—he'd said: "To achieve the survival of one great Canadian institution, I have given it into the care of another great Canadian institution."[2] The unwary believed he'd passed McClelland & Stewart (M&S) to U of T to have and to hold forever, that M&S would remain Canadian in perpetuity.

Wrong.

In fact, he'd created a brilliant method to free himself of the M&S albatross, to cash out while handing it off, piece by piece, to the largest foreign-owned publisher in the country. He'd found a way to get the federal government to declare this re-arranged M&S as "Canadian" in spite of the fact that its establishing agreements flew in the face of federal law and policy. That press conference actually signalled the slow-motion destruction of the nationalist publishing policy credited with making Canadian literature possible, a policy originated many years earlier just to keep M&S alive and Canadian, and the first step toward the submergence of M&S in the Bertelsmann media empire, headquartered in Gutersloh, Germany. By 2012, though the government kept saying the policy remained intact, foreign-owned companies dominated Canadian publishing and many independent Canadian publishers had bankrupted, were about to bankrupt,[3] or had been shut down. All that remained of M&S was its colophon—stamped anew on the spines of a few fresh titles each year and displayed on the website of Bertelsmann-owned Penguin Random House Canada. M&S now has a virtual life. Its name lives on though its corporate body has been subsumed within a foreign entity. The nationalist publishing policy, on the other hand, is just plain dead.

"I say that as a publisher," Bennett continued, as if I'd said nothing at all.

I'm sure Bennett is right. He has been spectacularly right about many things in the course of his long life. After all, who, other than the few people in the tiny Canadian book trade, would want to fork over real money for an inside baseball book about publishing? There is nothing more inside baseball—yet baseball free—than the story of how leading Canadian publishers of books and newspapers turned a policy created to protect them into a pale ghost.

And yet, though this tale is about a small industry that is shrinking like Alice,[4,5] it touches on much bigger issues, such as: the evolving idea of nationhood; how power really works in a country supposedly tamed by law; questions of identity we thought were put to rest but which have returned to bedevil us once more.

Canada's nationalist laws and publishing policies were born in the early 1970s, when this country was a rickety boat tossed on a sea of conflicts. Many in Quebec wanted a ship of their own. New rules and regulations were duly rolled out to counter what was happening on Quebec's streets. The hope was that it if Canada could become a richer, better country—a post colonial state—then perhaps

Quebecers would not want to leave. So: even as politicians and civil servants wrote laws that appeared to make Canadians the economic masters of our own house, they also negotiated free trade agreements to enrich that house through access to bigger markets, which made Canadians subservient to others peoples' rules. The result was contradiction and dissonance. On the one hand, Canada's national culture was protected by law and policy from foreign ownership, yet on the other, our borders were thrown open to investors from every corner of the planet. We touted cultural diversity as our strength even as we insisted that Canadian cultural products must be Made in Canada because our national sovereignty was at stake.

In the end, while sleeping dogs snored in public, hypocrisy went to work behind closed doors.

As I began work on this book, newly elected Prime Minister Justin Trudeau declared to the *New York Times Magazine* that Canada is a different sort of nation from all others. "'There is no core identity, no mainstream in Canada,' he claimed. 'There are shared values— openness, respect, compassion, willingness to work hard, to be there for each other, to search for equality and justice. Those qualities are what make us the first post national state.'"[6] He seemed to suggest that Canada is leading the way to a new political Jerusalem by becoming something never seen before—a state for which the usual norms of nationhood are irrelevant. I told my publishing friends to watch out, his statement signalled that change was on its way and they might not like its nature. But I also asked myself: was Trudeau right? Or was he dangerously wrong?

Among other countries, important ones, no such post nationalism was apparent. Instead, an old and familiar form had begun to climb back up out of the political dungeons of the 20th Century. Rhetorical flourishes from the Nazi period, including wicked words like *lugenpresse* and *volkisch*,[7] were being hollered at political rallies in Germany, Russia, Poland, Hungary, Greece, and would soon be heard even in the USA. Power was sliding from the grasp of a globalist old guard into the hands of those willing to say whatever it takes to win. China had set off on a course of old-fashioned nation building that included the creation of military islands in contested waters in the South China Sea. Russia had grabbed the Crimea and sent machines of war into Ukraine, allegedly to protect ethnic Russians, an argument all too reminiscent of Germany circa 1936. Waves of desperate refugees, fleeing from failed states in Africa and the Middle East to the borderless European Union, drowned by the thousands in the Mediterranean and the Bosporus. This made Europeans reconsider the virtues of fences. Britons voted for a bordered future. The Americans voted for America First.

The return of this old kind of nationalism is why I hope you will read this book even if you don't care about publishers, publishing, or those who make Canadian stories. The story I uncovered points to what can be expected elsewhere as legal walls go up and national borders are re-secured. I can say with assurance that these new rules will be turned inside out in short order, these new walls will soon be riddled with holes. The M&S handover makes that quite clear.

The M&S handover to a foreign owner was the direct result of laws and policies written to promote the opposite result. For a time, they worked as they were supposed to. For a time, they led to a flowering of literature about Canada by Canadians, some of it appreciated far beyond this nation's borders, some of it universal in its reach. But legal walls are like real ones: they call up great ingenuity from those with an economic need to circumvent them. Our laws and policies were soon hollowed out by those determined to advance their private interests, and by civil servants happy to assist.

In a way, then, the M&S story offers succor to those who argue that globalism is the future. Yet it also gives support to those who think a national culture is essential to sovereignty and security, and must be protected by law and practice. In other words, this M&S narrative has general application though, above all, it's a Canadian story, a story that could only have happened here. It demonstrates how Canadians wield power, how well-placed Canadians band together to do things forbidden to those who have none. It's about a smart, beloved/feared man who, seeking long-term redemption, teamed up with Canada's most able lawyers to get it; how a leading nationalist got around the rules shielding the sovereignty of the national mind.

It turns out that nothing could be more Canadian than that.

People who publish and distribute books in Canada have mythologized their business as a Social Virtue for close to 70 years. (In New York, they don't distinguish the book business from any other because in New York *all* business is Virtuous.) Books made in Canada, so long as they are not self-help tracts or cookbooks, are widely considered to be Good Things that any Right Thinking Person should purchase during the Holiday Season, the more the better. Civil servants who have doled out hundreds of millions of dollars over four decades to Canadian-owned publishing companies, in the form of grants and tax credits, take this one step further by adding the phrase "vital to national sovereignty."

On the Canada Council website, you can find (if you search hard) lists of Canadian-owned publishing companies that have been awarded many different kinds of grants to defend Canada's mental borders. The Canada Council's website has changed recently to reflect a new vision of who and what it wants to fund, but since the early 1970s, it has supported with public money things like author tours, the publication of literary fiction and non-fiction and its marketing and promotion. The Department of Canadian Heritage offers publishers support by various means, but especially from its Canada Book Fund—the Fund distributes about $39.5 million a year. Ontario, where two thirds of English Canadian publishing companies dwell, offers publishers grants from its own Arts Council. In addition, the Ontario Media Development Corporation administers another Book Fund and tax credits.

Yet Canadian-owned and controlled publishing companies are the endangered coral reefs in what federal civil servants call the publishing ecosystem. Reports on the publishing industry demonstrate that almost no Canadian-controlled publishing companies could survive without government aid.[8] In some circles, this tenuous existence is regarded as an inverse measure of social value which may be why owning the means to publish stories by Canadians has been treated as a cleanse by some who got rich through less laudatory means (such as manufacturing components for military vehicles or land development). Those in charge of handing out civic prizes, such as honorary degrees, Orders of Canada and of Ontario, have rewarded owners of Canadian publishing companies for their sheer endurance as they struggle to: meet payroll; assure whining authors that everyone interested *did* get a copy of their latest tome; explain why a third of the books they printed the previous year were returned unsold by the one dominant Canadian bookseller in the country (who gets a significant proportion of revenues from household goods and toys).[9]

I can't think of an industry with so little economic clout that is nevertheless so well-connected to the powerful. This connection could be described as transactional. On the one hand, Canadian publishers have a desperate need for government money which requires at least defensive familiarity with those who decide how much will be on offer. On the other hand, politicians need public platforms unsullied by voices other than their own. This perhaps explains the abundance of political memoirs written by people running for, leaving, or considering, public office.

Perhaps because funding is available, the number of Canadian publishing companies has been growing even as demand for their product has been shrinking: in 2013, there were three times as many Canadian publishing companies as there were 25 years before. (That number is expected to fall over the next five years.[10]) The number of Ontarians with full-time jobs in book publishing was about 1600 in 2012, but those jobs are precarious and the well-paid ones are the hardest to hang on to. Salaries are low according to an industry survey conducted by the trade publication *Quill & Quire* in 2013. That year, entry-level editorial staff earned between $25,000 and $35,000 a year while a person working as the president/publisher of a Canadian-owned company (half of which earn revenues of less than $1 million a year) was paid about $57,000. Their counterparts working for foreign multinationals earned about $138,000.

Multinational-owned publishing houses utterly dominate the Canadian publishing marketplace in spite of decades of support for Canadian-owned entities, and laws and policies aimed at changing that balance.[11] One foreign-owned entity—Penguin Random House Canada (PRHC)—has cornered 32% of the Canadian trade book market. (A trade book is one aimed at the general book buyer. Educational publishing is aimed at schools, universities, or specialists in their fields of knowledge.) This level of market concentration has drawn little attention from the Competition Bureau. Why? The Competition Bureau is mainly concerned about an abuse of market power that leads to rising prices for consumers. It doesn't appear to have investigated why retail prices for paper books have remained about the same over the last decade in spite of book unit sales declining[12] and in spite of the advance of smart and just-in-time technologies that should have made production, distribution, and marketing more efficient, and lowered costs. Yet such concentrated ownership does have a big impact on the diversity of ideas: two people[13] mainly dominate decision-making on what will be offered to the public by Penguin Random House Canada even as the rest of its staff play musical chairs for their jobs.

It should not be a surprise that just about everybody in the Canadian book business has met, worked with, or heard about everybody else. I can't think of a group whose members are more intimately entangled. Canadian publishers used to buy and sell pieces of each others' companies as they staggered to the edge of bankruptcy and back again. One market research firm believes that this consolidation phase is over and that any advantages from mergers have been squeezed from Canadian publishing.[14] Many employees who once had full-time jobs with some benefits must make do now with whatever freelance gigs they can patch together. They bounce from one bit of piecework to another, into the agency business and out again, carrying fresh gossip as they go. The result is that most people who work in Canadian publishing "know" far too much about their colleagues.

I put the word *know* inside quotation marks so you will understand that this is not nearly so reliable a form of knowledge as that required by the courts. To "know" in Canadian publishing circles means to gather tidbits about everyone else, the kind that make good stories. This should have made unearthing the facts concerning the central event in this book—the handover of McClelland & Stewart Ltd. to what is now Penguin Random House Canada—dead easy. Yet these facts remained extremely well hidden for fifteen years. When I asked officials at the University of Toronto (which owned the majority of the M&S shares for more than a decade), for information about this transaction, they behaved like witnesses to a gangland slaying. They knew *nothing*. No one still working at U of T who had anything to do with the initial gift, the management of the gift, or the subsequent sale of the University's shares to Random House of Canada, would submit to an interview or even answer questions by email. Others who signed the contracts involved and who did speak to me were unable to recall the most basic details, the kind that usually remain forever on top of business minds, such as how much money changed hands.

Yet publishing people *can* tell you what one famous M&S executive was paid—a remarkable $250,000 a year—because his former wife spilled the beans at a party. They will also tell you that a famous publisher threatened to withhold all future charitable gifts from a certain institution if that institution refused to do his bidding. (While he may have threatened, that famous publisher continued to make major gifts to that institution well after it failed to do his bidding.) They "know" these things because most of them (but not all, which is why this book is in your hands) live and work in Toronto, go to the same parties, restaurants, bars, coffee shops. They fall in love with each other, marry, fall out of love, whisper about who is sleeping with, or has slept with, whom. They fight, schmooze, hire, fire, and point fingers at this one's failure or that one's surely undeserved success. They can be kind, yet prone to snobbery which is usually defined as taste. They can be vain, yet appear as humble as an old shoe, especially when accepting an award on behalf of an author unable to attend a ceremony. They can be helpful and cooperative and considerate of each others' feelings, yet wily and competitive. Some are Canadian-born persons who have spent their professional lives producing the best Canadian books possible though they work for foreign-owned entities. Some are foreign-born persons who have spent their professional lives producing the best Canadian books possible for Canadian-owned companies. In other words, there are no villains here.

Some Canadian publishers say that Canadian book publishing is a glamour business. Well, one former publisher said so—Avie Bennett. This reminds me of that old joke about the man who ran away from home to join the circus.[15]

There are certainly a lot of parties, literary festivals, prize brunches, lunches, and galas that publishing people attend, if that's what glamour means. Some of these events are sufficiently well publicized that Important People like Hilary Weston and a Big Bank have bought naming rights. Consider that annual televised unreality show, The Scotiabank Giller Prize. Publishers who have brought forth nominated books get invitations. And they go, dressed in their best. They are seated at tables peopled with real celebrities and "people of influence" who are invited to attend the show in order to drag the public's attention toward Canadian writing. Nominated writers, on the other hand, have been known to appear at The Giller like so many Cinderellas in rented or borrowed finery. In 2013, some Canadian publishing people—Avie Bennett for one—got to attend a Nobel Prize Ball, thanks to Alice Munro's Nobel Prize, though McClelland & Stewart, the company that published a lot of her work in Canada, had by then become just another imprint owned by Bertelsmann SE & Co. KGaA.

This brings me to another fact about Canadian book publishing that should be better known. The industry's operating revenues amounted to about $1.7 billion in 2014, way down from over $2.1 billion in 2006.[16] Are you surprised to learn that only about seven percent of those revenues[17] were paid out to writers as royalties?

No writer will be. The average annual gross income for writers in Canada in 2015 was a munificent $12,879, which was 27% lower than their average income in 1998 (after taking inflation into account). It was $36,000 below the average income earned by Canadians in general. Female writers (the majority) made only 55% of what male writers earned. A similar pattern of decline in revenues and increase in the poverty of writers is evident in the US and the UK. This pattern parallels the intense worldwide consolidation of the publishing industry and the withdrawal of important copyright protections.[18]

I tell you these things so you will understand something of the world that Avie Bennett bought into when he purchased M&S in 1985, and which he washed his hands of fifteen years later.

Every public policy, like every person, has a history. Major public policies are usually born in the sunshine of a fresh political morning, the brainchildren of brand new governments. Such policies eventually die in the darkness of what former British Prime Minister Harold Macmillan is said to have called *"events, dear boy, events."* The birth of Canada's nationalist publishing policy was different. It was not a new government's splendid baby: it was in fact birthed by events, "on the fly,"[19] as one writer put it, a small part of the various policy responses to the dangerous events and electoral requirements of the early 1970s.

It was basically an add-on to a larger strategy devised by federalists shaken by the rise of radical separatism in Quebec. Small nationalist policies were offered to English-speaking Canadians as vaccinations against a more serious political infection.

By the late 1960s, nationalist ideas had become very attractive to the English-speaking boomer generation—a generation so large and volatile that it decided elections. English-speaking boomers (yes, I am one) were well-educated, ambitious, and utterly disdainful of the fear of ethnic nationalism and political radicalism ground into our parents by the Great Depression and World War II. We were both fascinated and repelled by the separatists in Quebec: repelled because they wanted to leave us, yet fascinated because their anti-colonialist ideas resonated. We weren't all the descendants of British immigrants emotionally tied to the Mother Country and the Queen: many of us had different roots, neither French nor English. We were fed up with being under the economic thumb of American multinational corporations whose decisions about investment, research, and development were made at head offices in New York or Chicago or Houston, leaving Canadians with dominion over nothing. And while we were no longer a colony of Britain, we weren't free of it either, and wouldn't be until the repatriation of the Constitution in 1982. We had become a comfortable Puerto Rico North, a resource-rich protectorate of the American Empire. As various government reports and commissions had made clear since the 1950s, about 30 percent of Canadian businesses were subsidiaries of American multinationals, and by 1973, a staggering 90% of Canadian oil and gas revenues went to the foreign-owned multinational oil companies known as the Seven Sisters.[20] Young

English-speaking Canadians wanted to change that, to become *maîtres chez nous* of a new Canada, if we could just figure out what being Canadian meant.

When I was growing up, English-Canadian magazines and newspapers constantly posed this question to their readers: what is the Canadian identity? Is a Canadian just a Briton without the class antagonism? Is a Canadian an American without the right to pursue happiness? French-speaking Quebecers knew who they were because they remembered themselves *en Français*, which made them marvellously distinct in a sea of *les maudits Anglais*. English-speaking Canadians shared a language with the Americans, the British, and the entire Commonwealth. With the exception of First Nations, we were immigrants or the descendants of immigrants. What cultural touchstones were ours alone? We remembered next to nothing about ourselves because hardly anybody wrote about us. The Americans next door, along with our former masters, the British, treated the Canadian book market as extensions of their domestic ones. Our textbooks and trade books were mainly written abroad. Our scholars and authors usually had to find a foreign-owned publisher if they wanted to get their ideas into the world. Pierre Berton's first book was published by a foreign-owned publisher: the same was true for Farley Mowat and W.O. Mitchell.[21]

In 1971, one year to the day after the FLQ Manifesto was read out on the CBC during the height of the October Crisis, Prime Minister Pierre Trudeau rose in the House to issue a counter manifesto. It was presented as a response to the recommendations of the Royal Commission on Bilingualism and Biculturalism published two years earlier, but everyone knew it was more along the lines of a counterpunch. Instead of Canada as a nation founded by the English and the French alone, Trudeau proposed an image of Canada much closer to the truth, a wonderful mosaic made up of people from the four corners of the earth. Our multiplicity of ethnic identities would become Canada's real identity, he argued, with no one group representing Canada.[22] Instead of the US melting pot model, we would encourage Canadians to keep hold of their ethnic differences, all of which would have equal value. This Multiculturalism Policy, as it was called, followed major changes in immigration rules which had opened Canada's doors to anyone with the right qualifications, regardless of country of origin, regardless of ethnicity and race. The leader of the Official Opposition and the leader of the NDP rose to support Trudeau. Everyone seemed to grasp the need to promote a diverse society over one based on French versus English identities. This determination grew more urgent after the *Parti Québécois* swept to power in Quebec in 1976. Referenda on the break-up of the country loomed. The idea of diversity as the central fact of Canadian culture would either hold the country together or drive it apart, no one really knew.

One thing everyone did know is that no one could create an identity out of a multiplicity of identities just by making a speech in the House. After the Massey-Levesque Royal Commission of 1949 to 1951 on arts, letters and sciences in Canada, policy makers in Ottawa had come to believe that English Canada's curious lack of identity was due to the absence of cultural mirrors. How could Canadians know themselves if they so rarely saw themselves reflected in stories, books, movies, songs, television shows, went the argument? And how could we see ourselves reflected if our cultural artifacts were made elsewhere for other markets? The CBC and the National Film Board had both been created with mandates to generate national conversations (in the case of the Film Board to make wartime propaganda films) so as to protect Canadian airwaves and film screens from an American cultural onslaught. Book publishing was different: Canadian publishing had been established early in the life of the country, yet by the time of the Massey-Levesque Commission, Canadian publishing had fallen on hard times. The first Canadian press, the Ryerson Press, was started in 1829, at around the same time and with the same purpose as Bertelsmann in Germany—to publish religious tracts. Then it began to find audiences with more secular works. Canadian publishing companies had done well publishing Canadian writers in the 1880s and done well again by producing patriotic books during World War I. Ryerson brought out 84 Canadian titles in 1930.[23] But while the publishing trade in Quebec grew rapidly during World War II, in English Canada publishers did poorly with Canadian authors. They relied instead on selling works originated elsewhere, and on educational publishing in which the number of buyers was guaranteed by provincial contracts.[24] Massey pointed out that the output of Canadian books had plummeted from that high point in 1930: in 1948, only 14 novels and 35 works of poetry and drama were published in English Canada by Canadian companies.[25]

The Massey-Levesque report led to the creation of the Canada Council in 1957 and the National Library of Canada. (The Commission found that more Canadian books could be found in the US Library of Congress and in other American libraries than in Canada.)[26] But getting more English Canadian companies to publish Canadian authors remained the hard problem. A state-owned book publishing company smacked of something the Soviets would do. The Canada Council only issued its first grants to publishers in 1972.[27]

Every trade book is a risky, stand-alone offering. Well known and successful authors produce books that fail, and in a market as small as Canada's, even a big success may fail to defray the costs of production, marketing and distribution. The problem was complex: how could Canadian-owned publishers compete with the foreign-owned publishers already active in Canada yet centred in much larger markets? The foreign-owned companies could amortize their costs over much larger sales in their much larger home markets. Foreign-owned trade publishers (as opposed to academic or educational publishers) active in Canada had no incentive to publish Canadian authors writing on Canadian subjects. How many US readers would want to buy a biography of Sir John A. Macdonald? Why would a British reader want a coming of age novel set in rural Saskatchewan? That's why book traffic moved in one direction only, from a foreign source to Canadian readers.

Canadian storytellers needed Canadian publishers willing to take the risks necessary to find Canadian audiences. But Canadian publishers could only make a go of it by acting as Canadian agents for foreign publishers, or, by printing textbooks ordered by provincial education departments. (For that story, read *The Perilous*

Trade by Roy MacSkimming.) It took the canniest and most determined of Canadian trade publishers, Jack McClelland, the owner of
McClelland & Stewart Ltd., to ignore most of these realities, to put
aside the profitable educational publishing business and concentrate
instead on finding and marketing Canadian authors of fiction and
non-fiction. By the early 1960s, McClelland & Stewart was the leading publisher of Canadian works, but every year was a struggle.

In 1971, McClelland realized that if he wanted his company to
survive, he had to attract serious support from governments. At
that point, there were no grants offered to publishers by any level
of government. McClelland & Stewart was in trouble: it was carrying too much debt, a hangover from doing too many books for
the Centennial Year, 1967, and McClelland's refusal of the offer of
a cash infusion from the Bronfman investment vehicle, CEMP, and
the McConnell family's Starlaw. The deal they'd offered would have
required McClelland to give up control.[28] Later, they'd backed an
M&S bank loan for close to $1 million with the Toronto-Dominion
Bank. He was having trouble paying it back.

He picked the time to make his pitch for help with great skill. John
Robarts, the handsome, fiery, and innovative Premier of Ontario,
had been replaced as leader of the Progressive Conservative government by former Education Minister, Bill Davis. In 1970, Davis had set
up a Royal Commission on book publishing due to concerns about
foreign textbooks flooding Canadian schools and the sale of the original Canadian publisher, Ryerson Press, and Gage, to foreign interests. Just as those hearings began, in February 1971, Jack McClelland
announced that he hadn't made any inroads on what had become a
$2 million debt. He said he needed immediate investment to the tune
of about $1.5 million or he would have to consider selling out—to
foreign interests.[29]

Jack McClelland was also a founding co-chairperson of the brand
new Committee for an Independent Canada. He'd been recruited
to the nationalist cause, along with Quebec publisher Claude Ryan,
in 1970 by M&S author and *Maclean's* Editor Peter C. Newman,
economist Abe Rotstein, and former Liberal Finance Minister
Walter Gordon. They were joined later by the Edmonton-based

bookseller/publisher Mel Hurtig and many others. The group had garnered 170,000 names on a petition which they sent to Prime Minister Trudeau asking the government to curtail foreign investment in Canada.[30]

Given the popularity of this new nationalism, and an election coming in Ontario that would turn on southern Ontario's boomer voters, those guiding the provincial government's re-election campaign decided that M&S couldn't be allowed to fail. Only one month after McClelland made his announcement, the Commissioners (one of whom was Dalton Camp, a leading Tory political organizer and a television personality) issued an interim report. They recommended that the Davis government should back a $962,000 ten-year debenture issue by M&S that would accrue no interest for five years and be convertible to shares, in order to keep M&S afloat. The Commissioners described the M&S publishing program as "a national asset worthy of all reasonable public encouragement and support."[31]

The Davis government accepted this recommendation. As Roy MacSkimming (to whom I am indebted for this material) put it in his fascinating history of modern Canadian publishing, *The Perilous Trade,* this ushered in

> ...a new era in Canadian public policy. Book publishing would no longer be regarded as a business like any other; it was a key cultural industry, producing what economists call 'merit goods,' things of intrinsic value to society that must not be abandoned to the mercies of the market. By throwing himself on the public's mercy, McClelland had judged the political mood with uncanny accuracy.

Davis's Progressive Conservatives won the election. In 1972, both the Canada Council and the Ontario government began to offer grants to Canadian publishers.

The Ontario NDP, like the Ontario Progressive Conservative Party, was greatly troubled by its own nationalists, a well-organized and noisy rump group known as the Waffle. The Waffle wanted Canada to nationalize foreign-owned oil and gas companies and to take back control of other key areas of the economy. It also supported an independent Quebec if Quebecers wanted out. James Laxer, one of the Waffle's leaders, had the temerity to run for the federal NDP leadership against David Lewis after Tommy Douglas was pushed to resign by Lewis's son, Stephen (who promptly ran for the leadership of the Ontario NDP). David Lewis may have thought the federal party crown would be his for the taking: after all, he had been the anti-Communist disciplinarian within the NDP from its inception, and before that for the international union movement, and the CCF. Yet the nationalist movement within the NDP was strong enough that Laxer didn't lose to David Lewis until the fifth ballot.[32]

Stephen Lewis soon organized the ejection of the Waffle from the Ontario wing of the NDP.[33] But that didn't mean nationalist ideas were ejected from Canadian politics. Southern Ontario had given the federal Liberals a great majority in 1968. But in the federal election of 1972, southern Ontario's boomers turned their backs on the Liberals: the Liberals returned to power as a minority—supported by David Lewis's NDP which had greatly increased its seats due to its campaign against corporate welfare bums. Lewis, who had almost been defeated by nationalists, promptly pushed Waffle-ish policies on the federal Liberals, starting with a demand for the creation of a national oil company.[34]

The Liberal Party had been split for many years between those who defined themselves as continentalists in economic and foreign policy, and those who styled themselves as independents or nationalists. Nationalists had been an unhappy minority until the Pearson years, but by 1968, they had begun to make gains.[35] The Canadian Radio-television and Telecommunications Commission was created to regulate Canadian broadcasting and communications. It set out a rule stipulating a required percentage of Canadian-made programs to be broadcast as a condition for licensing. In 1971, similar content rules on Canadian music were extended to radio. In 1972, American programs aired on Canadian television channels were required to be broadcast simultaneously so that Canadian television stations would get the benefit of Canadian advertising dollars. (Canadian periodicals eventually got postal subsidies and Canadian advertisers in those periodicals got tax benefits. Split run magazines—American magazines printed in both the US and Canada with American content but with Canadian advertising in their Canadian versions—were banned. Decades later, when that rule was defied by *Sports Illustrated*, foreign split run publishers were punished with a very high excise tax on their Canadian advertising revenue.)[36]

By late 1973, economic nationalists were gaining the upper hand in Ottawa. They got a boost from events. In August, 1971, President Richard Nixon had shocked the world by taking the US dollar off the gold standard, imposing a 90-day freeze on wages and prices, and a 10% surcharge on all imports—without notice to its best friend and largest trading partner, Canada. Then, after the 1973 Yom Kippur War in the Middle East, OPEC, the Saudi-led oil cartel, embargoed nations that had supported Israel, including the US, and cut production. The price of oil suddenly quadrupled, which drove up inflation while suppressing economic growth. The result was an economic malaise dubbed stagflation.[37] Worse, Canadians in Quebec and the Maritimes found themselves scrambling for winter home heating oil because Canadian energy policy and infrastructure had been configured for a continental energy market, not to protect Canadian security of supply. Most of the foreign oil that was available went to the American eastern seaboard first. Being Puerto Rico North was no longer comfortable at all.[38]

Canadian public opinion, especially among the university-educated boomers in southern Ontario, swung decisively to the economic nationalist side of the debate. Canadian boomers were outraged over so many things that the Americans had done or were doing: the Nixon surcharge; the awful carnage of the Vietnam War; America's presumed role in the overthrow of a democratically elected government in Chile;[39] the Watergate revelations which had been displayed for months via the televised US Senate Watergate Committee hearings.[40] Many boomers—me included—began to believe that a culturally, politically, and economically independent Canada was a really good idea. The one concern muttered out loud at dinner parties was this: what if the US marines came marching up Bay Street to protect their investments? The US had helped support Brazil's 1964 coup to protect American interests there, hadn't it?[41] The US had just helped get rid of Salvador Allende in Chile, hadn't it? How independent could Canada actually be?

In December 1973, the federal Liberal government, with the insistence of the NDP, threw a big nationalist bone to an angry (and fearful) electorate. It passed a law to create a government agency called FIRA—the Foreign Investment Review Agency.

FIRA was granted the power to screen all proposed acquisitions of control of Canadian companies by foreign entities. By April 1974, a few months before the next federal election, the new agency was in business. Though FIRA was aimed mainly at manufacturing and resource companies, Canadian-owned publishers were also protected by it. From 1974 forward, no Canadian-owned book or periodical publisher, or distributor, could sell control of itself to foreigners without permission from the Minister of Industry who could refuse to allow the transaction, or extract in exchange for that permission a significant benefit for Canada. Even indirect acquisitions of the Canadian subsidiaries of foreign-owned publishers were soon regulated by FIRA. Roy MacSkimming quoted the Minister of the day, Hugh Faulkner, who declared that: "The Canadian government believes strongly that the major segment of the book publishing industry in Canada should be owned by Canadians. Canadian books and magazines are too important to the cultural and intellectual life of this country to be allowed to come completely under foreign control, however sympathetic and benign."[42] Canadian companies were encouraged to buy control of foreign subsidiaries operating in Canada or to become controlling partners of the subsidiaries of foreign companies entering the Canadian market.[43]

On July 8, 1974, the Liberals were returned to power with a majority, winning back many of the voters they'd lost in Ontario and Quebec in 1972. David Lewis, leader of the NDP, lost his seat. The new nationalist policies of the government, along with the creation of FIRA, had proven to be vote getters for the Liberals, not for the NDP who'd promoted these policies first. Canadians embraced this Liberal form of nationalism, especially in cultural industries. We told ourselves this kind of nationalism was okay: after all, it wasn't based on ethnicity or religion, it wasn't exclusionary. Canadians come from everywhere: the stories reflecting us to ourselves would be multicultural too.

A decade later, the Conservatives came to power in a landslide, led by Brian Mulroney, the boy from Baie Comeau, Quebec. He had vowed to offer a friendlier attitude toward foreign investors, especially Americans, not that FIRA was ever much more than a paper tiger. "Canada is open for business again," is how the Prime Minister put it to 1,450 US executives at a dinner organized by the Economic Club of New York only a few months after he won the 1984 election. His government was there "to assist and not to harass the private sector in creating new wealth and the new jobs that Canada needs."[44] He also enticed a young political operative named Nigel Wright to leave law school at the University of Toronto in order to write speeches and work with his Senior Policy Advisor, Charles McMillan, whose assignments included reshaping Investment Canada, the new name for the old FIRA.[45]

The *Foreign Investment Review Act* and its agency were quickly renamed as their aims changed from holding off foreign ownership to encouraging it. Under the new *Investment Canada Act,* the Minister of Industry became responsible for making sure that certain new investments in Canada by foreign entities, or any shuffling of the ownership of foreign-owned Canadian subsidiaries, resulted in good things for Canada. The Minister got to review new businesses started by foreigners, and also the sale of Canadian businesses to foreigners, plus planned mergers between Canadian subsidiaries of foreign-owned companies. The real point of the new *Act* was to get net benefits for Canada from these sorts of transactions.[46]

But Mulroney was never so politically insensitive as to throw open the doors to foreign investment in cultural businesses. Foreign ownership of designated cultural industries remained off limits under the new *Investment Canada Act,* unless certain exceptional circumstances prevailed.[47] These rules applied to the entire publishing system, including the publication, distribution, and sale of books, magazines and newspapers.

Mulroney's *Investment Canada Act* forbade the establishment in Canada by foreigners of a new publishing company, or a new book distribution company, or even a bookseller, without the express permission of the Minister of Industry who would expect to see a net benefit for Canada. The *Act* also forbade mergers or acquisitions of the Canadian subsidiaries of foreign-owned publishers or distributors, even if they were part of larger transactions outside of Canada, without notification and ministerial review. Control of existing Canadian publishers, distributors, or even those stores primarily in the business of selling newspapers, books, and periodicals, could not be sold to a foreigner unless the Canadian company was in financial distress and no Canadians offered to buy it. Even if both of these circumstances applied, the Minister still had to review the transaction and extract net benefits for Canada before granting permission to proceed. And permission did not have to be granted.

The *Investment Canada Act* became law as the Free Trade Agreement with the US was being thrashed out in Washington's back rooms. The country was split on the virtues of the deal that Mulroney signed in his first term: the nationalists wanted no part of it, while continentalists were convinced it would make Canada wealthier, or at least save it from economic decline. The Agreement had to be ratified by both Parliament and the US Senate. So, in a bid for political support, well before the election of 1988, a new and even tougher nationalist cultural policy was announced. It was named after Progressive Conservative Prime Minister Brian Mulroney's hometown—Baie Comeau, Quebec. It was the brainchild of Communications Minister Marcel Masse, a Quebecer who took it as a given that any nation must have its own cultural life. Under this Baie Comeau policy, 51 percent of the shares of any foreign-owned publishing subsidiary in Canada acquired indirectly by another foreign entity had to be sold off to a Canadian entity within two years. Masse sold this new policy to his colleagues as a smart way to prove to Canadians that Canadian culture would be protected from the Free Trade Agreement, which required the same treatment for Canadian and US investors and industries in other areas.[48] The policy was politically astute: it defanged the arguments of the noisy and influential cultural community which worried that Canada's cultural gains, so painfully achieved under the *FIRA* and the *Investment Canada Act,* along with federal and provincial grants, would be swept away by an Agreement aimed at getting rid of protectionist practices, tariffs, and taxes.

The Baie Comeau Policy proved to be politically effective. Mulroney won the 1988 Free Trade election defeating the Liberals, led by John Turner, a former free-trade advocate, who converted to the nationalist side at the last moment, and for a time seemed close to carrying the day. The PC's pulled through with another majority, though their seats were greatly reduced, while the Liberals doubled theirs and the NDP won the greatest number of seats ever (until 2011). About two million more people voted against Mulroney and Free Trade than voted for them.[49]

The Free Trade Agreement was duly ratified. So was the North American Free Trade Agreement, followed by a series of other free trade deals including the most recent one with the European Union. In all these deals, Canadian cultural industries were allegedly, or at least publicly, kept off the negotiating table. Because: Canadian control of Canadian culture had proven to be the third rail of Canadian politics. No government could be seen to reduce that control without feeling the burn.

To recap the history: the first iteration of the nationalist Canadian publishing policy was nothing more than the guarantee of a small debenture by the Davis government in order to save itself from the nationalist fuss raised by Jack McClelland at the right moment. The second iteration was no accident, but cultural protection was not its main thrust. It was part of a much larger nationalist economic policy that helped Trudeau the Elder win back the votes of English-speaking nationalists in southern Ontario and Quebec, which he'd lost in 1972. The third iteration, the Baie Comeau Policy and the cultural provisions of the *Investment Canada Act,* allowed Prime Minister Brian Mulroney the political breathing room to complete the free trade negotiations with the US, quietly started by the Trudeau government years before, and to win a national election in which nationalism versus free trade was the central issue. The Baie Comeau Policy and the *Investment Canada Act* made it clear that Canadian culture would not be used as a bargaining chip in trade deals because Canadian culture is *vital to national sovereignty* in a way that softwood lumber could never be.

All iterations of this nationalist policy were rooted in the notion that Massey-Levesque had gotten it right, that Canadians could only develop a national identity if we could see ourselves reflected (in all our splendid ethnic diversity) in books, newspapers and magazines, on television and radio, in song, and on the stage. No such reflections would result if we had no means to help our artists find audiences or laws to prevent the Americans and the British and the French from flooding us with their offerings and buying up all our talent. Canada's evolving nationalist cultural policy embodied the belief that a country is built from words, images, and sounds, as much as from bricks, lumber, and steel, and that a shared culture is essential to national survival. Perhaps most important, this nationalist policy embodied the public will: there would have been no nationalist ownership rules if Canadian politicians hadn't believed that their political lives and agendas depended on them.

And so, Canadian book publishers became contractors building Canada. They became recipients of hundreds of millions of dollars in grants and tax credits administered with close attention by civil servants tasked with making the policy and the law work. The Canadian book publishing industry expanded its offerings from the miserable 14 novels and 35 works of poetry and drama produced in 1951. In 2014, according to Statistics Canada, Canadians produced 10,433 new titles.[50] That's a lot of mirrors.

Why the emphasis on publishers (and producers of film and TV and recordings), instead of on the artists who create those reflections?

Because, even as late as 1998 most Canadians did not have home computers,[51] and hardly anyone grasped that a global network called the Internet would soon connect everyone to everyone else across almost all national boundaries. Few policy-makers foresaw that this Internet would become a global territory where works of the imagination would be displayed, sold, or offered for free. Few (Avie Bennett was one of the few) understood that such a network would change all the rules of the cultural game, especially the boundary rules.[52] Even as late as 2008, writers, filmmakers, and musicians still could not get their creations in front of audiences by themselves:

they had to sell rights to publishers, producers, and record companies willing to invest in them and bring their works to market.[53] In spite of the rise of the blog, the availability of an endless array of online publishing formats, the success of Amazon, etc., the development of YouTube, Instagram, the whole Silicon Valley oeuvre, most professionals working in the book business still believe that unless the taxpayer bankrolls Canadian publishing companies, Canadian writers will be like so many fish out of water, gasping out their stories in quiet rooms, unheard.

And because of that, though Mulroney's *Investment Canada Act* has been amended over the years since the Baie Comeau Policy was announced, it has not fundamentally changed. In the last throes of the Mulroney government's political life, a new book policy was announced that was a lot like the old book policy. Liberal Prime Minister Jean Chrétien transferred responsibility for screening foreign takeovers in the cultural sector to the Minister of Canadian Heritage in 1999. The Conservative Stephen Harper government made a few changes to the *Investment Canada Act*: the federal government still reviews offers to purchase Canadian companies, but only if those companies have asset values greater than specific thresholds. These value-based and national security reviews were introduced after Chinese state-owned entities made one offer too many for vital oil sands projects. When it comes to cultural industries, especially publishing, the threshold value which kicks off a review is very low. In other words, the *Act* and the Policy still exist and still purport to protect publishing, and other cultural industries, from foreign ownership.

Yet on Canada Day, 2000, without public explanation or debate, Canada's nationalist publishing policy—dubbed the Book Policy in 1992—had actually been stabbed in the heart. That was the day that the U of T received the gift of 75% of McClelland & Stewart's shares while Random House acquired 25%, along with other more significant benefits. This transaction was the first step in the movement of control of M&S to a foreign owner. It was permitted by the very public servants who were supposed to make sure that control of Canadian publishing companies remained in Canadian hands. Only six weeks earlier, the civil servant in charge of such reviews in the

Department of Canadian Heritage—Michael Wernick—had testified to the Standing Committee on Canadian Heritage that Canadian control "of both publishing and the retailing sector is important to maintain," that it remained the government's policy, and that this policy had been successful.[54]

The knife had been inserted this way: the Liberal Government's Minister of Canadian Heritage, Sheila Copps, signed a Letter of Opinion that resulted in Random House of Canada agreeing to buy 25% of M&S's shares. The gift would not have been made without that sale, and Random House would not have bought those shares without that Letter of Opinion. The Opinion asserted that the Minister would still consider M&S to be a Canadian company after this transaction took place, and that her successors would be bound by that opinion too, unless the facts presented to the government to get the Opinion changed in a material way.[55] The issuance of this Letter led predictably to M&S's absorption into the global Bertelsmann publishing empire. Any senior civil servant who read the proposed contracts submitted for review by Avie Bennett's lawyers would have understood that if these transactions went through, M&S's transformation into another imprint in the Bertelsmann stable would be inevitable.

Yet at the press conference held to announce the transaction, Avie Bennett was praised repeatedly for his philanthropy and his foresight in giving control of M&S to U of T to hold for all Canadians. There were two rounds of applause to salute his "astonishing generosity."[56] University of Toronto's President, Robert Prichard, declared, in a University-issued press release/story, his admiration for Avie Bennett's "extraordinary commitment to the future of Canadian literature, one that utilizes the University as a trustee to perpetuate McClelland & Stewart's long-standing contribution to Canadian arts and culture." Margaret Atwood wrote a letter of praise. Michael Ondaatje described the gift as "remarkable." Three years later, this transaction was cited by the Governor General, Adrienne Clarkson, when she elevated Bennett to the highest office in the Order of Canada—Companion.

Since M&S had been the *sine qua non* for Canada's nationalist publishing policy, and even styled itself as "The Canadian Publishers," when U of T was permitted to sell its M&S shares to Random House of Canada in 2011, it marked that policy's last breath. The proof? Two years later, Stephen Harper's Minister of Canadian Heritage and Official Languages, Shelly Glover, approved Torstar's sale of Harlequin Books to Rupert Murdoch's HarperCollins LLC for $455 million. The *Investment Canada Act* provisions permitting such a sale were not met.[57] And no one blinked.

And now we come to the tricky part. I've spent most of my adult life working as an editor, journalist, and author—in other words, in the publishing trade. Canada's nationalist laws and policy, first *FIRA*, and then more explicitly Baie Comeau and the *Investment Canada Act*, allowed me to pursue what I laughingly call my career as a writer. So, I must declare that though I bring this narrative to you with a pure heart, it is nevertheless soaked in conflicts of interest and personal relationships. Good friends of mine work in the book business. I have had relationships with some of the companies, institutions, and people who played key roles in this story. For example: a few years ago I almost sold a book to McClelland & Stewart Ltd., but backed out because I didn't like their new contract. In addition, Random House of Canada has been my publisher on three projects, the first of which was very contentious and expensive for the company and from which a book failed to emerge, yet its officers and editors stood by me to the end. Its current staff, and its former publishers, editors, and Chairman, have my affection and respect. (For a list of my conflicts and entanglements, please read this endnote.[58])

Of course, it would be better all around if this story had been told by a reporter with none of these connections. But in the years since McClelland & Stewart, "The Canadian Publishers," ceased to be, no such person has stepped forward, though the M&S handover set off an under-the-table rewrite of Canada's cultural policies. Ten years later, hoping for a brand new political day, the Harper government did a more formal review of the book policy but backed away from acting on its findings.[59] Another rethink-and-renew process has been initiated by the government of Trudeau the Younger in the sunshine of its brand new political day. Everything is on the table, the

Canadian Heritage Minister Mélanie Joly, has said.[60] It might have been more honest to say that this has been the case since 2000, when the M&S gift/transaction got Ottawa's quiet approval. One of the law firms where Joly once worked (Stikeman Elliott) pointed this out on the law firm's blog in 2014.[61] The authors of the post advanced the theory that the policy had been dead for some time, itemizing each deal that went through ministerial scrutiny without a hiccup. They then invited foreign investors to consider making new forays into previously—but no longer—forbidden terrain, Canadian publishing.

Finally, burrowing into the M&S story showed me why it is dangerous to assume that vital laws are being enforced just because they are on the books, and why our access to information laws must be revised and the cloaking provisions in the *Investment Canada Act*[62] must be revoked. Thanks to Canada's remarkable and ridiculous propensity for treating matters of great public interest as secrets, flexible minds have found many ways to get around the public will without any of us being the wiser. Brilliant ways. Remarkable ways. You have to admire the cleverness, if not the result.

But, you ask, can you trust me to tell this story fairly?

You'll have to be the judge of that.

1

Citizens Beyond Suspicion

Any reporter can confirm that some questions are like the tide, they pull the unwary into a sea of a story from which there may be no return. Questions about one's own trade are particularly dangerous, but any reporter will also confirm that danger has the greatest allure. That's why that red flag waved at me by one canny Canadian publishing professional dragged me into this book. Blame him. I do.

It was spring, 2015. A federal election was coming. I'd been saying for some time to anyone who'd listen that Canada's national book publishing policy was dead: for one thing, in spite of hundreds of millions spent, and forty years of effort, the leading Canadian book publishing company had ended up in the hands of the foreign-owned mega-publisher which dominates the industry world wide. How did *that* happen was the question that kept coming at me. The reporter in me bellowed: find out! Good story!

But how? Many had tried, and many had failed due to the fact that the relevant documents remained safely hidden behind the secrecy rules of the *Investment Canada Act* and the *Access to Information Act*. Also, I was unnerved by the whiney person in the back of my head who kept whispering that any investigation in this area would finish off whatever was left of my career.

Nevertheless, that May I found myself hemming and hawing through what I told myself were just pre-interviews with people more knowledgeable than I am about the publishing business. I'll publish what I find where no one will read it, on my blog, I assured myself.

I did take note that those people who agreed to talk to me in those early days did not want to be quoted for fear of losing *their* livelihoods. But that was another good reason to inquire. Fear infests any marketplace dominated by a few big players who can squash anyone fool enough to make the wrong noises. In such circumstances, almost everyone walks very softly and carries no stick whatsoever. A dominated marketplace is an unhealthy one: didn't my livelihood depend on a healthy market for Canadian stories?

Still, it rattled me that those few who talked to me off the record had to screw up their courage even to do that. One agent I've known for decades refused to confirm even off the record that there had been a meeting of leading literary agents to consider the anti-competitive situation in which they found themselves mired. It was getting damned hard to sell book rights at reasonable prices, especially to the multitudinous imprints controlled by Penguin Random House Canada. In the past, its various imprints had competed against each other for agents' offerings. That's why earnings for agents and authors had been lush in the 1980s, reasonable in the 90s, fair in the 00s, but rarely any of the above in the last few years. The alternative buyers for bigger budget books in Canada were the two other Canadian subsidiaries of major foreign companies: HarperCollins Canada and Simon & Schuster Canada. Simon & Schuster was new and quite small. It had been permitted by the Minister of Canadian Heritage to enter the Canadian publishing business in 2013,[63] just in time to publish Prime Minister Stephen Harper's hockey book.[64] HarperCollins was shrinking. It had dispensed with its Canadian distribution warehouse business and the position of CEO, last filled by the legendary publishing executive, David Kent. No need for a Canadian CEO when distribution is moving to the US, said one of its executives without even bothering to explain how it could move to the US when the law forbids that.[65] As for the Canadian-owned publishers, they offered advances so low that an agent's share wouldn't keep him/her supplied with wine sufficient to drown sorrows, let alone pay staff and rent.

And then there was that former book editor, recommended to me as a possible source, who had been made to sign a non-disclosure agreement when let go from a job in a major foreign-owned publishing house. Why? It was hardly news that editors were losing their jobs. The publishers' announcements on that score appeared in email missives extolling the virtues of executives given new titles after corporate rearrangements—otherwise known as cutbacks. These notes made their way around the circuit with considerable regularity.[66]

In those early off-the-record interviews, I tried to pinpoint when Canadian book publishing began to collapse on itself like an origami version of a black hole. I knew that smart people had been running for the exits for the last few years, closing their publishing companies—sometimes ahead of the bailiff, sometimes not—leaving the agency business to learn a more useful trade, or setting themselves up in New York. Statistics Canada data showed that total revenues earned by foreign-owned and Canadian-owned companies combined had shrunk from $2.1 billion in 2006 to $1.7 billion by 2014. Things had gotten very tough after the recession of 2008: but the more people I talked to, the more the year 2000 seemed to have been the beginning of an ending. As with any black hole, first came concentration, then the implosion.

Concentration became intense in 2000 when Chapters, then the dominant bookseller in the country with more than about 65% of the market sewn up, set up a wholesale/distribution system called Pegasus and began to squeeze publishers for larger discounts.[67] After Christmas 1999, Chapters returned unprecedented numbers of unsold books to publishers while also holding back payments that had been owed to some for as long as two quarters. Several publishers were pushed to the brink of bankruptcy.[68] As these issues became public, Chapters' share price fell like a rock—from a high of $35 in early 1999 down to $7.95 by mid 2000.[69] All of this engendered a set of hearings by the Parliamentary Standing Committee on Canadian Heritage to find out what in hell was going on in book publishing. Few Canadians paid much attention, not even writers in the throes of finishing a book (such as me), possibly because the important information was imparted during *in camera* sessions by people afraid to rat on the big boy in public.[70]

The Committee published its report in June, 2000. I doubt many noticed that either.[71] However, the book world did pay attention on June 26, 2000, when the University of Toronto announced that Avie Bennett, the long-time owner of McClelland & Stewart Ltd., was donating to the University 75% of his company's shares and Random House of Canada was purchasing the remaining 25%. In a side deal, Random House signed a multi-year contract to market and administer M&S. A press conference was held to explain it all.[72] The gift/sale was scheduled to come into effect on July 1, Canada Day.

You had to admire Bennett's chutzpah. Who else would have had the nerve to sell a big chunk of "The Canadian Publishers" to a foreign-owned competitor on Canada Day, and give the rest to a university? On the other hand, the date might have been picked to keep the fuss to a minimum. There is no more forget-about-the-news-get-me-another-beer-day on the Canadian calendar than July 1. Most of the University's students and faculty were on vacation, on sabbatical, or just wallowing in the joys of summer. University of Toronto President Robert Prichard, who had advised U of T's Governing Council to accept the gift, became President Emeritus the same day. The new President would not take up his position until the fall. The paperwork to close the deal would be completed under the University's summer executive authority.[73]

The setting for the press conference conveyed an aura of great cultural authority.[74] It was held in the U of T's Simcoe Hall, a Federalist/Beaux Arts-style carbuncle on the faux Roman temple known as Convocation Hall. Simcoe Hall is the location of the University President's office and Convocation Hall is the site of many important cultural events as well as the bestowal of degrees.

It was made clear that day, and in the University's press release on the gift, that the University's Governing Council was the recipient of the M&S shares, not the University of Toronto Press. This was weird. The Governing Council, the University's ruling body, is not a publisher. The Council is made up of University officials along with faculty and student representatives, plus sixteen (out of fifty) worthies who are appointed by the Lieutenant Governor in Council—basically, the Premier of Ontario.[75] The Governing

Council of U of T is the kind of classy public vehicle which can advance the profiles of prospective and former politicians: an appointment to it is also a means by which big donors can be acknowledged, giving them a title to affix to their c.v.s like gold stars. The University of Toronto is, to put it mildly, a politicized entity, with only a narrow road separating it from Queen's Park, Ontario's seat of government. It was created and is ruled by its very own provincial statute. This is why any list of the outside members of its Governing Council reads like a Who's Who of the English Canadian business/political establishment (see who ruled at the time of the gift of McClelland & Stewart in this end note.)[76]

Avie Bennett, M&S's owner for 15 years, explained the whys and wherefores of his gift. He was getting on—72 years old!—and as his kids weren't interested in the business, he needed an exit plan, one that, according to the University's press release, had taken him five years to work out with U of T.[77] His problem was that the *Investment Canada Act* would not allow him to sell the whole company to a foreign entity, yet no Canadian companies had offered to take M&S off his hands.[78] According to one of my informants, who was present at the press conference (I was not), Bennett named Anna Porter, of Key Porter Books, and Jack Stoddart, controlling shareholder of Stoddart Publishing, General Publishing, and General Distribution Services, as Canadian publishers to whom he had unsuccessfully offered the company. Porter was an unlikely buyer, as Key Porter was a small operation by comparison to M&S, which was then publishing more than 100 books a year.[79] But by 2000, Stoddart's operation was the biggest Canadian-owned book publishing and distribution machine in the country, so that claim was taken seriously.

Only the year before, Stoddart had also been the dominant partner in Macfarlane, Walter & Ross (MWR), the publishers of Stevie Cameron's bestseller *On the Take* (about corruption in Mulroney's government), and the major non-fiction hit *Boom, Bust & Echo* by David Foot with Daniel Stoffman. *Boom Bust & Echo* would sell a remarkable 300,000 copies.[80] By 1999, however, MWR's cofounders—John Macfarlane, Gary Ross and Jan Walter—no longer saw eye to eye with Stoddart. They had asked him to sell MWR to McClelland

& Stewart. Stoddart did the deal with Bennett and got $1 million for his 51% of the company, even though he retained MWR's very valuable backlist. (A backlist comprises all the books published by a company to which it retains future publishing rights. A good backlist is a continuing source of revenue, in this case a continuing source of a lot of revenue.)

You had to ask: why had Bennett bought another publishing company even as he was devising his exit strategy from M&S? Was he trying to buy up the competition to make M&S more attractive to a buyer? If so, why leave the MWR backlist on the table?

If that question was raised at the press conference, no reporter recorded it. People seemed to worry instead about whether M&S would remain Canadian. Reassuring words were uttered by M&S's Publisher and brand new President, Douglas Gibson. Gibson was the long-time publisher of Alice Munro, so who could be more committed to Canadian literary culture than Doug Gibson? To much applause from those gathered at Simcoe Hall, Gibson praised Bennett's "astonishing generosity." In addition, Margaret Atwood issued a prepared statement lauding "Bennett's 'thoughtfulness, thoroughness, and integrity' and encouraging authors to feel confidence in the new arrangement," according to Roy MacSkimming, who wrote about the transaction in *The Perilous Trade*.[81]

Still, reporters asked what the deal meant for the independence of McClelland & Stewart, The Canadian Publishers, since Random House had bought a quarter of its shares and would handle its sales and marketing. And what about that law—the *Investment Canada Act*—forbidding foreign-owned companies from buying Canadian publishers without government approval?

Approved in advance by Ottawa, Brian Bethune of *Maclean's* was told.

And, Bennett explained, he'd chosen Random House to manage M&S's business because U of T's Governing Council is not a publisher and Random House is a terrific publisher, the ideal partner. Yet he insisted M&S's independence from the much larger Random House would be guaranteed.[82]

How? Reporters wanted to know.

The U of T's story on the gift pointed out that M&S would be overseen by a board of directors with five representatives from the University versus two from Random House. Bennett would represent U of T's interest as the new M&S board chairman. Douglas Gibson would also represent U of T on the board. Other citizens of sterling reputation would likewise defend U of T's interest. *Maclean's* named them as: former University of Toronto President Dr. John Evans, University of Toronto President Emeritus Robert Prichard, and Arlene Perly Rae, author, book reviewer, and wife of former Ontario NDP Premier Bob Rae. No one in her right mind would question their commitment to Canadian culture. *Of course* they would ensure that the University of Toronto controlled M&S, not Random House. "You have to be a real conspiracy theorist to see this board as a rubber stamp," Gibson told *Maclean's* Bethune.

But Bethune must not have been convinced, because he asked how long U of T had promised to hold on to its M&S shares, a critical question.[83] Douglas Gibson insisted to Bethune that the terms of the agreement required U of T to hold all of its shares for at least three years, and then only sell them in their "entirety" to another Canadian entity.[84]

In sum: the main thrust of the press conference was that Avie Bennett had done something amazingly generous. He had safeguarded M&S's Canadian-ness by placing it in the bosom of a great Canadian institution, one that would hold it close for many years to come. This long-term commitment was reiterated by the University's own story on the transaction, in which it described itself as a trustee to "perpetuate McClelland & Stewart's long-standing contribution to Canadian arts and culture." That word, perpetuate, seemed to suggest the University would hold M&S for a very long time.[85]

Yet questions nagged: how did a contractual requirement to hold the shares for three years fit with keeping M&S Canadian for many years to come? And didn't this gift/sale represent further concentration of the book publishing business, what with MWR and the children's publishers, Tundra, nestled within M&S, and with M&S now under the capable arm of Random House? And why would the government of Canada have had anything at all to say about this gift/sale? Random House had only bought 25%, while the University of

Toronto was given 75%, which satisfied all governmental requirements concerning Canadian ownership and control of publishing companies. In fact, 75% Canadian ownership and control was
then the requirement for a Canadian publishing company to qualify
for grants from the Canada Council. It is still the requirement for
any publishing company seeking grants from Canadian Heritage's
Canada Book Fund and the Ontario Book Fund.[86]

After the press conference was over, prominent people in book
publishing were asked for comment. Some expressed depression at
the declining state of the Canadian book industry. Some worried
that U of T might sell its interest to Random House piecemeal. Jack
Stoddart was much more blunt.

"I think it can be demonstrated very clearly that Random House
will have control of this company," he said.[87] So far as Stoddart was
concerned, he who controls the marketing and the money controls
the company, so Random House had been given effective control of
M&S, which violated the spirit of the law. In addition, he asserted
that Random House would now control 45% of the Canadian publishing market, which was far too high. Ridiculous, replied John
Neale, Chairman of Random House. He insisted Random House
only had 20% of the market before this transaction, and M&S had
9%, but that included its agency business which had been retained
by Bennett.[88] Other publishers told Bethune they admired Bennett
for extricating himself from M&S.[89] Kim McArthur of McArthur &
Company hoped the government would show similar flexibility to
other publishers who, as Bethune put it, are "all entombed in the
same velvet coffin. The federal regulations that protect them from
takeover also make it impossible for them to sell their companies."[90]

Douglas Gibson seemed particularly upset that these ground-
less fears and gripes were obscuring a remarkable gesture. "I have
never seen a gift horse have its teeth more microscopically examined," Gibson told *Maclean's,* sounding as though his own teeth were
clenched. "The point is the gift—Avie Bennett has made a generous,
imaginative gift that will keep M&S going as a Canadian entity."[91]

Usually when an important business changes hands and a press
conference is called to announce it, the sale price is the first thing

trumpeted. It's the way business people keep score. Yet nowhere in the contemporaneous press reports of the gift/sale, or even in Roy MacSkimming's book on the publishing trade published years later, was there information on how much Random House had paid for its 25% of M&S. MacSkimming, writing in 2007, said it was for an "undisclosed sum, rumoured to be large."[92]

Which made sense. M&S had published most of the authors whose works constitute the CanLit canon, everyone from Margaret Laurence to Alice Munro, from Michael Ondaatje to Margaret Atwood, Leonard Cohen, Mordecai Richler. It had also published major non-fiction authors such as Peter C. Newman, Pierre Berton, Farley Mowat, writers who had produced books about every Canadian subject imaginable. The M&S backlist will sell for as long as anyone is interested in Canadian stories.

Of course, as *Maclean's* also pointed out, Bennett's gift to the U of T would earn him a significant charitable tax credit, in effect a gift of cash or a reduction of taxes owed, courtesy of Canadian tax-payers. How much? *Maclean's* reported that estimates ranged up to $15 million, but no one knew what that number was either.[93]

The M&S story was pushed aside that July 31st by one which sig-nalled extreme concentration in another area of the Canadian reflec-tion business—newspapers. That day, Hollinger International Inc., the owner of the biggest newspaper chain in the country (and the third biggest in the world), put out a release saying it had reached an agreement to sell its Canadian chain along with several other media properties. This transaction concentrated Canadian media owner-ship to an unprecedented degree, one that David Olive, writing in the *Toronto Star,* described as unequalled in any other G-8 country. Some called it a danger to democracy.

Ownership of the Southam daily papers, including the *Ottawa Citizen*, the *Montreal Gazette*, major papers in Calgary, Edmonton, Vancouver, and Winnipeg, half of the *National Post* and a host of regional and municipal papers, was transferred, at the price of $3.2 billion, from two right wingers to a third.[94] Conrad Black and David Radler, who controlled Hollinger International Inc. through a holding company called Ravelston, sold these properties to Israel Asper and his family. Asper, a right-wing Liberal and a friend of Prime Minister Jean Chrétien, was the dominant shareholder of Canwest Global Communications, which already owned a Canadian television network and other media properties in Canada and abroad: this deal gave Canwest a huge voice in the Canadian marketplace of ideas just months before a federal election would be called.[95] Canwest soon insisted that all its newly acquired papers had to follow the editorial line emanating from its head office in Winnipeg. That editorial line was pro-Liberal, pro-Chrétien. Two years later, Canwest fired Russell Mills, long-time publisher of the *Ottawa Citizen,* for running an editorial calling on Prime Minister Chrétien to resign over the Shawinigan affair.[96]

And finally, just one day after the November 27, 2000 federal election returned the Liberals to power, the bookselling side of the cultural reflection industry imploded. Chapters became the object of an all-cash takeover bid from the owners of Indigo, the much smaller chain of booksellers. Publicly traded Chapters (234 stores) received an unsolicited offer for 43% of its shares from the main shareholder of Indigo (14 stores), a private company called Trilogy Retail Enterprises L.P.[97] Trilogy had already purchased 9.5% of Chapters' shares on the open market, so if Chapters' shareholders took up this offer, Trilogy would own 53% of Chapters and be able to merge it with Indigo.[98]

Trilogy was and is controlled by Gerald (Gerry) Schwartz, husband of Heather Reisman, the founder and chief executive officer of Indigo. Both had been leading Liberal fundraisers[99] and would be again. Nigel Wright, by then a lawyer with degrees from U of T and Harvard, and still an active Progressive Conservative operator, had also become a managing director for Schwartz's publicly traded equity investment company, Onex, and acted as an officer of Trilogy.[100]

Starting Indigo in 1994 had represented a distinct shift in Heather Reisman's career. A niece of Free Trade Agreement negotiator Simon Reisman, she'd grown up in Montreal and spent a short time at McGill before marrying and starting a family. After her marriage broke up, she worked with her brother to grow his IT company, and then became a business consultant.[101] Gerry Schwartz was introduced to Reisman by her boss when Schwartz came to Montreal on business. They fell in love. According to the arbitrageur Andy Sarlos in his autobiography, *Fireworks,* when Gerald Pencer, a Montreal businessman who had been one of Reisman's clients, bought the small financial services company Financial Trustco in Toronto, in 1981, Reisman became a director and Schwartz became one of Pencer's investors. When Schwartz created Onex, Pencer became one of Onex's lead investors. But after growing very fast on a diet of Drexel Burnham Lambert junk bonds, by 1988 Financial Trustco was in trouble. And things got worse that fall when reporter Philip Matthias revealed in the *Financial Post* that Pencer had once been a tad too close to the Montreal mob. A decade earlier, Pencer had given *in camera* testimony to the Cliche Commission about his friendship with William Obront.[102] Obront had been a money launderer for mobsters Vic Controni and Paolo Violi before his arrest in 1983 for selling massive amounts of Quaaludes in the US.[103]

Ed Clark (a former federal civil servant involved in devising the National Energy Programme and later, the CEO of TD Bank and advisor to the Ontario government) had just been brought into Financial Trustco as chairman. He proceeded to sell the company before it could be bankrupted. Pencer retreated to a family business, a practically moribund soft drink company called Cott Corporation. In 1990, Reisman became President of Cott Corporation. Thanks to deals made with President's Choice and Walmart, Cott soon became a major stock play. According to Sarlos, the share price zoomed up quickly from $4 to $60. Reisman stayed at Cott until 1992, but there was a small problem concerning her failure to declare, in a timely way, that she had sold some Cott shares. An offer to serve on a major business board failed to materialize, apparently due to her relationship with Pencer.[104] She resigned from the company just as Pencer brought in the former lead marketer for President's Choice, Dave Nichols.

It was two years later that Reisman decided to get into the book business. She heard that Borders, a US-owned big box bookseller, was interested in expanding to Canada.[105] She formed Indigo and, in 1996, asked the federal government to let Indigo partner with Borders. The government refused—the *Investment Canada Act* requires Canadian booksellers to be Canadian controlled.[106] This refusal was surprising given the social, political, and economic clout Reisman and her husband had by then accrued. Both were politically active Liberals, raising money, and in Reisman's case, offering policy advice to Ontario Premier David Peterson. Schwartz had taken on the job of bagman-in-chief for the federal Liberal Party when it was led by John Turner, raising millions to retire its debt. They later raised a lot of money for Paul Martin when he ran for the Liberal leadership.[107] Perhaps that is why the proposed Borders partnership found no favour in Ottawa. By 1996, Chrétien was watching warily as Martin, his Finance Minister, maneuvered to replace him.

Schwartz seemed to be an even less likely bookseller than Reisman. Book selling is a low-margin business. Schwartz had spent his adult life pursuing high margins. He grew up in Winnipeg, went to law school and articled there with Israel Asper, then a renowned tax lawyer. Later Schwartz went to Harvard Business School to get an MBA. While studying at Harvard, Schwartz met Bernie Cornfeld who gave a speech at the school's Speakers' Bureau, which Schwartz ran. (Apparently Schwartz also ran a number of small prairie businesses on the side.) Cornfeld was the founder of Investors Overseas Services, then the world's largest group of mutual funds, a money tsunami that would soon collapse. Schwartz spent one summer working for Cornfeld out of the IOS mansion in Geneva where, according to Peter C. Newman in *Titans* (to whom I am indebted for this material), very attractive women were made available to moguls who stopped by in search of a deal. According to Newman, Schwartz found this sort of behaviour repellent, but learned a lot from watching Cornfeld deal with major business people.[108]

After receiving his MBA, Schwartz went to work in the investment business in New York at Bear, Stearns Inc. There he had a desk beside Henry Kravis, who later became a founding partner of the legendary leveraged buy-out firm Kohlberg, Kravis, Roberts (KKR). Schwartz wasn't happy with the money he was making in New York, so he returned to Winnipeg in the late 1970s, and rejoined

Asper. Together, they created Canwest Capital Corp., which grew very quickly by making smart acquisitions. By 1981, Schwartz and Reisman had moved to Toronto. Schwartz began developing, along with other Canwest investors, the precursor to Onex.[109] But in 1983, Schwartz and Asper parted ways over the sale by Canwest of an insurance company, Monarch. Schwartz turned his full attention to raising money to create Onex, then a leveraged buy-out vehicle.[110]

Onex now owns and manages about $22 billion in equity investments around the world.[111] On its website it boasts a 28 percent internal rate of return. Schwartz is by far its largest shareholder, and owns all its multiple voting shares as well as 17.6% of the subordinated voting shares. This arrangement allows him to retain control of Onex no matter what.[112] He is both the President of the Corporation and its CEO as well as its board Chairman. Onex buys control of, reorganizes, and then holds or resells companies. Some are publicly traded, some are privately held. Onex also runs investment funds with partners. These funds buy shares of companies active in favoured lines of business such as real estate and casinos. Onex earns management fees and interest from these funds. Onex likes to say it has hundreds of thousands of employees worldwide, a number that governments certainly pay attention to, but it's less a direct employer and more like an octopus. Its managers control the boards which control the management of the companies it buys into. Onex employs a tight-knit group of managers based in Toronto, New York, and London.

The Onex way of doing business is premised on the notion that aligned interests lead to better outcomes. Its managing directors, directors, and associates (mainly men but lately several women) must invest their own money in the companies Onex invests in and which they oversee, as well as in Onex itself, so that their personal interests are aligned with their investors' and employer's interests.[113] They have to keep reinvesting fees earned until they have acquired at least one million Onex shares, which they must hold until retirement. Schwartz has said on the record that in searching for opportunity, he avoids risk and seeks control. He takes home a remarkable amount of money—in 2014 he was the highest paid CEO in Canada, earning $87.9 million through various forms of compensation.[114]

The board of Onex comprises very accomplished and powerful persons, including Peter Godsoe, former Chairman and CEO of the Bank of Nova Scotia, Robert Prichard, former President of University of Toronto, and Heather Reisman. Robert Prichard has served on the board of Onex since 1994, the same year Reisman founded Indigo.[115]

Trilogy Retail Enterprises LP., Indigo's majority shareholder, is located in the same Bay Street building and on the same floor as Onex.[116] Schwartz owns a lot more shares of Trilogy, and therefore Indigo, than Reisman does,[117] which suggests that Indigo has value beyond any dividends earned from selling books, toys, and pillows.

In November, 2000, when Indigo made its offer for Chapters, its CEO, Larry Stevenson, did not want Chapters to be taken over by Trilogy/Indigo or anyone else. He had very quickly built Chapters by acquiring other bookstore chains and had just set up his distribution warehouse/wholesale operation, Pegasus.[118] He fought back by appealing to the Ontario Securities Commission, alleging he needed more information about Trilogy/Indigo's financial situation, though they were offering cash. However, by early 2001, after failing to get the Ontario Securities Commission to stop the Trilogy offer, his strategy changed.[119] The two parties agreed to merge.

This merger would plunge the book-selling end of the English Canadian book business into the economic condition known as monopsony, a wonderful word that my word processor doesn't recognize but is well known to economists. It would eventually leave English Canada with only one big English language bookstore chain, a chain that also owned its own wholesaler/distributor and that had been demanding large discounts from publishers, dumping large numbers of books back into publishers' laps, and failing to pay for months on end.

The merger was therefore investigated by the Competition Bureau. After investigating, the Competition Commissioner took his concerns about it before the Competition Tribunal whose ruling is on the public record (except for the secret part that is still withheld).[120] Legal analysts of Canada's competition policies would later point out that the Bureau's investigation of this proposed merger is one of the very few instances in which the problem of monopsony has been addressed by Canadian competition authorities.[121]

Monopsony refers to the economic circumstance in which there is only one buyer in a market. That buyer can abuse its position because it controls the destinies of all its suppliers, in this instance, Canadian trade book publishers. Such a buyer can dictate to its suppliers the terms of trade, can demand outrageous discounts, and can hold back payments in order to squeeze better terms. Traditionally, the Competition Bureau has not been concerned with the abuse of suppliers, so it was interesting that monopsony became an issue. The Competition Tribunal that heard the case was led by Mr. Justice Marc Nadon, appointed to the Federal Court by Prime Minister Mulroney, and appointed to the Tribunal in 1998. (He was later appointed to the Supreme Court of Canada by Stephen Harper, only to have the Supreme Court rule that he did not have the specific qualifications required for Quebec appointees.[122]) The Tribunal ordered that several conditions would have to be met in order for the merger to proceed. Chapters and Indigo had to divest certain stores; refrain from building any new superstores for two years; and institute certain practices—a behaviour Code—for dealing with publishers, all under the eye of a Monitor. Terms of trade, including the size of discounts, returns permitted, etc., were included in the order and were to be in force for the next five years.

Reisman quickly invited respected persons onto the merged entities' new board. They included movie maker Robert Lantos, of Serendipity Point Films, formerly of Alliance-Atlantis (which Schwartz had invested in in 1994[123]), and Senator Michael Kirby, a very well connected Liberal. Nigel Wright, an officer of Trilogy, also became an Indigo director.[124]

Another instance of monopsony that drew the attention of the Competition Bureau a few years later also concerned Wright and Onex. It was the proposed purchase of Famous Players by Cineplex-Galaxy. At the time of the merger offer, in July, 2005, Onex controlled Galaxy, which had in turn bought the remains of Cineplex out of bankruptcy. Paul Martin, whose leadership of the Liberal Party had been supported by Schwartz and Reisman to the tune of $315,000,[125] was by then the Prime Minister of a minority Liberal government.

Martin's family had an indirect interest in the transaction. Nellmart, a family investment company that dated back to Martin's father's time in government, owned some movie theatre properties in Vancouver leased by Famous Players. The management of Nellmart was in the hands of Martin's sons.[126] The Competition Bureau's analysis showed that in some markets the purchase by Galaxy-Cineplex of Famous Players would result in the combined Cineplex-Galaxy-Famous Players entity owning 100% of the local movie theatres.[127] The purchase was permitted anyway though divestitures were required. Perhaps not oddly at all, Nigel Wright, still serving Trilogy and on the Indigo board, also managed Onex's interests in the movie screen side of the cultural reflection business.

Wright stayed on the Indigo board until April Fool's Day, 2006.[128] By then, Stephen Harper had become the Prime Minister of a minority Conservative government and the Indigo Code of Conduct was no longer in force.

By early 2001, five years after Amazon sold its first book online,[129] Chapters was under Indigo's control. But its newly achieved monopsony turned out to be a mixed blessing. Chapters had invested about $50 million in its wholesaler Pegasus, but it was an unmitigated disaster. In addition, foreign-owned Walmart, Costco and Toys"R"Us, had gobbled up almost 17% of the bookselling market.[130]

As Heather Reisman would tell the Standing Committee on Canadian Heritage in March, 2001, as the Chapters-Indigo merger proceeded she found herself holding the keys to a rotten empire. Pegasus, she told the Committee, was broken. "I can tell you, I have been in there for a month. I am very familiar with logistics...This facility is plain, ordinary broken. It does not work."[131] She had no idea how she was going to get unsold inventory out of there, whether publishers would accept books squirrelled away in unmarked boxes for more than a year as returns, or whether she'd have to dispose of them some other way.

Indigo staggered as it struggled to put two very different companies together and to deal with publishers according to the Code. It staggered again as technological innovation, the success of online selling through Amazon, the spread of the Internet, the great increase in speed of downloading, the rise of social media, the creation of ebooks, disrupted all media including the selling of paper books. Indigo continued to lose market share to non-traditional booksellers like Walmart and Costco, neither of which are affected by the provisions of the *Investment Canada Act* because selling books is not their main business.

In 2009, Indigo began to invest heavily in a new e-reader system called Kobo.[132] In January, 2010, Trilogy, its majority owner, sold two million of its Indigo shares to a Bay Street equity group with a US counterpart operation for a price not made public.[133]

In March, 2010, on learning that Amazon was asking for permission from the Minister of Canadian Heritage to set up a distribution warehouse in Canada, Reisman made it clear that something had to give with Canadian publishing policy. "Supposing I should decide three years from now that, in order to expand some of my capability, I'd like to partner up with a foreign company," Heather Reisman told the *Globe and Mail*. "I do not want to be disadvantaged."[134]

Perhaps it is just coincidence, but that same month, Prime Minister Stephen Harper called Nigel Wright at Onex and asked him to become his Chief of Staff as of January 1, 2011. He would replace Guy Giorno who would run the Conservatives' campaign in the coming federal election. Wright asked Schwartz for permission to take a leave of absence, and in April, he got it.[135]

In April, 2010, the Minister of Canadian Heritage, James Moore, gave Amazon permission to set up a book distribution warehouse in Canada. "This signals a government of Canada policy change confirming that a company no longer needs to be Canadian-owned to sell books in Canada," said Reisman to the *Globe and Mail*.[136] The Minister followed that decision with another that permitted Apple to set up an iBookstore in Canada. In July, the Minister and his department announced it had begun a review of the "foreign investment policy for the book industry" as one law firm's bulletin put it.[137]

Concentration in the newspaper side of the publishing business increased to the point of implosion in July, 2010, as the Canwest papers changed hands once more. Canwest had become insolvent, then bankrupt. That month, the corporate remains were sold to a group led by the *National Post's* publisher and prominent Conservative, Paul Godfrey. The price paid was $1.1 billion, the great bulk of it borrowed.[138]

Most of the money for the purchase was loaned to the buyers by a US hedge fund called Golden Tree Asset Management. Most of it went to pay off Canwest's creditors. Some newspaper watchers were concerned that the renamed and soon-to-be publicly traded Postmedia Network Canada Corp. Inc. would be eaten alive by the interest costs imposed by Golden Tree and end up in bankruptcy just like Canwest. Its assets could then be scooped by its creditors—such as Golden Tree. In effect, these critics argued, these loans gave a foreign-owned hedge fund effective control over Canada's largest newspaper chain. Yet the government did not interfere: it would have been hard to interfere. The actual ownership of the newspapers had moved from one group of Canadians to another. While Golden Tree Asset Management owned more than 30% of Postmedia's shares, the shares it owned had fewer votes attached than those of other share categories.[139]

By November, 2010, Nigel Wright was working in Ottawa, though his appointment would not begin for two more months. His leave of absence permitted him to keep his Onex shares and options earned over 14 years of service: his leave was to be for a term of two and a half years. This continuing relationship with Onex created ethical issues. Wright was examined by members of the Standing Committee on Access to Information, Privacy and Ethics[140] who were concerned about how he could run the Prime Minister's Office without resigning from Onex given Onex's reach across whole swathes of the Canadian economy and beyond. The federal conflict of interest rules also required a cooling off period for high level appointees upon leaving government. By taking a leave instead of resigning from Onex, Wright not only kept his wealth growing uninterrupted, he avoided having to endure that cooling off period. He explained to the Committee that the Ethics Commissioner and senior Privy

Council officials had instructed him on how to erect an ethical wall to prevent him from making decisions regarding his personal interests, which he had revealed to the Commissioner as required. He said his subordinate would keep certain files away from him. These were in the following areas: aerospace, special taxation, taxation in the Canadian private equity sector, tax deductibility. Wright insisted that in his experience, Onex had few direct contacts with government, so conflicts would be minimal.[141]

Certain committee members found that statement very hard to swallow. Some opined that there was no area the government of Canada overlooks in which Onex had no interests and there were at least 40 companies in the Onex kingdom whose interests were clearly connected to government departments, including cultural entities like "Cineplex and Indigo." Carole Freeman, BQ Member for Chateauguay—Saint-Constant asked: "Do you not find it odd that you are moving from the largest private corporation in Canada to the most influential position in the country, second only to the Prime Minister? It appears that your mandate will be relatively short, following which you will be returning to the private sector with privileged information and contacts, and that raises an ethical problem."

Mr. Wright did not find it odd. "I've sent a memorandum to political staff throughout government and through PCO, through deputy secretaries... I have asked that no information come to me that in any way relates to Onex or its business or the other areas..."

Still, Freeman persisted with her question. Given that Wright had asked to be kept away from such a lot of files, he would constantly have to recuse himself, so how could he carry on his Chief of Staff duties and advise the Prime Minister on key areas? Pat Martin, the NDP Member for Winnipeg Centre, put this most succinctly: "You can't even order pizza for the PMO... Onex owned CiCi's Pizza Parlor. Every move you make, every breath you take puts you in a conflict of interest."[142]

Nevertheless, Wright became Chief of Staff on January 1, 2011. By then, Indigo's monopsony had badly frayed. A graph of Indigo's share price shows a consistent pattern of falling and struggling back up, falling and struggling back. Its share price used to be about $20. In

2015 it had sunk to about $10. By 2016 it was back up to about $16. The federal election took place on May 2, 2011. Just before, Trilogy Retail Enterprises LP, Indigo's owner, sold a lot more of its Indigo shares, retaining only 51.78% of shares outstanding as of May, 2011.[143] Were Schwartz and Reisman anticipating a large Conservative majority, and thus a major change in the book policy? If they were, they were disappointed. Though the Conservatives won, their majority was small, several ridings' results hotly disputed. The NDP under Jack Layton had done so well they pushed the Liberals to third place and became the loyal Opposition. Not surprisingly, though the Harper government had consulted the industry on changing the Book Policy in 2010, no changes were announced. The Minister of Canadian Heritage proceeded as his predecessors had done, hands off the third rail, approving application after application, the exact nature of net benefits extracted from each deal approved covered up neatly by the secrecy provisions of the *Investment Canada Act*.

In November, 2011, the Minister approved Indigo's sale of its Kobo ebook publishing business to a Japanese company called Rakuten. The sale price for Kobo was $315 million.[144] The company was certainly not in trouble and apparently had not been offered to Canadians first, yet the deal went through.

And at the end of 2011, the Minister of Canadian Heritage permitted Random House to buy the University of Toronto's shares of M&S.[145]

Another not-for-attribution informant regaled me with book industry stories one hot spring day. We were sitting at a small table in a small coffee house named for a dead fascist poet. Soon my informant began to lay out his frustrations with the Canadian book publishing business, which in his view has stayed "stuck in the Medieval period." For example, while ebooks enjoy about 30% of the US bookselling market, in Canada the percentage is about 13%,[146] though that is just a guess, no accurate data is kept. There are no returns with ebooks, so you would think that small Canadian publishers, in thrall to a monopsonistic bookseller, would have gone heavily into ebooks by now. Yet most have continued to ship the bulk of their production as paper books at discounted prices, waiting for the inevitable returns. Why inevitable? Because: only the foreign-owned publishers can afford to pay for prominent display space in Indigo's stores. Publishers must buy marketing position for the books they want to push in the same way cookie manufacturers buy shelf position at Loblaw.

As another informant had already explained, once upon a time, the publishers of leading Canadian authors (e.g., Atwood, Shields) paid Chapters or Indigo a great deal of money for prominent table position for their new works. They spent a great deal too on other forms of promotion, buying newspaper ads, paying for big tours. In those golden days, Canada's booksellers allowed books to sit for six to nine months on their shelves before they were returned. Indigo shortened that period to about 30 days. Thirty days is not a lot of time for word of mouth to spread about a book, and word of mouth is the main form of advertising for Canadian books nowadays, unless an author is already well known, or wins a big prize. Thus, many books meet the fate described by philosopher David Hume when he bemoaned the reception afforded to his first, his *Treatise on Human Nature*. It fell "dead-born from the press without reaching such distinction, as even to excite a murmur among the zealots."[147]

Then, my informant got to his main point. He believed that since the final handover of M&S by U of T to Random House, Canadian authors had become window dressing for the foreign-controlled entities operating here, companies which make the bulk of the money they earn in Canada by selling brand name international authors published originally elsewhere.

To illustrate, he told this story. He had attended a party held by Random House of Canada about a year after it took full ownership of M&S in 2012. The occasion was the celebration of a big prize won by an M&S author—a writer born in Canada, so therefore a Canadian, but who had mainly lived elsewhere. The book had originated in New York, which is where an M&S executive heard about it. Canadian rights had not been sold, so the executive made an offer and M&S got them for a song. Yet at the party, this coup was being lauded as another Canadian triumph by Random House, with M&S's bird dog role in the background. This inspired someone to ask the

M&S people at the party why U of T had sold its M&S shares to Random House. One of the M&S editors had just stared and said nothing. Another said M&S was so deep in debt there was no other way out.

In debt to whom, my informant asked me rhetorically? Hmmm?

2

Hints and Allegations

On a blue-sky day later that spring, I found myself at a certain senior publishing professional's front door. He lives in a Toronto neighbourhood in transition, meaning caught in a class war. I'd been given his email address by an informant who demanded to remain nameless. Knows everything, I'd been told. Go see him.

I was still at the first stage in my research, just curious, just poking here and there, trying to figure out why I was so interested in the handover of M&S, why the story kept yanking at my knees like a hungry child. I had no inkling, then, that I wasn't just inquiring into the life and death of a publishing company and the national publishing policy. I was on the edge of a larger narrative about the way our politics work, about how control of what Marx might have called the means of reflection had been gathered in so few hands with such firm links to power.

A few blocks away, a well known author and his wife live in a beautifully renovated home on a 19th century street where Mercedes and Audis preen at the curbs. The city gardens there are small but perfect. This man's street was not so advanced in its rejuvenation. On one side, there was an array of painted row houses. On the other, an old woman who appeared to be fresh from the bars staggered up the path to her rooming house.

I could hear dogs breathing heavily behind his door. He'd warned me about them, but not about his incendiary views: perhaps that's why he too had demanded to remain anonymous.

As his dogs buffeted my knees, I made my way through the narrow front hall into a slightly down at heels living room which would have

been unremarkable in Bloomsbury circa 1935. It was designed for the
comfort of people who read, and who talk about what they read. A
deep couch and three upholstered club chairs were set around a circular coffee table, its tiered surfaces hidden by mounds of books and
marked up manuscripts. The dining room beyond glowed in the late
afternoon light. A majestic Edwardian sideboard shimmered behind
a gauze of dust motes. It was a home from another era, yet the man
in front of me was youngish, certainly younger than me. Dishevelled
hair; flushed, yet pale skin; a bit on the heavy side, as if he spent too
much time at his desk; clothes of no distinction and not artsy black.
One of his dogs flopped on my feet, demanding petting.

He'd responded to my first email with a digital screech:

Who are you? What do you want?

Who are you was a good question. Yet it was impossible to answer.
I'm too old to reduce myself to a few sentences. He could have
zeroed in more tightly on my political beliefs, but they are no easier to spit out. My understanding of things has been revised and
revised and revised again through the years. He could also have
asked if I think that Canadians need cultural mirrors to reflect our
shared multicultural identity, and whether such reflections must be
guaranteed by a national policy enforced by the State. What would
my answer be?

I think I believed in all of that while learning my craft as a journalist at *Maclean's* in the 1970s. As I sat in one of his club chairs trying
to figure out what to say, I remembered the exhilaration I felt when
I began my career there. We were making an ideological commons,
a home for stories that Canadians could immerse themselves in just
by picking up the magazine. Magazines are small countries. They are
always changing and evolving, they are both creative and reflective.

What do you want? It was an even harder question to deal with.

What *did* I want? I was painfully aware that the time I have left is
shrinking, and should not be wasted on stories that will be forgotten before they wrap the fish. Maybe this M&S story was much ado
about who cares.

I stuttered out some sort of answer. By contrast, he had no difficulty describing himself to me. Liberal, he said. He'd been a student of the works of both Hugh MacLennan and Louis Dudek, who had been teaching at McGill, just before the Americans took over the English department and these giants of Canadian literature went out the door. Everything he said marked him as a Canadian nationalist to the core.

We tussled for a bit over the current state of Canadian publishing. I said something provocative like: what's in it for authors anymore since we give up 90% of the take to booksellers and publishers who can't get our books reviewed, let alone sold? I told him I'd just self-published a book that had been bought but then offloaded by Penguin, and it had been an interesting experience and probably the way things will go in future. He asserted that self-publishing would never substitute for a Canadian publishing industry because it would never produce literature. He, as a publisher/gatekeeper, brings to his authors the years he spent at university training his mind, his tastes, and his methods, not to mention all his subsequent years of experience. This is why his authors' books get nominated for prizes, year after year.

Big deal, I wanted to say, what have prizes got to do with it? I've been on prize committees, I know how choices are made. But I held my tongue, because I decided I liked him. He was so certain, so passionate. I used to be certain and passionate too. Maybe that's why I confided in him as if explaining my present self to a younger version. I told him I was still kicking the tires on a story about the death of Canadian publishing policy beginning with the handover of McClelland & Stewart, but was finding it hard to clear a path through my entanglements. I laid them out, especially the problem of writing about Penguin Random House Canada, once such supportive publishers, now something else again. On the other hand, these changes were what had made me think this was a story I should tell. The publishing policy's story arc ran parallel to my own career as a writer. It had shaped me, it made my working life possible.

I explained that I started my career just as the policy was born. I was hired as a researcher and then editor at *Maclean's* when Peter

C. Newman was Editor. He was finishing the first volume of *The Canadian Establishment* and pushing—along with his publisher, Jack McClelland—for government support for Canadian storytelling, and especially for Canadian periodicals like *Maclean's*. By the time I got to work in the morning, Newman had been at his desk for hours, plowing through transcripts of his interviews as jazz blew through his headset. He was writing about the Canadian business elite as it then was, introducing the rest of us to those who had been running the country, often on behalf of foreign masters, for generations. His next volume would be about the people he called acquisitors who were poised to buy the old guard out, people I too found myself reporting on only a few years later. We—the more junior editors and writers on *Maclean's* staff—knew that our job was to discover, present, promote and critique Canadians of every sort, from politicians to cowboys to feminists, from musicians to writers to scientists, to give them platforms to propound their ideas, to shape national debates, to make sure there *were* some.

As I said these things out loud to my informant, I was hit by a wave of sadness. Too many of my colleagues from that time were no longer above the grass. They'd died, just like many of the ideas we'd shared.

One of my jobs at the magazine had been editing the book review pages and excerpting new books for the feature section of the magazine. I had excerpted a reissue of a non-fiction book written by Hugh MacLennan. I had also set up *Maclean's* first bestseller list at the behest of one of *Maclean's* more senior editors, John Macfarlane (who went on to a long career leading several national magazines and co-founded the publishing company Macfarlane, Walter & Ross). To create that list, I had to set up relationships with booksellers across the country who we could call once a month to find out what was selling. Remembering how tricky it had been to get that list going was why I found myself gritting my teeth whenever I opened the shrinking book sections of my weekend newspapers to scan their bestseller lists. These days there are two: one labelled 'Bestsellers,' the other, below, labelled 'Canadian.' While there is no text explaining the difference, it is pretty clear that the bestsellers lists record the books selling in the greatest numbers in Canada. While Canadian authors telling Canadian stories sometimes appear on the bestsellers lists, it is getting rarer. Lately, they mainly record the success of works originated elsewhere.

I told him that just looking at these lists made me feel as if we had come full circle, back to when Canadian meant *lesser.* Yet as I said these things, I wondered why I was making such a fuss. In my *Maclean's* days, no one pooh-poohed Canadian so-called literature more loudly than I did (only to be shocked to find that Alice Munro really is as great as everyone said). I read the books I sent out for review, and most of them did not appeal. Hadn't I gone to the trouble of getting a magazine job offer in Los Angeles as soon as my husband found television work there? We were thinking that L.A. is where we should be, because Canadian journalism, and Canadian film and TV, were patently inferior to what was produced down South. Hadn't I hunted up a New York literary agent? Would I have done that if I believed in the value of Canadian stories told to Canadians? And yet it was also true that when I wrote for a foreign audience, I found myself at sea. My touchstones were Canadian: my metaphors were Canadian; my context was Canadian. It was Canadian stories I wanted to tell.

All of this just poured out. As I listened to myself explain and contradict and explain again, I realized that the reason this M&S handover story would not let go of me was because it was personal. I didn't want to say that to him: reporters should avoid inquiry into that which is personal. So, I fell back on saying that I was troubled that the *Investment Canada Act*, though still on the books, seemed to be ignored, that the deals permitted were getting bigger and bigger. How come? A law is supposed to mean something, isn't it?

"You're right," he said. "I need to get my glasses so I can look at you. I see why you were sent to me."

He rose from his chair to go find them. He turned and wagged his finger.

"But be careful, be very, very careful," he said. Then he disappeared into the hall.

What in hell did he mean by that, I wondered.

He came back with his glasses perched on his nose. "You are treading where angels fear to tread," he said, wagging that finger again, lips pursed as he sank into his chair.

Never tell a reporter don't go there, because of course she will. Never tell a reporter that the people she is interested in are very dangerous, because she will have to throw herself at them to find out why.

He proceeded to tell me that the definition of a Canadian publisher had been adjusted after the gift/sale of M&S so that M&S, in spite of being bankrolled, administered, and marketed by Random House, could still qualify for membership in the Association of Canadian Publishers which represents Canadian independents. The requirement for membership had been 80% Canadian owned until 2001, he insisted, but then someone changed it to keep M&S on board. And, he added, there were friends of M&S in official places who had made sure that M&S got public money it wasn't entitled to. He'd tell me all about that later, he said. But first, he offered an anecdote.

In the summer of 2000, someone he knew at *Quill & Quire*, the book trade publication, told him that M&S was being given to U of T, and that Random House was to take over marketing and administration. There was going to be a press conference. He'd called up people at the University of Toronto Press, assuming they'd know more, only to discover that they knew nothing about it. They had "scrambled to attend" the press conference because they hadn't even gotten the press release. My informant went to the press conference too, with his boss.

He'd listened to what was said about Random House taking on the management of M&S's marketing and sales, while M&S's independence would be guaranteed by the creation of a new M&S board. "I said to colleagues at University of Toronto Press, it's a fucking lie," he said. Then someone, he couldn't remember who, asked Avie Bennett how this deal fit within the rules about Canadian ownership of publishing companies. Bennett, my informant said, replied that "he'd offered the company to Jack Stoddart and Anna Porter, and they had declined."[148] My informant knew Jack Stoddart pretty well. He'd heard nothing from Stoddart about any such offer.

He stopped. He looked at me, his eyes narrowed. You know Avie got a huge tax credit, he asked?

How much? I asked.

It was $15 million or in that realm.

Is that known, or rumour?

That's what he'd heard, he said. And from that, he'd figured that M&S must have been valued at a total of $45 million in order to justify such a huge tax credit. As I wrote down his claim, I did my own calculation. Since Random House had bought 25% of the shares, and U of T got 75%, if the $15 million tax credit figure was correct, then the value of the company must have been more like $20 million, not $45 million. I began to listen to him a little more skeptically.

So, he said, after the press conference he went back to his office and called up Jack Stoddart at his cottage. He'd asked him flat out if Avie Bennett had tried to sell M&S to him. "'You know better,'" Stoddart had replied. And then he'd called Anna Porter. "Anna said something along the lines of, 'Trust me, if I had been offered it, I would have found the money to buy it.'"

"Now flash forward to 2004," he continued. He was at the Canadian Booksellers Association convention. He was in a booth across the way from McClelland & Stewart's where there was a display of a book on ways to cook with pork fat. This outraged him.

How many Jews died so you could publish this? He'd hissed at an M&S colleague. His colleague told him to play fair, he said, with a sniff. "I thought I was," he said.

"What are you talking about?" I asked.

So he explained, and when he'd finished explaining, I checked. Not long after the 1998 purchase by Bertelsmann of the then-American-owned Random House (which had long since acquired Knopf and Doubleday and Dell, plus various other famous American publishing companies), ugly accusations about what Bertelsmann did under the Nazis during World War II were aired in the press. The general allegation was that Bertelsmann had greatly benefited from the Nazi State: specifically, the charges were that it had run printing plants with slave labour, and it had published millions of propaganda tracts and books for the Hitler Youth and the German army. An Austrian journalist named Hersch Fischler and American journalist John S. Friedman published these claims in *The Nation*—Fischler had published them first in a Swiss newspaper called *Die Weltwoche*.[149] Bertelsmann's official history said something quite different. It had been written by a man who had helped publish the fraudulent Hitler diaries in *Stern* magazine (owned by Bertelsmann). The official corporate history claimed that the company had been shut down by the Nazis in 1944 because it was a political thorn in the side of the Nazi state.[150]

In response to these claims, Bertelsmann decided to open its company archive to a group of independent historians, led by a history scholar at University of California Berkeley, Saul Friedlander.[151]

In 2002, the independent scholars published their 800-page report.[152] They had determined that Bertelsmann's war-time controlling shareholder, Heinrich Mohn, the father of Reinhard Mohn who by 2002 ran the foundation controlling Bertelsmann, had indeed printed millions of tracts and books for the Hitler Youth and the German army. Its contractors had made use of slave labour in Lithuania. In fact, the company, which had got its start in the 19th Century publishing religious materials, had thrived in Nazi Germany by publishing its propaganda. Heinrich Mohn had also been a donor to the SS. After the Allies invaded Germany, Bertelsmann had got back on its feet quickly because British officials were told that the Nazis had shut the company down in 1944 for political reasons. Bertelsmann was therefore given a license to get back in business. The Commission found the Nazis had indeed shut Bertelsmann down, but not because it was politically unacceptable. It was due to the suspicion that it was illegally stockpiling scarce paper.[153]

Ohmigod, I said. I had no idea.

Now my informant veered back to what he really wanted me to think about.

"Meanwhile, M&S collected millions from the Canada Book Fund, the Ontario Media Development Corporation, the Canada Council, the Ontario Arts Council."

What are you saying? I asked. Are you saying they didn't qualify for grants but got them anyway?

Yes, that's what he was saying. "And they got millions," he said again.

But the granting agencies only give money to Canadian publishing companies that are *owned and controlled* by Canadians, I said. The qualifying level of ownership for some of the programs in Ontario is 75% and M&S was 75% owned by a Canadian institution. Why wouldn't they qualify?

But was it *Canadian* controlled, or was it controlled by Random House? He asked.

In addition, he asserted, M&S had been, in his belief, over-funded by officials at the Canada Council who misapplied certain formulas in its favour. My informant had pointed out to officials that certain books published by M&S had been funded as if they were new, when they were in fact being reissued (new works earn a higher grant than reissues of books from a backlist), and that certain books had been funded as works of fiction (which earn a higher grant than non-fiction) when they were not, books such as *Canada: A Peoples' History*, he said. My informant had been irritated enough to file access to information requests about this which had produced documented evidence from the Canada Council that books that should have been treated one way had been treated another. When he pointed this out to officials by reference to the database recording the matter, an official "corrected" that database. And he was warned to back off or be cut off.[154]

Just go back to what you said before, I said, your allegation that M&S got grants it wasn't qualified to apply for. Explain that.

From the moment Random House bought 25% of M&S, he explained, it was well known that the company no longer had "its own bank account" and that Random House issued cheques on behalf of M&S. This, in his view, spoke directly to the issue of control. M&S's distribution was also moved to Maryland though books sold in Ontario must be distributed by Canadian companies. Canada, he said, had done a bad job of building institutions, which was a legacy of being a colony: only the Crown matters, he said.

He was suggesting that rules don't matter as much as they should in government agencies: friends matter more.

I asked him about the net benefit undertakings given to the Minister of Canadian Heritage when Random House bought

U of T's shares of M&S in 2011. And I asked about the undertakings made when Random House was allowed to merge with Penguin Canada in 2013.

"The undertakings are basically 'while you screw us, wear a condom,'" he said dismissively.

As far as he could tell, the whole publishing system, including enforcement of the national publishing policy and the *Investment Canada Act* had begun to go wrong after the Free Trade Agreement. "When the air is poisoned, so is the sealed room," he said. The government policy encouraged foreign-owned publishers already active in Canada to start publishing Canadian authors, and from that point, Canadian independents could not compete for those Canadian authors who found an audience. "Coach House [authors] were getting poached," is how he put it. His company's authors were getting poached too. He had tried to keep up and to compete. At one point, he made an offer on a new project written by a suddenly famous novelist who had begun his career with small Canadian independents. The most he could muster was $6,000. The advance offered by a foreign-owned publisher was $120,000. If the provincial governments bought Canadian novels for the schools, he said, instead of more famous American books such as Harper Lee's *To Kill a Mockingbird*, "I wouldn't need grants."

The more he talked, and complained, the more it seemed to me that the most dangerous thing he'd told me was that after the gift/ sale of M&S, it got grants it no longer qualified for because Random House controlled it. I asked again for clarification.

Not just a few, he said, but more grants than any other Canadian publishing company. He wagged his finger in time with each word.

Surely he didn't mean that, I thought. So I asked him again. Did he mean it?

He didn't answer directly. Instead he said the Chapters-Indigo merger should never have been allowed. Beware this person and beware that one, he said, tossing names around like petals, well-known names, names with many honours attached. A certain institution in town accepted gifts that were fakes, producing questionable tax credit receipts, he alleged. Even though there had been great difficulty getting a favourable opinion on the authenticity of one such gift, nevertheless, a gigantic tax credit receipt had been issued. He had information from the inside, he knew what he was talking about and he had voiced his opinion loudly at a dinner party. The person sitting next to him had taken umbrage, said he knew the man being defamed very well, who would be told, and my informant would be sued. No lawsuit ensued.

Are you saying that there's a practice among certain charitable institutions of letting big donors get away with things? I asked.

I was trying to get him to say something that I could check, a number, a date, something substantial, not just these hints and allegations. But whenever I pressed for details, he just offered another allegation.

Where can I check on these grants to M&S? I asked.

He said I should look up the annual grant reports published by the federal and provincial governments and I should ask the bureaucrats to help me get the facts and figures. "If you put it that you're writing a *success* story, they'll be all over you," he advised, bitterly.

How much money are you saying M&S got that it wasn't entitled to? I asked.

"It's millions," he said.[155]

3
Dragged In

I sat in my car scratching down phrases, words, descriptions. I was shaken: these allegations, these names he had thrown around—were these just rumours taken too far, or actual facts? Was this man trust-worthy, or not?

The character question bedevils reporters whenever a stranger hands over a ticking bomb in the guise of a story. Does the person saying 'dangerous, beware' actually know something? Is his judg-ment good, is he legitimately pointing to matters of public interest or is he trying to suck the world, via the reporter, into his personal quagmire? My informant was clearly smart, and knowledgeable, and committed to his work and his country, but he was also angry. Was his anger a character flaw or was it legitimate fury at the private manipulation of the public system? He'd declared himself to be a Liberal so there was no anti-State ideology at work. He approved of the rules enacted to protect Canadian publishing and publishers, and he approved of the grants and tax credits that keep them in business. He was no libertarian fixated on the evils of government, convinced that all who apply for help are fraudsters. Yet I found it very hard to believe that M&S had illegitimately gathered millions from govern-ment programs, and that civil servants had conspired to help.

You're supposed to be a reporter, I said to myself. So get down to it. Find out if he's full of crap or not.

He'd said I should read the government's own reports. Well that was easy. But I decided I should also check everything else about this story from the beginning, starting with the gift of M&S shares to the

U of T. I decided to check when it was accepted, by whom, whether there was any record of any tax credit receipt issued to the tune of $15 million, the lot.

I called University of Toronto Press to ask whether they'd been involved with the gift of M&S. The executive I spoke to confirmed that his colleagues at the Press had known nothing about the gift until it was made in 2000, and they still knew nothing of the details because the shares had been given to the Governing Council of the University, not to the Press. He said that records of Governing Council meetings are available. Perhaps I could learn more by reading them.

The good thing about my *alma mater*, University of Toronto, is that it puts up a good show of being transparent. The bad thing about University of Toronto is that when you dig beneath the surface, transparency can disappear.

The Governing Council's meeting minutes, and the minutes of certain of its committees, such as the Business Board, are available online, as are the University's annual financial statements.

I found the minutes of the Governing Council meeting when the resolution to accept the gift was passed. The date was June 29, 2000, only two days before the agreements surrounding the gift were set to take effect and three days *after* the University had issued a press release announcing it, which seemed odd. Why bother to hold a vote at all? I could see from the resolution that the gift had involved an agreement between four parties, the Governing Council of U of T; Random House of Canada; First Plazas Inc; and McClelland & Stewart Ltd. It was clear Avie Bennett must control First Plazas Inc., and that First Plazas Inc. owned the publishing assets of M&S. As part of the transaction, First Plazas had transferred ownership of some (but not all) of the assets of McClelland & Stewart Ltd. to a new company also called McClelland & Stewart Ltd. The University got 75% of the shares of this new entity. The 25% sold to Random House of Canada was not mentioned in the resolution, but it did refer to an agreement between McClelland & Stewart and Random House of Canada regarding "administrative services and financial support." I later confirmed that First Plazas Inc. retained the agency business by which the old M&S had acquired rights to sell books in Canada on behalf of foreign publishers. A few hours of Googling showed me that a few months after the gift/sale, First Plazas Inc. sold this agency business to a former executive of M&S,[156] Kenneth Thomson. Thomson renamed this business Stewart House Publishing Inc. and Stewart House Distribution Services which rented a large warehouse in Markham owned by the publishers Douglas & McIntyre. Stewart House also set up a US operation. But within two years, all facets of this agency business had gone bankrupt.[157]

The resolution mentioned that a summary of the terms of the gift had been given to the Business Board the week before and approved. It also gave the Council's permission for the University's President to sign an undertaking with the federal government in order to close the deal. Specifically, this undertaking was to be given to "the Director of Investigations, Investment Canada" but there were no details about what it entailed.[158]

So, I looked up the Business Board's minutes thinking the summary might be there. It was not. The terms of the gift had been discussed at an *in camera* portion of the meeting of June 22. The minutes of the next meeting of the Business Board, held the following October, referred to a question put to a university official, Michael Finlayson, then head of Human Resources. Would University of Toronto students be able to serve as interns at McClelland & Stewart, someone wanted to know. Finlayson had answered that the company was to be run as a business completely independent of the University. As I read those minutes, I found myself wondering: how could the University control a company run completely independently?

I turned to the university's annual financial statements. I thought that the value of the gift—75% of the shares of a company that published about 100 books in 2000—would likely be recorded there, if only in a footnote. And I thought the same would be true for the sale of those shares in 2011.

There was nothing recorded regarding the value of the gift of M&S shares in the 2000 report. I looked at the report for 2011. There were several categories under which earnings from the sale of those shares to Random House might have been listed, but there was no specific reference to the transaction, no footnote, no endnote. Maybe it was included in 2010, I thought. Or 2012? No. Nothing in those reports either.

So I sent an email to David Curtin, the Director of Communications in the office of Meric Gertler, President of University of Toronto. I also called and left a voice mail. Curtin responded that he had no knowledge of these events and so my request had been handed to a person named Althea Blackburn-Evans.

While I waited for Blackburn-Evans to respond, I asked a few knowledgeable friends about how gifts of a private company's shares are normally handled by charities such as the U of T's Governing Council. (These were not formal interviews, so I am not entitled to give you their names.) One friend, a lawyer with extensive experience as a donor and a board member in the charitable sector, was surprised to hear that the gift of the shares of a private company had been accepted by University of Toronto back in 2000. Due to the difficulty of establishing the value of a private company's shares, he didn't think such a gift was allowed at that time.

Well it happened, I said to him, are you sure it wasn't allowed?

He was sort of sure.

I called another lawyer who I've known for a great many years. He is very experienced in the ins and outs of donations made to charities, especially universities, having worked for over a decade at a large Canadian university to bring in large gifts.

He said that while it was definitely legal to donate the shares of a private company to a registered charity and get a tax receipt, it was rarely done. We almost never accepted gifts like that, he said. Too damned expensive, he said.

What do you mean, expensive?

Well you have to get one or two different opinions on share value from professional business evaluators, he replied. It can take months for them to go through the company with a fine tooth comb, and it costs a lot of money, and usually it just isn't worth it.

You're sure?

He was sure.

Oddly, the news stories about Bennett's gift had not mentioned such concerns. Yet if these knowledgeable friends were correct, at minimum this gift of shares to the University was very unusual. Valuation seemed to be the big problem, so I thought I'd better focus on that. How had it been done? Surely there was some place where the value of the gift had been recorded.

Usually universities are happy to publish the names of their big donors and the size of their gifts because it encourages others to give more. The gift of M&S shares was not anonymous: Avie Bennett had participated in a press conference to announce it and explain it. Yet no matter how I searched, I could find nothing in writing in Governing Council documents or the financial statements on the value of the M&S shares. I did find resolutions of the Governing Council appointing people to the board of M&S, and resolutions regarding the University's indemnification of these appointees against all manner of possible legal difficulties. I found a hint that the value of the shares was high in the minutes of the October 2, 2000 meeting of the Business Board. The total gifts and pledges to the University in sums greater than over $250,000 between May 1 and July 31, 2000, had been a great deal higher than normal. The man then in charge of big gifts, Jon Dellandrea, the University's Vice-President and Chief Development Officer, explained to the Board that the average total of gifts per quarter was between $7 and $10 million, but between May and July 31, the total had soared to $83 million. Dr. Dellandrea had been duly congratulated.[159]

Had the value of the M&S shares pumped up that number? Or had there been a whole lot of big gifts to honour Robert Prichard as he took his leave from the Presidency? Prichard had presided over a massive increase in donations to the University's endowment, raising a total of about $1.4 billion during the 10 years he was in office, a blistering track record.

Look up Dellandrea, I thought. He'll know what happened. He was so successful at raising money for U of T that he had been hired in 2008 by Oxford University in the UK to launch their $2.5 billion fundraising campaign.[160] I found him working his magic for Sunnybrook Foundation. I wrote an email, left a voice mail.

No response.

A reporter working on a story doesn't proceed sequentially, waiting for one set of questions to produce answers before proceeding to the next. We cast out our lines in various directions all at once. As I delved into the University's records, I also asked for information from both the federal and provincial governments about the grants they give to Canadian publishers. I started with the Department of Canadian Heritage and the Canada Council. Both the Department and the Canada Council make various kinds of grants to publishers, everything from support for interns, to grants for nominated authors to attend the Governor General's Awards, to export and translation grants. The Department hands out $39.5 million a year to 235 Canadian publishers, and the Council gives about $19 million.[161] Oddly, the Canada Council has a softer definition of Canadian ownership and control for grant-making purposes than the Department of Canadian Heritage. Heritage requires that recipients of its publishing support and publishing business support grants must be 75% Canadian owned and 75% controlled. To get Canada Council grants, a Canadian publisher must only "have its head office in Canada, maintain editorial control in Canada and be at least 75% Canadian owned." Editorial control is not the same as control as defined in the *Investment Canada Act*. When I asked a Council official what editorial control means, I was told it means that "acquisition decisions and editorial processes are controlled by the publisher."[162] I could see from the list of grantees on the Canada Council website that McClelland & Stewart, Tundra, and Macfarlane, Walter & Ross, had all received annual Block Grants, as well as grants for author promotion tours, etc. Macfarlane, Walter & Ross was closed down in 2003. But M&S and Tundra continued to be awarded grants until the University sold its shares to Random House in 2011.

I also asked for information about grants from the Ontario government. In 2005, Ontario began to issue Book Fund grants to publishers. It also certifies tax credits (with a cap of $30,000 per eligible book, only Canadian authored books eligible) through the Ontario Media Development Corporation. As well, it gives small grants to publishers through its Arts Council. Only Canadian-owned and controlled publishers qualify. However, the OMDC definition of control is rooted in section 26 of the *Investment Canada Act* which assumes that control lies with ownership of the majority of voting shares, though it also requires "control in fact," not just control on paper. Yet an Ontario publisher applying for a tax credit is also defined as Canadian according to the rules of the *Income Tax Act*—to be a Canadian publisher hoping for a tax credit, only 51% of the company's shares must be owned by Canadians.

I did a rough total of grants given to M&S and Tundra from the Canada Council's Block Grant and the OMDC Book Fund between 2001 and 2011. The Canada Council gave Block Grants to M&S and Tundra that totalled $1 million between 2001 and 2006, and $1,595,300 more for the period 2006 through 2011, for a grand total of $2,635,000. I had to appeal to an information officer at the OMDC to find out how much each Book Fund recipient was given as these figures are not available on the website. Ontario's Book Fund gave $547,046 to M&S and Tundra from 2006 to the end of 2011. Combined, the Canada Council Block Grants and the OMDC Book Fund grants came to well over $3 million. A rough total of author promotion grants to M&S and Tundra from the Canada Council came to another $100,000. I didn't bother with the Ontario Arts Council because its grants are tiny by comparison. It took a while, but eventually I got a list of Heritage Canada's grants to M&S and Tundra (with the help of an official and a new policy requiring it to make public its grants and contracts over $25,000). I wanted the totals for each year beginning in 2000. What I got was the amount given to M&S and Tundra between the third quarter of 2006 and the third quarter of 2011: in that period, Canadian Heritage gave M&S and Tundra $3,519,537.[163] Remember: Canadian Heritage has the strictest requirement for eligibility, grantees must be 75% Canadian owned and controlled. The grand total from both levels of government came to close to $7 million and that did not include tax credits, which are secret.

So my informant had been correct: M&S *had* garnered millions in grants after Random House began to manage it. M&S was entitled to the grants it got from the Canada Council, regardless of whether or not Random House controlled it. But when it came to the OMDC's grants and tax credit certificates, the entitlement was less clear. As for the Heritage Canada grants, the largest by far, if Random House had control-in-fact, M&S's entitlement was not clear at all.

Though press stories at the time of the gift mentioned that Bennett had received approval for the transaction from Ottawa, I could find nothing on the Canadian Heritage website to show that the Canadian Heritage Minister, Sheila Copps, had reviewed the gift/sale and approved it. I did find notice of Heritage Minister James Moore's decision to allow the sale of the University's shares to Random House in 2011.[164] But I could find no mention of the undertakings given by Random House which caused the Minister to conclude the sale was of net benefit to Canada.

So I inquired about those undertakings. I was informed by Harold Boies, the official in the Department of Canadian Heritage who presides over these matters, that undertakings are confidential—unless the company making the acquisition chooses to publish them. This confidentiality requirement means it is not possible for anyone outside government to track whether or not foreign investors are living up to the promises they've made, or, if the government enforces them.

So my informant was right about that, too.

I found Sheila Copps thanks to Google. She has a website. When I sent her an email she answered quickly. She was the Minister of Canadian Heritage from 1997 until she decided to run for the Liberal leadership in 2003. She published her second memoir with McClelland & Stewart in 2004. As an M&S author, I thought she'd surely remember if permission had been sought from her to do this gift/sale, not that I could figure out why anyone would have needed her permission. Besides, as Minister of Canadian Heritage in 2000, she had just acquired the responsibility for cultural industries applications under the *Investment Canada Act* along with a new power to determine whether a company is Canadian for the purposes of the *Act*.[165] If something had come before her, I was sure she'd remember it.

I asked Copps if I could talk to her about the M&S gift/sale to the University of Toronto and Random House of Canada.

"I don't think it happened under my watch," she wrote back. "What year?"

The summer of 2000, I said.

She suggested I speak to the man then in charge of book publishing policy in the Department, Allan Clarke. She thought he would know if the Department had made a decision about it. So I contacted Clarke, by then Director General in the Policy wing of the Department of Aboriginal Affairs and Northern Development. He remembered nothing about the M&S gift/sale either, but pointed out there is what is called a Chinese wall between the officials in the Department who handle the *Investment Canada Act* issues, and everybody else. In other words, secrets were kept even within the Department.

The fact that neither Clarke nor Copps remembered the transaction, though the University's Governing Council resolution had referred to an undertaking, puzzled me. So I re-read the resolution. It said that the President and/or the Secretary of the Governing Council had been authorized to execute instruments to affect the transaction, including "an undertaking by the University of Toronto *in favour of the Director of Investigations, Investment Canada.*" (italics mine)

Aha! I thought, the University of Toronto, not Bennett, had made some sort of pilgrimage to Investment Canada. But why? Responsibility for vetting foreign investments in Canadian publishing companies resided with Heritage Canada, and this transaction involved a Canadian publishing company being handed to a Canadian institution. Why would the University have to give any sort of undertaking to Investment Canada to accept the gift?

I contacted Investment Canada (whose name had changed by then to Industry Canada) for an explanation. I was told, to my amazement, that there is no such person as the Director of Investigations, Investment Canada and there had been no such official in 2000. Further, there was no undertaking by the University of Toronto relating to the gift of McClelland & Stewart shares found in the records of the Department. And yes, they double checked.[166]

Finally, Althea Blackburn-Evans, Director, Media Relations at the University of Toronto, got in touch. I explained that I had tried but failed to find a record of the sale of the M&S shares to Random House of Canada in the University's financial reports. Could she tell me where to look?

You won't find it in the annual report, she said. It was just a transfer of the shares. I only have the Random House [press] release, she said.

A transfer of shares? What does that mean? I asked.

She said there were huge financial issues.

Well okay, but what did you sell the shares *for*? Isn't every asset sale included in the University's annual report?

You won't find anything in the annual report, she reiterated.

She asked me to write her an email describing what I wanted to know. As I explained what I was interested in, she began to complain about how much time it would take to answer my questions. It was all in archives, people involved had left the University years ago, could I please specify who I am, and who I'm writing for.

So I wrote an email to her explaining I intended to publish what I learned on my blog or in a magazine, that I have been a journalist and non-fiction author for many years and she could look me up if she was worried about wasting the University's time. Then I asked the obvious questions. How did U of T value the M&S shares when they were first received by the Governing Council? What was the size of the tax credit receipt issued by University of Toronto? What voting rights were attached to University of Toronto's shares of M&S? I asked for a complete list of those who'd served on the board of M&S representing the University. I also asked again for the price paid for the University's shares by Random House in 2011.

But even as I typed the email, I remembered she'd said the shares were "transferred." That implied that no money had changed hands when the U of T's shares became Random House's. But how could that be? Surely a company with a backlist like M&S's must have been worth a considerable amount of money even if it had fallen on hard times.

It took almost a month before a short reply from Blackburn-Evans appeared in my inbox:

Apologies for the delay.

The University of Toronto is proud to have acted as a steward of McLelland [sic] & Stewart during a difficult time for the publishing industry as a whole.

We can confirm that we accepted 75% of McClelland & Stewart on July 1, 2000, and transferred our shares to Random House on January 10, 2012.

The University did not receive any financial compensation when the shares were transferred to Random House, given that Random House provided all of the financial support for period during which we held the shares.

As the shares were in a privately-held company, the university is not offering any specific details about them. The university used its ownership position to ensure the stewardship of the cultural heritage, but did not provide any financial support.

That was a stunning piece of news. "The Canadian Publishers" had passed from the hands of its steward to Random House for nothing! I couldn't understand it. The backlist would surely have been worth millions even if the company carried a load of debt, if that's what she meant by "financial support." And why was it under a load of debt when at minimum $7 million in grants and goodness knows how much in tax credits had flowed into M&S's coffers?

I had asked for the names of the directors who had represented University of Toronto on the McClelland & Stewart board. She had replied with a list of people she characterized simply as "the board of directors."

Avie Bennett, Chairman, Dr. John Evans, Chairman Torstar Corp., Mr. Brad Martin, COO and Executive V.P., director of sales and marketing Random House of Canada, John B. Neale, Chairman Random House of Canada, Ms. Catherine J. Riggall, Vice-President Business Affairs, University of Toronto, Ms. Arlene Perly Rae, Mr. Douglas J. Pepper, President and Publisher McClelland & Stewart Ltd.

This list did not distinguish Random House directors from U of T directors, and several names were missing, as I knew from reading the resolutions of the Governing Council appointing U of T directors. My list also included: Robert Prichard, former President of the U of T; Felix Chee, former Vice-President, Business Affairs at the U of T; Trina McQueen, former CBC public affairs executive, lately Adjunct Professor at the Shulich School of Business at York University and soon-to-be Vice-Chairman of TVO; Judith Wolfson, Vice-President International, Government and Institutional Relations at the U of T; and last but not least, Douglas Gibson, formerly Publisher and President of McClelland & Stewart Ltd. Yet when I asked about these missing names, I was told that "our records indicate that neither Felix Chee nor Rob Prichard were members of the board; they were not included on the board meeting membership or attendee lists."

When I pressed her to check again, she replied that they had not come up with anything further and could not without "extensive archival work."

I concluded that the University had decided to stonewall, or at least not to dig too deeply on my behalf. How else to explain its refusal to offer simple facts that should have been publicly known? When a charity like the University of Toronto's Governing Council issues a tax credit receipt, it means that the University has asserted to the government that a gift given to it has a specific value and the government should forego tax revenue in that amount, or, if no tax is owed by the receipt holder, should remit money according to that taxpayer's situation. The government uses charitable tax policy to advance charitable—as in *public*—purposes. And why on earth would the University fail to answer a basic question about the voting rights attached to the shares it owned? Why couldn't it produce a complete list of its own representatives on the M&S board? Why didn't it distinguish its own directors from those affiliated with Random House?

Yet Blackburn-Evans had managed to convey one bizarre fact. The University had decided that McClelland & Stewart, owner of the best Canadian backlist in the country, was without any value whatsoever when it re-gifted it after 11 years of "stewardship."

When M&S was handed over to Random House, "The Canadian Publishers," the point of origin for Canada's cultural policy, the recipient of millions of dollars in grants and tax credits from the public purse, was, as my grandfather would have put it, not even worth a mark on the page.

4

About Canadian Control

On the surface, the University of Toronto seemed to have acquired control of M&S when Avie Bennett gave it 75% of the company's shares—that's certainly what the word "stewardship" implies. Yet the University had hidden most of the basic facts about the M&S gift and its subsequent transfer to Random House. Why? Was it because its stewardship was *not* the same as Canadian control? The meaning of Canadian control is as variable as summer weather in Saskatchewan. As any prairie person will tell you, one minute it can be blue sky and sunshine as bright as a nickel, and the next the thunder clouds are rolling in on a howling wind. Similarly, under one statute, Canadian control can mean ownership of 50% plus one of the voting shares of a company, while under another, it can mean ownership of 75% of those same shares. Some *Acts* require that those who own 51% of the shares of a Canadian company must not only be entitled to a Canadian passport, but that they must also be Canadian residents. Example: your Auntie who lives in California and owns 51% of the family business means that your company is *not* Canadian when it comes to qualifying for a certain kind of tax credit. In other words, just as the rules for who qualifies for grants differ, the same company can be Canadian under one rule, and non-Canadian under another. Then there's the concept of de facto control (meaning control in fact) whose meaning has been articulated by various court decisions in various circumstances under various statutes. De facto control can be wielded by a minority shareholder in certain circumstances. That's why, as any commercial lawyer will explain to you if you can bear to listen, questions and answers about Canadian control depend on who is asking and in what context.

The more I thought about it, the more the M&S gift/sale began to remind me of business stories I'd covered in the 1980s and 1990s. One familiar theme was the suspicion that a minority shareholder actually controlled the company. Another was the sudden transmutation of valuable assets to worthlessness. For those readers too young to remember, or who were not yet born, let me sketch that raucous, big-haired epoch in which only business seemed to matter and old truths no longer seemed to apply.

Take money.

Money, if newly made, once interfered with social standing. But by the 1980s, new money had become the more interesting kind and those who made it acquired celebrity status. In Canada, and elsewhere in the Western world, political power was moving from the centre-left (those who thought power should be wielded by the State), to the hard right (those who wanted all power, along with profits, to remain in private hands). It was the age of Margaret Thatcher. (There is no such thing as Society.) It was the age of Ronald Reagan. (It's morning in America, so let's help the Contras take back Nicaragua from those Commie Sandinistas. Who cares if Congress said no? We don't need Congress's money: we'll use "friends" to trade illegal drugs for arms, and route and sell some of those arms to Iran, which is at war with Iraq and sponsors terror, and with whom we have no relations and we'll just dang well lie to Congress about all of it.)

The Cold War was fading away. Dictators in Latin America were losing their grip. Chinese officials were getting set to fly business class. Gorbachev's restructuring of the Soviet Union had transformed its creaky Communist kleptocracy into an oligarchic kleptocracy running a smaller state named Russia. One political scientist had the nerve to declare that we had arrived at the end of history. Switzerland's private banks bulged with stolen money—old Nazi loot as well as to up-to-the minute transfers from developing States into the private accounts of their leaders. Oil-producing nations were awash in riches. Canada opened its doors to those seeking safe haven for such gains. Come hither with your money, cried Canadian traders, you have to put it *somewhere*. Don't leave it in jurisdictions where there is no rule of law, where currencies can't be traded or where their values fluctuate with glorious Leaders' moods. Put it into reliable currencies, commodities, commercial real estate, or into companies with head offices in places more stable than Beirut, Cairo, Riyadh, or Moscow, companies whose shares can be publicly traded without too much scrutiny. Bring it to Canada![167]

And they did.

By the early 1990s, the new Russian oligarchs and their *Mafiya* friends were buying Canadian mansions, listing Canadian publicly traded companies (one with former Ontario Premier David Peterson on its board),[168] giving generously to Canadian politicians (one of whom, Paul Martin, was the Minister of Finance and would later become Prime Minister).[169] One night in Toronto's posh Bridle Path neighbourhood, shots were fired through a mansion's gates, an escalation of the war in Moscow for control of the new Russia.[170] Yet for the most part, the thing that made Canada such a fine haven for dubious wealth was that few outside this country paid attention to who did what and with whom behind that veil known as the Canadian border.

In the same period, control of Canada's widely held, publicly traded corporations was being pried from the hands of an old guard by a new one—by land developers, investment bankers, and media moguls. People who might not have had much to do with each other in an earlier period began to do all kinds of business together. For example: Onex Capital Corporation was set up in Toronto in 1983. Gerry Pencer's Financial Trust Company was the second-largest investor in Onex's first $50 million private placement. The largest investor was the public/private Canada Development Corporation, started by the federal government many years before to buy up foreign-owned resource companies active in Canada.[171]

Financial Trustco raised money through Drexel Burnham Lambert which sold its junk bonds to the unwary. The Lambert name in Drexel Burnham Lambert derived from a Belgian holding company known as Groupe Bruxelles Lambert. The Groupe's American subsidiary had merged with Drexel Burnham, a long-established

American brokerage house, in 1976.[172] Drexel Burnham Lambert soon acquired Canadian connections. For example: Groupe Bruxelles Lambert controlled an oil company called Petrofina S.A. Maurice Strong, formerly founding chairman of Petro-Canada, stickhandled the sale of Petrofina's Canadian subsidiary to Petro-Canada in 1981. The directors of Petrofina's Canadian subsidiary sold their shares into a market rising on rumours that Petro-Canada would make an offer (the correct price appeared in the newspapers long before that offer materialized).[173] There were accusations of insider trading, followed by investigations by three Canadian provincial regulators which went nowhere. Some time after that deal was completed, Power Corporation of Montreal (which had employed Strong, future Prime Minister Paul Martin, and many other political actors) bought a significant position in Groupe Bruxelles Lambert and then Petrofina S.A. Through its position in the Groupe, Power Corporation, controlled by the Desmarais family, also became large shareholders in Drexel Burnham Lambert. Paul Desmarais pulled back from becoming Drexel Burnham Lambert's controlling shareholder just before the company was charged with serious misbehaviour.[174] Drexel Burnham Lambert later pleaded guilty to three counts of stock manipulation, three of stock parking, and its former chief rainmaker, Michael Milken, was indicted for racketeering and securities fraud, pleading guilty to lesser securities and reporting violations. He paid a $600 million fine, was sentenced to 10 years in jail, and was barred from any securities trading for the rest of his days. Drexel Burnham Lambert ended in bankruptcy. But thanks to Paul Desmarais' decision not to invest another dime in Drexel, Group Bruxelles Lambert avoided disaster. The Groupe went on to buy a large chunk of Bertelsmann AG in 2001, shortly after 25% of M&S was purchased by Bertelsmann's Canadian subsidiary, Random House of Canada. Andre Desmarais served on the Bertelsmann board until 2006. Thus, Canada's most politically connected company came to enjoy significant influence over a European publishing company, which controlled an American publishing company, which controlled a Canadian subsidiary, which may have had effective control over Canada's iconic publisher, M&S.

And then there was a Delaware-based company called Barrick Petroleum Corporation. It was founded in the early 1980s from the merger of small US oil companies owned by certain Saudi investors, among them Adnan Khashoggi. The same investors owned a large portion of a Canadian subsidiary called Barrick Resources. Barrick Resources was led by Peter Munk, who would later transform it into the global mining giant Barrick Gold. At that time, Munk had newly returned to Canada from London and Asia where he'd partnered in resorts with Khashoggi, also known as an arms dealer and fixer for the Saudi royals. Barrick's investors included some of those Saudi royals, among them a former chief of Saudi intelligence.[175] By 1984, Munk had acquired a listing for Barrick Resources Corporation on the Toronto Stock Exchange. It was trading at $1.39 per share when Adnan Khashoggi came to Toronto with a huge entourage. He was wined and dined by the province's political and business elite, including former Premier William Davis, who hoped to interest him in other Canadian opportunities. As Marci McDonald hilariously recounts in *Yankee Doodle Dandy*, Khashoggi went to the Toronto Stock Exchange and made a public show of buying into the Barrick—on margin!— though he already owned a significant piece of it.[176]

Peter Munk was not Khashoggi's first Canadian partner. In 1977, Maurice Strong, then still chairman of Petro-Canada and the Canadian government's International Development Research Centre as well as a prospective candidate for the Liberal leadership, was invited to take over AZL, a US company Khashoggi controlled. AZL was a publicly traded conglomerate with African oil and gas interests, American cattle and land holdings, a commodity trading operation, and a bank. Khashoggi wanted Strong to take over because he was unable to be in the US at that time: he was avoiding a subpoena. Some US officials believed that the huge commissions Khashoggi had been paid by American manufacturers selling arms to Saudi Arabia amounted to illegal bribes paid to Saudi royals. The US Securities and Exchange Commission wanted to have a serious chat.[177]

With so much new money coming to Canada in search of safety and good returns, it is no surprise that several Canadian-based corporate raiders (Sam Belzburg, Israel Asper and Gerry Schwartz at

Canwest, the Edper Brascan group, commercial real estate developers such as Robert Campeau and the Reichmann family's Olympia & York Developments) began to strike terror in the hearts of CEOs everywhere. They bought publicly traded companies the way the rest of us might pick up a second-hand car. Toronto-based arbitrageur Andy Sarlos gathered blocks of shares for these clients as they went after mining giants, oil companies, distillers, utilities. So did Jimmy Connacher[178] through a company called Gordon Capital. Gordon Capital bought and sold blocks of shares, or entire public offerings in what were called bought deals. Acquiring control of a publicly traded company through the careful accumulation of blocks of its shares is a salami strategy: what one can't buy all at once can often be acquired piece by piece, especially if stealth is employed. Acting for groups of buyers cooperating with each other, Connacher's traders pulled in shares sufficient to gain control of target companies. Successful raiders then demanded seats on the target company's board commensurate with the shares (and votes) acquired. Old CEOs were dumped and new CEOs appointed to do their bidding.

Sometimes the point wasn't to own the company, but to shake it down—to make the company buy back its own shares at a high price. This was known as greenmail. First a raider accumulated a nice chunk of shares on the open market or in private deals with institutional investors. Then the raider would make a well advertised offer to buy the majority of the company's shares for a less-than-welcome price. The company's executives would either pay a big premium to buy those shares back, or, find a "white knight" to make a higher offer. Either way, the raider made money. Some takeover artists went after companies that would be worth more broken up than as going concerns. Most used leverage (borrowed money) to acquire shares, using the shares as collateral for the loans. If they won the bid, they'd sell off company assets and use the gains or the company's cash flow to pay off their lenders, often leaving wreckage in their wake. Those who got wind of planned takeovers could make fortunes if they were willing to ignore laws against trading on inside information. And they did. People working in places like Gordon Capital who knew that their company was about to execute a big trade could buy shares in advance at a lower price and make money selling their shares as their company's purchase drove up the market price. This was called front-running.

From the early 1980s until the harsh recession of 1991/1992, hostile takeovers of publicly traded companies were often front-page stories. As narratives, they had it all: fear, greed, white knights, black hats, raiders who lived so grandly that Gatsby was put to shame. Former Winnipegger J. Ross Johnson, CEO of RJR Nabisco (who tried to take over his own company but lost out to KKR) was reputed to have asked his secretary to "get me an inch of fifties,"[179] before heading out to shop in New York. He and his wife happened to be good friends with Prime Minister Brian Mulroney and his wife Mila who, according to author Stevie Cameron in her remarkable *On the Take,* also enjoyed shopping with thick envelopes of cash.[180]

Hostile takeovers were often adjudicated in the courts or by securities regulators. Some journalists turned themselves into minor Boswells writing books about these business 'warriors' who found fame to be a useful business tool. Raiders and traders had the ears of those in power because they contributed extremely generously to political coffers. Some also took care of politicians by offering them seats on boards when they were no longer in office. They knew each other, worked with each other, became mortal enemies of each other, married and left each other, just like publishing people. Some of them became publishing people.

The M&S story brought to mind a particular takeover struggle I covered, one that indirectly dragged me into the book business. It unfolded in 1985—the same year Avie Bennett purchased his first chunk of McClelland & Stewart.[181] It too was the by-product of insiders' maneuvers to get around inconvenient government rules. It, too, involved suspicion about who was in control of whom.

In January, 1985, Union Gas, one of eastern Canada's largest energy utilities, spun out a publicly traded holding company called Union Enterprises. Because utilities are essential, they have traditionally been granted geography-based monopolies. Because they are monopolies, they are overseen by regulators who allow them to earn reliable returns. In Ontario, by law, no shareholder was allowed to own more than 20% of a regulated energy utility. But the law was silent on whether or not the holding company of a utility could be majority owned by one entity. Because Union Gas enjoyed a steady stream of cash year after year, when Union Enterprises was publicly listed for trade, it immediately became the target of a takeover.

Union Gas was well connected to the ruling Ontario Progressive Conservative Party, which was about to lose power for the first time in 42 years. Within a few months of the takeover bid, the Conservatives would be replaced by a Liberal minority government led by David Peterson with the guaranteed support of Bob Rae's NDP. The Union Gas takeover was a business war with cultural and political implications.

The company that made the offer for Union was called Unicorp. Hardly anyone had heard of it. Its chairman, a dapper fellow named George Mann, had owned a smallish real estate/financial services company in Toronto years before, but had made a recent fortune in the US by buying real estate investment trusts, their value growing from about $40 million to over $400 million in record time. Unicorp's President, Jim Leech, had previously worked for Commerce Capital Corp, a company with newsworthy Liberal connections.[182] When Unicorp announced its takeover bid publicly, it had already acquired close to 30% of Union Enterprises' shares with the help of Jimmy Connacher's Gordon Capital and a $60 million line of credit from Continental Bank of Canada. Many shares were made available after Leech had conversations with certain managers of the Brascan/ Edper group which had been trying for some time to unload its Union shares at a price higher than the market said they were worth. When Mann offered to buy them for a combination of preferred shares and warrants of Unicorp, the deal was done in one day. Unicorp then made a public offering with the same terms.

This takeover bid was treated by Union as a boil on the body politic. It tried to lance it through appeals to the Toronto Stock Exchange, the Ontario Securities Commission, the provincial Cabinet and an obscure official in charge of the Business Corporations Act. It even bought Burns Foods (the same Burns Foods that had sued Gerald Pencer before he bought Financial Trustco) with new shares in order to dilute Mann's shareholdings.

Nothing they tried worked. So the Cabinet ordered the Ontario Energy Board to conduct a hearing, at which point the OSC held a second hearing, a secret one. The parties reached a settlement, but the OEB hearing went ahead anyway. The prime concern appeared to be, who is this guy George Mann? Who does he think he is to try and gain control of a great old Canadian utility?[183]

As reporters covering the story soon learned, control is a complicated issue that cannot be defined solely by reference to who owns the majority of a company's voting shares. Though George Mann owned the majority of Unicorp's shares, this question slithered through Bay Street brains: who controlled George Mann?

The Ontario Energy Board's counsel soon dragged out into the open the names of those who'd bought Union shares to offer to Unicorp. Many turned out to be entities belonging to, or allied with, the Edper/Brascan group of companies. Edper/Brascan was mainly owned by Edward and Peter Bronfman, cousins of the children of Sam Bronfman of Montreal, but run by Trevor Eyton, a well-regarded securities lawyer close to Prime Minister Brian Mulroney, and Jack Cockwell,[184] a South African-born accountant and extremely able strategist. Edper had been buying control of major companies for years, most notably acquiring Brascan, a venerable operation that made its first fortune building tramways and power stations in Brazil. When Brascan sold most of its Brazilian holdings, leaving itself flush with cash, Edper captured control through a tricky deal mainly executed in New York. At the time of the Union takeover, Edper/Brascan owned important positions in the mining giant Noranda, London Life, a financial company called Trilon, a developer called Trizec, 20% of a bank called Carena-Bancorp, plus a chunk of the Continental Bank which had provided Unicorp with its $60 million line of credit. By 1985, the Edper/Brascan group, along with another affiliate called Hees, controlled about $30 billion in assets,[185] $10 billion more than Onex controls now. The hearings made clear that the Gordon Capital people had called the Edper/Brascan people to find out which of the many companies they controlled might buy Union shares and tender them to the Unicorp offer. The takeover bid could not have succeeded without their participation.

One buyer of Union shares was a numbered company, 499977 Ontario Inc. Lawyers at the hearing demanded to know who owned it. Counsel to the OEB asserted that it was an unrelated party, so no name needed to be disclosed. Jimmy Connacher said the same thing in his testimony. But after a *Maclean's* story to the contrary, the OEB panel determined that there *was* a relationship between the numbered company and the Edper/Brascan group. The owner turned out to be Olympia & York Developments. O&Y's Executive Vice-President, Paul Reichmann, enjoyed a reputation for religiously inspired probity. While Eyton, Cockwell and Connacher had to give their testimony to the OEB in person (Connacher hiding his face from the press like a perp, Cockwell threatened by the head of the OEB panel that he'd better show up, or else), Paul Reichmann was allowed to give testimony by affidavit. Reichmann claimed that he had bought into the deal after George Mann came to see him because it was a good investment. At Reichmann's request, Connacher had bought $20 million worth of Union shares for O&Y's numbered company which were then tendered to the bid. Reichmann said that he did not feel connected to the Edper group or anyone else. However, he agreed that O&Y did have two people on the boards of Edper-controlled Trilon and Trizec. (That relationship went back to the 1970's.)[186]

In sum, the OEB hearings revealed an informal yet extremely powerful network that was reshaping the Canadian economy by methods subtler than acquiring ownership of the majority of a company's shares. I compared it to the Golem, a figure out of Yiddish folklore made of mud and dust that could be called upon to do its master's bidding in time of need, only to return to dust when its mission was accomplished. The players in this network, while independent, also moved in concert when it suited them, and it had suited them to deliver Union to Mann, one slice at a time.

The Unicorp takeover marked a turning point in Canadian business, a shift in social, political and economic power from the hands of the WASPs who'd been in charge in Ontario since 1793, to more recent immigrants, children of immigrants, French Canadians, Catholics, South Asians, Jews. The Jews included the Bronfmans, the

Reichmanns, Israel Asper, Gerry Schwartz, George Mann. All of this was deeply resented by some.[187]

So, who controlled George Mann? Most of Bay Street believed that Edper/Brascan did, especially after Mann kept Edper/Brascan people on the board of Union in spite of the fact that they had sold all their Union shares.[188]

And how did it drag me into writing books? After I published a two-part magazine story on the takeover, *Toronto Life* magazine asked me to do an exhaustive article about the origin of the Reichmann family and Olympia and York Developments. O&Y and its subsidiaries had begun to buy publicly traded companies, taking advantage of the former Liberal government's policies promoting the purchase by Canadians of foreign-owned assets, especially energy assets. The story of their early years in Hungary, Vienna and Tangier had not been unearthed. The project proved to be complex, fascinating, and it screamed non-fiction book.

By the time the magazine story was published in *Toronto Life,* in November, 1987, the struggle to manage M&S's debt had finally overwhelmed Jack McClelland. He and his investors had sold their shares to Avie Bennett. Yet the rest of the book industry was doing well, and growing fast. Agents were negotiating handsome advances for Canadian authors. The foreign-owned publishing companies that had previously been uninterested in Canadian writers were offering large sums for non-fiction books even to writers without a track record who had a story to tell, writers like me. Nancy and Stan Colbert sold the Canadian book rights to the Reichmann story, which I called *Absolute Trust*, to Random House of Canada, and the US rights to Viking in New York before the magazine story hit the stands.

The Colberts had refused a very good offer from an independent Canadian publisher, Lester & Orpen Dennys. They didn't believe the company would be able to withstand pressure if the Reichmann family took offence. It turned out the Colberts were wise. The Reichmanns did take offence. A few weeks after the magazine story appeared, several Reichmann family members and their company, Olympia & York Developments, sued me and my colleagues at

Toronto Life for libel claiming damages amounting to $102 million. Only a few months later, Lester & Orpen Dennys was in such dire need of fresh capital that it went looking for a buyer. Avie Bennett kicked the company's tires, but Louise Dennys thought he just wanted to buy the company so he could close down a competitor. She and Malcolm Lester sold the company instead to Michael Ondaatje's brother, Christopher, who bought it through his investment company, Pagurian Corporation.[189] Only four months later, Pagurian merged with Edper/Brascan's Hees International Bancorp. Ondaatje became Vice-Chairman of Hees, which had little interest in a break-even publishing company. Lester & Orpen Dennys soon withered on the vine. After it published Christopher Ondaatje's book, *Leopard in the Afternoon,* in the fall of 1989, Ondaatje turned his back on the company and Hees soon put it up for sale. In 1991, Hees sold its assets—its contracts and inventory—to Key Porter.

That same year, after too many legal motions, *Toronto Life* ran though its insurance money.[190] My colleagues and I agreed to a settlement, which included an abject apology. Random House of Canada accepted the loss of my book with grace and kindness. Not long after that, there was a major recession and a real estate crash. Olympia & York went into reorganization and bankruptcy protection in Canada, New York, and London, leaving its massive Canary Wharf project unfinished (until a Saudi prince came to the rescue). Banks around the world were left holding large outstanding loans. I got calls from foreign journalists who wanted an explanation: how had a multibillion dollar empire made of real buildings and publicly traded companies just gone poof?

Over-leveraged, I said. Assets declining in value, loans made on trust instead of close perusals of the books, a grander version of the eldest Reichmann brothers' problems in Morocco and Montreal in the late 1960's.[191]

Edper/Brascan's real estate empire came a-cropper too: control of Trizec was later bought by Peter Munk.[192]

It was all that business history still living in my head that made me wonder: could there have been an unwritten understanding between University of Toronto, Avie Bennett, and Random House that gave

Random House effective control of M&S? My informant thought so. Jack Stoddart thought so, too. There was a certain logic to it: why else would Random House buy a minority interest in a Canadian publishing company better known for discomfiting politicians at election time than sending dividend cheques to investors? It certainly wasn't a case of buying the competition to shut it down, as Louise Dennys had feared when Bennett made an offer for Lester & Orpen Dennys. M&S had continued on for 11 years.

But then I found myself thinking about it from Avie Bennett's side. Why had Bennett—a vociferous nationalist—decided to sell even a part of M&S to foreign-owned Random House? U of T could have signed a management agreement with Random House or another publisher to run the company. Why hadn't Bennett just given all of it to U of T?

I raised this question with my husband at the kitchen table one day. Clever husband instantly replied that Bennett needed Random House to buy M&S shares to put a market value on the gift. No market value, no tax credit.

Well that explains what Avie Bennett wanted, I said, but what did U of T get?

He had no answer. Neither did I.

5
When in Doubt, Ask

You will not be surprised to learn that I've known Douglas Gibson, renowned editor, and former Publisher and President of McClelland & Stewart, for years. Who better to tell me whether Random House effectively controlled M&S (and Tundra, and Macfarlane, Walter & Ross) from 2000 on, as my informant had alleged? Gibson had run the place for quite a while and he'd served on the M&S board as a representative of the University of Toronto. I thought he also could explain whether or not anyone in government *had* blessed the initial gift/sale, as stated in the original press reports, but which had now been denied, as they say, by Moscow. It's always awkward to interrogate a friend. But we are friendly colleagues more than social friends. No dinner parties would be spoiled.

I think we met in 1974 when he was the newly appointed editorial director of trade books at Macmillan. By then, I was editing the *Maclean's* book review section (along with the other opinion columns at the back of the magazine). Maclean-Hunter, which at that time owned *Maclean's, Chatelaine,* and numerous trade publications, had bought Macmillan of Canada from its UK parent, outbidding Jack McClelland to get it in 1972.[193] So we toiled for the same owner when he stuck his head around the edge of my office door one day. He introduced himself with a big, loopy grin, and began to praise his upcoming books which he said I should be sure to send out to be reviewed. I thought he was charming in a book-nerdy way. His round face hid behind a big beard. He moved in awkward lurches, first here, then there, ending up leaning against my bookcase where

review copies and galleys were piled. He was tallish, blondish, and Scottish, with a kindly burr, and he was very enthusiastic. Now he is less tall, less blond, and his accent is a Canadian/Scottish palimpsest, but he is still very enthusiastic.

He arrived in Canada after studying at St. Andrews University in his native Scotland, and Yale in the US. He worked for McMaster University, then Doubleday Canada,[194] and then moved to Macmillan where he inherited a sterling backlist and a list of leading Canadian writers previously published by his Macmillan boss, John Gray, such as Robertson Davies and Morley Callaghan. But he soon found great Canadian authors on his own. Gibson enticed Mavis Gallant to Macmillan and also attracted Alice Munro. In those days, writers stuck to editors who treated their books with care, following them if they moved to a new company (so long as the new company offered advances as good as the old). Writer loyalty made leading editors major commodities to any publisher wanting to grow a better publishing list.

In 1986, Gibson left Macmillan for M&S, after Macmillan's cherry-picked assets (but not the company itself) had been sold by Maclean-Hunter to Ron Besse, who'd merged them with Gage. There'd been a press conference that time too. Gibson, who became Publisher at Macmillan, assured concerned writers and fiery nationalist publishers who claimed the merger was a disaster for Canadian publishing, that all would be well.[195]

Gibson moved to M&S because Avie Bennett, its brand-new owner, offered him the chance to start Canada's first personal book imprint, the eponymous Douglas Gibson Books. When Alice Munro, W.O. Mitchell, Robertson Davies, Jack Hodgkins, and Mavis Gallant followed him there, Gibson proved himself to be a very valuable person. Two years later, Gibson replaced Adrienne Clarkson (later the Governor General) as the M&S Publisher.[196]

After I left *Maclean's*, I didn't see Doug much until, after his divorce from his first wife, he married the best friend of one of my friends. Then we began to run into each other at a local swimming pool. Summer after summer we exchanged hi-how-are-ya's and bits of gossip on the deck of an outdoor community pool in Toronto's

Rosedale—just around the corner from Heather Reisman and Gerry Schwartz's house.

I searched for him on LinkedIn and arranged a call.

At first he carried on with such enthusiasm about his current occupations that I couldn't get my questions in. He is an author and storyteller now, he explained. After he retired from M&S in 2009, he wrote a book or two. He was finishing his latest, *Across Canada by Story,* which he described as "a coast to coast literary adventure" in which he tells tales of his encounters with the wonderful storytellers he's worked with.

Who's publishing it, Doug? I asked.

ECW, he said (a growing Canadian independent).

Not M&S?

He muttered something about how he'd thought it best to go with someone else. Then he segued back to the fun he was having as a literary performer and how he was trying to raise money for the Alice Munro Chair in Creativity for Western University where she had once studied.

Enough pleasantries, I said to myself. Get to it.

I told him I couldn't seem to find documented evidence for a number of assertions made at the time of the gift of M&S to U of T. Neither could I discover obvious facts such as the value of the gift and the size of the tax credit receipt. Could he help me on that?

"Well your man is Avie Bennett," he said, in a tone that suggested real pleasure that this cup would now pass from him. "He owned 100%."

But why did Bennett give those shares to U of T? I asked. Do you know? I mean he was Chancellor at York University at the time. Why not York?

A keen and loyal U of T alumnus, Gibson said, with a certain *edge.* (In fact, Bennett attended the University of Toronto but did not graduate.) Have you seen the Bennett Gates on Harbord Street, he asked? (Actually, the Bennett Gates are off Hoskin Avenue.) He wanted to preserve this national asset into the future, Gibson continued. And, he added, "I think he wanted to find a way out."

We began to talk about what it had been like to work at M&S in his early years there. "Avie was the chairman, there was no president,"

he said. McClelland & Stewart had been physically relocated from its suburban office on Hollinger Road to the 9th floor of the former Maclean-Hunter building on University Avenue. Doug had one corner office and Avie Bennett had the other and they spent a lot of time together plotting the company's future.

So what were the annual revenues in those days? I asked.

I would say several millions, he said.

And debt? Was there a big debt?

Not sure there was a big debt, he said. On reflection, he didn't think so. Yet it was always a struggle to make a profit, and sometimes even to break even. From 1988 to 2000, he said, they took very seriously their title of "The Canadian Publishers."

What happened in 2000 that made Bennett want out? I asked.

"My memory of 2000 in the publishing business, we were terrified of the dotcoms and the electronic problems that never really happened...."

You mean the millennium thing where all the computers were supposed to die?

That's what he meant. But by the time Bennett handed off M&S that threat was long gone.

How did Random House get into the deal? I asked.

At some point, Gibson said vaguely, Avie Bennett went to John Neale, then head of Random House of Canada, formerly of M&S, and said he planned to hand the company to U of T, and he "would like you guys to be involved... He also went to the government to say here's what [I'm] planning to do... He lined up his ducks and got U of T."

Do you think he wanted to sell part of the company to Random House to establish a value for the shares? I asked.

Could be the reason, Gibson said, but also, he wanted publishing expertise on the new board.

Now why would that be, I wondered, as I scribbled notes. Surely Bennett and Gibson had sufficient publishing expertise? They were both on the new board.

How long did these negotiations go on and when did you hear about them? I asked.

I became aware quite late, he said.

Really? How late? I asked.

I was busy bringing out books, he said. He seemed to be apologizing for something. But what? That Bennett hadn't told him what he was planning to do until it was almost done?

So, like you heard about it the day before? I found myself asking.

A little in advance of it, he said. And there he stopped.

Amazing, I thought. Gibson was the Publisher, and he was working in an office down the hall from the owner, and the owner had told the public that he'd worked on this deal for five years, but the owner seemed to have made these arrangements without telling Gibson until they were almost complete. Yet the arrangements had included Gibson becoming President of the new version of M&S.

Can you explain to me why there would be no reference to the value of the shares, the size of the tax credit receipt issued, or even the final sale of the shares to Random House of Canada on University of Toronto's website? I asked.

He was silent. I waited a moment, then tried another tack.

Okay then, tell me about the board of M&S, I said.

He said that John Evans was on it and Rob Prichard. "At one point, I was on it too." He listed other names he could remember: Avie, Arlene Perly Rae. Then he stopped. "I'm blanking," he said.

How long was Arlene Perly Rae on it? I asked. She'd always struck me as an odd choice.

From the start, he said. She was an M&S author.

There were lots of those, I pointed out. Why her?

"She was Toronto based," he said. "Ask Avie."

A short while later, he remembered the name of another board member, Trina McQueen, who had once worked at CBC. "And another was Felix Chee, he was a financial man from U of T, and John Neale and Brad Martin, at the same time."

Do you remember saying to the press at the time of the gift that the University had promised to hold its M&S shares for three years? I asked. Why three years? Isn't that kind of short?

Three years? He repeated. "That rings a faint bell…"

We had arrived at the tricky part. I made the suggestion to him that the initial gift/sale might have been stage one of a salami strategy, the beginning of a slice-by-slice takeover of M&S by Random House whose eventual result had been envisioned from the beginning.

"There was talk about a transfer," he said. "I do know conspiracy theorists who think it was a conspiracy from the start. If so, I was not aware."

He sounded irritated, dismissive. So I thought I'd better get to the tricky part, the control issue, before he decided he'd had enough of my questions and hung up the phone.

There is a theory that Random House was really in control of M&S from 2000 on, I said. Was that the case?

"I was working hard to maintain M&S's independence as a separate company," he said. "We had our own sales conference at Hart House (at University of Toronto). After I left, it went inside Random House."

When was it that you stopped running the company?

He explained that he'd been moved sideways out of the management of M&S in 2004. He had been allowed to stay on running his Douglas Gibson Books imprint through which he brought out up to ten books a year. But in 2009 he'd been retired from that too. When he was in the M&S President's chair, he said, he'd been careful to keep a distance from Random House, but after that, the distance lessened and the separate sales force disappeared.

I've been told that all M&S payments were made on Random House cheques from 2000 onwards. Is that the case?

"It could be true," he said. "They took on the central administrative role."

Now why can't he answer that definitively? I wondered. He'd been the President of the company for the first four years: surely he had signed company cheques? You'd think he'd remember whether or not they were drawn on an M&S account. On the other hand, if they were Random House cheques, maybe someone directly employed by Random House signed, not him.

Why did you leave the presidency? I asked.

I was moved sideways, he said. The board wanted a change.

Did the board change?

He said he wasn't sure.

Well according to U of T's records, I said, Douglas Pepper took your place on the board and was listed as Publisher and President of M&S.

Pepper came from Crown, Gibson said, and then he fell silent again for a moment, as if to let that fact sink into my head, as if to say, without saying it, that Crown, being a subsidiary of Random House US, meant that Pepper had been an employee of Random House when he took Gibson's job.

Sounds like part two of a salami strategy, I said.

"When I was moved sideways," he continued, "and Pepper came in, there was alarm in the author and agent world."

Why?

He replied that the fear was that there would be no more competing bids for projects from the various Random House entities. They said no, things would be as before, and they were for a while. "Then, suddenly, they were no longer going to compete... it became public very fast, it might be in 2006 or 2009. It became the policy and they acknowledged the policy."

Again, he was saying something without saying it. He was suggesting that Random House began to treat M&S as just another imprint of the company long before the University's shares were actually handed over. He was also waving a red flag about an emerging publishing monopsony—actually the more precise term would be oligopsony. Random House, which controlled so many imprints, was by far the largest and certainly the highest price buyer of fiction and non-fiction publishing rights in the Canadian market, and if its imprints stopped competing against each other for projects, that would drive down advances.

On the other hand, Gibson said, as if to remove the sting from his own remarks, Booknet had a dampening effect on advances too, because publishers were able to look up and see exactly how many copies of an author's previous books had sold, and agents couldn't use smoke and mirrors to drive up prices anymore. (Booknet is a non-profit organization that gathers and shares information on book sales for subscribers, both publishers and booksellers. Its creation was instigated by the federal government. Subscribers get accurate weekly data about book sales from Indigo and other large sellers, but not from independents, Amazon, Apple, or ebooks, so its reports cover less than 75% of total market transactions.)

But surely the market share is more important, and what about the fact that two people drive decision making in a company with so many imprints? I said. Back in 2000, you and John Neale said Random House's market share with M&S included was way less than 30%. Don't they have a much bigger share now?

"I thought I was right then," he said. "Bigger companies have got much bigger in the interim."

I was tired of hints and red flags. I wanted the former President of M&S to answer on the record about who had effective control of M&S, and from what point in time.

"When did control actually pass from the University of Toronto to Random House?" I asked. "Was it in 2004?"

"I was off back in my Douglas Gibson Books corner and not involved in corporate strategy."

I asked again. "Is that when control transfers? 2004?" I asked.

"I think so," he said. "The replacement of Douglas Gibson with Douglas Pepper, a long-time Random House employee, speaks for itself."

"Does that mean that any government grants and tax credits M&S received, as a Canadian-owned and controlled company, were invalid after 2004?" I asked.

I expected him to say something like *don't be ridiculous*.

"It's an issue worth raising," he said, to my shock.

Why did no one protest at the time? I asked. Why did no one say anything?

"Yeah," he said. "No one says anything."

I can tell you that the University of Toronto says it transferred its shares to Random House in 2011 for essentially *nothing*, I said. Apparently, there was a huge debt.

There was another silence at his end of the phone. Was he thinking about what the backlist should have been worth? Who would know that better than Douglas Gibson?

"I can't understand it," he said.

Was a dividend ever paid to the University of Toronto by M&S?

"Not that I'm aware of," he said.

What was in it for U of T? I asked.

No answer.

Do you know whether there was a debt problem when you were moved sideways?

"The first year was a very good year. Some years were better than others. But [we were] breaking even."

That didn't answer my question. He seemed to be saying there was no big debt in the years when he was President and reading the financial statements. At least that's what he seemed to be saying. Try again, I thought.

In the years after you left the M&S board, I asked, could M&S have accumulated a debt so huge that it wiped out all of the value in the backlist?

"You're asking very interesting questions," he said. "The key to this is Avie Bennett."

Avie Bennett, he went on to say, was an exemplary owner of the publishing company who never said no to a book that Doug wanted to do and who provided financial stability to the company for years. "He deserves all kinds of credit for that," he said.

Bennett was in his late 80s, but Gibson said he still went to his office every day. He said I should call him there. He gave me the number.

I didn't expect Avie Bennett to take my call. We weren't friends. If we'd ever met, that moment was no longer stored in memory. When I left my message, I expected his people to call back, if any call came at all. After all, Avie Bennett is a very important person with an illustrious career who has advanced to the highest level of the Order of Canada for his services to the community.[197] In this country, in these times, it is routine for important people to find it inconvenient to talk to journalists. We are asked to email our questions. We are expected to print whatever is emailed back, usually a statement conveying few answers, yet positioning that person, or his/her organization, in a manner satisfactory to a public relations expert. These missives are usually as interesting as watching paint dry.

Bennett called me back the next morning.

Long time since we last spoke, he said.

I racked my brains. When *was* the last time? Had we *ever* spoken? As I tried to remember, and nothing came up, I told him Douglas Gibson had recommended that I speak with him. I said I wanted to come to his office and ask him a lot of questions about his gift of M&S to U of T.

"Are you gonna be friendly?" he asked.

Only one other person has ever asked me that question when I called to request an interview: it was Patrick Gossage, former Press Secretary to Prime Minister Pierre Trudeau. He was then the Minister of Public Affairs (a nice title for the chief press guy) at the Canadian Embassy in Washington, D.C., when I asked him if I could meet with the Gotliebs—Allan and Sondra—for a magazine article. Allan Gotlieb was then the Canadian Ambassador to the United States, and a very unorthodox one. He was stalking the halls of the US Congress, buttonholing the elected officials about the evils of protectionism as practised by the US against Canada, and giving public speeches pumping the virtues of trade with the Good Neighbour to the North. His wife Sondra organized dinner parties for the power brokers who she then wrote about in a droll column for the *Washington Post*. Quiet Diplomacy had been replaced by this Public Diplomacy, which was very controversial, especially when Sondra slapped her social secretary in view of the press at a dinner for Prime Minister Mulroney.[198]

Of course I'm friendly, I said to Bennett. (I meant it: all journalists are friendly or we can't get a foot in your door.) But I knew that was not what he meant. He was asking: will you listen to my story with a sympathetic ear, or are you on a mission to trap me in my own words?

We set a date. Bennett was concerned that he might have to change it for a medical appointment. I said my schedule was flexible, no worries.

I hung up the phone thinking come on, you must have talked to him at one time or another, or he wouldn't have said that. But when?[199]

The next day, I got a call from a person on Bennett's staff. Could I please telephone Avie Bennett's daughter? She had some concerns about the interview.

I was given the phone number and I called.

Bennett had health problems, his daughter said. It would be appreciated if I would postpone the interview until his long-time assistant, who had just left on vacation, returned. So I rearranged the date with Bennett's associate. I was told Bennett would be informed.

But the next week, just minutes after the time set for the original appointment, Bennett called me.

Where are you? He said.

He sounded annoyed.

I'm not supposed to be there today, I said, the appointment was changed. We rescheduled so your assistant can be there. Isn't that okay?

No one told *him*, he said. He sounded hurt as well as angry. He made it clear that he was not pleased about waiting, that he had wanted to get it over with.

I'm *so* sorry, I said. But then I thought: why would he want to get it over with? Was he anxious about it?

I had to wait more than a month to find out.

6
Monopsony / Oligopsony Revisited

On the last Saturday in June, 2015, I sat down at the kitchen table and opened my *Globe and Mail*. Usually I read the front section—News—first. Yet I opened the Arts section first, and promptly forgot the News entirely.

Everybody who writes, edits, designs, publishes, or sells books, and who read the newspaper that morning, probably did the same thing.

Mark Medley, the *Globe and Mail's* books editor, had written a feature story about Penguin Random House Canada. It sprawled across three full pages. The story made it clear that, just as I had been saying for years, just as Doug Gibson had confirmed, Canadian book publishing, not just bookselling, had become a monopsony—okay, okay, an oligopsony—although Medley did not use either word. He used the word monopoly. "It is a near monopoly, able to dictate financial terms to writers who now face fewer places to publish their work," he wrote. He also used the word control: he suggested to Brad Martin, CEO of Penguin Random House Canada, that his company controls "the domestic market."[200]

The piece started with this line: "The most powerful man in Canadian publishing is leading me on a tour of his new cubicle." For reasons unknown, Brad Martin had decided to give Medley (and *Globe* readers) a tour of the merged entity's new offices down on Toronto's Front Street. Martin made it clear that he and one other person, his second in command, President Kristin Cochrane, make the important publishing decisions for the whole entity, leaving a question mark for some about editorial autonomy and competition among imprints, "despite pledges." Medley did not reference in the *Globe* where those pledges had been made, but maybe he was referring to a story he had written for the *National Post* in June 2012, six months after U of T's shares of M&S ended up in Random House's hands. That story had been based on a press release issued by Random House that declared that McClelland & Stewart and Doubleday had been put together in one publishing group under the leadership of Kristin Cochrane. The claim made then was that "editorial identities of the imprints will remain distinct," though in the same story, Medley quoted Brad Martin saying "there will only be one bid coming out of the group. There will not be competing bids." This was the admission of non-competition that Doug Gibson had referred to.[201]

In this article for the *Globe*, Medley focused at first on the fact that the largest trade publisher in the country had moved its merged self to an open plan office. The pictures that ran with the story showed a space indistinguishable from the back offices of a bank except for the occasional feature wall displaying books. The work spaces of the editors of Penguin Random House's 18 different imprints were tiny cubicles behind waist high walls. Even Brad Martin, the commander of this 229-person empire, now including Knopf, Doubleday, Random House, Penguin, McClelland & Stewart, Tundra, Douglas Gibson Books, Signal, Allen Lane, Vintage, Anchor, Emblem, Hamish Hamilton, Appetite, etc., had been reduced from book-lined, private office grandeur to a cubicle. While there were meeting rooms and booths scattered throughout, personal offices were no more.

How to work in this new environment seemed to bewilder most of the PRHC editors who spoke to Medley. A leading Publisher on the Random House side of the merger had formerly enjoyed a private room big enough for a couch, table and chairs, as well as a decent-sized desk. While Penguin's old space had been cramped, its offices at least had walls. Open plan ignores the basic nature of book creation in favour of reducing square footage costs. Book making requires editors to have long, quiet, careful conversations with sensitive authors, or long, quiet, careful conversations about sensitive material. Neither can be done well in a big room crowded with people trying to do their own work. So the office design conveyed an interesting message. It said Bertelsmann, like other publishing conglomerates, takes an industrial approach to the business.

Medley asserted that Bertelsmann had reported a 25.2 percent increase in revenue (to about 3.3 billion Euros), in its worldwide Penguin Random House operations (employing about 12,000 people) between 2013 and 2014. But my own reading of the annual report itself showed that this increase was mainly due to the merger with Penguin. The addition of Penguin's revenues to Random House's had caused "portfolio effects," according to the report. This meant that the combination of the revenues of the two companies made it appear that book publishing revenues were growing, when in fact they were not. That year, book publishing revenue had actually dropped from being the second largest to the third largest segment in Bertelsmann's holdings.[202]

While Bertelsmann had bragged in its 2013 report about Alice Munro's Nobel, claiming her, and her Nobel, as its own,[203] Canada got one sentence in this 2014 report. It asserted that PRH Canada had a large number of Canadian bestsellers that year. But no Canadian revenue numbers appeared: they were either included in the US figures, or were in the "Other" section of a graph showing publishing revenues by geographic area.[204] No Canadian was listed as a member of the senior management team pictured in the annual report either. Though Martin attested to Medley that the Canadian end of the company is profitable, he showed no evidence to support that claim. In other words, Penguin Random House Canada is so small in the Bertelsmann scheme of things that if it vanished entirely it would leave no significant gap at all in future Bertelsmann earnings.[205]

Martin was not content with offering Medley a tour. He also explained to Medley the way in which the merged businesses would be run. Reading Martin's words, I found myself wondering if Martin was banking on the Harper government being re-elected in the November, 2015 election. The Harper government, which was fairly friendly to foreign investment, had shown little interest in enforcing net benefit promises, and only a marginal interest in reshaping national publishing policy. Or did Martin believe that if the Liberals won, they might scrap the publishing policy entirely? He must have considered his company to be in a no-lose position either way because he proceeded to grab the third rail of Canadian politics, give it a hard yank, and dare whoever formed the next government to come and get him.

Martin confessed to Medley what every agent had been whispering about for years. He made it very clear that he had done away with competition for projects by price between his imprints. Price competition had been replaced with something one of his editors called *"vision"*—otherwise known as the editor's plans for a book. Martin also made it clear that the number of books published by Penguin Random House would be reduced in future, that "...I would rather publish two books instead of three, and give both of those books a chance to win, than publish all three of them because it's a numbers game."

While this honesty was harsh, it wasn't what made the world of agents, authors, and other publishers gasp in astonishment. It was what Medley drew out of Martin about his main requirement for projects he would be pleased to consider. PRH Canada had only published 542 books in 2014 with its staff of 33 editors. (The entire worldwide Penguin Random House operation, with its 250 imprints, published 15,000 books that year.) Martin wanted it known that unless one of his editors could mount a major case—a big *vision*—in support of a project, "I'm not interested in a book that is going to generate less than $100,000 in revenues."

I could almost hear a collective, ragged *whaaaa?* rise from the throats of book industry readers across the country when I got to that paragraph. It certainly rose from mine.

In order to earn $100,000 in revenues (he surely meant net revenues), the average Canadian hardcover book would have to sell more than 6,000 copies, thanks to the high discounts demanded by booksellers (about 50% at Indigo or Amazon, for example). The average paperback priced at $20 would need to sell 9,000 copies. A Canadian non-fiction hardcover needs to sell about 5,000 copies to get on bestseller lists, sometimes fewer. Most Canadian trade books do not make the bestseller lists. Sales of about 1500 are high for Canadian fiction. As one independent publisher would later tell me, only six percent of all the nearly 200 books he's published so far have sold more than 6,000 copies, meaning, 94% of his books would not have met Martin's criterion for publication by Penguin Random House Canada. An advance of, say, $85,000, would require sales of 35,000 to 40,000 books for the author to earn enough royalties to pay the advance out. In practice, if a book doesn't sell well enough for the author's royalties to do that, no further offers would be made from that company to that author, or, any new advance would be much, much lower.

As Martin explained to Medley, before getting a go-ahead to make an offer on a book project, a PRH Canada editor would have to show him and Cochrane that a proposed non-fiction book would sell at least one thousand more copies than the average bestseller. An editor afflicted by "vision" would have to show that though a project might not hit that target, it would build a big audience for the author's next book. With jobs disappearing, how many editors would make that pitch? This meant that Penguin Random House intended to focus in future even more than it did already on well-known, foreign-originated works supported by the bigger publicity machines in the US and the UK. The corollary of this policy was that writers (like me) who had been previously published by PRH Canada, and made it to the bestseller lists, and sold foreign rights, and/or won major awards, would still likely get no offer on new projects, unless, as one agent put it to Medley, HarperCollins or Simon & Schuster Canada also made an offer. How else would a PRH Canada editor demonstrate that a book could pull in $100,000? And even if those counter-offers appeared, and PRH countered the counter-offers and won the bid, that PRH offer would be lower than before—because there would be only one coming from all its imprints. (Are you paying attention,

Competition Bureau? Falling prices paid to suppliers by a dominant company is indicative of oligopsony.)

I drew the obvious conclusion. Writers like me would have to take their projects in future to the poorly financed Canadian independent publishers. But for writers like me, this is no future at all. Canadian independent publishers subsist on a thin gruel of government grants, tax credits, and, in Ontario, the power to direct a small grant to writers from what is called the Writers' Reserve. They simply cannot afford to offer significant advances—for example, advances of over $30,000 for Canadian rights alone—even if they believe that a book will sell 10,000 copies. The risk is too big. That kind of advance may be sufficient for fiction writers, but complex works of non-fiction require a lot of money up front. Non-fiction usually involves extensive research and often extensive travel, not to mention a lot of time, and granting agencies award money to writing projects only after the writing has begun. They insist on samples. While academics might be able to publish interesting non-fiction with small independent publishers, because they are paid salaries while they do their research and can earn academic grants as well, people like me would be out of luck. Non-fiction Canadian works will therefore mainly be replaced by non-fiction works of non-Canadian origin. In fact, if you listen carefully to the few remaining radio and television shows that still interview non-fiction authors about their work, you will note that books originated in the US and the UK are featured much more often than they used to be. That's because the production of Canadian non-fiction has already been reduced.

And there is another corollary. Smart Canadian agents will desperately try to make their first sale of a Canadian project to publishers in the US or the UK, in order to prove to PRH Canada that a project will bring in a nice pile of dollars. But US or UK publishers are even less likely than they were 40 years ago to buy books focused on Canada, Canadians, or the Canadian experience. For one thing, unless the Canadian writer also writes for newspapers, magazines or online journals in the US or the UK, they have no platforms from which to publicize their new works and to build an audience for them. And then there's the xenophobia factor: Britons like to read about the British. Americans like to read about America and Americans. Canadian writers aiming at foreign markets will be encouraged to scrub Canadian themes and issues and geography from their stories, in the same way that movies made in Canada for foreign release pretend to look as if they were shot in New York, or LA, or London. The world, as Bono has said, may well need more Canada. But the purchasing editors of the world are not convinced that Canada sells.

So where will that leave the Canadian reflection business?

When Medley suggested to Martin that his company, thanks to the merger with Penguin in 2013 and its absorption of M&S in 2012, controls the Canadian publishing market, Martin did not like the suggestion and responded that his market share is only about 32%. Yet that is just below the 35% share that the Competition Bureau defines as dominance. At that point, investigation will begin to determine whether practices have become abusive.[206] As if to add fuel to that fire, when Medley noted that Penguin Random House imprints in the US and Britain still compete against each other on price, Martin insisted that in Canada, PRH would play by other rules.

"In Canada... that's just the way it's going to be," he told Medley. "Why would you bid against each other? Scale is supposed to mean something. This is a small market."

And growing smaller. After all, when Avie Bennett and Doug Gibson ran McClelland & Stewart, it published more than 100 books a year.[207] As just another imprint of PRH, M&S brings out about one tenth that number. Martin had made it clear there would be even fewer books from PRH imprints in future.

I put down the newspaper in despair. Canadian book publishing, in spite of forty years under protective laws and policies, was even worse off than I'd imagined. Thanks to governments' failures to enforce their own rules, it was now dominated by two oligopsonies, both of which are *fragile*. PRH Canada's future depends on it keeping its costs low and its sales revenues sufficiently high that its foreign owner will let it live another year. Indigo is utterly dependent on its owners' deep pockets and their willingness to keep selling books even at substantial loss. If either one fails, much of the Canadian book business will go with it.

I wondered: would the Competition Bureau launch an investigation of PRH Canada given Martin's public announcement of its determination to suppress competition, which seemed to fall within what the Bureau calls "reviewable practices"?

There was no point even calling to ask (though I did), if any such investigation had taken place.[208] That information is secret by law.

7

Avie's Version

My appointment with Avie Bennett was at ten in the morning on a midsummer day so cool it felt as if fall had arrived early. I parked near the University of Toronto's main campus and walked south. The sun was bright but not warm, the wind brisk yet erratic. It blew my hair in wild circles while plastic bags and paper napkins and Tim Horton's lids piled up against the curbs. All I could see of the homeless people sleeping rough on University Avenue's ceremonial median were tufts of hair and stockinged toes jutting from their sleeping bags.

Names that kept cropping up in this story were emblazoned here and there along the way, reminding me that at the top, Canada is a small town in which our leaders' lives cross-link like a Deep Learning neural net.[209] There is a newish stone building on the campus, north of Simcoe Hall where the M&S press conference took place in 2000. It resembles a shrunken version of the Supreme Court building in Ottawa. It's called the J. Robert S. Prichard Alumnae Building and is named for the most successful endowment builder in U of T's history,[210] some say in the history of Canadian universities. The Bennett Gates, named for Avie Bennett who has donated millions to University of Toronto (not just shares in M&S),[211] open onto the pathway called Philosopher's Walk. The Gates are just behind University of Toronto Law School where Robert Prichard once presided as Dean. The Law School would confer an honourary degree on Gerry Schwartz in 2016, his introduction made by Prichard. Schwartz served on the University's Governing Council and its Executive Committee between 1986 and 1995, when Prichard was Law School Dean and then U of T President.[212] (The current Dean, Ed Iacobucci who is also the James M. Tory Professor of Law and an expert on competition law, is the son of the Honourable Frank Iacobucci, a former Justice of the Supreme Court of Canada. Frank Iacobucci taught Prichard at the Law School, became an interim President of U of T when another President left early, became Chairman of the Torstar Board after John Evans stepped down, which made him Prichard's boss. Now Iacobucci and Prichard both work at Torys, which makes them associates.)[213]

On the west side of University Avenue, a big sign on the side of Mount Sinai Hospital says Schwartz Reisman Emergency Centre. The size of the gift conferring these naming rights was $13 million.[214] Schwartz and Reisman gave another $15 million to expand the centre and create an Institute of Emergency Medicine. Across from the mirrored Hydro building lies MaRS, the brainchild of John Evans, also a former President of U of T. MaRS is supposed to marry the University's scientific bright lights to Bay Street's investors so as to birth high tech start-ups. It is not nearly as successful as John Evans was. He co-founded McMaster Medical School. He ran for Parliament for the Liberal Party in Rosedale in 1978, and though he lost, he failed upwards, becoming the first non-American chairman of the Rockefeller Foundation. In 1993, Evans also became Chairman of Torstar Corporation, then the owner of the *Toronto Star*, the country's largest circulation newspaper, as well as Harlequin Books, the world's most successful publisher of bodice-ripper fiction. Robert Prichard was hired by Evans and the Torstar board as President and CEO two years after the University accepted Bennett's M&S gift.[215] Both Evans and Prichard served with Bennett as representatives of U of T on the M&S board.

And then there's Peter Munk's name on the cardiac care centre at Toronto General Hospital and the Munk Centre on the campus—but Munk is only tangentially involved in this story.

The pillars beside the main door of 481 University Avenue have brass plaques affixed. They say:

McClelland & Stewart House

Not anymore and not for many years, I thought, as I entered the lobby. Nothing seemed as it did when I first walked into this building, age 24, hoping to be hired at *Maclean's*. Then, 481 University was Maclean-Hunter's head office. Then, I was filled with anticipation, taking my first step toward so many joyful times practising a wonderful trade. Now, there was an old woman reflected in the elevator doors, an old woman masquerading as me, who actually was me, but still filled with anticipation because I thought my questions were about to be answered.

I took the main elevator to the third floor. The doors opened on the expansive reception for B+H Architects. Bennett's office was around a corner and down a narrow hall. There were two small brass plaques beside his door. One said Avie Bennett. The one below said First Plazas Inc.

Stepping into the reception hall was like dropping through a wormhole to the 1980s, the era of Edper-Brascan/Olympia & York/Unicorp. There were vertical blinds, pink walls, deco-style leather armchairs. Diana Massiah, Bennett's tall and elegant assistant, led me into a small conference room and offered me food and drink. No thanks, I said, as I pulled out my notebooks and pens. I amused myself instead by gazing at Charles Pachter's portrait of Margaret Laurence which covered one wall. Pachter had painted her as if she were a member of a panel discussing some important subject, except she was covering her mouth in disgust and turning her back on the person beside her. Pachter had painted over that person—him? her?—with a great blob of black paint.

I waited for Bennett to appear. And waited. Finally, the main door opened and he came in on his daughter's arm. I went to the hall to greet him. His once dark hair was homing in on white, his face seemed too lean, a not-at-all-well sort of lean. His goatee had turned white too, so at first I thought he was clean-shaven. He wore a dark blazer, with an Order of Canada pin in his lapel, a striped shirt without a tie, dark pants. He was tall enough to loom over me as he leaned in close to shake my hand with a roguish grin.

Don't want to do this here, he said to Diana, spurning the conference room. We'll do this in my office.

Diana, who was the reason we'd put off this meeting for a month, was not invited to sit in.

As I followed him down the hall I tried to figure out who he reminded me of. It came to me as I settled into a chair across the desk from him.

He looks like the father of Frasier and Niles Crane of television fame—
the retired cop who drives his over-educated sons crazy with his work-
ing-man's tastes and ideas. Not that there is anything unsophisticated
about Bennett: it was the limp as he walked, the way he tilted his head to
one side to size me up, the way he emanated a friendly openness alongside the impatience of a smart man with a short fuse.

His office was large, with two sets of windows down one wall, but
it was not grand. He sat behind an ordinary desk in a large, leather
office chair. Behind me, two dark couches faced off across a coffee table.
Bookshelves lined the walls, shelves filled with McClelland & Stewart
editions. Above, there were many framed photos: Avie with a very young
and happy Prime Minister Brian Mulroney standing in a line of men that
included Eddy Shack; Avie with Prime Minister Pierre Trudeau; Avie
with Prime Minister Jean Chrétien in the Prime Minister's office—I recognized the panelling. On the coffee table, there was a picture he particularly wanted me to see right away. It was Avie in white tie and tails at a
Nobel Prize ball, a pinnacle moment. There was nothing I spotted that
spoke to his years as a developer, though First Plazas Inc. still seemed to
be a going concern with employees at work down the hall.

Why am I thinking of him as Avie instead of Mr. Bennett? I asked
myself as I settled in. Was it the way he made himself seem like an
old friend, as if we'd known each other for years? I'd certainly known
of him for years, ever since he bought McClelland & Stewart back
in 1985. I'd never heard of him before that. Many of my journalist
friends, who had never heard of him before either, had been curious
about his motives for taking on M&S.

Which is why the first question I asked him was why he got into
McClelland & Stewart in the first place, whatever had possessed him?
I'd wanted to ask him that for years.

"It's a story I've never told publicly," he said. "I'll tell you the truth and
how it happened. My late daughter-in-law Alison Gordon, and because
late, I don't like to be public about this, was writing a book for M&S called
Foul Ball!: Five Years in the American League. She was the first woman to cover
baseball. She worked for the *Toronto Star*. The book was heavy on being a
reporter in the major leagues, first woman in the dressing room. She just
died. She came to Friday night dinner complaining of mistakes at M&S."[216]

He stopped for a moment to be sure I caught the reference to Friday night dinner, which of course I did. Friday night dinner for Jews is like Sunday dinner for Christians: it's when a Jewish family welcomes the Sabbath. When I grew up, our Friday night menu was chicken soup ("better it should run under bridges" is what my father infamously said to my mother over her first effort), roast chicken, salad, and pie. The subject was usually the politics of Medicare.

"At that time, Jack [McClelland] was looking for public financing."

It was the summer of 1984. By then, Linda McKnight was running M&S for McClelland, who had stepped back a bit. John Neale—who would later buy 25% of M&S for Random House—was head of marketing. While the company had shown a small profit in 1983, M&S would publish 91 books in 1984 and was about to post a loss of $2 million. The prime rate at CIBC was 12.50%[217] and M&S was spending way too much on interest. McClelland told everyone he was on the financial ropes again in spite of the loan made to him by the Province of Ontario ten years before, which had kicked off Canada's nationalist book policy. Was his timing political? The federal election that would bring Brian Mulroney to power would be held four months later, and a provincial election would follow eight months after that.

So, once again, the M&S debt was refinanced by the province on the condition that McClelland find some new investors. He raised $1.1 million in return for 36% of M&S.[218]

"It was a bond issue," Bennett said.

Actually, it was more along the lines of a debenture that was done under the auspices of Ontario's Small Business Development Corporation.[219] Investors were to get back 70% of their investment over a 10-year period, payments waived for the first two years. As the book trade publication *Quill & Quire* put it later, the remaining 30% was already "returned to them in the form of an Ontario tax rebate or tax credit." Several writers who had done very well by M&S, such as Margaret Atwood, Pierre Berton, and Farley Mowat, bought into it.[220]

"I decided to buy a piece as a public-spirited thing," Bennett said.

How did you hear of it? I asked.

He said it was in the papers that he was looking for money.

And money is something Avie Bennett had in abundance by 1984, more than enough to be very generous to others, though very few others have been as generous as Avie Bennett. In 1983, Bennett and his wife Beverly and lawyer W. Norman Ross of the law firm WeirFoulds LLP, set up the Bennett Family Foundation.[221] (I think Ross is also public-spirited, though I cannot be sure as he did not respond to my phone messages or emails. Stephen Harper appointed him to the board of the Canadian Mint. He previously chaired the boards of the Canada Development Investment Corporation and the Canada Hibernia Holding Corp. He also served on the Chapters board.)[222] The Bennett Foundation has had assets ranging from $28 million to about $19 million between 2005 and 2015 (earlier information is no longer available.) Some years, the Foundation gave away as much as $7.5 million, others less than $1 million, depending on the vagaries of markets, how much Bennett spent on administration and professional advice, and the assets Bennett moved into the Foundation where they are protected from tax.

According to the Foundation's information returns, favourite recipients have been: University of Toronto, York University, the National Ballet, the United Way, and the Art Gallery of Ontario. The Foundation's 2015 return differs from the rest. In 2015, while I was researching this project, Bennett gave $11 million in receipted gifts, reducing total assets to about $5 million. The U of T got $4 million, York University got $2.5 million, and smaller gifts were made to a long list of other organizations. An anonymous recipient paid about $170,000 each year, through WeirFoulds, got $550,000. By then Ross had stepped down as a director, and Avie Bennett's assistant, Diana Massiah, had taken Ross's place. She is listed, as Ross had been, as being at arm's length to the Bennetts.[223] The Foundation's returns show that between 2005 and 2015, Bennett gave the University of Toronto over $8 million, though in 2006 and in 2013 he gave U of T nothing.[224]

So how much money did you kick in? I asked Bennett.

Don't remember the amount, he said, which I found surprising. Others have reported that it was about $100,000 and that his was the second-largest investment in the M&S debenture. "He asked me on the board. Others were on it already… I said I'd be happy to help if I could."[225]

This was not the first time a developer had come to the rescue of M&S. Senator Leo Kolber, who managed the holding company, CEMP Investments, which stewarded the fortunes of Sam Bronfman's children, had helped out after the company came close to bankruptcy following a blowout publishing year in 1967. Kolber was chairman of the board of the developer Cadillac Fairview and for years led fundraising efforts for the federal Liberal Party.[226] Kolber's wife was then an unknown poet. When M&S was desperately seeking capital in 1967, it published a book of Sandra Kolber's poetry while asking at the same time for project finance support from CEMP. (Eventually, CEMP and the McConnell family backed a large bank loan for M&S.)[227] Mordecai Richler had riotous fun with a Kolber-like figure in his satirical novel, *Solomon Gursky Was Here,* which was *not* published by M&S but by Viking Canada in 1989.

Bennett was made a member of McClelland & Stewart's finance committee. He helped organize an extension of a credit line with the Royal Bank. As Bennett remembered it, when he got a look at the books he could see that the company was *not* in big trouble.

"Not doing well, but not serious trouble," he said.

Yet one day, Jack McClelland called him up and said he was done with the whole damn publishing business.

"He said 'I promised the Royal Bank $300,000 on Friday.' I knew it. I'd spoken to the bank. He said 'this fucking business is driving me up the wall. I used the money, don't have it to give.' I said Jack, do you want to sell? He said 'I had enough.' I said maybe I'll buy it. I had no knowledge I was going to do this. It was very spontaneous... Within a day, we made a deal."

Do you normally act that fast? I asked.

What's the word, he said, searching for the right one to describe his action.

Impulsive? I asked.

"It was unusual. I was impetuous."

Well maybe. But by then he'd had a deep look into M&S's financial situation and in 1985, the economy was on a tear with lucrative "bought" deals and hostile takeovers like Unicorp's setting Bay Street on fire, with commercial real estate values rising to a peak. A man who had just made large gains in his development company could make good use of a company that could reliably incur losses far into the future. The fact that Bennett bought out all the other investors, as well as Jack McClelland's voting shares, suggests he wanted to incorporate its losses into his development business. As Jack McClelland put it at the press conference when the deal was announced, Avie Bennett "can afford to own M&S."[228] Former publisher Jack Stoddart, who later took Bennett out for lunch at his club to welcome him to the business, said that Bennett explained to him that however dire M&S's situation, his investment in it had already paid for itself many times over. Why? If he hadn't bought M&S when he did, he wouldn't have sold a large retail plaza to the Murray Frum Development Group. If he'd waited, it would have cost him $100 million because the retail real estate market soon went down. As Stoddart put it, even if Bennett threw $1 million a year into M&S for years, that wouldn't amount to the interest earned on that extra $100 million. Besides, he told Stoddart, he didn't want to spend his days playing cards or wintering in Florida. What he liked doing is business.

What Bennett now told me is that the real reason he bought M&S was that he was bored with the development business. By 1985, the deals he was doing were small, while the only deals that were "good" were big ones. "We had done large deals," he said. "We had 100 draftsmen and architects, it was a large organization." He didn't want to spend his evenings going before City Council to "plead for rezoning" on itsy bitsy projects. And none of his children (he has six) were in the business.[229]

What was the name of that business? I asked. I'm not sure why I asked. I'd just seen the sign for First Plazas Inc. outside the office door.

He shot me a look, as if to say, you're trying to embarrass me. "Principal Investments," he said. That's when I realized that he had been referring to a previous big company, not an earlier phase of First Plazas Inc. "It went into receivership. It was a big story. We were the biggest real estate developer in Canada, then we were flattened out completely."

Why flattened? I asked.

"We borrowed too much money," he said. "Peter Newman wrote it as a cover story in *Maclean's.*"

Later, I hunted for Newman's story. I searched the periodicals index from the 1970s onward and couldn't find it—that's because, as I would soon learn, the bankruptcy of Principal Investments had occurred way back in the early 1960s. I learned that only because, while I was searching for the Newman story, I found a cover story about Bennett by business writer David Olive. It had been published in *Toronto Life* in June, 1988. As soon as I got the magazine up from the stacks and opened it to Olive's article, I remembered that my colleagues and I had read the piece avidly when it came out. That's the problem with getting older. Memory is an active process. Unless you revisit your memories again and again, they just get buried beneath an onslaught of new ones.

As Olive told the story, Bennett's first couple of years running M&S had not been smooth. In the beginning, he hired a former bra salesman to handle marketing—not a good idea. People wondered: was he trying to kill the business? Is that why he bought it? Or is he just inept?[230] Jack McClelland left M&S after Bennett's first year running it, though he'd said he'd hang around as an advisor for five.[231] Also, early in 1987, Bennett let go several people who were very experienced and then he held a fire sale of the books published the previous fall which had failed to sell. The howl that went up from writers and agents was loud and long because royalties are calculated as a percentage of a book's sale price. Bennett's response: "In the slow season every other business has sales, so why is the book business sacrosanct?" This was an outsider's question, a retail plaza czar's question whereas insiders knew that the book business is in many ways irrational and not like any other business at all. Out of the blue, Bennett hired Adrienne Clarkson as his Publisher, though her publishing experience was no greater than his. She had just finished her stint as Ontario's Agent General in Paris. Apparently she called him one day, they went to lunch at Il Posto and realized they were on the same wavelength on many things, like being left of centre, like being Canadian nationalists.[232]

Bennett explained to me that he hired Clarkson because he didn't care at all "for being in the public eye... this public thrust my life had taken. I felt it wasn't me. And Adrienne fit into the picture… she had a public persona."

But that relationship didn't last long, either. Clarkson went on to other things (eventually becoming Governor General) and Doug Gibson took her place.

So: why had we read Olive so avidly? Because by June of 1988, some of us in the publishing business—magazines, newspapers, books—had passed beyond curiosity about why a successful developer such as Avie Bennett would suddenly buy the most important Canadian independent publisher. By then, we were in a full-blown state of fear that something bad was happening to the Canadian publishing business, that reporters were being blocked from publishing that which really needed to be published.

By the spring of 1988, some developers and other major business figures had begun to face off against journalists and authors in a series of libel suits. Olive, then a staff writer for *Toronto Life,* set to work on his profile of Bennett only a few months after several members of the Reichmann family (not the eldest brother who I had interviewed extensively) and Olympia & York Developments, sued me, my colleagues, and *Toronto Life* over our November 1987 story on the family's history. They also sued the *Globe and Mail* and the *Toronto Sun* for their *coverage* of our story. Some of us feared that the courts were being used to suppress information important for the public to know. And some of us also feared that a clever way to derail an upsetting forthcoming book would be to buy the publishing company that had contracted for it, refuse to publish it, and then refuse to release the manuscript for someone else to publish without payback of the advance.

These fears were not wholly irrational. The Reichmann/O&Y's statement of claim against the *Globe and Mail* revealed that a writer named Leo Heaps had written a book about Samuel Reichmann under a 1984 contract with M&S. M&S had refused to publish it in 1986, not long after Bennett acquired the company. Heaps had apparently researched the business done in Tangier during World War II by Samuel Reichmann, progenitor of the brothers who later founded Olympia & York Developments. Adding one developer to another developer to make a conspiracy theory, some wondered if Bennett had bought M&S to kill that book. Years later, Bennett told Anthony Bianco, the author of another book on the Reichmanns, that Heaps had asked him and Jack McClelland to convey what amounted to blackmail demands to the Reichmanns. Bennett said that Heaps had asked them to tell the Reichmanns that if they paid him $1 million, he would destroy his manuscript, and if they paid him $250,000, he'd write a different book.[233] Heaps denied that charge and published his allegations about Samuel Reichmann in British *Esquire* in 1992. He and the magazine were sued. But then O&Y went bust and Heaps died.

As Olive researched the Bennett story, I was revising my book manuscript about the Reichmann family and their business interests, under the direction of my Random House editor, Ed Carson. After a while, I was not allowed to work on it in my own office. Random House's lawyers insisted that I must always leave the evolving manuscript in Random House's control in case the court ever ordered me to turn my drafts over to the Reichmanns' lawyers. And sure enough, a motion was filed demanding the manuscript. *Toronto Life's* lawyer, Julian Porter, Q.C., argued, to no avail, that if I was made to turn the draft over as I was still working on it, this would be like sticking a straw into the mind of the writer as she wrote. Yet the court did so rule: eventually I had to turn it over. But in the meantime, I had to drive every day to the warehouse/editorial offices of Random House of Canada, which were then located in an industrial zone not far from Pearson airport. I worked at a computer in the office of a junior editor named Douglas Pepper—the same Douglas Pepper who would become the President and Publisher of McClelland & Stewart in 2004, replacing Doug Gibson. As I corrected facts, juggled syntax, and made cuts, I worried that something I did might be misconstrued by the Reichmanns' many lawyers and blow back on me, my colleagues, and the magazine that employed them. I spent hours deleting phrases that were apt in favour of phrases that were safe.

One day, a woman I'd never seen before came up to me in the Random House lunchroom and asked me if I was very, very afraid. Afraid of what? I asked. The people suing you, she said. I told her I was not, and tried to get away from her, but she followed, and kept asking. There was something about the way she persisted that I read as a threat. When I told my editor about it, it was discovered that she was a brand-new hire. Now we had to consider: had she been sent in to get a look at the manuscript? Or to intimidate me? Or none of the above? How would we ever know? *Toronto Life's* lawyers had learned by then that a very well known detective agency, Kroll Associates, had been hired by the plaintiffs to go over every facet of the *Toronto Life* story, and every detail of the Reichmann brothers' parents' lives in Tangier, Paris, Vienna, Hungary. During the first three months of 1988 alone, the Kroll bill reached $844,000. (The investigators' work continued for two more years involving as many as a dozen agents at one time, each paid $1500 per day.[234])

But the truth is that I *was* afraid, as were many of my colleagues. Kimberley Noble, who had been writing in the *Globe and Mail* about the Edper/Brascan/Hees group of companies, was threatened with legal action if she proceeded with a planned book on the group's history.[235] *Globe and Mail* reporter Jock Ferguson had so many developers suing him that he and the *Globe* parted ways. Conrad Black sued. Garth Drabinsky was litigious. Many years later, these two would be found guilty of certain crimes and end up going to prison, but then they were aggressive in their use of the courts to secure their reputations.[236] Some of us who had been sued began to think that these lawsuits, emanating from people who sat together on important business boards, were about more than individual reputations: these suits represented a business strategy to discourage reporting about important interests, unless that reporting was of the fawning variety.[237]

So, Olive's article was read by unhappy libel defendants with close attention. It provided an answer to that whispered question: why *had* Bennett–a developer!—bought the leading publisher of Canadian fiction and non-fiction? Had a fox bought the henhouse?

As Olive saw it, and as he compellingly told it, Bennett's motive had nothing to do with any of that, and everything to do with redemption. He had taken on a company in trouble that was considered to be vital to the sovereignty of the nation, as if to atone for the failure of his family's development company, the biggest in the country, more than twenty years earlier. Bennett told Olive that he "would keep McClelland & Stewart as an important force in Canadian literature…

if profits were the underlying motive I wouldn't have bought the company, because there are a lot of easier ways of making money. It's not worth my saving McClelland & Stewart unless I try to save what Jack started."[238] According to Olive, it had taken Bennett 17 long years to make his comeback, 17 years to earn a seat at important tables, like the Governing Council of the University of Toronto to which Premier Peterson appointed him in 1987, as well as to its Business Board later.[239] He would be inducted into the Order of Canada as a Member by 1991, his ownership of McClelland & Stewart cited as the reason.[240]

Olive described meeting Bennett in First Plazas Inc.'s modest offices, then located above a Winners store in Toronto's Lawrence Plaza. Bennett's father and uncles had built some of Canada's earliest shopping plazas, first in Toronto, and then across the country. They had talked the Woolworth's chain into leasing properties and eventually became Canada's biggest commercial landlords, owning most of the Famous Players theatre buildings, leasing back 150 branch offices to Canadian banks. One of Bennett's uncles started the Fairweather chain of ladies clothing stores. Bennett had been so excited to become a part of the family empire that he left the University of Toronto without graduating to set to work. The business was worth about $200 million by the early 1960s—a vast sum of money in those days—but it was over-leveraged. And then there was a sharp economic downturn.[241]

Olive, unknowingly writing a prophecy, described the Bennett family's business this way: "The Bennetts had been the Reichmanns of their day."

Only a few years after Olive's story was published, the Reichmanns' Olympia & York Developments was also flattened by too much leverage.

The Bennetts' problems were touched off thanks to $6 million borrowed from the Mercantile Bank. The Mercantile Bank was bought by the First National Bank of New York, now known as Citibank. First National called the loan. Principal Investments owned a lot of land, but had no free cash. As Olive put it:

> In his frantic efforts to pay the bank off, Avie offered it the corners
> of Bloor and Yonge, and Yonge and St. Clair—land packages with

staggering appreciation potential. But the bank wasn't willing to let the Bennetts sell off some of their properties in order to slip out of their bind, choosing instead to force the entire Principal empire into receivership.

The assets were sold by the receivers to pay creditors, which is the way it works in capitalism: first the business grows slowly, then it expands through borrowing, then in an economic contraction lenders call their loans, which is often followed by business failure and the recycling of assets at bargain basement prices. Some of Principal's properties were picked up by the company that became Cadillac Fairview, and by other developers who would have similar problems in a later business cycle. Bennett's father and uncles retired, leaving Bennett to pay off $1 million of Principal's debt that he'd backed personally. As Olive wrote:

> ...Bennett's empire today—dubbed First Plazas Inc... is a ramshackle collection of 12 or so properties, some of them prized from the Principal receivers' grip... including a part interest in McClelland & Stewart's new head office building...

In other words, Bennett owned a piece of 481 University when he moved M&S into the building.

After he finally got back on his feet, Bennett helped others out of their own troubles, according to Olive, stabilizing the Tanenbaum family fortune when Max Tanenbaum suffered a stroke, and bankrolling Jerry Goodis' comeback.

After making his impetuous offer, Bennett bought M&S from Jack McClelland and the other investors for about two million dollars. After McClelland left, he settled down to run the business and make it work.

"I enjoyed the stimulation of the business," Avie told me.

But suddenly, he jumped right out of the chronology of his entry into the publishing business, to the way he'd managed his exit. He gestured toward a small photograph, framed, hanging on the wall between the windows, where he could see it easily from his chair.

Do you know who those people are? He asked.

I got up and went over to look at the photo. Yes, I know who they are, I told him. And you would too: arrayed in rows were several creators of the CanLit canon. There was Margaret Atwood, her husband Graeme Gibson (I read him before I'd heard of her), Rohinton Mistry, Alistair MacLeod, Alice Munro, Anne Michaels, Michael Ondaatje, even John Fraser, Editor of *Saturday Night Magazine* when Conrad Black owned it. Fraser had by then become Master of Massey College at U of T and was trying to be a novelist. Standing among them was Avie, a much younger, heavier Avie, and his assistant, Diana.

"They phoned Diana and asked [can we] take Avie and you to lunch to thank you for what you did for Canadian publishing?" he said, "just authors, to show respect... A very rewarding day."

There was a date inscribed on a tiny brass plaque on the frame. It said January 5, 2001, six months after he gave those M&S shares to U of T and sold the rest to Random House. These writers appeared to be smiling down upon him, blessing him and all his works. Pointing this out was clearly his way of saying: will you get to the point, already? You can see that what I did passed muster with the people who count.

So why did you give M&S away? I asked.

He'd been in the business for fifteen years, he said. It was time for a change. And he was 72.

You didn't get out because it was getting really tough to be in publishing? I asked.

I'd assumed it was brilliant business timing on his part. Knowing when to sell is as important as knowing when to buy. I'd been reading the testimony given to the Parliamentary Standing Committee on Canadian Heritage in their hearings on the state of Canadian publishing in the spring of 2000. Other publishers and their association had made it clear to the Committee that some were in dire straits due to their books being returned by Larry Stevenson's Chapters, with no payments for as long as two quarters. Some were at the edge of bankruptcy.

It had nothing to do with Larry Stevenson, Bennett assured me. He never had any trouble with Larry Stevenson. "Nothing pushed me out," he said.

And yet I'd also found a report of a speech Bennett had made in the fall of 1999, concerning the disaster about to befall Canadian trade book publishers—due to the rise of Amazon. *Maclean's* called it a "dire warning." The occasion was the group launch of McClelland & Stewart's fall books. This event was held at the Art Gallery of Ontario. Bennett had just bought the *Canadian Encyclopedia* from Mel Hurtig in order to help out Hurtig whose company was going under. (The Encyclopedia lives on at Historica.ca and is available online. It receives very significant grants from Heritage Canada.) Bennett's M&S had just bought Macfarlane, Walter & Ross from Jack Stoddart. By the fall of 1999, consolidation seemed to be a favourite strategy in the international book business. Random House had merged with Doubleday, and then been bought by Bertelsmann. Putnam had merged with Penguin.

When Bennett made his speech, he pointed out that returns to Canadian publishers from booksellers had increased by 12%, which was bad, but that the biggest problem was the territory-busting behaviour of Amazon. Bennett said he'd just done a test to see if the American edition of a Canadian originated book (Alice Munro's *The Love of a Good Woman*) would be delivered to a Canadian address if ordered from Amazon US online. It had been. He concluded that "we and other Canadian publishers are losing millions of dollars in sales that way..."[242]

I reminded Bennett of that speech.

Giving away M&S had nothing to do with any of that, Bennett insisted, nothing and no one had pushed him from the business. M&S was profitable on and off, he said. He just felt he needed "an exit strategy," just like anyone else who owned a Canadian publishing company.

Why?

"The obligation to keep Canadian ownership and there were no Canadian buyers," he said.

Did you try to find some? I asked. I remembered what my informant had asserted, and what Jack Stoddart had confirmed when I called him to check. At the time of the gift and sale in 2000, Bennett had claimed that he'd offered M&S to Stoddart and to Anna Porter, but both had turned him down. Stoddart called this "an utter fabrication."

"No, I didn't try," Bennett said now, to my surprise, "but nobody knocked on the door. I thought I needed an exit strategy at some point."

Yet he didn't actually exit from M&S after he gave it to U of T. He stayed on its board as Chairman for another 11 years until U of T handed the shares over to Random House of Canada. He'd also told me that he was bored with the development business when he bought M&S, but he hadn't gotten out of the development business either. First Plazas Inc. was still involved in deals.

Did you go to Random House first? I asked.

"I went to U of T first," he said.

Another surprise. That meant my clever husband had got it wrong. He is rarely wrong. Who did you see? I asked.

At first, he said he didn't remember. Then he remembered. He said: "I went to Mr. Prichard."

Robert Prichard, the President? How did you know him?

I was on the Board of the U of T, he said. It seemed logical.

He'd been on the Governing Council and its Business Board for two years when Prichard, Dean of Law, became President of the University of Toronto.[243] The Governing Council that appointed Prichard to the Presidency included Gerry Schwartz, who, like Bennett was appointed to the Council by Premier David Peterson. After Premier Peterson lost the election of 1990 to the NDP, Peterson served as a director on various corporate boards, including as chairman of the board of Chapters.[244] Peterson was still on the Chapters board when Gerry Schwartz and Heather Reisman, through Trilogy, made their takeover move.

What happened?

"It was receptive," Bennett said. "I felt it was in good hands. I thought it was a way out. And it was."

What about the valuation of the gift for the tax credit? I asked. Did that come from the sale of shares to Random House?

"U of T put a value on the company. That was the value we used for the government valuation of the tax credit," he said.

I sat back in my chair. I explained that I understood that when the shares of a private company are given as a gift to a registered charity, it's very difficult to get their value properly assessed for the purpose of issuing a tax credit receipt, and that I had heard some universities were reluctant to take such gifts because the last thing they want is trouble with the Canada Revenue Agency. In fact, one large university got more than one independent appraisal by professionals, which entailed a lot of time and expense and involved running through the company and its books with a fine-tooth comb…

Oh, we did none of that, he said, cutting me off with a hand wave.

And the University issued a tax receipt?

It did, he said. "There was no hocus pocus. The Random House deal was at that point."

He went to Random House because he thought that the U of T Press was not a well-run company and he wanted some kind of arrangement that would ensure M&S would be well managed. "Didn't need to have an appraisal," he said, "needed a better back room to work with U of T…" And, he said again, it had nothing to do with what was going on in the publishing realm, it was "coincidental" that it happened in that period, there was no pressure on him at all, not from U of T, Random House, or anybody else. "Random House liked the idea. And I knew Neale, [then Chairman of Random House of Canada] a good guy."

So you're sure that U of T valued the company itself, they didn't use the sale of the shares to Random House to value the gift? They didn't send auditors to poke into the company?

I kept asking this question because I was so surprised at his answer. But he was adamant.

"None of that valuation happened," he said firmly.

Who did you clear it with when you went to Ottawa? I asked, thinking at least I'll find out now whether he went to see Sheila Copps, or someone else, or no one at all. Because I can't find a record of any of that, I added.

"I don't remember going to Ottawa. Did talk."

Do you remember who to? Was it with a man named Wernick?

"The name Wernick rings a bell," he said. But then the said: "I'm not sure."

Did you try offering it to any other foreign-owned publishers? I asked.

"At that point, Random House was the top Canadian [foreign-owned] publisher. I didn't have to go anywhere else. They said yes."

This is *not* the way the sale of a business is normally handled. Usually the seller wants to maximize value in the eyes of prospective buyers, and the best way to do that is to find more than one interested buyer. On the other hand, how many business owners give the control block away as a gift to a charity, and then try to sell the minority to a business that will run it?

Okay, I said. So you did the deal and then the years go by and in 2011, U of T decides to transfer its shares to Random House. What can you tell me about that?

"The final deal we weren't aware of till it was finished," he said. "I was as surprised as you were."

That made no sense either. He'd been on the board at the time, in fact he'd been the Chairman of that board, voting the University's interest.

Remind me who else was on the board, I said.

He began to speak with pride about some of the people who'd served with him. Its members had included John Evans, a former president of U of T, and Rob Prichard.

Why those two? I asked.

"A certain glamour to the business that appealed to them," he said with just the tiniest hint of a glint in his eye. And then there was Arlene Perly Rae.

Why her? I asked.

"She was a bright woman and the right sex," he said. Trina McQueen, who replaced Perly Rae when her husband Bob Rae ran for the leadership of the federal Liberal Party in 2006, was "the brightest board member." McQueen was once a leading figure at both CBC and CTV, but by then was a director on the CBC's board. Later, she became an adjunct professor at the Schulich School of Business at York University. He knew her from the board of Historica. And he rhymed off the others on the board, including Doug Gibson.

So why did you stay on as Chairman of the board of a company you didn't own any shares of for so many years? I asked.

"It had a certain prestige," he said. "It gave me an opportunity to keep an eye on the undertakings, to make sure it continued," he said.

No, he wasn't talking about making sure that the University would sell its shares only to a Canadian. That wasn't part of the agreement because it was the law: "It was taken for granted. So not in the agreement," he said.

There is a written agreement? I asked.

"Yes, there is a written agreement," he said.

Can I see it?

"No, you can't see the agreement," he said.

About the tax credit you got for giving U of T 75% of the shares of the company, I said. Did that matter to you?

It mattered, but it was not a big deal, he said.

How long was U of T supposed to hold onto its shares? I asked. From the press conference given at the time, it sounded as if you were giving it to the university to hold in perpetuity. But Doug Gibson told *Maclean's* three years.

He looked at me for a moment and said nothing, as if he was reconsidering his estimate of my general level of intelligence.

Forever is a long time, he finally said. On the other hand, "they didn't go into it with the idea you'll sell it," he said. "It was to be there a long time. They carried out all obligations the way they were supposed to. I have no criticisms of the way Random House or U of T handled the deal."

What if I told you that when the University got rid of its shares, there is no record of that transaction in U of T's annual reports, and its spokesperson says that is because it was handed over to Random House at the cost of zero. And her explanation is that there was a huge debt.

I can't tell you, he said.

Was there a three-year hold agreement as Doug Gibson said at the time?

Yes.

Can you show me?

Get it from U of T, he said.

What would you say if I told you that Doug Gibson believes that actual control of M&S passed to Random House long before the University's shares did, like sometime in 2004–2005?

I thought his answer would be definitive. He had been Chairman of the board for the whole period, from the time he made the donation to the final transfer of the shares. No one was better placed to confirm or deny what Gibson had said about who had control.

"I think Doug is correct," he said.

A bit later, I asked him again, to be sure. Was it fair to say that M&S was not Canadian controlled from 2004 and therefore not eligible to apply for certain grants and tax credits?

"I can't comment," he said, [whether or] not [it was] Canadian controlled from 2004 on. I don't know…"

I was confused. Had he just changed his tune? I asked again: I need to know, I said, because if it was not Canadian controlled from 2004, it shouldn't have been able to receive certain grants and tax credits.

"I would have guessed 2005," he said.

And a little later, as he considered these questions, he said: "This is a book no one will read. I say [that] as a publisher."

I'm not doing a book, Avie, I replied.

But from that point forward, though I meant to publish what I learned in my blog, I began to think perhaps I should do a book or at least a magazine story. Because: I had two people who were in a position to know agreeing that actual control (meaning the minority shareholder was able to make vital decisions even though the majority of the voting shares were owned by U of T) passed from the hands of a Canadian institution to the foreign-owned Random House in 2004–2005. Nevertheless, M&S had continued to apply for grants requiring U of T to have that control for another six years—as if nothing had changed. (I didn't know then that the government had no problem with the transfer of de facto control of M&S to Random House: in fact, it had blessed it from the start.)

What do you know about the M&S shares being passed over to Random House by the University for essentially nothing? I asked.

I can't comment because I don't know, he said.

Did you know that Bertelsmann had a Nazi past?

First I've heard of it, he said. But he thought that probably was the case for many German companies. They had been cleaned up so they could move forward.

The tax credit—what was the size of it? Can you tell me?

"I don't remember the size of the tax credit," he said. "But [I] think it's a personal matter between an individual and the government."

I could see he was getting tired. It was time to go. He had answered the vital question about when control changed hands, but just to be sure, for the record, I asked him one more time.

So, I said, when did effective control of M&S pass from U of T to Random House? (Effective control is simple English for the legal term de facto control.)

"[From] 2004—basically it's Random House's baby," he said.

I threw my notebook and pens into my bag and thanked him for his time. But instead of saying goodbye, he said he wanted me to go to the far end of his office and pull a book bound in red leather off the shelf and read what it said on the inside cover.

I did as I was told. I found the red book. It was Pierre Trudeau's memoir. I had been told that Avie Bennett used to have a box at the Big Owe (the stadium built for the 1976 Olympics) in Montreal and that Pierre Trudeau would sometimes watch Expo games with him there. I opened the book to the first inside page. In Trudeau's hand were scrawled these words, "thanks for the advice." I could see why Bennett would want me to read it. It showed that he had a warm relationship with the Prime Minister who brought Canada into the fullness of nationhood, who brought forward and passed the law that made the sale of Canadian publishers to foreign entities illegal unless certain exceptions pertained.

I walked out into the cool sunshine thinking I could use some wise advice myself. My informant had been right about many of his allegations, and now Bennett had given me one more thing to chew on—that the University had done no deep investigation of the value of M&S when they issued him a tax credit receipt for shares.

What kind of story had I been pulled into?

8

For an Exit Strategy, Call...

When I got home, I called Robert Prichard. I couldn't just take Bennett's word for it that the University of Toronto had put a value on the M&S shares *without* reference to the sale to Random House, and that the University had issued a tax credit receipt *without* sending in the accountants to examine M&S's books and prospects.

I left a voice mail message on Prichard's line, and on his assistant's, explaining that I needed to check facts about that gift.

I did not expect Prichard to call back, though I had to try. He has been hip deep in the pool of power coagulating around Queen's Park and Bay Street for more than a quarter of a century, a member of a charmed circle of accomplished people who have blessed Canada with their intelligence and their determination to serve. I expected his assistant to ask for an email she could forward to him: I thought I would probably have to wait for hell to freeze over before I got a response.

Consider his astonishing curriculum vitae. He was born in Britain, grew up in Toronto (his father taught law at the University of Toronto). He earned a B.A. from Swarthmore, a US Little Ivy League school that ranks higher than most real Ivies, an MBA in Finance and International Business from University of Chicago, an LLB from University of Toronto, where he graduated with the gold medal, which is no small feat. He did an LLM at Yale, became Dean of Law at University of Toronto in 1984, its President in 1990. He has, as an upper-class Brazilian scholar of my acquaintance would say, a proper formation.

And then his life got busier, though there were downs as well as ups. In 2002, Prichard was appointed President and CEO of Torstar. Under Prichard's direction, Torstar bought its competition—20% of the conglomerate CTVglobemedia, and Black Press. By the time Prichard resigned from Torstar in 2009, the CTVglobemedia investment had been written down from $200 million to $95.7 million, and Black Press to zero. There had been layoffs, Torstar's share price had dropped from about $20 to $6, and the dividend was cut (though do not cry for Prichard: he left with about $10 million in severance,[245] bonuses, and shares).[246] Torstar's decline cannot be laid at his feet: newspapering everywhere was under assault from the relocation of ads from newspapers' classified pages to the Internet, from the relentless bleed of major advertisers to Google and Internet platform providers, from the emergence of smart phones and tablets with an ever-expanding array of apps, from the rise of social media that have changed how most people get their information about the world.

Prichard was then appointed Chairman of the newly formed board of Penguin Canada (there'd been a sex scandal and the company had been placed under the sharp eye of Penguin US). He was also appointed President and CEO of Metrolinx by Ontario Premier Dalton McGuinty, but quickly became Chairman of its board. Metrolinx plans, builds and runs transit systems linking the municipalities forming the Greater Toronto Area and the Greater Hamilton Area. This creates serious political flack. Metrolinx decisions can make developers happy or sad, and municipal and provincial politicians happy or sad, and can drive voters to punish or reward. For example: Metrolinx opened a new station in 2015 with bright lights around its perimeter and buses rolling in and out by night. The station was placed right behind a residential neighbourhood with big backyards. The hue and cry made the papers. Prichard went to check it out himself and changes were made. Similarly, Metrolinx miscalculated the fare to be charged for the trip between Pearson Airport and Union Station on its new, dedicated UP Express line, which is supposed to be like the fast, cheap transport systems offered to air travellers in London and Paris, etc. But the fare was set so high that hardly anybody used it, which meant it could never pay for itself. Eventually, the fare dropped and its CEO was replaced. In other words, Prichard presided over the problems and the solutions.

During his tenure at Torstar, Prichard added new corporate directorships to a list that already included Four Seasons, Onex, and Imasco. Prichard had joined the Imasco board in 1993, while he was President of U of T, the year before he joined the Onex board. Imasco's Pension Fund had been one of the earliest investors in Onex. Imasco was an investment vehicle for the cash flowing from its ownership of Imperial Tobacco of Montreal. As President of U of T, Prichard apparently accepted so many gifts to the University from Imasco that those who disapproved referred to it as the University of Tobacco. (That's a nicer name than Prichard's Palace, Seymour Schulich's epithet for U of T after Prichard accepted Joseph Rotman's donation to the management school, not Schulich's.[247] Schulich had to settle for York, according to Peter Newman in *Titans*.) Prichard also served on the boards of Brascan (now called Brookfield Asset Management), Moore Corporation and George Weston (Loblaw). These days he is on the board of Peter Munk's Barrick Gold and is Chairman of the board of the Bank of Montreal (the BMO Financial Group). But what you really need to know about Robert Prichard is that soon after he left Torstar, he became the non-executive Chairman of Torys LLP, which was once called Tory, Tory, Deslauriers and Binnington.

Torys is a corporate lawyer's idea of heaven. Not only do its partners include some of the great lawyers in this country, but it promotes the role of women in the profession, advocates about righting the wrongs done to First Nations, and about the roles lawyers play in safeguarding democratic institutions. Former Ontario Premier William Davis was Counsel to the firm for many years after he left public office. Frank Iacobucci became Counsel to Torys after retiring from the Supreme Court of Canada.[248] Lawyers who have "matters" with Torys lawyers rarely have bad words to say about them.[249]

Torys' major client has been the Thomson Corporation. John Tory (the father of the Mayor of Toronto who is also named John

Tory) along with his twin brother James, led the expansion of the firm founded by their father from the 1950s onward. In 1973, John Tory left the firm to work with Thomson Corporation's founder Roy Thomson, 1st Baron Thomson of Fleet, who had become a Fleet Street mogul by buying newspapers and media outlets in the UK (including the prestigious *Times* and *Sunday Times*). Tory maintained this *consiglieri* relationship with Thomson's son Kenneth, and for a time with Kenneth's son David. Together, they built Thomson from a smallish newspaper chain (Thomson bought his first paper in Timmins, Ontario, for about $200)[250] into a globe-spanning information giant with a little oil business on the side. Meanwhile, the law firm remained in the hands[251] of John's twin brother James and partners. The name change occurred when the firm merged with a New York law group. It has also set up branches across Canada.

That Prichard presides over Torys speaks of the high regard in which he is held by his peers, but also of the rain he can make. Prichard is an economic advisor to the governments of Ontario and Canada. He has served on too many boards and commissions to mention. He has been recognized for his service by being named a Member of the Order of Ontario and an Officer of the Order of Canada.[252] (But not a Companion: Avie Bennett is a Companion. If Prichard wants to be a Companion, he might consider buying what's left of M&S from Penguin Random House.)

The only time I have seen Prichard in the flesh, as opposed to the pages of my newspapers, was one hot summer night at a restaurant in my neighbourhood—a very ordinary restaurant—eating dinner by himself. He was dressed the way most of us dress when we're by ourselves on hot summer nights, in slacks and a shirt of no importance. He wore a frown too, the same one that usually appears in the newspaper photos under his tousled crop of fair hair. The frown is like a long divot dug between his eyes, eyes that angle sadly down at their outer edges. Why does he frown? Is he considering so many things at once that he forgets to tell his face to take it easy? He told one magazine interviewer that he has a farm outside of town where he relaxes over a book on weekends. I believe he has a farm. But I doubt he relaxes anywhere.[253]

I offer as proof, this: I got a call back from Rob Prichard the same day I called him, at about 5:30 in the afternoon. I was astonished, and at first thought this boded well, that he would say yes when I asked if I could please come down to his office and speak with him about Avie Bennett's gift of M&S to U of T.

No, he said.

Why not?

"[It's] not a great idea to meet with you. There's a cardinal rule at University of Toronto. Former presidents should be seen and not heard."

Yes, I'm sure, I said, but my questions are about what you did as President and no one else can explain that but you. (And besides, I should have said, here you are being heard though not seen. But that only occurred to me later.)

"Well if it's something prior to 2000…," he said.

It happened in the spring of 2000, I said, in your last couple of months as President.

I was pretty sure he would still say no, so I told myself I should just treat this phone call as a face-to-face interview because it was probably as close to Prichard as I was going to get—unless I stalked him at a public meeting. I once tried that on Marshall (known as Mickey) Cohen, former Deputy Minister of Energy, Mines and Resources and former Deputy Minister of Finance, who was at that point working for the Reichmanns' at Olympia & York Enterprises[254] as they acquired companies—such as Gulf Resources.[255] Canadian investors had been encouraged by the federal government's National Energy Programme and certain interesting tax provisions to buy the Canadian subsidiaries of foreign oil companies. Cohen had helped form these policies, along with Ed Clark, and while working at Enterprises, he was executing them. Cohen had refused to be interviewed. So I went to an annual meeting he had to attend and tried to corner him. He'd walked backwards very fast and got away from me. I thought Prichard would probably do the same if I stalked him. Besides, a face-to-face interview was not essential. Physical context and personal attributes are the main reasons why journalists ask for meetings, though listening to a person on the phone is sometimes more revealing: important signals may be missed when you are sitting with your head down over your notes on the other side of someone's desk. Besides, I already knew what Prichard looked like and I had spent time inside Torys. I had endured mediation there during the end game of the 'Robertson 1' electronic rights class action, so the setting was still fresh in my mind. So was the Torys lunch, delivered by pushcart loaded with a charming array of soups and wraps and other treats set out on white swoops of china, surmounted by edible flower accompaniments. The art in the conference room had seemed so appropriate to Torys: an actual wasp's nest displayed under glass on a white plinth.

So, as Prichard pondered whether he would speak to me at all, I simply remembered entering the south tower of the Toronto Dominion Centre, one of six black, sleek, featureless totems to commerce whose placement and style were designed by Ludwig Mies van der Rohe at the suggestion of architectural maven Phyllis Lambert (daughter of Sam Bronfman). They were built by Fairview, forerunner of Cadillac Fairview, which controls them.[256] I remembered the slippery granite floor in the entry hall, the express elevator that zoomed up to Torys' 33rd floor reception. I remembered the reception area's vertiginous views of water and sky. Tory's ten floors are interconnected by a floating staircase, the whole space redesigned by KPMB in 2008 in a carefully conservative version of the modernist style.[257] I remembered my way down a wide hall with beautiful planked flooring, past glass-walled meeting rooms with wood-panelled sliding doors, past a series of Ed Burtynsky's arresting images, hung on white walls, of the devastation wreaked upon the earth by corporate hands.

I imagined Prichard sitting in a big, light-washed room, one lanky leg flopped over the other (did I mention he is tall?) with the lake behind him as moving wallpaper.

As he did not hang up on me, I began to quickly explain what I'd learned from Gibson, from U of T, and from Avie Bennett, which was why I'd called.

I told him that I had just been to see Mr. Bennett and we had talked about his gift of 75% of M&S to U of T. (Prichard interrupted to say he still considered it to be a magnificent phil-anthropic gesture.) I told Prichard that I had asked Bennett about the valuation of the shares for the tax credit receipt issued by U of T, and Bennett had said that, contrary to what I had been told about how other universities deal with the gift of shares of private companies, U of T had done no independent valuation of the M&S shares, and that the sale to Random House had *not* been used to establish their value.

There was a brief silence and then an intake of breath followed by a strong statement delivered in a wrap of pure sarcasm. Prichard said that he was sure that in my fairly busy life it wouldn't surprise me to learn that such a thing—issuing a tax credit receipt for a gift without independent evaluation—would be "beyond the competence of the president" of a university.

In my business, that is what is called a non-denial denial.

Well, I said to him, I'd thought, thanks to clever husband, that the tax credit value must have been based on the sale of 25% of the shares to Random House of Canada, but Mr. Bennett had assured me that was not correct, and yet, he had also said there had been no combing through the business of M&S by the University either.

"My recollection is Mr. Bennett sold 25% of M&S at the same time, or before the gift to us, I forget... They paid a fair market value." And that was the basis of the valuation, he said, "a contemporaneous market transaction. That is my recollection."

So how would you suggest that I determine what actually happened, I asked, as the two of you disagree? How do I know whose recollection is correct?

"[If I were you] I'd go back and get the files," he said. "It would show the basis of the receipt."

"Which files?"

"The Development Department's. The President of the University can't do that," he reiterated. By which he meant, the president of a university is not in charge of issuing tax credit receipts for gifts. People working in development departments do that.

I asked him if he could just try and walk me through how the gift had happened, how the proposal had come to him in the first place.

"Avie told me that he wanted the company in different hands. He proposed to sell 25% to Random House, for the benefit of [its] back offices, distribution, early [adoption of] digital, and to put 75% of the shares in the University to maintain Canadian ownership in U of T's hands."

Okay, I said. So you had no problem with that idea.

"He was a friend and a prominent man for many years. He made the proposal. We did the gift. We made the agreement public at the time. The terms under which he gave the shares may not be public."

He was certainly right about that: I'd been searching for those terms for some time with no success. They had been well and truly buried. I told Prichard that Bennett said he had spoken to people in Ottawa. I told Prichard I didn't get that. It wasn't as if Bennett was trying to sell control of the company to a foreigner. So why talk to Ottawa at all? I asked.

"We had to get Ottawa's support," he said.

But why? I asked, and from whom? The law requires that Canadians control Canadian publishing companies, there's nothing in it prohibiting the sale of a minority share to a foreign owner.

"Heritage Canada," he replied. "I went to Ottawa myself. I think the issue was the sale of 25% to Random House."

Again, I said I didn't understand why that would be. Why would Ottawa have been concerned with this at all? Random House wasn't buying control. And why did *he* go? He was the president of a Canadian institution getting the gift, he wasn't the seller of the shares. And by the way, I added, there is no record of any application having been made, and Sheila Copps didn't remember it coming to her.

"This was 15 years ago," he muttered, annoyed.

Yes, I said, and I'm sorry to ask you about it now because I know if you asked me about something I did 15 years ago I'd be at sea. But please try to recall.

"I have a clear memory of discussions in Ottawa to ensure U of T had control though Random House had control or influence on parts of the business. I do a lot with Heritage Canada. I dealt with them and Penguin Canada. I may be conflating."

Penguin Canada? What about Penguin Canada?

And then I remembered. He had been appointed Chairman of a brand new board of Penguin Canada three years before its merger with Random House.[258] The *Investment Canada Act* required Penguin and Random House to get permission from the Minister of Canadian Heritage to merge their Canadian subsidiaries after the parents merged. Such permission was not guaranteed. So he seemed to be telling me he had helped escort two publishing companies through the thickets of the Department of Canadian Heritage's Book Policy and the *Investment Canada Act*. Yet when he became chairman of Penguin's board, he'd made much of being a Canadian nationalist. He had told John Barber of the *Globe and Mail* that "he sees his role as keeping the Maple Leaf flying with the company's new internationalized operations."[259] That flag did not fly long. Later, when I wrote to Penguin Random House to inquire as to whether the independent Penguin Canada board still exists, no one bothered to reply.

I told him that the minutes of one of the University's Governing Council meetings had referred to an undertaking to be made by the University to the Director of Investigations, Investment Canada. I explained that when I'd followed that up, I had been assured by officials that there had never been such a person as the Director of Investigations and there was nothing on file about any undertaking given by University of Toronto in this matter.

He listened to me carefully. He said he was pretty sure that the discussions he had were with Heritage Canada, and the issue had been this: though Random House had influence, U of T had control. The *Investment Canada Act* and the *Income Tax Act* are concerned with the difference between influence (a large say in how a company operates) versus control (the right by the majority shareholder to appoint directors who will have complete sway over corporate decisions). In other words, "that it was not a transfer of Avie indirectly to Random House."

He seemed to be saying that he'd assured someone in Ottawa that the gift/sale was not the first step in a salami strategy devised to get around the *Investment Canada Act*.

How do I check this? I asked.

He suggested that I speak with Avie's lawyer, but he could not remember the lawyer's name. He seemed a bit uncertain about whether he went to Ottawa by himself or with others.

"I could be wrong," he said. "Avie may well have come with me."

I said I still didn't understand why anyone had talked to Ottawa at all.

The issue, the question, was about control, he said again. On paper it looked as if U of T had control, but the bureaucrats wanted to know, was that real? The answer was yes, Prichard told me. On its face the gift/sale "does not require approval. But Heritage wanted to know that the ownership of U of T was real."

And of course it didn't hurt that he, the President of U of T, was the man giving the assurances. It would have helped too that he could say that he and John Evans, a former President of U of T, would be on the M&S board helping to safeguard U of T's control.

And yet it was also specified that Random House would run the business. "We were clear we did not intend to invest in the business if a drain on the University's resources," he said.

Do you remember any of the terms of the agreement, how long the University undertook to hold on to the shares? I asked.

No, he did not recall any terms. But there had been no intention to receive the shares and then sell them. "But things change," he continued. "Retail is difficult, ebooks are difficult, consolidation is a powerful force…"

How would I be able to find out what the terms were? I asked.

"Look at the contract," he said.

How would I do that?

"Was it public?"

No, I said, it was not.

"If not, make a freedom of information request."

I almost snickered. The federal government had long been notorious for failing to respond to such requests for months, even years, and then producing pages of blacked out material, along with an invitation to file an appeal. Besides, universities are not covered by the federal *Access to Information Act*.

File an access request with whom? I asked.

Ontario's universities have been brought under the aegis of the provincial *Freedom of Information and Protection of Privacy Act,* known as FIPPA, he said. He advised me to make a provincial filing.

By the way, I asked. What did the University get out of this?

There was a pause. "The University's interest was the promotion of writers published by M&S, like Margaret Atwood..." he said. Like Michael Ondaatje, he added.

I thought that was an odd response. Neither author needed help to promote their work. Neither would have been denied publication if control of M&S had not been given to U of T. Any publisher would have been thrilled to get them as they had been on bestseller lists and selling internationally for many years.

So, to reiterate, I said, how was the value of the M&S shares established?

"I believe the Random House sale was the valuation, a market transaction for a percentage of the company."

And how large was the tax receipt?

"I don't know the value of the tax receipt issued."

Who would it have been issued by?

"By the Department of Development. The lawyers and accountants there would insist it conform to the CRA [Canada Revenue Agency] requirements." And, Prichard said, all of this would have been handled correctly. There could never be a hint or suggestion that the valuation was inappropriate. It was a "very public transaction much commented on by many interests."

I told him I found it amazing that I could find no mention of the subsequent transfer of the University's shares to Random House in the University's annual reports. I told him I'd been trying to reach Dr. Naylor, who was President of the University at that time, in order to ask about it. Did he have advice on that?

He said Dr. Naylor might not talk about it and I should write instead to the current president, Dr. Meric Gertler. And by the way, he added, he still considered Avie Bennett's gift to the U of T to be a "wonderfully generous act of philanthropy and Canadian nationalism." He was still "happy to be a part of that. It was a second way that U of T could be involved in Canadian publishing. [My] view hasn't changed."

Did you know that the M&S shares were transferred to Random House at a cost of zero? I asked him. M&S owned the best Canadian backlist in the country, the best part of the Canadian literary canon, which should have had spectacular value. So how could it have been worth nothing?

"I can't help on that," he said, after another pause. "Write to Meric Gertler and inquire as to who to speak to. He may answer. Or not."

9

The Gift that Kept Not Giving

I hung up the phone, checked over my notes, threw up my hands.

How on earth could I find out what had really happened when two of the people who did the deed—both of whom enjoyed spectacular business experience and public honours—contradicted each other? Was the tax receipt issued by U of T based on the sale of 25% of M&S to Random House? Or was it based on Avie Bennett's say so?

Who had spoken with Heritage Canada, Prichard or Bennett? And if one or both had done so, why did Sheila Copps, the Minister at the time, have no recollection of it coming before her? Why did the University's records refer to an undertaking given to an office that never existed in a Department with no record of any undertaking asked for or given? It still made little sense to me that the federal government would have been asked for its opinion. The University of Toronto, already the owner of one Canadian publishing company, had been given 75% of another. The *Investment Canada Act* does not forbid the transfer of control of Canadian publishing companies to other Canadian entities. Yet Prichard's statement on that point had been instructive. He said he'd gone to Ottawa to give assurances that the University would have *actual* control of M&S, whereas Random House would have *influence*. These are lawyer words for concepts deeply embedded in the *Income Tax Act* as well as the *Investment Canada Act*. In a general way, actual control means that a shareholder has the ability to enforce decisions to direct a company's operations. Influence is a more complex notion: it means that a minority shareholder has sufficient clout, gained by means other than the votes attached to its shares, to steer decisions made by a company. These words have been construed and stretched in myriad ways to suit all sorts of creative business arrangements dreamed up by lawyers earning $750 an hour, and their practical implications have been parsed differently according to particular facts in particular cases heard by the courts.

Bennett had said the tax credit receipt was important to him, but not vital, and the sale of shares to Random House had nothing to do with its value. However, I was willing to bet that the ins and outs of tax law, as well as the rules of the *Investment Canada Act,* had played a lead role in how his gift was made.

A visit to the Canada Revenue Agency website (followed by help from its media people) made it clear (as clear as the mud-like prose of the *Income Tax Act* permits) that when the gift of a private company's shares is made to a registered charity, if those shares are sold by that charity to some other party within 60 months of receiving the gift, the CRA can revisit the original estimate of their value.[260] If they are sold for less than the tax credit receipted value, the CRA can revise that tax credit downwards, affecting the tax situation of the original donor. On the other hand, nobody even has to file a report to the CRA if a charity sells its shares *after* 60 months (and for less than $50). So I was willing to bet that the University had been required by some provision in the Unanimous Shareholder Agreement to hold its M&S shares for 60 months plus one day. Bennett had said he stayed on the M&S board for the glamour and to make sure that promises were kept. He'd assured me that U of T and Random House had lived up to their obligations. I was willing to bet that some of those obligations had to do with how long U of T had to hold its shares.

But there was even more intriguing information on the CRA website that suggested my lawyer friend who'd wondered if such a gift could be made, had a point. While it has always been legal to give a charity the non-trading shares of a private company, there can be a problem when it comes to issuing a tax credit receipt. A share issued by a private company is called a non-qualifying security. A tax credit receipt may only be issued by a charity for a non-qualifying security if that security is also what is called an "excepted" gift. To be an

excepted gift, *all* of a list of legal criteria must be met. A key requirement is that the donor (in this case, First Plazas Inc., controlled by
Avie Bennett) must be at arm's length to the donee (University of
Toronto) *and all its directors and officers.* There have been many legal
cases concerning the meaning of arm's length. But: since Bennett,
who controlled First Plazas, the donor, had been a member of the
Governing Council of U of T, and of its Business Board, and represented U of T on the new M&S board, and Prichard was an officer of
U of T when the gift was accepted and became President Emeritus as
well as a representative of U of T on the new M&S board, from the
Income Tax Act point of view, the gift of M&S shares may not have
met the arm's length criteria sufficiently to be "excepted."

The CRA website's information on court decisions regarding the
meaning of arm's length shed light on Random House's role too. The
courts have held that parties are *not* dealing at arms' length if: there
is a common mind that directs the bargaining for both parties to a
transaction; the parties to a transaction act in concert without separate interests; there is de facto control.[261] De facto control essentially
means control acquired in some manner not related to a shareholder's
voting power. De facto control has been defined by Canadian courts
in the following way: "excessive or constant advantage, authority or
influence can constitute de facto control (that is effective without legal
control). This situation can bring parties into a non-arm's-length relationship. It is important to note that this advantage need not be exercised to be a factor; the mere ability to do so is sufficient." As a lawyer
for the Department of Canadian Heritage, named Jeffrey Richstone,
had explained to the Standing Committee on Canadian Heritage, the
Department is very alert to the issue of de facto control, which can
be measured by many things, including things like financial support.[262]

As Prichard had made clear, the U of T took no role in the business of M&S after the gift was made. As U of T did not operate
M&S, and Random House did, it seemed to me that Random House
may have acquired de facto control from the time it purchased its
minority interest in M&S.

And there was an even more basic problem with the gift: I could
see how Bennett benefited from this arrangement (he got a tax credit

receipt and an exit plan while retaining association with a "glamour" business). I could see how Random House benefited (it may have acquired de facto control of former competitors). Yet in spite of Prichard's claim that control of M&S was in the University's interest, I couldn't see how the University, the donee that issued the tax credit receipt, had actually benefited. Apparently, no dividends had been paid to U of T while it owned the M&S shares. It got nothing for its pains when it transferred those shares to Random House in 2011.

And most puzzling of all: why couldn't these two men, whose brilliant careers were built on their business skills, remember the terms, or the *value* of the gift? Prichard had run a university that winkled great gobs of money from people with very deep pockets. Every big donor must have thought long and hard about how much money to give to U of T, and had probably paid for a lot of expensive advice on how to arrange things so as to maximize the ensuing tax credit. Woe to any university president who failed to remember exactly how much each big donor had given, and to treat that donor accordingly.

Prichard's proven skills in this area were so obvious, and the public profile that came from leading Canada's best university so high, that he had been elected as a director of many major publicly traded companies. Directors of large companies are paid large sums to oversee shareholders' interests, to carefully watch what is spent and what is earned. Onex pays its directors an annual retainer of $240,000 US and expects them to own a significant number of shares. Prichard owns subordinate voting shares and deferred share units of Onex amounting to a value—as of May, 2016—of $7,582,502. (By comparison, Heather Reisman's shares had a value of $105,997,207 and Gerald Schwartz's shares were worth $1,056,273,307.)[263] It was hard to believe that Prichard could not remember what those M&S shares were worth. Getting a donation of 75% of the shares of a private company was unusual: surely he would remember their stated value?

I was quite sure Bennett remembered how much he received in the form of a tax credit receipt in exchange for his generosity. By 2000, the normal exit strategy for the owners of Canadian publishing businesses did not include sizable tax credits. It involved a fire sale or bankruptcy. And besides, though he had made many other

very generous gifts totalling many millions to many charitable institutions during the previous 17 years, it was this gift that had distin-
guished him sufficiently to raise him to the position of Companion
in the Order of Canada, the highest level on offer. He was elevated
on October 30, 2003. He was by then serving his second term as
Chancellor of York University, and had been awarded an honourary
doctorate from York, but this was the prick over the i as a Danish
friend of mine would say. "A bold and unprecedented act of largesse"
is how the Governor General Adrienne Clarkson characterized his
gift to U of T. She went on to say: "This carefully crafted endowment will ensure that the company remains proudly Canadian and all
income that the University receives will be used to secure a vibrant
future for our artistic community."[264]

Bennett had said the size of this receipt was none of my business.
But since the gift itself had been made public, a major public honour had been bestowed, a tax credit receipt issued, and millions in
grants paid out subsequently, I could not see why that value ought
to remain hidden. So I asked *Maclean's Magazine* to assign me to the
story. I explained that the two leading figures who had run M&S had
told me on the record that actual control passed to Random House
of Canada in 2004–2005, yet M&S had continued to apply for and
receive grants until 2011—grants that require Canadian control of
the company asking for them. In other words, millions of taxpayers' dollars had been paid out that possibly should not have been. I
wanted to find out why. I had no idea—then—that the government
had waved a magic wand over its own rules and made them disappear.

Too many unanswered questions, was the business editor's reply.

Well yes, I said, but isn't that what journalists are supposed to do,
answer the unanswered questions?

I decided to pursue them myself and publish what I learned on
my blog.

I kept badgering the communications people at U of T. Finally, in
order to explain to me why the University had received nothing for
its shares from Random House, I was given a letter written on July
4, 2011, by Catherine Riggall, then the Vice-president of Business

Affairs for U of T, to Missy Marston-Shmelzer, Director of Cultural
Sector Investment Review at Canadian Heritage. This letter asked for
permission for U of T to transfer its shares to Random House. It had
kicked off the favourable Ministerial review of the transaction under
the *Investment Canada Act*.

In this letter, Riggall, then one of U of T's representatives on the
board of M&S, offered that word stewardship again when describing
the University's role in M&S. However, she said, the time for stewardship was over as it no longer served the interests of the University. The
letter asserted that the only means available to the University to promote its own interests was either to have M&S cancel its shares (leaving Random House with control of the company), or to sell its shares
to Random House "for a nominal amount." In that way, the University
could accomplish its own objective while "providing the infrastructure
and support needed to engender the future success of M&S."

Riggall then touched on one of the hidden terms of the agreements between the parties. She wrote:

> ...if M&S generated a profit, after all outstanding debt obligations
> were met, that profit would be divided between U of T and RHC in
> proportion to their ownership interests. Over the past eleven years,
> M&S has accrued significant debts and has earned a small profit
> in only two years. As a result, U of T's ownership interest in M&S
> has not resulted in any financial benefits to the University. In fact,
> U of T concluded some years ago that there was no hope of making
> a return on the shares it held in the company and *wrote off the value
> of its holdings*. [Italics mine].[265]

She asserted that the U of T had looked for buyers for its shares for
some years, but no one had come forward with an offer. The U of T
therefore wished to "exit the investment while also ensuring that
M&S continues with an owner which is experienced in the Canadian
publishing industry and committed to the ongoing development of
the M&S business."

I read the letter over and over again. On first glance it appeared
to convey facts, but on closer inspection, it was basically fact free.

How big was the debt? Not stated. When was the value of M&S written down to zero? Not stated. Who was offered a chance to buy U of T's shares and when? Not stated. How could the value of the shares be written down to zero considering the value of the backlist? Not stated. The backlist was not mentioned, and the phrase *Canadian control* did not appear in the letter either. In fact, the letter slid very close to describing Random House as Canadian. But the biggest problem I had with this letter was that Avie Bennett, the chairman of the same board upon which Ms. Riggall served, had said he had no inkling that the transfer to Random House was going to happen—until it did. Was it possible Ms. Riggall had written this letter without conferring with Bennett and the rest of the M&S board?

I searched the Governing Council's minutes again to see if I could find any reference to the write-down of the value of M&S shares, or to a Governing Council decision to authorize the transfer of the shares to Random House. No and no.

I wrote more emails to the University's communications people asking in which financial statement issued by the University of Toronto this write-down had been noted.

While I waited for their answers, I also followed some of Rob Prichard's advice.

Prichard had recommended writing to Meric Gertler, U of T's current president. I did that. No response. I tried again to speak to Dr. David Naylor, the President of the U of T at the time of the transfer of its M&S shares to Random House. He had just produced a report for the federal government. I spoke to the federal media people charged with answering press questions about that report. I asked for contact information for Naylor. I was told that Naylor had instructed them not to give out his email address to anyone. They said they would pass on an email from me to him, but that was the best they could do. I sent them an email. No response. I tried to reach Naylor by email through the U of T where he has tenure. It did not bounce back, but I got no response. I asked for interviews through the U of T's communications people. Much later I was told no on Gertler, no on Naylor.

Prichard had said the development department would have been responsible for the tax credit receipt. Donations are utterly vital to a university's stature. That is why the man in charge of development at U of T when Prichard was President and this gift was received, Dr. Jon Dellandrea, earned significantly more than Prichard. The Sunshine List disclosed that in 2000, President Prichard made $250,000 plus $15,337.20 in taxable benefits, while Vice- President Dellandrea made $283,999.96 plus $11,780.04 in taxable benefits. Dellandrea is also a member of the Order of Canada, an honour awarded to him for his fundraising efforts at U of T.[266]

I tried Dellandrea again at Sunnybrook. This time, I spoke to his assistant. I was told he'd been away but he could spare fifteen minutes on the telephone.

When I got him on the line he asked: are you *that* Elaine Dewar? I confessed.

He confessed that he had worked for Mount Sinai Hospital Foundation between 1989 and 1994, prior to joining U of T, and that Albert Reichmann had been on its board "at the time of the meltdown," by which he meant the bankruptcy of Olympia & York Developments. Apparently, the lawsuit against me, my colleagues, and *Toronto Life* had been discussed in his circle. We then traded "do you knows" back and forth. As he waxed on about the lunches he had every quarter with the father of one of my friends, I figured he was trying to run the clock.

Can we talk about the gift of M&S shares to U of T, I asked. You were Vice-President of Development at the time of the gift I believe.

He said he could share what he could remember, but not things he was not engaged with.

I explained that Robert Prichard said the development department would have handled the details of the gift and the tax credit receipt.

He quibbled about his title, which had changed at a certain point from Vice-President of Development to include the term Advancement. He said he was one of three vice-presidents at the University at the time and stayed there from 1994 until June 30, 2005. Yes, he was in charge of the department that handled these matters, but it employed about two hundred staff, some of whom were law-yers who handled gift agreements and dealt with the CRA.

And they reported to you?

They reported to him, yes, but there was some shared respon-sibility with the Vice-President of Business Affairs who was Robert White for a part of the period. Or it might have been Felix Chee, possibly later, he corrected.

Do you remember the value of the M&S shares, the value of the tax credit receipt issued, and how that value was estimated? I asked. Were the financials of M&S reviewed? Was it unusual to accept the gift of shares of a private company?

"I remember nothing on this question of review of financials," he said. "I had no direct involvement at all. We had routinely gifts of private real estate, or a major book collections, [there were] well-established protocols [to evaluate] private holdings," he said. Among them, he said, was a clear requirement for independent evaluation.

I asked if he had any discussions with Avie Bennett about the gift, or with Robert Prichard.

He couldn't recall speaking with Prichard about it, but "was I aware of discussions with Dr. Bennett? Yes. The high points," he said. These discussions were in regard to a "drive on Bennett's part regard-ing succession and the future of a Canadian icon and would U of T be the appropriate custodian."

But that was all he could offer. He said I should speak to whoever was directly involved with the file: he was not. He was not involved with the value of the tax credit receipt issued either. What he could say with regard to the Canada Revenue Agency and its requirements was that there is a "high degree of rigour of what it will and will not accept on valuation."

Did he remember the size of the tax credit receipt issued or not?

He replied that he did not know the details of "the certificate."

Who was left to try?

Hah! The other side of the deal of course: Brad Martin, CEO of Penguin Random House Canada. I asked for an interview by email. I informed Martin in that letter that I had been told by

Bennett and Gibson that control of M&S had passed to Random House by 2004–2005, and that when the shares were transferred from the University to Random House in 2011, nothing had been paid for them. Could I please come and see him to find out how that occurred?

Martin's assistant informed me that same day that Mr. Martin would offer an appointment upon his return from his travels. A time frame was mentioned. I asked the assistant for a particular date, but was told that I would have to wait. The time frame passed without an appointment being offered. A phone call to get one produced no response. Martin never said he wouldn't speak to me. He just never did.

Okay, I thought. Try all the other M&S directors you can find. By then, I had compiled a complete list of those who represented University of Toronto on the M&S board. I got their names from the minutes of the Governing Council which recorded the appointment resolutions for every year from 2000 to 2011.

John Evans was dead, so I couldn't call him.

I'd spoken with Prichard.

I'd spoken with Bennett.

I'd spoken with Doug Gibson.

I tried to get a hold of Felix Chee. He had worked as Vice-President, Business Affairs of the University, but had long since left. I found his name on a list of the directors of a Toronto rehabilitation hospital: when I called, I was told he was no longer associated with it. The board secretary refused to give me his business address or business phone number. I soon found he'd also served on the board of Teck Resources. No one from Teck offered a forwarding email or address either. Chee had also recently led the Toronto office of the state-owned China Investment Corporation, which had made a huge bet on Teck. But Chee no longer worked there either.[267] The person I spoke to promised to send an email to him if I would send it to her. So I had done that. No response.

I thought finding Catherine Riggall would be easy. She became Vice-President of Business Affairs at the U of T after Chee left, and she stayed on the M&S board until the transfer of the University's shares to Random House. She had retired, but an online search showed she had been on the board of the YWCA in Toronto. I phoned and asked how to contact her. I was told the Y would forward a message. If they did, I got no response. I heard she had something to do with the Stratford Festival and lived in Stratford. There was no Stratford phone number for her so I called the Festival. She had a membership. I asked the membership people for her address or a phone number. They refused to give it to me. I asked if they could get in touch with her and ask her to get in touch with me. I told them to tell her why. They said they'd try. No response.

I decided not to call Doug Pepper because he works for Brad Martin. A call from me would put Pepper in the unfair position of having to say no if I told him I'd tried to speak to his boss first with no luck, which would make him out to be a coward. Worse, if he said yes, it might put his job in jeopardy as Martin had chosen to ignore me. I decided that since Doug been kind to me when he was young, he deserved kindness from me now. I resolved to try everyone else I could think of before trying to reach him.

I found Trina McQueen at the Schulich School of Business at York University where she has become Visiting CTV Professor in Broadcast Management (when I contacted her she was still an adjunct professor in the Arts and Media Department). She would soon also be appointed Vice-Chairman of TVO. She had started as an on-air journalist, rose to head CBC News, became the first president of Discovery Channel, President and COO of CTV Inc., and had been appointed to several highly political boards, such as the CBC's, Telefilm's, and the NFB's advisory group. She also served on other cultural boards, including Historica with Avie Bennett. She is an Officer of the Order of Canada. Her Schulich bio made mention of all these things, but not of her five years of service on the M&S Board representing U of T.[268]

The departmental secretary gave me her email addresses and McQueen got back to me quickly. I asked for an interview, but she preferred to take questions by email. So I sent her a long list. The ones she answered were helpful. The ones she ignored were interesting. The one she answered that I never asked was more interesting still.

I asked her when she was appointed, by whom, how often the board met, whether control transferred to Random House long before the University's shares did, as Doug Gibson and Avie Bennett had asserted. I asked about Doug Pepper's position, whether M&S was in debt when she was appointed to the board in 2006, whether she voted on instructions from the University, whether there had been an offer to purchase the U of T's shares from Random House that precipitated the transfer of the University's shares. Was she aware of the University having tried to find Canadian buyers for its shares? I wanted to know how she heard about the U of T transferring its shares to Random House: was it a surprise, as Bennett had said? What sort of net benefit undertakings had been given to the government?

She replied that she had been put on the board as a representative of U of T which she thought had four directors, but maybe five, when Arlene Perly Rae stepped down. It was Avie Bennett who proposed her as Perly Rae's replacement.

> The U of T agreed and I met with the incumbent Random House president [sic] John? (I can probably find his last name) who also approved, and I was duly elected. Early in my tenure John took retirement as planned and Brad Martin replaced him as President of Random house [sic] and on the M and S board.

In fact, John Neale, to whom she referred, was the retiring Chairman of Random House. It seemed strange that he would have been asked to approve a University of Toronto nominee.

In answer to my question about whether there were instructions given to her by U of T she wrote:

> My understanding of board membership is that one has a duty to the company, not to be a representative of other groups, and that is the way I acted. I did not consult with the U of T about any vote, and I was not asked by the university to vote in any particular way. I remained on the board through the sale, after which all board members resigned. The two U of T people on the Board were Judith

Wolfson and Cathy Riggall (sp?) Judith is still at U of T, but Cathy retired…

She thought Doug Pepper was on the board ex officio. In fact, he was a full-fledged director representing U of T, just like her. She thought the board met every quarter, but she wasn't sure. She refused to discuss any questions relating to the financial circumstance of M&S or the sale. She wrote:

> However I agree 100% with the press release issued at the time of the sale which said there were financial challenges. The intensity of these challenges worsened gravely during my time on the board. Given the changing models of publishing and bookselling, and the structures and needs of the two ownership groups, I personally saw no path to an outcome any different from the one which took place. I voted for it. We all did. But no one cheered. It was the least worst outcome.

As to how she heard about the sale of the University's shares to Random House, she said that Avie Bennett phoned her and told her. There was a board meeting and a vote. On the question of undertakings given to the government, she said she was so pleased that one of them involved M&S continuing to publish poetry. "I have little doubt that our prime minister [Stephen Harper] personally insisted on this," she wrote, "and I thank him. If I am wrong, I thank the anonymous bureaucrat who did it…"

Then she added something about someone I had not asked about at all: Brad Martin.

> Over the years, I developed a respect and affection for Brad Martin. He is a tough businessman, but never a mean one. And he is a reader. He always seemed happiest when he was discussing books, books, books, writers, writers, writers Canadian ones a lot of the time. One of my recollections is running into him, long after the sale, at Allen's restaurant on the Danforth. It was afternoon. He was at the bar, alone, except for a Scotch. And he was really down because his fight

to publish that year's Massey Lectures was not going well. A very admirable and Canadian case of the blues...

I wrote her back and repeated my unanswered questions: this time I also told her that a tax credit receipt had been issued for the gift, but that the University had apparently got nothing in the way of a dividend on its shares because no profits had been earned, and I had been told the shares were transferred to Random House for essentially zero. Could she confirm or deny? And though there may have been financial issues [I did not tell her that neither Avie Bennett nor Doug Gibson agreed with that] apparently a hugely valuable backlist had been handed over for nothing.

She responded by saying that even if she remembered more than a vague idea of the sequence of events, "it would be wrong of me to disclose financial details learned in my capacity as a board member..." She asked for my phone number in case she thought of something else and offered hers.

I sent a message to Arlene Perly Rae via Facebook. No response.

I tried Judith Wolfson, who was still employed by the University. I told her secretary what I was calling about, but Ms. Wolfson did not return the call. I tried again by phone. Ms. Wolfson was not available. And she never did become available.

I tried to find an address for Douglas Foot who had served for Random House on the M&S board after John Neale's retirement: no success. I asked Penguin Random House for John Neale's address and was told he was retired, so no forwarding address would be forthcoming. When I finally found a phone number for him, his wife—a journalist—told me to write him an email because he was in Florida. She gave me his email address. She said she was sure he'd respond.

I wrote to him.

He didn't respond.

But by then, I had long since decided there was only one way to find out how Bennett sliced the salami.

10

If Still in Doubt, FIPPA

I looked up the FIPPA legislation to see what my chances were of getting any information from the University of Toronto. Ontario's *Freedom of Information and Protection of Privacy Act* is an *Alice in Wonderland* legal instrument. It aims to make government-gathered information available to all, while protecting the privacy of those whose information has been collected. For every entitlement to access, there is an opposite requirement to withhold private information about individuals, or companies, or the high deliberations of the Governor-in-Council—the cabinet. Decisions to release information are made by officials according to certain rules, but they have a lot of room for discretion. In other words, the FIPPA is the land of the Red Queen.[269]

The Ontario law, like the federal *Access to Information Act*, appears to say that the default position is that the government must release whatever an applicant is entitled to see. Information may only be withheld if it falls under listed exemptions. However, there is some information that no department head can provide. He/she "shall" withhold information derived from the collection of tax information, or gathered for the purpose of determining a tax liability or collecting a tax.[270]

As I read that particular clause I found myself muttering: well there goes any chance of getting a copy of the Bennett/First Plazas Inc. tax credit receipt.

But I decided to file an application anyway because so many people involved in this gift/sale had acted as if they'd taken a vow of *omertà*. Their silence shouted: dig harder! Though all of Prichard's other suggestions had bombed (proof of my father's adage about free advice being worth what you pay for it), I had nothing other than his FIPPA suggestion left to try.

I contacted the University of Toronto's FIPPA office. I explained to its Coordinator, Howard Jones, that I was working on a story that would likely be published on my blog and that I needed information from the University's files. Jones told me that his office would evaluate my request after the payment of a $5 fee and give me an estimate of how much the search would cost. He also said I would have to pay half up front.

I wrote a long, detailed request for information about the gift of M&S shares to U of T and their subsequent transfer to Random House. I took it to the University along with my cheque for $5.

The University's FIPPA office is on the University's main campus in the McMurrich Building, a stone-faced structure whose front door is on Queen's Park Crescent. Earlier generations of doctors had learned their anatomy in this building, so it had once been a place where bodies remained unburied.[271] Now that's an appropriate place to bury the FIPPA office, I cackled to myself as I walked down the stairs into the building's basement and to the very last door at the end of a very long hall.

Howard Jones turned a little green around the gills at the size of my application. I explained that I needed to see everything the University had on file about this complicated and controversial transaction because the main participants differed on important facts, or couldn't remember them. The only way to find out what had really happened was to read the actual documents. I won't bore you with the list of questions I included in that application. But I will say this. I was pretty sure I'd asked for *everything*.

Some time later, Jones let me know that my curiosity was going to cost me about $1000.

No way, I said, that's outrageous! By then I had studied the appeals process as set out on the Information and Privacy Commissioner's website and learned that the cost of an application should not become a barrier to getting information, and institutions covered by the FIPPA must take many things into consideration when asking for payment, including the public interest. This is research on a matter of major importance to Canadian cultural history! I said to Jones. You need to reconsider.

After reconsideration, Jones informed me that the University had decided to cut its estimated cost in half—to a mere $500. I swallowed hard and delivered a cheque for $250. It soon bounced due to my failure to put enough money in the correct account. I made out a new cheque and took it to Howard Jones and his colleague Rafael Eskenazi with apologies. They were very kind. I resolved to bluster at them no more.

By the time I made that FIPPA application, I had already begun to publish on my blog what I'd learned about the gift and sale of M&S. I put up one post called "Avie's Version" in which I quoted what Bennett had said about control passing to Random House in 2004/2005. I calculated a very rough total of the grants that M&S had received just from the Ontario Book Fund and the Canada Council in the subsequent six years. I brought Bennett's statement and this dollar figure to the attention of the Ontario Media Development Corporation which is in charge of administering the book publishing tax credit (a maximum of $30,000 per book if the correct criteria are met) as well as the Ontario Book Fund. No one there could tell me if M&S had received tax credits because that's tax information and therefore secret. I asked for an interview and got a phone conversation instead with two OMDC officials—well, one official, and her book publishing advisor. I told them that the former Chairman of M&S had said that control of M&S was transferred to Random House by 2005. I told them that M&S continued to apply for and receive grants that required control of applicants to be in the hands of Canadians. I asked if they would therefore ask for the return of that money. They showed no interest in Avie Bennett's views on control. They referred me to the definition of Canadian control in the *Income Tax Act* when discussing how eligibility is established for the Ontario book publishing tax credit, though the website refers to the *Inverstment Canada Act* definition. The *Income Tax Act* deems Canadian control to reside with a Canadian shareholder who owns more than 50% of the voting equity of a company, and U of T owned 75% of the shares for the entire period. Besides, they said, they were sure M&S qualified as a Canadian-controlled entity because M&S had produced its own financial statements every year, although what that had to do with the issue of control I was unable to drag out of them. (Did they mean tax returns?)

I also reported in the blog post what Bennett had told me about how the value of his tax credit receipt had been determined—by the University, without reference to the sale of shares to Random House or by combing through M&S and its books.

But then, Erin Lemon, Executive Director of News and Media for the U of T, contradicted Bennett's assertions. She said there *had* been an independent valuation of the M&S shares. It was done for the University for the purpose of issuing the tax credit receipt by Ernst & Young Corporate Finance. Yet when I checked the Governing Council's minutes for references to Ernst & Young, I found they had been appointed as auditors to the University for so many years that this had given rise to a debate about whether they were still able to exercise independent judgment. While a review may have been done, was it really independent?

I put up another post with Robert Prichard's version of how the gift was made and valued.

I wrote as well about filing the FIPPA application. I said I didn't have much hope of getting useful information. Jones had warned that several things I'd requested could fall under the exemptions to the *Act*. I hereby confess that I also made bets with friends that I would get next to nothing back from the University in exchange for $500. I figured the money was as good as down the drain.

Publishing people began to read these posts on the blog. Some sent me notes. Months later I would ask myself: did the blog posts prod the University into changing its stonewalling ways?

The manila envelope containing the University's response to my FIPPA application was surprisingly thick. I ripped it open. Howard Jones had attached a cover letter. He wrote that the University had found records responsive to my requests, and:

> The University is pleased to grant full access to the responsive records, except for one minor portion of a legal opinion. Although

the entire legal opinion falls under solicitor-client privilege, the University is waiving privilege except for one paragraph that contains both legal advice and personal information that are exempt under FIPPA sections 19 and 21. For context, the University will also provide a Toronto Star editorial and a letter to the editor from former President David Naylor...

Of course, "responsive to your request" did not mean giving me everything I'd asked for. I focused on those weasel words immediately, which is why I was utterly unprepared for the first document in the pile.

It was a letter addressed to Jeffrey Richstone, Senior Counsel in the Department of Canadian Heritage, the same Jeffrey Richstone who had given testimony to the Standing Committee on Heritage about how factors concerning de facto control are considered. It was from Avie Bennett's lawyer N.W.C. Ross of the law firm Weir & Foulds. (The law firm was later styled WeirFoulds LLP. Ross was not just Bennett's lawyer, but was also listed as an arm's length director of the Bennett Family Foundation.) The letter, dated June 2, 2000, carried this admonition in bold:

PRIVILEGED AND CONFIDENTIAL UNDER
THE INVESTMENT CANADA ACT AND
EXEMPT FROM DISCLOSURE UNDER
THE ACCESS TO INFORMATION ACT

Apparently, that did not make it exempt from disclosure under the FIPPA.

The letter was a "Request for Opinion Regarding First Plazas Inc. Gift of 75% of McClelland & Stewart Business to University of Toronto and Sale of Remaining 25% to Random House of Canada Ltd." This request had been sent to Ottawa less than a month before the transaction was due to close, which suggested that Bennett and his lawyer expected unheard of speed from a Minister of the Crown.

The letter explained that First Plazas Inc., controlled by Bennett, had acquired control of McClelland & Stewart, created in 1906, and that Bennett began to "oversee its day-to-day operation as Chairman" in 1986. The letter outlined Bennett's problems.

> In recent years Mr. Bennett has been forced to confront several complex issues which do not lend themselves to simple solutions. These issues include:
>
> (a)   ensuring that control of the publishing program remains with Canadians:
> (b)   the difficulty of finding a dedicated and capable successor to purchase the entire business;
> (c)   coping with the significant losses which the business has suffered, particularly over the last number of years;
> (d)   identifying a group or groups that are capable of protecting and continuing to build one of the finest fiction and non-fiction programs in the country (particularly by supporting the McClelland & Stewart business on a secure financial platform);
> (e)   identifying a group or groups capable of allowing the McClelland & Stewart business to respond to the significant changes occurring in the publishing environment, including securing better access for McClelland & Stewart authors to international distribution.

This outline of Bennett's problems cleverly reframed the main thrust of the *Investment Canada Act*. It forbids the sale of existing Canadian publishing *companies* to foreigners, or foreign-controlled entities. Control of the publishing *program* by Canadians is not the legal issue: control of the publishing *company* is.

The other issues Mr. Bennett allegedly faced—the difficulty of finding a capable successor to "purchase the entire business" and "coping with significant losses which the business has suffered, particularly over the last number of years" were the required conditions for exemption from the *Investment Canada Act* and Book Policy. And yet both statements were direct contradictions of what Bennett had told me about the state of M&S in 2000 and whether he'd tried to find a Canadian buyer.

He'd told me that he had *not* tried to find a Canadian buyer. He'd told me that the company was doing fine, that nothing had pushed him out. He'd told me, and Doug Gibson had concurred, that M&S was profitable—not very profitable, but profitable—and not deep in debt.

The other concerns raised in Ross's letter—identifying a group capable of "protecting and continuing to build one of the finest fiction and non-fiction programs in the country (particularly supporting McClelland & Stewart business on a secure financial platform),'' and, finding a group that can allow M&S to respond to changes in publishing and get better distribution for M&S authors internationally—were certainly issues. But they were not *Investment Canada Act* issues, not issues that needed a letter of Opinion from the Minister.

So why were they raised in this letter at all? I think because Bennett had picked the timing for the execution of his exit strategy with Jack McClelland-like care. A federal election was in the offing when he threw himself upon the Minister's officials with his modest proposal. The phrases in this letter constituted a warning that the leading Canadian publisher was once again in dire straits, just like the rest of the Canadian publishing industry, something no one would want to see on the front pages of the newspapers during an election campaign. After all, the Associate Deputy Minister of Canadian Heritage, the person in charge of *Investment Canada Act* issues for the Department, Michael Wernick, had testified to the Standing Committee on Canadian Heritage only three weeks earlier. On May 9, 2000, he'd said that the government's book publishing policy was successful. A report on same was about to issue from the Standing Committee on Canadian Heritage.[272]

Ross asserted in his letter that Bennett's proposal to sell shares to Random House and give the rest to U of T had been discussed in two prior visits to Ottawa (no dates were given in the letter), one made by Bennett and Prichard, the other made by Ross and his partner, John McKellar. Bennett and Prichard had met with several officials, including Michael Wernick.

The letter explained that Bennett's First Plazas Inc. had already created a new Ontario corporation as a wholly owned subsidiary called McClelland & Stewart Ltd. This new entity would acquire from the old M&S "the following assets of the M&S business: book rights, inventory, prepaid expenses, a portion of the office lease, office equipment, trademarks and other intellectual property rights and goodwill (including the Tundra Books and Macfarlane, Walter & Ross subsidiaries). M&S will not acquire from FP any cash, receivables, payables, agency business, business relating to *The Canadian Encyclopedia* or any interest in Canbook Distribution Corp."

In return, the new M&S would issue to First Plazas Inc. all its common shares plus a promissory note in the amount of $1,000,000. This note would have a one-year term. If the new M&S was unable to pay back First Plazas as promised, then Random House of Canada would lend M&S sufficient funds to "repay FP," such loan to bear interest at the then "less than market rate of 6% annually." First Plazas would then donate 75% of the new M&S's common shares to U of T "by deed of gift" and sell the remaining 25% of the new M&S shares to Random House of Canada. U of T's Governing Council, the recipient of the gift, was described as a Canadian entity to which only Canadians could be appointed.

The new M&S would also maintain the publishing program (including Tundra, Macfarlane, Walter & Ross, New Canadian Library, etc.) "intact." New M&S would be overseen by a board of seven, five from U of T, two from Random House, with Bennett to be the "initial" chairman. There would be an agreement between the parties including: protection of minority rights, U of T's right to sell its shares to a third party, but a right of first refusal for Random House to buy the U of T's shares if such an offer was made (with regulatory approval, said the note) plus something in favour of U of T called "put rights respecting its interest in M&S."

I had no idea what these "put rights" were, nor did the letter spell them out.

As well, the new M&S would sign an Administrative Services and Financial Support Agreement with Random House, which "guarantees the independence of the publishing program under the Publisher." The first publisher would be the current McClelland & Stewart Publisher, Mr. Doug Gibson. Random House would be obliged to provide all loans required by M&S to operate the business at a lower than market rate of interest. U of T would not be required to provide any funding, and Random House would also provide administrative and back office support "at cost," including finance, human resources, computer, legal, royalty, production and inventory management services for "a ten-year term." And finally, editorial decisions would be made by its staff under the direction of its publisher "who will be a Canadian."

Eventually, the letter got to the real point of this request for a Letter of Opinion.

"It is a condition to RHC's investment in M&S," wrote Ross, "that M&S receive an opinion of the Minister of Canadian Heritage under section 37(1) of the *Investment Canada Act* that M&S will continue to be a 'Canadian' within the meaning of the *Investment Canada Act* after the implementation of the RCH investment, and, accordingly, that the investment is not notifiable or reviewable under the *Investment Canada Act.*"

The Minister of Canadian Heritage had been granted the right to declare companies to be Canadian at the same time she was granted the right to be notified and to review under the *Investment Canada Act* any proposed purchases (or mergers) by foreigners of Canadian companies in cultural industries. Such an Opinion is binding on successors provided material facts do not change. The point of the request for this Letter of Opinion was to have the Minister affirm that regardless of the facts of this deal, regardless of the nuanced meanings in law of "arm's length," "influence" and "de facto control," which might otherwise have been brought to bear given Random House of Canada's role, the new M&S would be treated by the government as a Canadian entity. The transaction would therefore not be subject to review under the *Act.*

The letter asked for this Opinion to be issued quickly since Bennett wanted to close this deal by July 1, 2000, that being "the ideal time in the year to complete a transaction of this nature." Why July 1 was ideal was not explained. All the underlying agreements between the parties had apparently been sent to Ottawa attached to this letter, but they were not attached to my copy.

Now I understood why Prichard and Bennett had gone to plead a case in Ottawa: Random House had demanded it. With such a written declaration from the Minister of Canadian Heritage (who is also responsible for the Canada Council, and its various grant programs), M&S would have no difficulty applying for federal grants and Ontario tax credits. And wool was pulled over no one's eyes: this letter subtly made it clear that this Opinion should be issued in spite of Random House gaining de facto control of M&S through this transaction. It itemized Random House's responsibilities to make loans and operate the business under a ten-year administrative and financial services agreement. As Random House was going to run the company's finances, it clearly would acquire de facto control. While the letter asserted that *the publishing program* would be run by Canadians and the owner of the majority of the shares would be a Canadian entity, the word "control" only appeared in the letter when referring to First Plazas Inc.

The letter confirmed that Bennett and Prichard had both spoken to people in Ottawa. What they hadn't told me, but as the letter made clear, is that they had gone to Ottawa because Random House had insisted on it, that the transaction was dependent on gaining this Opinion. They had not argued that Random House would have influence but not control: they had gone right around the control issue by asking for a declaration of Canadian status for the new entity. Their Ottawa meeting must have taken place after Wernick's May 9 testimony to the Standing Committee on Canadian Heritage, because Wernick gave no hint to the Standing Committee that M&S, the leading Canadian publisher, was in such dire straits that it needed the government to spit out this extraordinary Opinion.

Ross's letter neatly demonstrated Bennett's business brilliance. This Ministerial declaration of the Canadian nature of the new salami permitted all the slices that were to come. But three questions remained: what was the price Random House paid for its 25% of the new M&S? What was the size of the tax credit receipt issued? And what was this "put" in favour of U of T? A put is a contractual agreement between parties detailing the conditions and the price for which shares can be sold at a later date. But the letter did not provide these details.

The next item in my bundle showed that approvals had also been rushed on the University's side of the transaction. It was a memo labelled "strictly confidential to Members of the Business Board". It was dated June 20, 2000, only 10 days before the deal would close. The University's Business Board must review and recommend to the University's Governing Council "approval of receipt of major gifts and bequests with terms and conditions of an unusual nature." This memo summarized the terms of Bennett's proposed gift. The gift's sponsor was named as J. Robert S. Prichard, the U of T's President.

The memo said there had been a teleconference of Board members concerning this gift on June 8, 2000, six days after Ross wrote to Jeffrey Richstone in Ottawa. A motion had been put forward to the Board stating that the Governing Council should accept the gift, that the President and Secretary of the Governing Council should be given the authority to execute the agreements entailed by the gift, including "an undertaking by the University of Toronto in favour of the Director of Investigations, Investment Canada," as long as the documents were consistent with the terms and conditions set out in this summary.

The summary was light on details, but included in its highlights were terms of the gift not stated in the Ross letter to the federal government. For example, the memo said: "Any payments received by the University as a result of its ownership of the shares, including dividends and proceeds of disposition, shall be allocated to an endowment fund named 'the Bennett Endowment' and used by the University for the purposes of advancing Canadian literature, Canadian poetry and Canadian culture." In a section titled Financial Implications, the memo stated that the new M&S would be run as a for-profit corporation "and it is believed that it will become profitable with the administrative and financial support from Random House... If the University decides to sell its shares in the new M&S, it has various sale options pursuant to the unanimous shareholders' agreement."

This was a change in tone from the Ross letter of a few weeks before. In that letter, the implication was that without a deal, M&S's prospects were dim. As Ross had put it,

In recent years Mr. Bennett has been forced to confront several complex issues which do not lend themselves to simple solutions. These issues include:

(a) ensuring that control of the publishing program remains with Canadians,

(b) the difficulty of finding a dedicated and capable successor to purchase the entire business,

(c) coping with the significant losses which the business has suffered, particularly over the last number of years...

But here, there was the prospect of profits. No mention was made in the memo as to how long the University was required to hold on to its shares, nor was there any reference to the University exercising *control* over the new M&S. No author signed it, but three names were written by hand on the right-hand side: Tad Brown; Brian Davis; and Matthew Cockburn.

The next memo in my pile, dated the same day as the summary memo for the Business Board, had been sent by the same people— Tad Brown, Finance and Development Counsel for U of T; Brian Davis, a lawyer with Torys; and Matthew Cockburn, also a lawyer with Torys—to Robert Prichard. They identified themselves to him as outside and in-house counsel to the University of Toronto in connection with "the negotiation of a series of agreements..." relating to the gift. "We have also acted on behalf of the University in connection with the preparation of an undertaking (the "Undertaking") proposed to be provided by the University to the Director of Investigations, Investment Canada, in connection with Investment Canada's review of these transactions."

So, I thought, there *had* been an Investment Canada review, in spite of official assurances that no review had taken place, and in spite of the letter to Richstone seeking assurance that no review would be required. Three lawyers could not make a mistake about who they had to satisfy, surely?

The next paragraph insisted that everyone who got this memo had to keep it confidential because "the University is subject to binding agreements of confidentiality, the violation of which may be prejudicial to the interests of the parties and potentially expose the University to damage claims." This warning was set out in bold.

For the first time, I saw a mark indicating that a paragraph had been withheld from me under FIPPA sections 19 and 21. The missing paragraph seemed to refer to Bennett, characterized as a long-time benefactor to the University.

The memo described the reason that a Letter of Opinion had been sought from the Minister. It said:

> Under the *Investment Canada Act* a non-Canadian is prohibited from acquiring 'control in fact' of an existing Canadian publishing business. In order to ensure that the Federal Government accepts the proposed transaction as being in compliance with applicable law, an opinion has been sought confirming that, in the opinion of the Minister responsible for the *Investment Canada Act*, Random House has not acquired control in fact of New M&S. As of the date of this memorandum (June 20, 2000) the Minister's opinion has not yet been issued, but, based upon conversations with Justice Department representatives advising the Minister, we expect that the opinion will be issued shortly.

Interesting: this was almost an admission that rather than arrange the transaction to suit the law, the law was to be interpreted by the Minister so as to obscure uncomfortable facts, such as Random House acquiring de facto control of the new M&S. As Stoddart had said, he who controls marketing and the money controls the company, and this transaction clearly handed Random House control of both.

The memo laid out a more comprehensive summary of the terms agreed to by the parties, a summary much more specific than Ross's letter to Jeffrey Richstone. The gift would be 7500 shares of the new M&S. The University would promise not to sell its shares for "three years unless required by law or with the consent of First Plazas." And, the letter said, *the decision to sell any or all of the shares would have to be made by the Business Board acting on the recommendation of the President* [italics mine].

I had found no reference to any such decision by the Business Board when the shares were transferred to Random House in 2011.

The memo described how profits from the new M&S would fund a Bennett endowment. Then it got to the meat, the agreement to be signed between the shareholders. And that was where, at long last, I spied a *number*, what Random House had agreed to pay First Plazas Inc. for 25% of new M&S.

The memo declared that number to be *$5.3 million.*

The memo said: "This would give a notional valuation to the entire company of *$21,200,000.*"

The memo did not say what the tax credit would be: but it had to be 75% of $21,200,000 million, which would be a little more than $15 million. But was this notional value of the company correct? According to the Ross letter to the government written only three weeks earlier, Mr. Bennett had to cope with "ensuring that control of the publishing program remains with Canadians... the significant losses that the business has suffered, particularly over the last number of years"... and the "difficulty of finding a dedicated and capable successor to purchase the entire business." So how could it be worth $21 million? Nothing in the memo detailed how this valuation had been arrived at.

It went on to name the people who would serve on the board of the new M&S on behalf of U of T: Avie Bennett, John Evans, Robert Prichard and Doug Gibson—Arlene Perly Rae's name was not listed. The initial Chairman would be Avie Bennett. As to how this board would function, the memo said: except where specified, "board decisions would be by majority vote (thereby providing control in favour of the university)." But then the memo immediately backtracked about control in favour of the University to control in favour of Random House. It said: "A number of key matters require a majority of the University nominee directors and at least one Random House nominee director before they may be approved (thereby providing 'negative control' in favour of Random House for these matters)." The issues over which Random House could exert the power of No! included: approval of the annual budget and operating plan; changes in capital structure; any change in the business of the corporation; any payment of dividends on the shares of the corporation.

These were not trivial matters, particularly the last one. Though the University would own 75% of the shares, it could find itself unable to pay itself any dividends, surely a major reason for the gift, even if M&S was awash in profits, if Random House said no.[273]

The memo then described a series of actions that could be triggered by the University, or by Random House. Random House was not allowed to get rid of its share of the salami without the University's approval. If the University wanted to sell its shares to a third party, Random House could buy them instead at a price equal to 105% of whatever that third party offered.

Finally, the memo described two puts, though only one had been mentioned in the letter to Richstone of June 2. A put, you will recall, is a contractual requirement that allows one party to an agreement to force another party to buy or sell something at a fixed price at some agreed upon point in time. The puts outlined in this memo were complicated.

When the Administration Agreement between M&S and Random House terminated after ten years, said the memo:

> ...the University may require Random House to buy the University's
> shares or the University may require Random House to sell to the
> University its shares, in either case at a 'fair value' price per share.

Fair value per share was predetermined to be equal to 1.0 times the previous 12 months' net sales of the new M&S divided by the number of outstanding shares *and adjusted for any outstanding loans due to Random House* [italics mine].

Whoa! I muttered. A feature like that could provoke the kind of creative accounting for which Hollywood has become infamous. First, *net* is a concept that allows accountants to add or subtract costs at will, depending on the outcome desired, especially in a business involving returns. Second, this term would make it advantageous for Random House to make large loans to M&S because, if Random House was forced by the University to buy the University's shares, a towering stack of loans would ensure Random House paid rock bottom price for them, or nothing at all. And, as the backlist was not mentioned at all in the equation set out to determine value, by this agreement the spectacular M&S backlist had effectively been assigned a value of zero before the signatures were dry on the contracts.

The memo went on to say:

"On the fifth anniversary of the Shareholders' Agreement, the University may require First Plazas to buy the University's shares for the purchase price of $5.0 million."

In other words, by these agreements, the University could force First Plazas Inc. to buy back its shares for a third of their value 60 months after the gift was received, just past the point when the CRA could demand repayment of First Plazas Inc.'s tax credit. While Bennett would get a tax credit receipt for over $15 million for the new M&S shares, those same shares could be deemed by the University to be worth $5 million after July 1, 2005.

So: even if Random House permitted no dividends to be paid to the University, after five years the University could still get $5 million in cash from First Plazas Inc.

Huh, I said to myself, that was where benefit to the University lay, not where Prichard had suggested, in the promotion of Margaret Atwood or Michael Ondaatje, but in this $5 million put. And yet the University had not exercised it. Instead, it had held on to the shares until 2011 and transferred them to Random House for nothing.

Why?

The summary said that the Publisher was to have editorial freedom, and Random House's work in managing M&S would be subject to the decisions of the Board. Though the budget was to be prepared by Random House, it would be voted on by the Board. Random House loans would earn interest at 6% and Random House would be paid for its administrative, marketing, and financial services to the new M&S. The initial fee was set at 25.7% of net sales. Apparently, Bennett had assured one and all that such fees were cheaper than his old M&S's costs. (The publisher of this book assures me that Bennett was correct.) The scope of the publishing program of the new M&S was also set out in the Agreement with Random House and summarized as follows: "The Administration Agreement establishes a general framework for the size and scope of New M&S's ongoing business activities and establishes that it will publish annually an estimated range of 100 to 170 titles including original fiction and original non-fiction works. As a result, annual budgets will have to be prepared with these objectives in mind." Random House had also agreed not to poach M&S's authors or staff without permission.

This Agreement with Random House could be terminated in five years by M&S if it realized no profits in the three consecutive years after June 30, 2002. In other words, M&S could not get rid of Random House until 60 months after U of T accepted the gift, which was the same point at which the University could call its $5 million put, and the same point beyond which First Plazas Inc.'s tax credit could not be revisited by the CRA.

So far, Jack Stoddart's warnings about the real meaning of this gift/sale had been confirmed. Not only did Random House get to control the M&S budget, and loan money to the company at 6%, and get paid for the cost of its services from M&S's earnings, but because Random House guaranteed M&S's payment of that $1 million promissory note to First Plazas Inc., and could decide whether or not to collect repayment of, or interest on the debt incurred on M&S's behalf, Random House could push M&S into debt at the end of the Agreement's first year.[274]

It was very clear that the U of T's role in the new M&S would be nothing more than acting as a Maple Leaf-branded container for 7500 shares of M&S for five years. In return for holding itself out in public as M&S's Canadian steward, the University's reward would be at minimum $5 million if it called the put. Avie Bennett's First Plazas Inc. would get $6.3 million in cash, plus at least a $15 million tax credit, unless the put was called, in which case it would be left with $1.3 million plus the full value of the original tax credit. Random House would get government sanctioned de facto control of a major Canadian competitor, and a letter from the Minister to wave when applying on M&S's behalf for grants and tax credits.

And what had the government asked for in return?

The memo said the government was worried that the *Investment Canada Act* provides that a "crown agent" may "dispose of an interest in a Canadian company without complying with that *Act*." If the University declared itself to be a crown agent, it could sell its interest in the new M&S to a non-Canadian without restriction. "There has been no definitive determination of whether or not the University is a crown agent," said the memo.

And so, the government had insisted that the University—not First Plazas Inc. and not Random House of Canada—must give it an undertaking. The University had to promise that if it disposed of its shares of the new M&S, it would not, nor would it permit any purchaser to, rely upon the provisions "which exempt crown agents from the application of the Act... the effect of this undertaking would be to require any future purchaser of the University's interest in New M&S to be Canadian."

Next item in the file was a letter from President Prichard on University of Toronto letterhead, dated June 21, 2000, the very next day. It was addressed to the Director of Investments, Department of Canadian Heritage, attention Michael Wernick. Prichard confirmed that the University would not accept Bennett's gift without having delivered an undertaking "to the Director of Investigations, Investment Canada, that it will not, and will not allow any purchaser of its interest in M&S to, assert that the University is a crown agent in connection with any disposition of the University's interest in M&S." He hooked the provision of this Undertaking directly to the Minister issuing the Opinion that "the completion of the transaction will not result in the acquisition of control of a Canadian business by a non-Canadian." He promised not to proceed with the transaction without having delivered to the Minister prior to, or contemporaneously with the closing of, the transaction, "the Undertaking negotiated with the Director of Investments, Department of Canadian Heritage."

Prichard's promise immediately begat the requested Letter of Opinion. It was signed only two days later, June 23, 2000. This is amazing speed as anyone who has ever requested a Ministerial

Opinion will attest. While the *Investment Canada Act* requires the Minister to issue such an Opinion within 45 days after receiving sufficient information to form it, there is no time limit in the *Act* saying how long the Department may take to investigate the facts behind such an application. It took the Department just 23 days from receipt of the letter from Ross to put the Minister's signature on the Letter of Opinion. It was labelled "Protected—Inv-Act," meaning it should not be released for any access requests because the *Investment Canada Act* forbids such revelations. And yet here it was in my hands, written proof that if you have friends in high places in this country, the law will be adapted to fit your facts at warp speed, and no outsider will be the wiser (but also that if you follow the advice of Robert Prichard to file a FIPPA, such secret acts may be revealed). The Letter was sent to N. William C. Ross, Bennett's lawyer at Weir & Foulds, via mail messenger.

Sheila Copps, who signed herself Minister Responsible for the *Investment Canada Act,* wrote:

> I acknowledge receipt on behalf of your client, First Plazas Inc., of your letter dated June 2, 2000 requesting an opinion pursuant to subsection 37(1) of the Investment Canada Act (the "Act") as to whether the proposed investment regarding First Plazas Inc. gift of 75% of McClelland & Stewart Ltd to the University of Toronto and sale of the remaining 25% to Random House of Canada Ltd would result in the acquisition of control of a Canadian business by a non-Canadian. Documentation relating to this proposal was received on June 2, 5, 8, 12, 13, 15, 16, and 19, 2000.
>
> Pursuant to subsections 37(1) and 26(2.1) of the Act, it is my opinion, and I determine and declare, based on your representations and all the agreements and documents that you have submitted to date on behalf of your client, that McClelland & Stewart Ltd would be a Canadian entity following the proposed transaction.
>
> This opinion is conditional on the accuracy of the material facts submitted by you on behalf of your client and shall remain binding on the Minister of Canadian Heritage and the Director of

Investments for so long as the material facts on which this opinion is
based remain substantially unchanged.

So: contrary to what Sheila Copps had told me, the McClelland &
Stewart handover had not only happened on her watch, it had been
approved by her. (Or at least it appeared to have been approved
by her. Section 37(4) of the *Investment Canada Act* gives the
Department's Director and designated officials the right to issue
such Opinions in the Minister's name.)[275] It is definitely Copps' signature on the Opinion permitting the transfer of de facto control
of a Canadian publishing company to a foreigner, Random House
of Canada. She waved a wand over the transaction and said, regardless of the meaning of its agreements, that the new M&S would be
a Canadian entity. Due to the secrecy provisions of the *Investment
Canada Act,* she could rest assured that this Letter of Opinion and
its underlying agreements would remain cloaked from public view,
never to cause a political uproar. Only the parties, a few bureaucrats, and a lot of lawyers would know what really happened and
why would they tell?

So many lawyers had been involved in this remarkable adaptation
of the *Investment Canada Act* that I looked up the collective noun for
lawyers on Google. It coughed up a whole list: a disputation; an eloquence; an Escheat: a greed; a huddle; a quarrel. The lawyers involved
included: an eloquence at Torys; a disputation at Weir & Foulds; just
one at Macmillan Binch; a quarrel at University of Toronto: a huddle
from the Department of Justice; a greed at Canadian Heritage.

And how was this portrayed in public? The next document in my pile
was a University of Toronto and McClelland & Stewart joint press
release dated June 26, 2000, three days after Sheila Copps' Letter of
Opinion was issued, but before the parties had signed the relevant
Agreements, and even before the University's Governing Council
had passed a resolution to accept the gift.

The title read: "McClelland & Stewart Owner Donates
Canadian Publishing House to University of Toronto." Bennett
was quoted to the effect that after 15 years in the publishing

business, it was time for him to find a way "of ensuring McClelland & Stewart's future and preserving its past." He said the gift and sale was the culmination "of more than five years of planning with the University of Toronto. What better way can there be to safeguard a great Canadian institution, a vital part of Canada's cultural heritage, than by giving it to the careful stewardship of another great Canadian institution."

All very well, except the deal required U of T to be the steward of nothing except 7500 share certificates and profits unlikely to accrue. Prichard made the U of T's hands-off-the-wheel position quite clear in this release.

> Stressing that McClelland & Stewart will be run completely independently of the University of Toronto and will have no relationship with the University of Toronto Press, Prichard added that all income received by the university from its ownership interest in McClelland & Stewart will fund an endowment at the university in support of Canadian writing, poetry and culture.[276]

It also said that M&S would maintain its Canadian publishing programs "intact," including Tundra Books, Macfarlane, Walter & Ross and the New Canadian Library. That promise would be ignored when Macfarlane, Walter & Ross was shut down only three years later. The services agreement with Random House was mentioned, but its scope was downplayed. It was described as "a contract to provide some services under an administrative services agreement, including accounting, computer support and, ultimately, marketing and sales." No mention was made of Random House's contractual obligation to provide loans and run M&S's finances, its capacity to encumber M&S with debt within the first year, its negative control of the company due to its negative control of the budget process, its right of first refusal should any Canadian try to buy U of T's shares, and its entitlement to refuse to permit the issue of dividends to U of T. Nor did the press release refer to the sale price of the shares bought by Random House, the put, or the tax credit First Plazas Inc. would earn.

Instead, high praise of Avie Bennett was sung by John Neale, Chairman of Random House. (Why not? Bennett had crafted a great deal for Random House.) A list of important Canadian authors past and present published by M&S was hauled out like lipstick for the pig: Lucy Maud Montgomery, Stephen Leacock, Farley Mowat, Pierre Berton, Margaret Laurence, Margaret Atwood, Peter Gzowksi and Michael Ondaatje. "Since Avie Bennett bought the company from Jack McClelland in 1986, numerous other acclaimed authors, including Robertson Davies, Mavis Gallant, Anne Michaels, Rohinton Mistry, W.O. Mitchell, Jane Urquhart and Guy Vanderhaeghe have joined the M&S family," said the release, making it seem as if these writers were Avie's Picks, though everyone in the business knew they had been brought to M&S by Doug Gibson or fiction editor and newly named Publisher Ellen Seligman.

And then there was a quote from Michael Ondaatje: "This is a truly remarkable gift on the part of Avie Bennett—to ensure a great Canadian publishing house and its excellent publishing program will continue to flourish in the best way possible," he said.

Having just read the summaries of the transactions that permitted the gift and sale, as well as the Minister's Opinion, it seemed to me that Ondaatje's ambiguous adjective—remarkable—seemed apt.

Beneath the press release lay a letter of June 29, 2000, from the Governing Council's Secretary to President Robert Prichard notifying him that resolutions to accept the gift had been passed by the Governing Council that same day. (The details, referred to as confidential, were not recorded in the resolutions.) Beneath that lay the actual undertaking made to the Director of Investments, Canadian Heritage and signed by Prichard and the Council's Secretary. This document was also labelled privileged and confidential under the *Investment Canada Act* and exempt from disclosure under the *Access to Information Act*. It was a very lawyerly text. In it, Prichard, as President, promised that in regard to the M&S shares, the U of T would not say it was a crown agent and entitled to sell its shares to anyone, nor would it let anyone else do so. But as to whether it actually was or was not a crown agent, the letter said:

> "...the University expresses no view as to its status as an agent of Her Majesty in right of Canada or a province."

It was signed and sent to Ottawa on June 30, the last day Prichard was President of the U of T.

The Donor Agreement was next in the pile. It was signed by Prichard and Bennett on behalf of First Plazas Inc. and the U of T and also dated June 30, 2000. There was nothing on the document or in it requiring that it be kept confidential. It laid out the terms of the gift. It permitted the University to sell any or all of its shares without the permission of First Plazas Inc. only after three years had elapsed. It set up the rules for the appointment of five U of T directors to the M&S board. It established who the first directors would be (Bennett, Gibson, Prichard, Evans, and Arlene Perly Rae). The U of T President would recommend future directors to the Executive Committee of the Governing Council and there would be consultation over such names with existing U of T-appointed members of the board. Once again, it was clearly stated that decisions to sell any or all of its M&S shares could be made only on the recommendation of the U of T President with the approval of the Business Board.

Most of the document detailed what the University would do with any profits that flowed from M&S or from the sale of its shares.

Dreaming in Technicolor, I thought. They'd have had to call the put to see a nickel.

So why hadn't they?

I got up and went out for a walk. I was muttering to myself over what I'd read. Nobody in authority could argue that they didn't know the terms of this transaction. All of the agreements surrounding the gift and sale had been put in front of the responsible civil servants by very competent lawyers. The lawyers involved must have turned the *Investment Canada Act* inside out and upside down to find an acceptable undertaking for the Minister to demand. The fact that an undertaking was given had allowed the Department of Canadian Heritage folks to cover political derrières and it had also permitted Bennett to say don't worry, folks, we got Ottawa's approval. Most people wrongly assumed that Random House had given an undertaking when in fact it was the University of Toronto. In fact, the Minister's Opinion had given foreign-owned Random House indirect but open-ended permission to exercise control-in-fact over M&S. In return for this, Random House had given the government nothing.

I could see how all the parties got what they wanted from these deals. Random House got to control its competition. The University got to hold itself out as a steward of Canadian culture with the prospect of at least $5 million to pour its coffers one day. Avie Bennett got his exit strategy without having to give up the M&S glamour, as well as $6.3 million ($5.3 million from Random House, $1 million from the new M&S), a tax credit, and a lovely prize from the Governor General.

But what did Canada get?

Sometimes it's better not to find out what you thought you wanted to know. Knowledge can make you sad.

11

And One More Thing…

I opened the FIPPA file where I'd left off and turned the page. There it was, the share purchase agreement between First Plazas Inc. and Random House of Canada. The Administrative Services and Financial Support Agreement was attached to it. Like all the written records of these transactions, both were labelled privileged and confidential under the *Investment Canada Act* and exempt from disclosure under the federal *Access to Information Act*.

Both agreements took effect on Canada Day.

The agreement by which 25% of the shares of the new M&S were purchased by Random House at first seemed simple and to the point. Random House agreed to pay First Plazas Inc. $5.3 million. But then I got to the part about the Promissory Note. It said that on the first anniversary of this transaction, "the Purchaser [Random House] shall cause New M&S to pay the Vendor [First Plazas Inc.], and if necessary fund, the principal amount of the Promissory Note together with interest owing thereunder." In other words, New M&S had to pay that sum to First Plazas out of its earnings or borrow it from Random House.[277]

As I thought about the way money was being made to flow, I suddenly became confused. I couldn't understand why the new M&S had to pay $1 million to First Plazas at all.

Gradually clarity returned: because, I told myself, before 75% of new M&S could be given away, and 25% sold, new M&S first had to acquire the publishing assets of First Plazas Inc.—assets such as the backlist—all those books already published by M&S and still controlled by M&S for the duration of their copyrights, which extend for fifty years after the death of the author—plus all ongoing projects, all grant dollars owing, etc.

Yet that number, $1 million, nagged at me. How could all the publishing assets being transferred to the new M&S only be worth $1 million when, according to the lawyers' summary of the transaction, the value of new M&S had been set at $21 million? If 100% of the assets transferred were only worth $1 million (the amount new M&S promised to pay for them within the year) how could 25% of the same company, on the same day, be worth $5.3 million?

I went around and around that question until I decided that it probably had something to do with taxation rules: don't go there, I said to myself, that is a rabbit hole from which the sane may not emerge. Yet this was clearly important because it was step two—okay, slice two—of the salami strategy.

I looked at the agreement again and was struck by this phrase: "Purchaser shall cause New M&S to pay." How could a minority shareholder promise to make a company it does not control pay anything to anyone?

Answer: if the minority shareholder has *actual* not just negative control.

The means by which Random House acquired actual control of new M&S were detailed in the Financial Services and Support Agreement.

These terms had not been fully reflected by the memos and summaries given to various parties. For one thing, the initial ten-year term of this Financial Services and Support Agreement would be automatically extended for another five years, unless M&S failed to realize a net profit every year for three years after June 30, 2002. More important, though Random House was supposed to perform its duties of management, marketing and administration of M&S as an "independent contractor" (while being one of M&S's owners, giving new meaning to the word "independent"), M&S could not rid itself of Random House's services during that first five-year period—even if it failed to make a profit for four of those years.[278]

And, as my informant had alleged, this agreement gave Random House control of M&S's bank accounts. It said that Random House shall handle "all banking necessary for the due performance of the accounting and administrative functions of M&S and for the receipt and disbursement of all moneys of M&S pertaining to its operations required to be attended to by Random House under this Agreement. Random House shall have signing authority and shall deal with such cash, cheques and negotiable instruments in accordance with sound business practices so that M&S is adequately protected and receives reasonable income thereon." This allowed Random House to arrange matters so that McClelland & Stewart did not show profits, or did show them, as it saw fit. Random House could also make secured loans to M&S, starting with the loan that might be required for that promissory note payment to First Plazas Inc., and to "register its security under the *Personal Property Security Act*."[279]

This ability for Random House to register debt M&S owed to it was slice three of the salami strategy. He who controls the bank account can create a debtor. A secured lender can force a debtor into bankruptcy. The bankruptcy, or impending bankruptcy, of a Canadian publisher is one of the requirements for a Canadian publisher to get permission, under the *Investment Canada Act* and Book Policy, to sell itself to a foreigner. The other is that no Canadians want to buy it. A big secured debt would guarantee that prospective buyers would beware.

While this document asserted that Random House and McClelland & Stewart would compete vigorously, it also stipulated that there could be no poaching of authors or staff between the new M&S and Random House unless permission was granted in writing—on penalty of termination of the Agreement. In addition, neither side was to try and have the Publisher or any person working in either publishing department to "cease being so retained" without prior written consent.[280]

The rights and duties of M&S as publisher, and Random House as "independent" contractor, were further defined in Schedule A.

Schedule A turned out to be a magnificent display of sucking and blowing at the same time (an act most lawyers are familiar with) as well as being a document that would be of interest to the Competition Bureau. It demonstrated utter entanglement while professing arm's-length distance between the two parties. On the one hand, they agreed that M&S shall "be committed to being a publisher of works that are predominantly written by Canadians or about Canadian subjects." Yet there was no definition of predominant. They agreed that the Publisher and President of M&S would be determined by the Board, "acting in accordance with the Unanimous Shareholder Agreement" (which I had still not come upon) and "each will be a Canadian citizen ordinarily resident in Canada." Then it said that "in the event that the proposed President or Publisher is not dealing at arm's length with Random House, the directors who are nominees of Random House will not vote on the question, but will support the decision of the other directors." This meant that if Random House wanted to replace Doug Gibson with a Random House employee, then Random House would go along with the U of T members of the Board on that issue. And of course, in a few years, it did replace Doug Gibson with Douglas Pepper.[281]

While the Publisher's editorial independence was acknowledged, and the Publisher's duties and responsibilities were laid out, it was also clear that this editorial independence was totally constrained by Random House's complete control of M&S' capital, loans, accounts, and budgets. The Publisher would select works to publish; negotiate contracts and advances; edit and copy-edit; determine backlist titles that will be kept in print and their format; supervise design, typesetting, etc.; organize publicity campaigns; issue media releases; provide review copies. But all this would happen "within the marketing budgets established by Random House."[282]

Random House would: establish the annual budget for the amount to be set aside for advances against royalties (upon consultation with the Publisher). It would time and stage the production for all works published; determine the suggested retail price; and, in consultation with publisher, the number of copies to be printed, and the marketing budget for each work. In other words, control of the fate of every book the M&S publisher wanted to produce would reside in the hands of its "vigorously" competing independent contractor, Random House. In effect, M&S would function as an imprint of Random House from the start. If there were continuous disputes, the Board could decide the outcome.

Here's where vigorous competition became its opposite due to the magic of legal drafting:

> M&S and Random House recognize that there will be competitions for works between the parties. It is agreed that such competition may continue unless the final two competitors are M&S or one of its subsidiaries and Random House or one of its subsidiaries. Should this occur, then M&S (or its subsidiary if applicable) or Random House (or its subsidiary, if applicable) shall mutually agree as to the terms of the final offer to be made in respect of such work. The author (or the author's agent, if applicable) of such work shall then be given the option of selecting either M&S (or its subsidiary, if applicable) or Random House (or its subsidiary, if applicable) to publish the work.[283]

Like a non-denial denial, this was a non-compete compete clause, the very definition of how an oligopsony works, and exactly what the country's literary agents had worried about when the gift/sale was announced. I realized I had actually experienced this situation when I proposed a new book in 2005. My agent had offered it to Random House, my previous publisher, and to M&S, as well as to others. Only Random House and M&S made offers. M&S offered a bit more than Random House. I was surprised that Random House did not come up with the extra dollars to get the book, but instead, stopped offering. Now I understood. (I ended up not doing the project with M&S because I didn't like certain aspects of their contract, which differed from Random House's.)

Interestingly, Schedule A also gave the M&S board the power to decide how many works of each category would be published in any given year. There was a list that showed an expected range for: original fiction (10 to 20 a year); non-fiction (30 to 40 a year); Tundra (between 20 and 30); and Macfarlane, Walter & Ross (8 to 15 books a year), and the New Canadian Library series (1–9), along with trade paperbacks and various other formats. Altogether it came to less than the 100 books mentioned in summaries. But it was still a huge publishing program compared to the new books bearing the M&S imprint and published these days.[284]

This Schedule was to prevail if it differed from the Administrative Support and Financial Services Agreement to which it was attached.[285]

Having read both, I realized that Avie Bennett and Doug Gibson both knew that Random House had actual control of M&S from July 1, 2000.

How did I know?

Because Bennett had signed the Asset Purchase Agreement with Random House and Douglas Gibson had signed this Administrative Services and Financial Support Agreement on behalf of McClelland & Stewart.

The next document in the file was the Unanimous Shareholder Agreement, the one ring to bind them all, the master contract that tied the parties and the agreements together. The parties were First Plazas Inc., Random House of Canada, the new M&S, and the University of Toronto. It turned out that the U of T's interests were not so well protected by that 'put' as the summaries had suggested.

The contract set out the rules for the way the M&S board would function. The chairman would be selected from U of T's representatives. Employees of M&S, Random House, and U of T would get no fees for serving on it, and neither would other directors unless it became "necessary," at which point they would be paid "as a group," no more than $30, 000 per annum. The voting rules reinforced Random House's control of the accounts. It would take three U of T directors and at least one Random House director to decide on "disposition of all or substantially all of the assets of the Corporation," or to commit to capital expenditures of over $100,000 or an author advance of over $250,000, or to borrow funds over $50,000—except for loans Random House was obliged to make to M&S, such as that $1 million to pay off the promissory note to First Plazas. Random House could also withhold permission to issue securities or to redeem or purchase securities of the Corporation. In other words, M&S couldn't borrow from another party to pay off its debt to Random House without the permission of one Random House director. No meetings or votes could be held without at least one Random House director present.[286]

Random House could not vote on a person proposed to be President or Publisher if that person was not dealing at arm's length with Random House, *but*, if such a person was voted in, "such individual will sever his or her economic relationships with Random House, except to the extent that the board specifically determines that such relationships do not result in such individuals being controlled by Random House. If an individual selected as President or Publisher does not deal at arm's length with Random House, then the board will ensure that the individual shall not, as such, operate under the control of Random House and the U of T Directors will have authority by majority vote to remove such individual from his or her office and the Random House Directors will refrain from voting on the question."[287]

At first I thought hey, that's good. On the other hand the President and Publisher who mainly fit this description, Douglas Pepper, had been appointed as a *U of T director*, not a Random House director, which theoretically permitted him to vote on his own removal and on whether he had sufficiently severed himself from Random House.

Here's where the prospect of earnings from this gift became hopeless for U of T. The agreement stated that U of T and Random House would get dividends from the cash flow "only after payment of taxes, principal and interest on any outstanding debt, amortization costs, depreciation and other expenses (including any amounts paid or payable under the Administrative Services and Financial Support Agreement).[288] No surprise, then, that no dividends had been paid. If U of T did manage to find a buyer for its shares of M&S, that buyer would have to buy them all and make a loan to the company immediately so M&S could pay back 75% of the loans outstanding, plus interest to Random House. It would also have to assume Random House's responsibility for making new loans to M&S.[289]

These terms had not been spelled out in the summary given to the Business Board.

The U of T was also required by this agreement to keep reappointing Avie Bennett to the board (or another nominee from First Plazas) for "at least" five years, and as Chairman if that's what he wanted. There was nothing in this agreement that permitted the U of T to get rid of Bennett even if they didn't like what he did, or if he became incapacitated yet refused to nominate someone else from First Plazas in his place.[290]

If the U of T actually received an offer from an arm's length third party to buy *all* its shares in M&S, and that offer was for cash ("or other consideration which Random House is reasonably capable of matching and which specifically excludes shares or other ownership interests in the Proposed Purchaser") and not for shares in the purchaser, Random House got what is called a right of first refusal. Random House would have 30 days to tell the U of T (after receiving notice and being shown proof that the third party is "a Canadian") that Random House would pay the same price plus 5% for the U of T's shares; or, give the U of T permission to accept the third-party offer; or, require the third party to also buy all of the shares owned by Random House at the same price per share. Random House would have 150 days (or more if the U of T agreed) to obtain government approval of its offer for the shares. If it failed to get permission to buy them, it could then agree to the sale by U of T of its shares to the third party, or demand that Random House's shares be purchased too, etc. In other words, any Canadian brave enough to make an offer for the U of T's M&S shares would need very deep pockets and the determination to wait[291] half a year to get an answer.

And then I came to the clauses concerning the 'put.' They were far more complex than the summaries had suggested.

At the termination of the Administrative and Financial Services Agreement, U of T could require Random House to sell its shares to the U of T, or to purchase the U of T's shares so long as the government agreed and did not require "unreasonable undertakings" of Random House. Unreasonable undertakings were listed. They could include: undertakings lasting seven years or more; the provision of material benefits to some other party; requirements that the business be run in some new manner; an agreement to divest all or a portion of the shares at some future date at fair value (defined as net sales of the previous year). Either purchaser (the U of T or Random House) could pay for the other's shares in cash or with a subordinated promissory note, so long as not less than 20% of the purchase price was paid immediately in cash. Any subordinated promissory note issued by a purchaser would have to be paid over a five-year period. Fair value would be net sales of the previous 12 months less any debt owed to Random House.[292]

Finally, I got to what was called the Alternative Put, which had been referred to in the summaries. "Within 30 days after the fifth anniversary of this Agreement (but not hereafter)," it said, the University could send a notice to Random House and First Plazas Inc. indicating it wished to sell its shares for $5 million "provided U of T has not previously sold or otherwise disposed of any of its shares or any rights in respect thereto." In other words, in order to ever use this 'put,' the U of T could not sell even one share in the preceding five years.[293]

Random House would then have to indicate whether it wanted to buy the shares or not. If it wanted to, it would have 150 days, or however long it took, after getting an extension from U of T and First Plazas, to get governmental permission. If Random House did not want to buy, or was unable to get authorization, then First Plazas Inc. would have to complete the sale. If First Plazas was forced to complete the purchase, however, it would *not* have to pay back any debt to Random House or provide any new loans to M&S. In fact, the wording was intriguing. It said: "U of T will deliver the shares free and clear of any encumbrances."[294]

So was that why, though the U of T received no dividends from this gift, it never called this Alternative Put? Was someone at the University concerned that the minority Liberal government would turn Random House down if it applied to buy the whole company? At that point, the hot potato would have landed in Bennett's lap. Would someone at U of T have worried that with his exit strategy reversed, Avie Bennett would be so annoyed he would stop donating to U of T?

These documents did not answer such questions.

The Unanimous Shareholder Agreement was signed for U of T by Wendy M. Cecil-Cockwell (once married to Jack Cockwell of Edper/Brascan/Hees) in her role as Chairwoman of the Governing Council, and by its Secretary, Louis Charpentier. John Neale and Douglas Foot signed for Random House. Doug Gibson signed as President of McClelland & Stewart Ltd. and Avie Bennett signed as President of First Plazas Inc.

I was getting close to the bottom of the FIPPA pile. Yet I still hadn't found any document showing the independent valuation of M&S for the tax credit receipt.

I turned over the last page of the Agreement, and there it was, a memo on Ernst & Young Corporate Finance Inc. letterhead marked private and confidential and titled "Fair Market Value of Shares of McClelland & Stewart Ltd. Donated to the University of Toronto." This memo was addressed to W.G. Tad Brown, Finance and Development Counsel, U of T. It was dated August 4, 2000, one month after all the transactions closed on July 1, 2000. It had been prepared by a well-regarded, long-time employee of Ernst & Young named Ronald W. Scott. (How did I know he is well-regarded? I Googled and found a business valuator's prize supported by Ernst & Young in honour of Scott's career. He has retired.) He is both a chartered accountant and a certified business valuator.

In the few weeks that transpired between the day upon which the gift was made and the date on this memo, Scott could not have spent much time going through M&S's books and prospects. So Bennett had told me the truth about that, too. Yet Bennett was wrong about the assumptions Scott used to value the tax credit receipt. His memo made it clear he had based it in part on the $5.3 million paid by Random House for 25% of the M&S. *But it had also been based on the value Avie Bennett placed on the publishing assets he'd sold to the new M&S.* I looked everywhere in the FIPPA pile for that particular agreement—essentially an agreement between Bennett and himself. It wasn't there. Yet Scott appeared to have seen it so it must have been in the University's possession at some point.

Scott's memo summarized his views as follows:

> ...in our opinion the fair market value of the donated shares of McClelland & Stewart Ltd. as of the date of gift at July 1, 2000, may be taken as $15,900,000. This value represents three times the *arm's length price* [italics mine] paid by Random House for 25% of the Company. This amount is also 75% of the aggregate value assigned to the assets of the business in exchange for shares taken back by First Plazas at the time the operations were sold to the new McClelland & Stewart corporate entity. It is accordingly

our opinion that a donation receipt in the amount of $15,900,000 would reflect the fair market value of the shares received by the University from First Plazas.

There! Finally! The value of the tax credit receipt issued to First Plazas. And it was bigger than anyone had supposed.

What did Scott study to arrive at his opinion? He mentioned a number of the documents that were in the FIPPA file, but he did not list the financial statements of the old M&S. He said he also looked at information "in the public domain with respect to the donation transaction, similar situations in which publishing companies were acquired and information respecting the valuation of publishing firms in trading and transaction contexts." He also said he "met with representatives of the University and McClelland & Stewart to discuss the background to the donation and the associated transactions and arrangements respecting future operation of the business."[295] He did not say who he had these discussions with.

Then he listed the assumptions underlying his opinion, which would be offered to the Canada Revenue Agency if it came knocking on the University's door. He started by saying that Avie Bennett, the donor, is well respected and his donation was motivated by his interest in education and culture "and is accordingly more than a financial transaction." He said the agreements he'd read "provide an adequate description of the background to the donation and the plans for future operations of the business." He said "there are no contingencies, liabilities or commitments or other matters outstanding...." that would impair its capacity to perform as expected. And finally, he said "that representatives of management of M&S and the University have reviewed this letter and are aware of no matters which would render the assumptions and analysis employed in this report invalid..."

He described the operations and assets that had been moved to the new M&S as the premier Canadian book publishing business. He threw in a list of the usual suspects—bestselling and prize-winning authors—to show how important M&S was in the Canadian literary scene. He argued that putting the marketing and distribution (he made no mention of banking) in the hands of the larger Random

House would lead to cost savings. These would result from "synergy potentials that are inherent in the larger operating base of the total Random House Canadian and other operations—the company is part of the international book publishing business of Bertelsmann AG—and thus improve its financial performance from what had prevailed historically."

As to what had prevailed historically and how he knew it, he was silent. There were no numbers in this memo detailing M&S's past revenues and costs, nothing about whether it had been profitable in 1999, or running at a loss. He said such numbers wouldn't be relevant because of the new relationship with Random House which would change everything, as would the fact that the agency part of M&S's business had been retained by First Plazas. Though First Plazas could be forced to purchase the University's shares for $5 million, he didn't see that this radically reduced value for the M&S shares was reflective of the real value of the company, but as "relevant only in circumstances where the business under the new structure has proved to be significantly less than successful."

Then he worked through the various approaches to valuing a business and ruled out two: the cost approach, which he said was better suited to buildings, and the income approach, which didn't help in this instance because "the future operating basis for the business under the Administrative Support Agreement structure differs significantly from its historical basis of operations" so, estimating future income "on a reliable basis could be difficult." This left him with the "market approach," which he thought fit because of the "arm's length transaction in the shares of M&S in the form of the Random House acquisition" and his ability to compare that to other sales of comparable firms.

What comparable firms, I wondered? The only Canadian publishing company sold in approximately the same period, so far as I knew, was Macfarlane, Walter & Ross, which First Plazas had bought the previous year, shorn of its valuable backlist, for a grand total of $1 million. And how, after having read all the interlocked agreements, could he say that "control of the business resides with the University as the owner of 75% of the shares..." While Random House has some rights as a shareholder and contract provider of administrative and financial support services under the various agreements as described above, such rights are far from an ability to control the business or to affect the independence of the publisher in carrying on the key operations of the undertaking.[296] When does control of bank accounts, control of debt, negative control of decisions to sell or borrow or vote, *not* count as control of a company?

As far as Scott was concerned: the "overall valuation of the new M&S company that is implied by the Random House price is understood to represent 1.25 times the most recent year's net sales of the business—an approach to interpreting values for businesses of this sort which is widely employed."

He used the word "understood." That suggested to me that someone had told him verbally what M&S net sales were in 1999, but he hadn't actually seen a financial statement. The use in the agreements of 1.0 time net sales to establish fair value in future he referred to as a minority holding discount because the other businesses he'd looked at had sold at higher multiples of net sales. As examples he mentioned the purchase of a company in the UK, and the purchase by W.H. Smith of Hodder Headline in the US. The only Canadian comparison he used was the purchase by Canadian animation company Nelvana of a US company called Klutz. Yet none of these transactions fell under the *Investment Canada Act*: because only Canadians may buy Canadian publishing companies, the value of Canadian companies is diminished, and was the reason for this gift and sale.

In fact, he didn't refer to the *Act* at all, he referred instead to the book policy. He pointed out there are "cultural policy constraints on transactions in Canadian publishing companies..." He acknowledged these "policies impose a perceived constraint on both value and resale value for any investment of this sort." Yet he went on to say: "While prospects exist that some relaxation of the Canadian culture policies could take place at some point in the future as a form of response to the increased globalization of commerce and an increasing willingness of the country to compete fully with the world on the basis of its merits rather than market access controls, any attempt to predict the potential timing and dimensions of such a change is fraught with uncertainty."

Having speculated on the future, he drew back to more familiar ground, the dampening effect on English Canadian publishers' values due to the power of the US market next door.

In the end, his argument became a circle. The business was worth what Avie Bennett and Random House had said it was worth. "The fact that the sale transaction between First Plazas and the new McClelland & Stewart company—a transaction involving the whole business and hence a control basis of transfer—also took place on a basis reflective of the Random House share purchase values, tends to suggest that the latter were effectively viewed as a reasonable index of total value for the business at the time."

The tax credit receipt was duly issued to First Plazas Inc. on September 12, 2000 and sent to Avie Bennett by courier. In his cover letter, Tad Brown, of Finance and Development at U of T said: "Please find enclosed a charitable tax receipt in the amount of $15,900,000 for your gift of 7500 common shares of McClelland & Stewart Ltd. Thank you again for this extraordinary act of philanthropy. As you requested last week, the University will continue not to list your name as a donor in its publications such as the National Report."[297]

Well, well, I thought. Now you know why there was no public mention of the value of the gift in any U of T publications. Bennett had asked that it be kept quiet.

This note had been blind copied to two officials, including—aha!—Jon Dellandrea. He'd told me he had no knowledge of the tax receipt issued.

I found nothing in the FIPPA file explaining why the University of Toronto had failed to exercise the put until I came upon a memo near the bottom sent by Helen Choy, U of T's Manager, Accounting Services, to Pierre Piché, Controller & Director, Financial Services Department. It was dated April 26, 2006. At that point, the University's representatives on the M&S board were: Avie Bennett, chairman, John Evans, Douglas Pepper, Arlene Perly Rae, and Catherine Riggall. David Naylor was the University's President. The subject line said: Investment Write-Down for McClelland & Stewart Ltd.

The first paragraph recounted the facts of the gift and how Ernst & Young had valued U of T's shares in M&S in 2000 at $15,900,000.

As I read the second paragraph I thought my head would explode. Ms. Choy wrote:

> On January 21, 2001 [only six months after the gift was accepted], after careful review of the accounting implications, it was determined that the University does not control M&S, but it has the ability to exercise significant influence.[298]

Wait a minute, wait a minute! I shouted into the silence of my office. You can't do that! You can't tell the world that you have been given control of this company as a gift, and get a valuator to affirm that you have control and advise you to issue a tax credit receipt for $15,900,000 in part premised on that control, only to turn around a few months later and say actually, you don't have it!

But apparently if you are U of T, you can do exactly that.

As the memo went on to say:

> ...It was further agreed with Ernst & Young that the University would record 75% share of M&S's income at April 30 and disclose the basis of valuation of the long-term investments, without disclosing the value of the investment separately due to confidentiality restrictions stipulation in the agreement with the donor.[299]

What restrictions? I shouted. Where? I went back through the FIPPA file to find the agreement between U of T and First Plazas. There was no stipulation of confidentiality. There was a confidentiality provision in the Unanimous Shareholder Agreement, but not in the donor agreement.

Is anything wrong? yelled clever husband from his own office down the hall.

I'm fine, I growled, and kept reading.

> M&S has reported deficits from December 2000 to December 2005 and has not made any dividend payment to the University. Therefore,

the University has never reported any income in relation to M&S. The University has been reporting the value of these investments using the receipted value since these shares are not traded in the open market and their market values are not readily available.

Choy explained that the original estimate of their value relied on the price paid by Random House, but also "the fact that the University had an option to sell these shares within the first five years for $5 million. The five years' period ended June 30, 2005, but was extended to June 30, 2008."

Ah, I said to myself. Though she did not use the word 'put' and misdescribed its terms, it was clear that the 'put' had been put off until 2008 by the U of T. By then, the Conservatives were in power, with a minority. The Conservatives were friendlier to the idea of letting Canadian publishers be owned by foreigners.

She mentioned that she had five years' worth of revenue statements and that there had been no profits in any of those years (but these statements were not attached to this memo). She performed a calculation of 1.25 times 2005 net sales to get the value of 75% of M&S in 2006: $7.6 million. From this number, she said she had to subtract 75% of the amounts owing to Random House for what she referred to as the net shareholders' deficit as of the end of 2005. That brought the value of the University's shares down to $5.3 million. She wanted to further reduce the shares' value to $5 million "since that is the lowest possible price the University can get for the shares." She recommended a write down of $10.9 million.

But how to report this? Her suggestion: "…we will net this item and report it under the category: 'preservation of capital on externally restricted endowments.'"

And so it was done. And no one was the wiser.

In 2007, the issue of the 'put' came up again. By then, the U of T was represented on the M&S board by Bennett, Douglas Pepper, Trina McQueen and two U of T officials, Catherine Riggall and Judith Wolfson.

I clearly had not been given the first memo that set off the next chain of emails about the 'put' and a further write down, but it appeared that at some point, Pierre Piché had asked again about writing down the value of the M&S shares.

On October 23, 2007, Catherine Riggall wrote to Piché and said: "Unless there is a good reason to write it down, we think it should be left at $5 mm [sic] since the put does not expire until July 2008 and it is possible that it could be renewed."

The next item in the email chain was Piché's response: "Since June 30 is close to our year-end, the financial statements must reflect our intentions. These companies are in a deficit and therefore there is not a lot of value. The only reason we did not right [sic] it down to zero in 2006 was because of the put. If we let it expire, if that is our intention, then we need to write the investment down close to zero..."

Riggall responded with "we are not sure yet what we will do—."

She then mentioned discussions with a potential buyer but she offered no names.

On May 1, 2008, Pierre Piché asked Riggall once more about the write down. "Has the put option been extended or will we let it lapse requiring a write-down to zero for this investment?"

Riggall responded: "We will let it lapse in July this year."

At which point Piché told Helen Choy to write off the whole investment to zero. In an accountant's view of the world, since the backlist had no independent value from the time the gift/sale transaction closed in 2000, that almost made sense.

There was nothing more in the file explaining the University's failure to extend the 'put' or to call it. In fact, there was nothing much left in the file at all. There was a copy of that July 4, 2011 letter sent to me by the University before I filed the FIPPA. In it, Catherine Riggall, U of T's Vice-president of Business Affairs as well as a member of the M&S board, asked Missy Marston-Shmelzer, Director of Cultural Sector Investment Review, Canadian Heritage, for permission to transfer the University's M&S shares to Random House. There was another almost identical letter underneath dated two days later. There was no indication as to which version was actually sent. This time, Riggall's words about the University's "stewardship" of McClelland & Stewart took on a very different meaning.

Riggall wrote: "Over the past eleven years, M&S has accrued significant debts and has earned a small profit in only two years."

Wait a minute, I thought. In Helen Choy's memo on the first write down, she said no profit had been earned in any of the first five years. Who was right?

Due to the lack of profits and accrual of debt, Riggall continued, "U of T's ownership interest in M&S has not resulted in any financial benefits to the University. In fact, U of T concluded some years ago that there was no hope of making a return on the shares it held in the company and wrote off the value of its holdings."

That was not what the University had concluded in 2007. At that point, it had still been possible for the University to call the 'put' and get $5 million from First Plazas. But this letter did not mention the 'put' or say why it had not been called or extended. Neither did this letter mention that right from the start, the U of T had decided that *it did not control M&S which meant Random House did.* Instead, this letter positioned the proposed handover of its M&S shares to Random House within the exemption requirements of the *Investment Canada Act* and the Book Policy as if control would only pass to Random House in 2012. Dire financial straits and the University's failure to find a Canadian buyer were both invoked.

> U of T has been interested in divesting its ownership interest in M&S for several years, however, no purchasers, viable or otherwise, have emerged. The current proposed transaction is the only viable plan that has emerged for the termination of U of T's ownership interest in M&S. The proposed transaction will allow U of T to exit the investment, while also ensuring that M&S continues with an owner which is experienced in the Canadian publishing industry and committed to the ongoing development of the M&S business.

There was nothing in the FIPPA file recording the government's response. However, the public record shows that the Minister conducted a review and agreed to the transfer of the shares, after having extracted certain net benefits which of course were kept secret. What I did have in the file were emails between the President of the

University, David Naylor, and Brad Martin of Random House recording the fact that they'd had a meeting about the impending transfer which was deemed to be a better result than "the possible bankruptcy and disappearance" of M&S. They had apparently agreed on the PR words that would be uttered in public.

The University had also included in the FIPPA file a *Toronto Star* editorial of January 13, 2012. The editorial ran just after the transfer of M&S to Random House was announced. It called on everyone to celebrate a golden age of Canadian writing, brought to us by that good Canadian nationalist, Jack McClelland, and his company, McClelland & Stewart. Thanks to both, Canadian writing had taken its rightful place upon the front tables of Canada's bookstores and Canadian authors' names graced big prize lists in the rest of the world. "The takeover of M&S this week was mourned by many in the publishing world, and indeed it is the end of a long and honourable chapter in Canada's literary life. Times are tough for publishers and booksellers, here and in other countries, as online sales and ebooks shake their traditional business model to its core. But for Canadian writing and Canadian readers, the outlook is overwhelmingly positive," said the *Star* without explaining how both could be true. While it called for vigilance to be sure that M&S, now under Random House's full ownership, would continue with its "unique programs" there was no call for an investigation as to how this all happened. Needless to say, no mention was made in this editorial that the *Star's* owner, Torstar, had embarked on its own end run around the *Investment Canada Act*, which would soon bear fruit.

Finally, the file included a Letter to the Editor written by U of T President Naylor in response to that *Star* editorial. Naylor proposed that everyone should praise Avie Bennett for rescuing M&S from "the brink of bankruptcy" in 1986, a decision "driven by cultural nationalism, not a business investment," sustaining it for 14 years, and then giving 75% of his ownership share of M&S to the University of Toronto, thereby "preserving Canadian ownership."

Random House acquired the other quarter and loyally poured millions of dollars into underwriting M&S. Another dozen years passed with M&S promoting Canadian titles and authors. Bennett continued to serve as volunteer chair of the board... if Avie Bennett had not stepped up 25 years ago to rescue M&S and keep Jack McClelland's dream alive, I am not sure there would be a "golden age" of Canadian writing to celebrate today.

As I closed the file, I realized I was hopping mad.

Reporters aren't supposed to get mad.

And yet: I felt disrespected as a reader. Naylor had spread a thick layer of congratulatory rhetoric—glossy as fresh butter on stale bread—over a set of arrangements he knew to be less than laudatory. He implied that the University had been public-spirited when it took on the ownership of M&S (he did not use the word control, but unwary readers would think that's what he meant). He quoted the *Star* to the effect that "ongoing changes in worldwide publishing" made it "impossible for M&S to carry on independently" though he must have known M&S had not been independent (as in, controlled by the U of T) for 12 years. He painted Random House as a splendidly generous organization by saying that it had poured millions into a losing cause, implying that its motive was sheer goodness, not the control and then absorption of a competitor. He announced himself "relieved that Random House has made firm commitments to preserve this iconic imprint and support its Canadian authors."[300]

12

Unanswered Questions? Pester!

I closed the FIPPA file. When I went to bed that night, I thought that I understood what I'd read and that I'd seen all the documents that mattered. It's always that way with me. I feel absurdly confident that I have mastered material I've just waded through once, though hard experience has taught me that all such convictions will vanish quickly, in the face of more questions.

The next morning, I rose wondering about things that had *not* been included in the University's FIPPA file. Certainty faded like the literary cat's grin.

For example: where were the follow-up questions that must have been engendered by the Minister's review of the transfer? Where were the emails discussing why the 'put' had not been exercised in 2005, extended to 2008, but not exercised at that point? Where were the minutes of the Business Board which, according to the contract between the University and First Plazas, was the only entity within the University with the power to decide, on the recommendation of the President, to sell the M&S shares? Where was that first agreement, referred to by the business evaluator, Ron Scott, by which First Plazas sold the publishing assets of old M&S to the new M&S? *Two* transactions had convinced Scott that new M&S was worth $22 million, not just the sale of a quarter of the company to Random House.

I searched the FIPPA file over and over thinking I'd probably mis-arranged the documents, these things had to be in it somewhere. But no, they were not. I sent another email to Howard Jones at the FIPPA office at the U of T asking for what I was sure the University had in its possession but for reasons unknown had failed to share.

About a month later, Jones sent me back one more document, saying the University believed it had now been responsive to my FIPPA request—in other words, that was all it was willing to hand over. He'd sent the Asset Purchase Agreement between First Plazas Inc. and the new McClelland & Stewart Ltd. Stamped on the first page was the usual warning: Privileged and Confidential Under the *Investment Canada Act* and Exempt from Disclosure Under the *Access to Information Act.*

This was the agreement that transferred to the new M&S most of the rights and ongoing business carried on by First Plazas Inc. under the names McClelland & Stewart Inc., Tundra Books Inc., Tundra Books of New York, and Macfarlane, Walter & Ross Ltd. This agreement noted that First Plazas was *not* selling to the new M&S: *The Canadian Encyclopedia*, the agency business and "the shares held by Vendor [First Plazas Inc.] in Canbook Distribution Corp," as well as something called First University Corporation Ltd., refundable taxes, and "Vendor's rights to royalties and to Book Publishing Industry Development Program payments such rights to be set forth in a transitional services agreement..." etc.[301]

I flipped right to the clause labelled Purchase Price. It said: "The purchase price for the Vendor Assets is the fair market value thereof as of the date hereof which the parties have determined to be $22,250,000." The parties meant the parties to this Agreement, First Plazas Inc.and the new M&S. Exactly 9,999 shares were to be issued by the new M&S to First Plazas Inc. with an "attributed value of $21,250,000" on closing, "such shares to be issued as fully paid and non-assessable." The Purchaser (new M&S) would also hand over a promissory note to First Plazas Inc. to pay $1,000,000[302] on the first anniversary of this Agreement, with interest payable at 6% on that date.

This may be what an accountant could call a fair market transaction, but you and I might take a different view as Avie Bennett was on both sides of the deal. This Agreement recorded how one very brilliant and creative businessman transferred assets between his right hand and his left. The right hand, First Plazas Inc., said these assets were worth $22,250,000. The left hand, the new M&S responded: absolutely, thanks very much, that is exactly what these assets are worth, please take these 9,999 shares in exchange as if they are worth $21,250,000 and keep them in a safe place until you sell some and give the rest away!

This was the weird meat from which the value of the new M&S was made—weird, as in magical. Capitalism can be magical: those who truly understand their business, or have excellent tax lawyers, are able to distill value out of very thin air. It was this Agreement that created the framework for the gift to the U of T and sale to Random House, which followed a few minutes later. It positioned the salami for the knife.

There were of course implications regarding the taxes that would be owed by First Plazas Inc. as soon as this transaction was complete, even though $21,500,00 had not actually found its way to First Plazas Inc.'s bank account. Since First Plazas had not paid $22 million to acquire M&S in 1986 (First Plazas had paid about $1 million to the other debenture holders, and about the same again to Jack McClelland for his shares of the old M&S), a lot of capital gains tax would be owed. Unless...

This is where an interesting aspect of the *Income Tax Act* came in. Further down in the agreement, it said:

> The Vendor and Purchaser agree to report the purchase price of the Vendor Assets in any returns required to be filed under the *Income Tax Act* and other taxation statutes in accordance with this Section 2.3 and Sections 8.1 and 8.2.

These sections of the Agreement referred to what is called an election under Section 85.1 of the *Income Tax Act*. When assets are transferred in return for shares between related parties (for example, when a new holding company is created so that the originating company can avoid paying a lot of tax on a capital gain), an election permits the buyer and seller to agree on a price *which is not the same as fair market value* and to be taxed accordingly. It can be higher than fair market value, or lower, in this case the parties agreed to an election "whereby the aggregate proceeds of the disposition to the Vendor of the Vendor Assets and the aggregate cost thereof to the Purchaser shall, to the extent required by the Vendor, be the aggregate adjusted cost base of the Vendor Assets to the Vendor for the purposes of the Act." How much was recorded for tax purposes? I have no idea.

This Agreement was signed by Avie Bennett for First Plazas Inc. It was signed for the new M&S by Bennett's employee, Doug Gibson, who had just been appointed by Bennett as the President of new M&S. Though Gibson had denied knowing what Random House paid for its 25%, or the amount of Avie Bennett's tax credit, he certainly knew what the company was worth at the time of these transactions—$22,250,000. His signature was right there, on the last page of this Agreement.

The fair market value of the new M&S, as set by Bennett at $22,250,000, was high for a Canadian publishing company shorn of its agency business. But the only real money that changed hands in this deal came from Random House—the $5.3 million paid to First Plazas Inc. for 25% of the new M&S shares, plus the $1 million it would loan to the new M&S so it could pay that sum to First Plazas one year later. It was hard to say how much—if any—real money First Plazas would receive thanks to the tax credit receipt for $15,900,000. That amount would be determined according to a formula related to the income of First Plazas. It would either reduce First Plazas Inc.'s tax owing, or, if no tax was owed, a cheque would be forthcoming from the Canada Revenue Agency.

In other words: though the claimed value of the new M&S was $22,250,000, Random House acquired control of a competitor for $5.3 million in cash plus $1 million loaned to the new M&S. What Bennett got due to the tax credit receipt remained hidden in the murky deeps of Canada's tax rules.

I wrote again to Howard Jones and asked again for any notes or emails about the University's decision to transfer its shares to Random House in 2011, any responses from the federal government, and any minutes showing that the Governing Council's

Business Board had decided to hand over the University's shares. Since he had not said such documents did not exist, I had to assume they did and I said so.

He wrote back to say the University had decided to send me some more emails as well as the actual Share Purchase Agreement with Random House.

This whole process had begun to feel like a striptease. If I whistled and hooted, a glove came off and was flung toward me. If I hollered and stomped, off came the blouse...

But this time, when I opened the new documents, I was sure the show was over, that the University had stripped to its skin.

The Share Purchase Agreement between the U of T's Governing Council, McClelland & Stewart, and Random House had absolutely nothing stamped on it declaring it to be exempt from disclosure. The Agreement was dated December 30, 2011. By then, the political situation in Ottawa had shifted once more. The Conservative government had been re-elected with a small majority the previous May. The Minister of Canadian Heritage had allowed the U of T to give its McClelland & Stewart shares to Random House for $1.

An opening background section of the Agreement recounted the pertinent facts. It spelled out that the buyer (Random House) and the Company (McClelland & Stewart) were parties to an Administrative Services and Financial Support Agreement dated July 2, 2002, and amended on April 1, 2004. That was a surprise: the University had only produced the original version of this Agreement, which was dated July 1, 2000. Clearly, the Agreement had been renegotiated twice. What had changed? But I forgot that question as soon as I got to Point E in this Agreement. It was so shocking, I dropped the papers on the floor.

It said:

As of November 30, 2011, the Company was in arrears to the Buyer under the Administrative Services Agreement for approximately $16,274,170 (including current accounts) which debt is secured by a General Security Agreement dated October 25, 2005, granted by the Company in favour of the Buyer and registered under the Personal

Property Security Act (file no: 619229727, reg. no: 20050927 1511 1590 4705).[303]

How could that debt have grown so huge?

M&S must have done extremely poorly over the previous 11 years, in spite of the millions in public money it received as grants and tax credits, in spite of the synergies that were supposed to result from having marketing, administration, distribution, and finance taken over by the much larger Random House of Canada. Bennett had asserted that these services offered by Random House would be cheaper than the ones M&S had incurred when operating independently. While its revenues must certainly have dropped, and dropped again—it had published far fewer books each year after Macfarlane, Walter & Ross was shut down—its costs should have gone down as well. Doug Gibson had said there was no large debt owing when he was moved sideways in 2004. So could it have been incurred in the subsequent years? I did a rough calculation: if I added the debt of $16,274,170 to what Random House paid for its 25% of the company—$5,300,000 plus a loan of $1 million for that promissory note—it came out to $22, 574,170, about $374,000 more than the "fair market value" First Plazas had attributed to the new M&S in 2000.

I noted too that Random House first registered this debt on October 25, 2005, a few months after the 'put' was extended for three years. From that point on, as a secured creditor, Random House had the right to put M&S into bankruptcy if Random House failed to cause M&S to pay it whatever M&S owed. Clearly Random House had decided shortly after the Conservatives won a majority in 2011 that the time had come to threaten to exercise that right.

How did I know that? The Agreement said so. "In light of the financial difficulties of the Company, and in lieu of exercising its rights as a secured creditor at this time, the Buyer proposed to buy the Seller's shares with a view to continuing the operation of the company as a division of the Buyer."[304]

In other words, Random House had demanded the U of T's shares in exchange for not bankrupting M&S. How would the U of T's stewardship look if the iconic Canadian publishing company it apparently controlled went bankrupt under its watch? No doubt this appalling debt had also enabled Random House to get government consent to "the acquisition of control of McClelland & Stewart Ltd... in accordance with the *Investment Canada Act...*"[305]

No wonder no Canadian buyer had been found. What prospective buyer would have been stupid enough to pay $16 million to a competitor, Random House, as it took possession of M&S, which it would have to do under the terms of the Unanimous Shareholder Agreement?

Attached as a schedule to this Agreement were copies of a letter to Missy Marston-Shmelzer of Canadian Heritage from Brad Martin, Random House CEO. It was dated October 11, 2011, and confirmed that Random House would live up to the undertakings listed on the next page in return for "the transfer of control of M&S to RHC," (control Random House already had). This note had produced a letter of permission on November 14 from the Minister of Canadian Heritage, James Moore. It was of course marked Protected-Inv. Act, though Moore merely asserted in it that he was satisfied after review that "your investment is likely to be of net benefit to Canada." After giving his approval, Moore went on to say: "I would like to take this opportunity to welcome your decision to invest in Canada and to express the hope that your investment will be successful." He could have been writing about any generic investment in any company, not the takeover of the iconic McClelland & Stewart.

The Agreement showed how the 11-year-old arrangement had ended. Avie Bennett, Trina McQueen, Judith Wolfson, Catherine Riggall, and Douglas Pepper (a U of T director as well as being an officer of McClelland & Stewart and its subsidiaries), had all resigned from the M&S board and the boards of its subsidiaries. Thus, the Agreement that transferred the shares to Random House from the University was signed by the Random House directors, Brad Martin and Douglas Foot, on behalf of both Random House and McClelland & Stewart. Oddly, Catherine Riggall, the U of T's Vice-President of Business Affairs, had signed on behalf of the Governing Council of the U of T. Usually the Chairman and the Secretary sign for the Council. More on that, later.

The Random House undertakings were also attached and were interesting. They had a five-year term ending December 30, 2016. Random House promised the government that it would: provide a written report on performance when asked by Heritage Canada; keep proper books, accounts and records at the "principal place of business of the M&S business division (the "Canadian Business") of Random House. It promised to "maintain current staffing levels at the Canadian Business." It promised to offer M&S employees Random House's enhanced employment benefits. While M&S would be amalgamated with Random House, "it will be operated as a separate business division within RHC. The M&S name and the names of its imprints will be maintained, the M&S business division will continue to produce separate financial statements, and the executives in the M&S business will have the same level of autonomy as the executives of other RHC business divisions, namely the Doubleday Canada Publishing Group and the Knopf Random Canada Publishing Group." In order to "ensure support for diverse Canadian authors, it would continue to support the existing imprints of the Canadian Business, including: McClelland & Stewart, Emblem Editions, Tundra Books, Fenn/McClelland & Stewart, New Canadian Library and Signal." It would also ensure "that the Canadian Business maintains an active publishing list, commensurate with the current list, continue to promote the backlists of Canadian titles published by RHC and the Canadian Business, commensurate with backlist sales in 2010." There were also guarantees about treating Canadian-based suppliers fairly and that "a majority of the management and staff positions in the Canadian Business will be held by Canadians. To ensure autonomy of the Canadian Business, the Canadian Business will designate a representative to participate as a full member of the RHC Executive Committee. This representative shall be an individual Canadian employed in a senior management role at the Canadian Business."

The rest of the undertakings were more general and related to things RHC would do for itself in the normal course of business. It promised to digitize M&S works, to continue to publish and seek out Canadian authors, etc., to continue to publish the winners of the

Journey Prize and to publish two books of poetry a year, to keep up the internship program and also to establish a new annual lecture in conjunction with the University of Toronto on cultural subjects.

And then, at the bottom was a list of what the government was entitled to say about these undertakings, if, in its wisdom, it needed to justify its approval of this transfer of the University's shares. It was a short form version of the longer version above. The lecture series was included while the promises about publishing Journey Prize winners and poetry books were not.

One of these undertakings had been abandoned within months of being accepted. For example: Random House promised to operate M&S as a "separate business division within RHC." Yet M&S was merged with the Doubleday Canada Publishing Group only six months later: Doug Pepper then became Publisher of Signal/ McClelland & Stewart, while Ellen Seligman became M&S Publisher, both reporting to Kristin Cochrane, the new head of the Group (formerly the head of Doubleday).[306]

At the end of August, 2011, one month after Catherine Riggall wrote to Missy Marston-Shmelzer at Canadian Heritage to say that U of T wanted out of M&S, Avie Bennett had apparently gotten in touch with President David Naylor by phone. He had just learned of the University's plan to transfer its shares. He objected. He wanted Naylor to make a suggestion about how to arrange things in a different fashion. Howard Jones had sent me a series of internal emails, which resulted from Bennett's phone call.

Naylor wrote to Catherine Riggall and to Judith Wolfson, another U of T official on the M&S Board, on September 1, 2011.

> Dear Cathy and Judith:
>
> Avie Bennett called. As I expected, he felt [words withheld here under section 21 of FIPPA] the way the M&S deal unfolded. I was out of the loop as you know, and commiserated. He shares the view that there are benefits, and I underscored them. However, Avie notes that (a) government grants may not be accessible, so that Canadian content will be diluted, and (b) there will be a reputational hit—i.e.

the University will be seen to be selling 'Canadian family silver.' I don't know enough to opine on (a), but I agree on (b). He wondered if a 'shell' of some type might be constructed to mutual benefit. I think this is worth considering, and at the very least given that M&S was part of this great man's life work, please give him a very careful hearing on the potential options.

Best wishes

David[307]

Riggall replied to Naylor, copy to Judith Wolfson, six days later:

I will give Avie a call and see what he has in mind. Judith and I spoke briefly on this and do not hold out great hope that there is a solution. This is the only way to keep the bradnd [sic] alive. Randon [sic] House could just call their loans and pull the plug on M&S, which would definitely be the worst result possible.

Cathy[308]

To which Naylor replied the next morning as follows:

Thanks Cathy

Avie argued today in a conversation at a Campaign Steering Committee that a 'shell' with a structure that gives U of T 51% ownership would maintain the grant and avoid any reputation issues. He does understand the vulnerabilities.

I don't think he will easily let this go—he seems more sad than angry, but I believe he will not rest until there is a meeting with some of the decision-makers at Random House.

I understand his views.

D.[309]

This suggestion by Avie Bennett made it clear that he believed Random House was foolish to grab all of the U of T's shares, that he wanted the situation to continue basically as before. He had certainly understood when he crafted this deal that Random House would eventually become the 100% owner of M&S's shares. But he seemed to think that Random House didn't understand its own interests as well as he did, that U of T didn't understand its public relations peril at all. He seemed to think that if Random House limited itself to 49% ownership, then M&S could still qualify for some grants. M&S would certainly still qualify for Ontario tax credits. In other words, in Bennett's view, Random House was throwing away its right to continue to milk the cow, and U of T would end up with a public relations black eye.

This email also confirmed that Avie had told me the truth, that there had been no prior discussion with him or the M&S board about the U of T's decision to transfer its shares, or even about Riggall's letter of July to the Department of Canadian Heritage. Communications had gone direct from Random House to the U of T, from the U of T to Canadian Heritage.

Riggall snapped back at her boss, Naylor, copy to Wolfson, making it quite clear that by 2011, some people at the U of T were very unhappy about Avie Bennett's gift.

> Avie seems to forget that we have had a 75% ownership of what is effectively a shell company for over 11 years.
> Random House do [sic] not wish to continue with anything less than 100% ownership.
> And as I mentioned, they could just pull the plug and walk away, leaving us with the mess.
> This does not mean I will not talk to Avie, but you do need to know the reality.
> The Board will be discussing this at the next meeting on the 23rd, and the two Random House officials will naturally be there.
> Cathy.[310]

I was surprised at her very blunt use of the word shell. Yet I should not have been. After all, only six months after it accepted Bennett's gift, the University had declared to itself that it did *not* control M&S. It had made that decision as a consequence of Bennett's request to withhold from public view the value of his tax credit receipt. Then the University had failed to exercise the 'put,' the only means by which the

University could have wrung value out of its ownership of the shares. It made sense that an official of the University and member of the M&S board would characterize the University as the owner of a 'shell.' A shell company is a flow-through device. The University's ownership of the M&S shares had been waved before the world like a Maple Leaf flag, though M&S was a husk through which millions of dollars in grants and tax credits flowed as Random House managed its finances: none of that money had benefited the U of T in any way.

Catherine Riggall got a one-word reply to her sharp note from David Naylor, her boss.

Understood.[311]

Other emails revealed that on September 26, 2011, Avie Bennett, Naylor and Brad Martin of Random House had had a meeting. Apparently, by then, Bennett had bowed to the inevitable. They agreed on the PR posture all three would take in public. These were the emails I had been sent earlier, but they read very differently in this new context.

Naylor wrote to Brad Martin, CEO of Random House, an email labelled "confidential."

Dear Brad,

It was good to meet you this morning and understand more about the plans involving a shift to full ownership of M&S by Random House.

Avie Bennett and I both came away reassured that the path ahead includes many safeguards, not least, maintaining the M&S brand within the Random House family, sustaining Tundra as an imprint, and ensuring continuity in a variety of the uniquely Canadian activities of M&S. This is obviously very much preferable to possible bankruptcy and disappearance of M&S.

I am glad we agreed to work together on communications in this transitional period. Avie clearly would like to have a say, as is only appropriate given his pivotal role in saving M&S years ago. I am therefore copying not only the U of T executives on the Board

(Cathy Riggall and Judith Wolfson) but Michael Kurts, AVP Strategic Communications, and Laurie Stephens, Director of Media Relations and Stakeholder Communications for the University.

Best wishes

David[312]

Martin replied:

David

I think the meeting this morning was very constructive and I am glad that you and Avie are comfortable with our course of action. Tracey Turriff our person in charge of corporate communications will contact Laurie this week. She will also contact Avie for his input. The theme will be much as we discussed this morning. The timeline I gave Tracey dovetails with this timing. Please do not hesitate to call if there are any questions.

It was a pleasure to finally meet you.

Brad[313]

I didn't need to look far to discover what Martin meant by "theme." The theme was the burial of the distasteful under yards of lavish praise. This theme was also displayed in Howard Jones' cover letter to me, the one that accompanied these documents.

Jones wrote:

From 2000 to 2011, the University preserved McClelland & Stewart during a time of decline for Canadian publishers. The Corporation was overseen by the Board on behalf of the shareholders. It was operated using expertise provided by Random House to give it the best opportunity of success. This useful arrangement, *providing for control by the University*, [italics mine] is what was colloquially referred to as a shell in Catherine Riggall's email of September 11 [sic] 2011. Regrettably, the hoped-for income to support a charitable endowment never materialized.

The University remains pleased that through its stewardship of the Corporation, it was able to sustain and preserve as much as possible an important element of Canadian publishing culture. The University remains grateful for the generosity of Mr. Bennett in thinking of the University and its educational mission when he made his original donation of the McClelland & Stewart shares.[314]

Note to the PR person who penned this nonsense for Howard Jones. In the future, first read the material already sent out in response to a FIPPA so as to avoid making spurious claims, such as the one above about control. This claim was disowned by your own officials 15 years earlier at the request of the donor praised here. And if you're going to praise that donor, extol him for what he did do—devise a plan of remarkable cleverness and foresight to deal with a law and a policy that damaged the value of his investment, an investment made to promote the public good and redeem earlier failings. The only reason your organization failed to get any benefit is that it failed to exercise its right to make that donor cough up $5 million. And most of all: don't second guess a former Vice-President of Business Affairs in her use of the word 'shell.' As a former member of the M&S board, she is better able than you to describe exactly how the new M&S functioned.

I sent an application under the *Access to Information Act* to the Department of Canadian Heritage, asking it to produce any notes and memoranda with regard to the purchase of 75% of McClelland & Stewart from the U of T by Random House of Canada. Eventually, I was sent briefing notes for the Minister providing answers to probable questions about his review and decision. One of the notes was prepared in the middle of November, 2011, far in advance of the public announcement. It said that the Minister, if asked about Random House's acquisition of McClelland & Stewart, should say: "this investment is compliant with the *Book Policy* and will secure the future of one of Canada's most important publishers." Another advisory dated January 10, 2012, added that the Minister should say that it was compliant with the *Investment Canada Act* as well as with Canada's "longstanding policy on investment in the book sector" and that any further questions should "be directed to the investor or Canadian business."

A similar document with similar answers was prepared January 20, 2012, after the announcement of the sale to Random House was finally made public. It offered the same suggested phrases as to how this acquisition was fully compliant with the *Investment Canada Act* and fit within the Book Policy. But it added that not only was the Book Policy still in place, the Minister was advised to say " this investment is compliant with the Book Policy and it will secure the future of one of Canada's most important publishers."[315]

The Minister was advised to say something quite ambiguous after the *National Post* reported on the merger between Doubleday and M&S six months later. The *Post* story appeared on June 20, 2012. If asked if Random House was allowed to combine M&S with its other operations, the Minister was advised to say: "Random House of Canada is aware of its obligations under the *Investment Canada Act*. I have no reason to believe these obligations will not be met. Any further questions should be directed to the investor or Canadian Business."[316]

The Department of Canadian Heritage also sent me an undated document labelled only as Q and A. Though there was no indication as to who was asking and who was answering the questions set out, or who had prepared the document, the answers given permitted Canadian Heritage to brag about the $39.1 million it spends on 230 Canadian-owned publishers, helping them to publish 6500 Canadian books by 4000 Canadian authors every year, and to suggest that this Canadian cultural industry is both protected and yet open for sale so long as there are net benefits to Canada. But the answers to the first three questions on this sheet were withheld due to provisions of the *Access to Information Act*.

Q: How could the Minister allow the publisher that was the birth-place of Canadian literature to be bought by a foreign company?

A: *This answer was withheld under section 24(1)*

Q: Doesn't this decision violate the Foreign Investment Policy in Book Publishing and Distribution?

A: *This answer was withheld under section 24(1)*

> Q: What is the status of the Department's ongoing review of this policy?
>
> A: *This answer was withheld under section 21(1)(a).*

The last page in this thin pile of documents had nothing on it at all except this: "Pages 14–439 are withheld in their entirety under subsection 24(1) of the *Access to Information* Act." These 425 missing pages were not identified in any way, but they likely included all the correspondence and memos between federal civil servants in the Department of Canadian Heritage and the U of T and Random House over the final fate of M&S. That's right, the brand new federal government, committed to openness and transparency according to the Prime Minister's ministerial mandate letters, kept secret 425 pages of documents related to the final handover of M&S to Random House.[317]

Your tax dollars at work.

13

The Accountant

I went to see Ron Scott, the retired business valuator from Ernst & Young, on the first bone-chillingly cold day of 2016. The sky was the colour of a wet hockey sock and a minor snowfall had evoked bumper-to-bumper traffic all over Toronto. Scott had warned me via email that he could remember next to nothing about his opinion on the value of Bennett's gift, but I was welcome to come and see him anyway. I had decided I needed to give him the opportunity to explain what he'd done.

Because: I thought his opinion on the value of the tax credit receipt for First Plazas Inc. was absurd. Basic facts had been ignored, others glossed over. I was prepared to confront and accuse. Long experience has taught me that it is best to do that in person.

Scott lives in Leaside, close to a gorgeous park overlooking the Don Valley. For those who have only seen Leaside on home reno TV shows, I can tell you that it was once a Sunday-is-for-family-dinners suburb where kids played softball on winding, tree-blessed streets. Now Toronto has a bylaw forbidding street play. The renos of Leaside sport kitchen counters in marble too beautiful to mess up with food, greatrooms with fireplaces that do not burn wood, master retreats, six-piece baths, dressing rooms. If a renoed Leaside home is sold to an unrelated party, the vendor will earn enough to buy two Canadian publishing companies, with plenty left over for glamour lunches at Il Posto. Of course, if the Leaside home vendor is so stupid as to actually do that, said vendor deserves to end up homeless.

Ronald Scott's house was therefore a surprise. It has changed little since the 1970s. The kitchen floors are made of a practical material, there is broadloom elsewhere, there are pictures of children and grandchildren. There is a den with a lot of books though Scott has pruned his collection, sending 70 banker boxes to University of Toronto's bookstore. He calls himself a book addict. He wears aviator-style glasses, his white hair is cut Roman style, he is neither tall nor short, he has a large square jaw. He said it wasn't that cold out when I complained: he said he knew about cold because he grew up in Sudbury and "this is Canada." He reminded me of a friend, the scion of one of Canada's great newspaper families. There is nothing at all grand about my friend, either, which is where the resemblance lay.

But I had expected someone slick and tricky, like that accountant whose bill collector appeared in biker garb at clever husband's office one day to demand payment for services never rendered. This man was so clearly the sort of person most Canadians aspire to be that I knew right away what he would say about his opinion. He would stand behind it. And he would have a good argument.

We sat down at the kitchen table. I handed him my copy of his letter of opinion. He read it with one hand over his mouth. The wife of the friend he reminded me of, a person of rare insight, has often told me that when people cover their mouths like that, they are trying to hide something. But he was just holding his hand over his mouth.

"Reads like a rationalization," he said after a few moments studying his own handiwork. "It's an opinion, an expression of view."

Did you do this sort of valuation for the University before? I asked.

He said he sometimes got involved in gift-based tax deals where someone was "trying to rip off the tax department." The kind of work he had mainly done for the U of T involved estate problems, for example, getting the University out from under a requirement for the continuing use of a gift when that was at odds with the condition of markets. He figured this particular letter of opinion for the U of T had probably been a first for him, though he did valuation work for Ernst & Young for many years, back to when it was still Clarkson Gordon. This opinion, he said, had been written to explain how the fair market value of the gift was established because the shares were not publicly traded. "Someone had to say this thing is worth this number… It's a list of rationalizations. The CRA could have said something else. So we gave a fairly conservative value."

He thought the request for his services came from Tad Brown, counsel in the U of T's Finance and Development Department, but he had various connections to the U of T. He had worked on its audit back in the 1960s. He thought that it was likely that Tad Brown got to him by calling the audit partner at Ernst & Young.

So, I said. I need to ask you. You listed the documents you studied, but you didn't mention seeing M&S's financial statements. Did you see them?

"Not sure I did see financial statements for McClelland & Stewart," he said. But if he hadn't, that really didn't matter because the value in this case had been based on market information and "the dominant thing here clusters on the transaction between Plazas and Random House."

I showed him the Agreement by which the U of T transferred its shares to Random House, which stated that M&S had run up over $16 million in registered debt by 2011. I told him the $5 million 'put' he'd also relied on to establish the gift's basic value was never called. In fact, I explained, my alma mater had got nothing from this gift at all.

He said he couldn't say why M&S had run up such a debt, though he thought it would be fairly easy to do since it amounted to about $1.6 million per year for ten years. The only way to understand those ins and outs would be to look at the financial statements.

Well Random House is not going to give them to me, I said. They won't talk to me.

"Ask U of T for the financials," he said. "If you own 75% of a company, you want the annual financial statements. Ask them."

For some reason, the perfect sense of his suggestion went in one ear and right out the other. I was focused instead on the end result of the gift, the failure of the University to get anything from it.

"Strange things go on," he said.

We went back to his opinion. I wanted to be sure I understood it. I wanted to know why he'd mentioned the government's book policy as a constraint on the sale of Canadian publishing houses, but not the

Investment Canada Act, and why he had suggested that a rule change could be coming. Why had he put that in? Where had that idea come from? Did someone tell him to do that?

You couldn't *not* say that, he said, because "the nature of international markets of the time was, the barriers are coming down. You've got to allow for it. It would allow value [to be] added." What he was concerned about was writing an opinion that would withstand any Canada Revenue Agency review. This was a "transaction framed by trading prices."

I told him that I had an informant who knew how gifts like this were treated by other universities. That informant had said that having only one opinion on the value of donated private shares was unusual. Was it unusual at U of T?

"Getting multiple people to evaluate would not be common," he said. "The CRA, if concerned, would have put their own people on it..." But if the CRA had wanted to challenge the opinion, he said, they'd have had to say they didn't care about the price paid by Random House for 25% of the company, but were mainly interested in future prospects of the business. This was "an arm's length transaction," he said. "The first part of this deal has to be at fair market value." By the first part, he did not mean when First Plazas sold assets to the new M&S in return for shares and a promissory note. He meant what Random House paid for its 25%.

To his way of thinking, that $5.3 million was the most significant evidence (of value). "We looked at revenues and how this price related to revenues. There are rules of thumb. People trade businesses on multiples of revenues. Implicit is a return on sales of x percent, a return on investment of y percent. Transactions are done on that basis."

But the situation of Canadian publishing companies is unlike that of other book businesses in other countries, I said. So, why had he compared this sale to sales in the US and Britain?

He said he'd looked at sales in the US because they were the only ones to look at. "It's a disciplined guess," he said.

He'd mentioned in his memo that he had spoken with officials at the U of T and at M&S. I wondered if it was Bennett who had assured him that M&S would do better in association with Random House than on its own. Did you meet with Avie Bennett? I asked.

"I can't remember," he said. "It's just not embedded."

So then I told him that the University's M&S shares had ended up in Random House's hands for one dollar, notwithstanding that M&S owned the best backlist in the country as he'd mentioned in his opinion. What do you think of that? I asked

"I'm surprised they sold it for a dollar," he said. "It could be looked at that the business is a liability if losing money..."

Could he think of any reason why Avie Bennett would not want the size of the tax credit receipt that he received to be disclosed?

He asked if Bennett disclosed his other gifts. He himself did not.

Yes, I said, he did.

No, he said, he couldn't explain it.

I told him about the U of T recording this transaction in a place where the size of the tax credit receipt would not become public because Bennett had insisted on it. I asked whether Random House could have appropriated the cash that flowed to M&S from grants and tax credits.

It could have, he said, but he'd be surprised if it had. And then he asked me a question.

Is publishing still protected? He asked.

Yes, I said, it is. Sort of. The law is still in place, but deals are getting done anyway.

The marketplace is owned by international publishing companies, like the oil business, he said. He did not appear to have an opinion on whether that was a good or a bad thing. It was just a statement of fact.

One more thing, I said. Avie Bennett told me that he arranged this gift with the U of T first, and the Random House deal came after that. He told me the value of the tax credit was *not* based on the Random House sale.

"The Random House deal *has* to be in place before he does this deal with Plazas," he said vehemently, referring to the transfer of shares for assets between First Plazas and new M&S, the first deal in the value chain. "The likelihood that Random House came out of the blue after this valuation deal is zero. There's no way."

He meant that Bennett had to establish what Random House was willing to pay before he transferred assets to the new M&S and asserted their value to be $22,250,000. The CRA must have agreed with him on that, otherwise they would have challenged the tax receipt. Revenue Canada, he said, clearly hadn't seen that as necessary. "[It was] sufficiently arm's length that [they said] we'll buy the numbers, like I did."

"And," he added, looking me right in the eye, "if the CRA had challenged this, I'd have fought them tooth and nail. Because it's defensible... It's a warranted opinion."

I was getting ready to leave when he asked me if M&S published Margaret Atwood. Clearly, he'd forgotten his own opinion in which he'd listed Atwood as one of the writers published by M&S who made it valuable.

Of course, I said.

I don't read fiction, he explained. "I called her Peggy when we were at Vic [Victoria College of University of Toronto] together."

And then he asked me this question: "Why do you care?"

This was a variant of "Who *are* you? What do you want?" put to me by that informant who'd turned out to be right about so many things.

The truth is I was no longer sure why I cared.

I muttered something to Scott about how it just seemed strange to me that the oldest and best Canadian publisher, owning the country's most important backlist, had ended its days in the bosom of the biggest publisher in the world, in spite of a law devised to prevent that, in spite of a policy that says telling Canadian stories reflecting the Canadian experience is in the national interest. Our policy and our law had delivered us instead a great, big, foreign-owned publishing oligopsony.

"Oh, *that* argument," he said. "It's always the same argument. This one is culture, but it could be jobs. On the other hand [Joe] Stiglitz [winner of the Nobel prize in economics] says it *does* matter, that you don't get innovation without it and Stiglitz is smart."

And as I went to the door, he said: "We do like our big companies."

By the time I got into my car to drive home, the sun was out. As I drove away, I replayed in my head what Scott had told me. That's when I remembered his suggestion that I should get the M&S financial statements from the U of T. It made me blush. What kind of reporter are you? I yelled at myself. In all your careful crafting of that FIPPA application, in all your follow up emails with Howard Jones and his colleague Rafael Eskanzi, that was the one thing you failed to ask for.

As soon as I got home, I wrote up another FIPPA and took it to the U of T. I asked for all financial statements and quarterly reports of M&S for the 11 years during which U of T owned 75% of M&S's shares, and any documents or notes regarding that registered debt. I also asked once more for any notes or memos or emails setting out why the 'put' had not been exercised.

I didn't have much hope that they'd give me what I'd asked for, but I had to try.

Because: I had decided it didn't matter why I cared. I'm a Canadian, and I'm entitled to care.

And so, the FIPPA clock began to tick once more.

14

Back to the Board

While I waited for the second FIPPA to be processed, I kept trying to think of other means to get those financial statements. I wasn't sure the U of T would produce them. I wasn't sure I'd get memos about the 'put,' either. In fact, I didn't understand why I had been given things that the University had the right to withhold under the FIPPA and in the case of some of the contracts, the duty to keep back. I was grateful, but wary. It was as if someone high up in the administration of the U of T had decided that parts of this story needed to be aired regardless of contracts and solicitor-client privilege, perhaps as the means to settle a score. Such documents can create false confidence that everything has been shared. But a document withheld can change the meaning of those handed over.

I decided to try other board members once more. After all, in our civil system, board members are responsible for what a corporation does. At a minimum, each board member should have gotten copies of annual financial statements and should have been aware of the reasons for major decisions taken. I decided to try Arlene Perly Rae on Facebook again. Perly Rae had been on the M&S board through most of the important changes—such as the renegotiations of the Administrative Services Agreement, the extension of the 'put,' the registration of the M&S's debt. I thought maybe, just maybe, she'd kept copies of the financial statements or that she would remember board discussions about the 'put' and the debt. This time, she answered my Facebook message. We made an arrangement to speak on the phone.

To my disappointment, she told me she had long since purged her M&S notes and documents.

She confirmed that it was Avie Bennett who had invited her to represent U of T. She had known him for years. She used to review books, children's books, and he had asked her for advice on several projects, even on whether or not M&S should buy Tundra Books. But mainly, she knew him socially. She had been friends with his daughter-in-law, Alison Gordon, whose complaints had spurred Bennett to buy a piece of M&S in the first place. She and Alison went back a long way: they had travelled to Egypt together after Prime Minister Begin of Israel and President Sadat of Egypt had their "rapprochement." She and Gordon had figured that might be the opportune moment for two Jewish girls to go to Egypt, in Gordon's case, to return, because she had lived in Cairo as a little girl. (Perly Rae didn't tell me why, but I looked up Gordon's father, J. King Gordon, later. He had served there as a diplomat after World War II. Before that he had been a Rhodes Scholar, a co-writer of the Regina Manifesto and a co-founder of the CCF, a United Church Minister, a journalist covering the UN for the CBC.) Perly Rae thought she'd first met Bennett when her friend Alison married Bennett's son, Paul. That was shortly after she married Bob Rae, in 1980.

Yet in spite of their long relationship, Perly Rae had been surprised to be asked to join the M&S board. She had no management experience. All her previous board appointments had been to non-governmental organizations, charities doing good works. She'd deferred to Rob Prichard and John Evans on budgets and other financial issues because they were so much more knowledgeable on the business side than she was. "I felt I was there for the authors, Michael Ondaatje, Margaret Atwood, Munro. I loved the group M&S [book] launches."

She remembered discussing specific books at board meetings, for example Brian Mulroney's memoir, should it be published as one volume or two. She remembered there was an Asian guy on the board representing U of T who didn't say anything. She remembered that Doug Gibson took charge and then was replaced by Doug Pepper. How often did the board meet? She thought maybe every two months. She thought the board was strong. "Avie brought in staff to discuss

planning and accounts," she said. She thought it was her job to advocate to keep authors in the fold "and reassure them. Others felt that
too. Avie was our saviour to keep it going as the key Canadian publisher. We spent a lot of time to make sure it stayed Canadian."

I read her what U of T officials had said in 2001 regarding the fact
that they had no control, only influence over M&S. She said she felt
the U of T had a strong presence, though Random House did too.
She did not remember the company reporting a profit. She remembered every year as a struggle. Grants were very important to keeping the company going.

I read to her from the correspondence of April, 2006 between
U of T officials Helen Choy and Pierre Piché regarding a write down
of the value of the U of T's shares to $10.9 million. She was still on
the board at that time. Did she know about that write down?

No, she couldn't remember any discussion like that. That just
wasn't her area of interest.

What about debt? I asked. The same letter said that the net shareholder's deficit was $3.1 million in April, 2006. Did she remember
discussing that? Did she know anything about the debt rising to $16
million after that?

She couldn't recall the company being millions of dollars in debt.
"I just can't remember," she said.

Did you see financial statements? I asked.

Yes, she said, she did, but nothing with those kinds of millions in
them.

And what about the 'put,' I asked. Did you understand there was
a $5 million 'put' in favour of the University that it could call?

"Never heard the word 'put' before. I'm sorry."

Well that was interesting. One of the longest serving board members had no idea what a 'put' is, let alone knew that the U of T could
have called its 'put' to get value out of its M&S shares. That 'put' had
been extended when Perly Rae was still on the board. Either the board
had not discussed it, or she'd missed that meeting, or she had simply
not understood what it was about when it was being discussed. The
latter possibility seemed very unlikely. Arlene Perly Rae is very, very
smart. If someone had raised the issue of extending the 'put,' she'd

have asked questions until she understood what was going on. I was willing to bet that it had not been discussed by the board, but had been handled off stage somehow by Bennett and Random House and people from the U of T. On the other hand, the Unanimous Shareholder Agreement had to be amended to permit that extension, and M&S was a signatory to the Unanimous Shareholder Agreement. So she should have seen memos about that. But clearly, she had not.

Did you think that control was passing to Random House when Doug Pepper came on board? I asked. Did you see this as a kind of salami takeover, one slice at a time?

She'd never heard of a salami strategy before, either. When I explained it, she did *not* agree that that was what had gone on. She said it had been important in the early years to keep Doug Gibson there because he kept the big authors. But Doug wasn't a finance guy. She thought Doug Pepper was more a business guy than Doug Gibson. "That's why we got Doug Pepper," she said. No, she didn't realize Pepper had spent his career to that point as an editor for Random House, the prior decade working in the US for Crown.

"There was a feeling that Random House was taking more of a role," she said, "storage, distribution, to save money, not to duplicate..." But it wasn't a takeover, it felt "very positive, Random House [was there] to help, not to absorb." In fact, she felt M&S lasted longer than it might have (because of Random House's involvement.) As far as she was concerned, it felt as if they were all doing a good deed, keeping those authors (Ondaatje, Atwood, Mistry, Munro) in print "and it was kind of nice to have this Random House injection, though [there was] fear in the community, like, oh, oh, better to have it subtle than to lose that brand and history... [these] men of great integrity, Avie, John, Rob—the stuff you're talking about is out of my league."

Do you remember why you closed down Macfarlane, Walter & Ross? I asked.

"The sales were bad and there was a tough decision about letting it go," she said.

And yet by contract among the parties in 2000, Macfarlane, Walter & Ross was to be kept intact, and to publish between eight and fifteen books a year, certainly not to be shut down only three years later for failure to make profits, profits it would have made if Avie had purchased its backlist, profits that could have alleviated M&S's debt.

Perly Rae resigned from the board in December, 2006, because her husband, Bob Rae, had decided to run for the leadership of the federal Liberal Party. She had to get off most of the boards she served on at that time. She thought I was making something nefarious out of something that just was unfortunate, like the rise of Amazon and Costco, and then there was that woman who ran Indigo, what was her name? Whoever she is, said Perly Rae, until she came along, booksellers did not return author signed books, but she changed that. They had all been trying their best.

Well that was interesting, I thought when I hung up the phone, but not exactly definitive. Who else to try?

Wait a minute, wait a minute: I hadn't raised the debt question or the 'put' question with Doug Gibson when I spoke with him because I didn't know about either one. He had been the President of M&S. He must have read the financial statements. He must have helped Random House prepare them.

That very day I got something in the mail from the Writers' Union saying that Gibson was going to lead a seminar on publishing for its Toronto chapter. There would be beer and conversation about the business at a pub just down the street from Indigo's flagship store. I contacted Doug and asked if I could do a follow-up interview the day after. He said fine.

We arranged to meet in a shopping mall on the corner of St. Clair and Yonge, probably one of the corners owned by Bennett's Principal Investments before it went bust.

It was wet and sloppy and dank, too warm for winter, not warm enough for spring. I found a place to park, walked into the mall. There were two floors, one at street level, another, below, connecting to the subway. There was a stairway, an escalator, and several other points of entry. A bevy of Canadian flags hung from the atrium overhead. I figured the best place to watch for Doug was right underneath those flags. That allowed me to monitor all entry points in case he came in and didn't recognize me.

Because: the night before he hadn't, though I was standing right in front of him reaching out to shake his hand. I'd sat at one end of a long table in the pub listening as he did a masterful job of explaining the finer points of the publishing business to the writers who'd gathered to hear him (and to cheer each other up). Many were older than me. One man, a doctor Doug had once published, said he was 94. Some said they were exploring self publishing. Some complained of the way they'd been treated by large publishers—their work contracted for, then rejected, followed by demands to return the advance, or, demands that they pay for editing. Doug seemed surprised to hear that the business had grown darker and less generous.

I was thinking he'd forgotten our appointment when he loped in late through a side entry, wearing a thin anorak and a loose scarf around his neck. He looked around and decided he didn't want to sit in the mall, so we went up to St. Clair to a small coffee shop he likes.

By the time we got there we had had the usual conversation, the normal one now, the one about who is ill, who is dying, who passed away. He told me that when offered a choice of dates for events, he always takes the earliest, because he never knows anymore where he'll be next month—as in above the grass or below? Up close I could see the grey in his hair, which was, as always, awry, and I'm sure he could see the same in mine.

I told him what I wanted to know, and why, and he got a certain look, a trapped look, like a man who, as a matter of principle, wants to tell the truth, but really did not want to remember let alone dwell on these particular truths. It wasn't that he had taken a vow of *omertà*. It was more as if he believed this whole story did not properly reflect the way he sees himself: as a business naïf; as a man who works with artists, for artists, as a literary person.

I asked him again if he knew the size of Avie Bennett's tax credit receipt when he gave the shares to the University of Toronto.

He said didn't know.

But you signed those agreements, the ones that listed the full value of the new M&S, I said. See? I showed him the Asset Purchase Agreement between First Plazas Inc. and the new M&S.

"If I knew, I've forgotten," he said.

Do you know what a 'put' is? I asked. Did you know there was a 'put' that gave the University the right to demand $5 million in exchange for its shares from First Plazas?

He said he knew in general what a 'put' is, "but not in this context."

How is it possible that two of the first members of the M&S board had been unaware of the 'put'? Wait, I said to myself. He must have known about the 'put,' it was in the Unanimous Shareholder Agreement.

"Did you sign the Unanimous Shareholder Agreement?" I asked.

"Can't recall," he said.

This was amazing forgetfulness, unbelievable forgetfulness. Yet I'd always thought of Doug as an honest person. I pulled out my copy of the Unanimous Shareholder Agreement and showed it to him. I showed him his signature.

But then, instead of badgering him, I let him off the hook. Why? I like Doug, which is the reason why reporters should not interview friends and colleagues, it's too hard to maintain objectivity, too hard to move in and grill when you should. Instead, I laid out what I knew and how I knew it. I told him the size of the tax credit receipt, the value created in the new M&S by the transfer of assets for shares with First Plazas. I showed him that agreement too, I showed him his signature.

"I'm impressed at the value of $22 million," he said, as if this number was brand new to him. And he did have a surprised look on his face. And yet he'd signed the document in which this value was set out. Which meant he must have known as well how much Bennett's tax credit receipt was for, and how much Random House had paid for 25% of M&S's shares. It was math so simple even I could do it.

Why are you impressed by that number? I asked.

While M&S had certainly acquired rights to some big books, he said, "the drawback was it was very hard to make a profit in a given year. Twenty-two million seems like a lot of money." On the other hand, he didn't know what publishing companies are deemed to be worth.

Did you see M&S's financial statements?

He said he did see the financial statements and the budget for the year.

And do you remember what net sales were in 2000? I asked.

"No, can't recall," he said. Though there were also monthly financial reports supplied by Random House, he said, his colleague Krystyna

Ross, then the general manager of M&S, would be better able to talk about them. He advised me to look her up. The financial matters really weren't what he focused on. On the other hand, from the time he became Publisher of M&S, after Adrienne Clarkson left in 1988, he could say that every year was hard, and his chief reaction to the sale/gift in 2000 was "relief, another few years to make a go of it."

Did he know that Random House paid $5.3 million for its 25% of M&S? I asked.

No, he did not.

Did he remember McClelland & Stewart, the company he was running, paying $1 million to First Plazas at the end of the first year of the new arrangement?

He did not. "Going back 10 years," he explained. "I cannot remember barrel loads of cash... The circumstances are that every year it was hard work to get a profit... Some years we did and some we didn't. We were trying to meet the budget every year."

What do you think net sales might have been in 2000? I asked again. I was thinking if I took that number and multiplied by 1.25, as Ronald Scott had suggested was a way to value a publishing company, that would be one way to measure the real value of new M&S. It would, or it would not, equal $22 million, and that might tell me something important.

"I was thinking $4 million or $5 million for annual sales," he said.

Multiplying that by 1.25 came nowhere close to $22 million. It came close to $5.3 million though, what Random House had paid for its quarter of the company—and effective control.

And what about the debt, the size of the debt? I asked. Do you remember the company being in debt to the tune of about $3.1 million in 2006?

He thought a debt of $3.1 million in 2006 "sounds about right," but he was no longer in charge by then. "You're aware of Doug Pepper's background," he asked.

What about a debt of $16 million in 2011?

He looked stunned.

"A $16 million debt is a surprise," he said.

He seemed miserably uncomfortable with these questions and his inability to answer them. I told him that Arlene Perly Rae had responded the same way to similar questions, and that she'd explained that, like her, he had mainly been interested in the books, not the business.

He was pleased to admit that what Arlene had said of him was "absolutely true." He'd relied on Krystyna Ross to take care of all of that, he said, and though she was not a board member, he even took her to board meetings to explain things to the other board members.

But that first year, 2000, I said. What can you tell me about it?

"I thought we made a profit in the first year," he said. "We won just about every prize going. [Margaret Atwood's *Blind Assassin* won the Booker that year.] I worried the directors would think publishing was easy. We had a spectacular fall season, won lots of prizes and the sales that went with that. To make more than a $1 million profit would be spectacular. We used to say, my God, if [we were] doing this well in another country we'd be rich and [could] afford new shoes."

I was pretty sure that Doug Gibson had been able to afford new shoes whenever he wanted them from the moment he went to work for Avie Bennett in 1986, which was probably why I told him then that the U of T had written down the value of the gift twice, the last time to zero.

Did you know about the write downs? I asked.

"Not aware of any of the write downs," he said.

Of course, by the time of the first write down, he had already been pushed out of the President/Publisher's job. However, he did insist that when he was the President/Publisher, his editorial control was never compromised. He would tell me later he was not even challenged when he decided to shut down Macfarlane, Walter & Ross. No one asked him to do that. "This is on me," he said. There was no conspiracy to kill the competition: he did it because they were losing money, a lot of money, and he couldn't see anything on their list of projects to come that would make that "curve" turn the other way. He'd done it between board meetings, and just announced it to the board. They'd made him justify it, but they hadn't stopped him.

So then Doug Pepper came on board, I said. Tell me about that.

He smiled. Not a happy smile. More like a grimace. There was a board meeting, a lengthy board meeting with an *in camera* session, he said. The next day he had a meeting with Avie Bennett who said "'we think it's [time for] the Douglas Gibson days to end, continue working on the Douglas Gibson Books and we will find a new Publisher, and he mentioned Doug Pepper who I barely know. He'd gone to Crown, a Random House company [in the US], for a number of years, so [he was] off the scene."

The relationship with Pepper was "correct. He behaved politely and recognized it was difficult, a relationship with the guy he'd replaced."

This happened early in 2004. At that point, he thought that John Neale also left and Doug Foot joined Brad Martin as a Random House representative on the M&S board. He knew it was 2004 because he was 61 at the time and in 2008 in the late fall when his 65th birthday came up, Pepper "wrote a polite note that my contract was not to be renewed." He was fairly sure the company was not doing well by then. [Of course it wasn't, nobody was doing well by then except Goldman Sachs. The worst recession since the Thirties had arrived with a bang that September, right after the University failed to call the 'put' that had been extended to July, 2008.] "It was hard not to personalize it and my dismissal caused a lot of dismay in [the] author world so a number of authors jumped elsewhere."

When I asked him about the non-compete clause in the Unanimous Shareholder Agreement, he said that was never used in his day. "Since those days, things have tightened hugely in Random House so competition between imprints is tightly regulated."

I asked a question that had niggled at me for some time. I'd wondered if Arlene Perly Rae had been placed on the M&S board as a kind of bouquet to a Liberal government that had allowed this scheme to go forward. I'd wondered if her presence was both a thank you and a guarantee that M&S would publish certain Liberals' political books, such as Bob Rae's third book, and Sheila Copps' second memoir in 2003. Rae's first two books had been published by M&S in the middle 1990s when he was reinventing himself after the Ontario NDP government's electoral defeat in 1995. He published his third book with M&S just before he announced his intention to run for the leadership of the Liberal Party, after which Arlene Perly Rae stepped down from M&S's board. Rae's last book was published by M&S four years later, in November, 2010.

"I'd regard it as coincidence that M&S published Rae's books with Arlene on the board," Gibson said, "because he was an attractive, well-selling author. I would see Arlene's presence as coincidence." And the same was true of Sheila Copps. There was no board pressure to publish her, or not to publish her.

"We had a proud record of publishing political books from all over the political spectrum. Mulroney, Trudeau, Crosbie. Sheila was a saleable commodity and I was happy to publish her. And that was me," he said.

I raised again the extraordinary level of debt accrued by M&S between the years when he last saw the financial statements in 2004 and the sale of the University's shares for $1 in 2011. I explained that the 'put' and debt provisions of the Unanimous Shareholder Agreement he'd signed had made it very unlikely that any Canadian publishing company would ever offer to buy M&S's shares from the U of T. I explained that if the University sold its shares, the contract specified that the debt to Random House would have to be repaid immediately and $16 million was a lot to repay immediately.

"Are you suggesting that Random House was deliberately running up the debt?" he asked.

I said I wasn't suggesting anything until I looked at the financial statements. But did it make sense to him that a debt of that size could have piled up in six years?

He said he couldn't see how.

"Question," he said, pointing a finger at me. "How many books were published in the last year? In the 1990s it was about 100 books a year. Take a look at the 2003 and 2004 catalogues. [*But I couldn't. There are no post-2003 catalogues to be found in any Canadian library, not even at Library and Archives Canada which is supposed to hold them. PRHC website's catalogues start at Fall 2011.*] Then, as you know, after I left the company, it shrank and shrank. Editors [were] fired. We had 50 [staff] under me. Now what is it—about 10?"

What he meant by his question is this: as the number of books published went down, and staff was let go, costs should also have gone down. Debt should have gone down too. But on the other hand, revenues would also have dived. So should the debt have climbed like that? Or not?

He thought it shouldn't have. He also thought the government simply wasn't enforcing undertakings, its Policy, or the law anymore.

"Look at Torstar's sale of Harlequin. It illustrates how the government is very reluctant to get involved."

I could see that I would get nothing more out of Doug Gibson. I was being asked to believe that he'd either forgotten everything I wanted to know, or, he'd paid no attention in the first place. He was very determined that I should accept the latter explanation as the truth. We were on our way out of the coffee shop when he asked me if I'd spoken to Avie Bennett.

Of course I have, I said. I explained that Bennett had refused to tell me the size of the tax credit.

That's when Doug said that he'd seen Avie himself.

Significant pause.

When? I asked.

"Three weeks ago, at that old folks place he's moved into," he said.

I knew Bennett was living in an assisted living residence. I even knew which one because my mother lives there too. I'd run into Bennett at a Sunday brunch, dining with Diana, his assistant. He was so gallant to my mother when I introduced them that she asked him if he played bridge. He'd played one afternoon as her partner.

"How did you find him?" I asked. I thought Bennett's memory had been just fine at the bridge table, but Doug had brought this up for a reason. Calling it an old folks' home was a subtle way of saying that Avie Bennett's memory might not be reliable when it came to certain details, although the previous summer Doug had assured me that Bennett was just fine, still going to work every day and I should ask Bennett all the questions I had about this gift and sale. "Are we talking about his memory? How did you find it?"

Doug made a slippy-slidey gesture with one hand, as if to say, it comes and goes.

Right, I said, that's why I'm relying on the documents the University gave me, documents that they could have withheld. Sometimes I wonder why they gave them to me at all. The fact is, I'm so used to people refusing my requests, I don't know how to take yes for an answer.

He laughed, and said goodbye, and went on his way.

Two weeks later, I was told the FIPPA #2 documents were ready.

15

FIPPA #2

The envelope was much thinner this time. Inside, the cover letter said the University had combed through its files and come up with 45 pages of records "responsive to your request…" However, it had decided to produce only 42 of them. Though the University had included a one-page memo protected by solicitor-client privilege in the package, the University had withheld another three-page memo "which contains legal advice that is exempt under FIPPA section 19."

And they hadn't given me all the financial statements, either.

> Please note that the University had access to financial statements of McClelland & Stewart Ltd during the relevant time period [the 11 years during which the University owned 75% of the M&S shares] but now only has the 18 pages of financial statements that are being disclosed to you in its custody or under its control.[318]

That was interesting language: "had access to"; "under its custody or control." This meant that the financial statements probably exist, but are stored elsewhere by someone else. Somehow this reminded me of the legal advice given to Random House and to me so many years before—that I should leave my working manuscript of the Reichmann book at Random House's offices, lest the court demand I turn it over. By 2006, the FIPPA had been extended by law to include Ontario's universities. Without looking at the financial documents provided, I made a bet with myself that the financial statements produced would only cover years before 2006. And I figured that the three-page memo they'd withheld must have had to do with the failure to call the 'put.'

I studied the wording of the letter carefully, trying to figure out if I should appeal to get access to that memo. At first I thought I could at least argue to the Commissioner that since the University had given me other documents protected by solicitor-client privilege, in effect it had waived this privilege entirely and should therefore give that memo to me. But on reflection, I didn't think that argument would win the day. The FIPPA is designed to give the institutional keeper of information maximum flexibility to determine what to show and what to withhold. What they'd done before would not necessarily shape the Commissioner's decision on appeal.

I rifled through the package. As I expected, there was nothing in it that explained directly why the U of T had failed to call the 'put' or its alternative, and collect $5 million from Random House or First Plazas. The financial documents recorded no transactions in any year after December 31, 2005 either.

I'd won my bet, but I was not pleased.

Among the items enclosed was a memo written by the U of T's in-house counsel Tad Brown, to Felix Chee, then the Vice-President, Business Affairs at the U of T, dated November 18, 2003. Chee had apparently asked Brown when the University could sell its M&S shares. Brown's memo explained the University's rights and duties as laid out in the donor agreement between the University and First Plazas, and in the Unanimous Shareholder Agreement between all the parties. He told Chee that though the agreement between the U of T and First Plazas required the U of T to refrain from selling its shares until July, 2003—after which it could do as it pleased—the 'put' clauses in the Unanimous Shareholder Agreement said that the University could *not* exercise the alternative 'put' if it had previously disposed of "any" share of M&S or "any rights in respect thereto." In other words: if the University sold even one M&S share before July 1, 2005, it would forfeit the right to ask for $5 million in cash from Random House or First Plazas. And there was only a narrow window during which the University could call the 'put'—the thirty days between July 1 and July 31, 2005. Brown also explained that any decision to sell the shares had to be made by the Business Board on the advice and recommendation of the President.[319]

July is a month during which the University's administration is in sleep mode. The Governing Council generally does not meet during the summer, (though it did in August, 2004, for an extraordinary vote, see below) nor does the Business Board.[320] Special summer executive powers must be voted on in advance by the Governing Council in order for the President to do specific things in the summer. To call the 'put' in July, 2005, the University would have had to get its ducks in a row several months in advance. The Chee query may have been the first step toward doing so.

The next item was Amendment No. 1 to the Unanimous Shareholder Agreement. It repealed the terms of section 5.6(1) of the original agreement and moved the date upon which the alternative 'put' could be called by the U of T to the thirty days following the eighth anniversary of the agreement. In other words, the 'put' could only be called between July 1 and July 30, 2008. The amendment was dated April 1, 2004.[321] That was way too early: why had they put that amendment through sixteen months before it was needed?

The next item in the envelope was a copy of the share purchase certificate recording the transfer of the U of T's M&S shares to Random House, dated December 30, 2011. It was signed by Brad Martin and Douglas Foot, acting by then as directors of McClelland & Stewart. It also included the articles of amalgamation between M&S and Macfarlane, Walter & Ross, plus an older bylaw passed by old M&S that was still in force. The amalgamation certificate showed that Macfarlane, Walter & Ross had not been officially swallowed by M&S for more than a year after it was shut down. The amalgamation took place on June 15, 2004, six weeks after the alternative 'put' date was changed. This certificate had been signed by Doug Pepper, as the new Publisher and President of both entities, and listed the directors of M&S at that time. They included: Avie Bennett, Felix Chee, John Evans, Brad Martin, Douglas Pepper, John Neale and Arlene Perly Rae[322] There was a resignation letter attached from Connie Fullerton that would not come into effect until May 3, 2005.

Housekeeping, I thought, as I turned the pages. Trivial. Why did the University send this to me?

But then I came to the page labelled McClelland & Stewart Ltd. bylaw No. 1 and marked "adopted on amalgamation on July 1, 2004."[323] This bylaw had been passed originally by the old M&S when it was still owned by First Plazas, and before the new M&S was brought into existence, its shares given to the U of T and sold to Random House. This bylaw had been passed in preparation for that gift/sale, because it referred to a unanimous shareholder agreement featuring Random House and the U of T. It set out the voting rules for meetings of the board of directors of M&S and for meetings of the shareholders of McClelland & Stewart Ltd. It said the chairman of any meeting of the directors had to be selected by "directors nominated by U of T." "Subject to any unanimous shareholder agreement, each question at a meeting of the directors shall be decided by a majority vote, and, upon an equality of votes, the chairman shall not have a second or casting vote." In other words, Avie Bennett could not push things through if there was an even split on any issue, which was interesting. But the important clause referred to the rules governing meetings of shareholders, not directors. It is the shareholders who ultimately control the fate of a company. The shareholders can overrule directors' and officers' actions taken or not taken. This clause said:

> A Quorum for transaction of business at any meeting of shareholders is present if there are at least two persons present in person or by proxy holding at least 90% of the shares entitled to vote at the meeting. No meeting shall continue with the transaction of business in the absence of a quorum.

In other words, in order for a meeting of the *shareholders* to decide on M&S business, only two people were required, one representing the U of T, one representing Random House. The way I read this, after Doug Pepper became President and Publisher of M&S, representing the U of T on the board of directors, he and one other representative of Random House could hold a meeting of the shareholders in the Random House offices without Avie Bennett being present. This explained how Avie Bennett could have been kept out of the loop until the last minute after Random House decided it wanted to acquire 100%

of the M&S shares. Yet Bennett must have understood that such a day could come because this bylaw had been passed by M&S when it was under Bennett's complete control. It was signed by Doug Gibson, as president of M&S on June 8, 2000, one week after Bennett's lawyer wrote his letter to the Department of Canadian Heritage asking for a Letter of Opinion, and the same day a telephone meeting was held by the members of the U of T's Business Board during which the terms of the gift were first outlined. It was adopted two weeks before the Board approved the gift, three weeks before the new M&S came into existence.

What difference did it make? In effect, after this bylaw was adopted by the amalgamated M&S on July 1, 2004, the takeover of M&S by Random House, a foreign entity, was final and complete—confirming Avie Bennett and Doug Gibson's recollections—long before the University's shares were actually transferred.

I turned back to the amendment to the Unanimous Shareholder Agreement adopted on April Fool's Day of 2004. It was signed by John Neale for Random House, Avie Bennett for First Plazas, Douglas Pepper for McClelland & Stewart, and Catherine Riggall, on behalf of the University of Toronto's Governing Council.

Why Catherine Riggall? I wondered. Riggall had just been appointed interim Vice-President, Business Affairs six weeks before, filling in for Felix Chee who had moved on to another assignment within the University. In January, 2004, Chee had been appointed the CEO of the University's Asset Management Corporation, though he remained a director of M&S.[324] At that point, Riggall had only worked at the University for two years and in another department, so she must not have had much knowledge of the M&S file[325] and her confirmation in Chee's old job was by no means assured. A search committee had been struck to find a new Vice-President, Business Affairs.[326] Why would an interim official sign such an amendment on behalf of the Governing Council? It arose out of a decision to postpone asking Random House or First Plazas to buy its M&S shares for $5 million: the gift had produced nothing for the University, so that decision must have been taken with some care. I would have expected the Governing Council's Chairman and Secretary, or the President, to sign. The President was certainly available. The

Governing Council held a meeting on March 29, 2004, only three days earlier, and the President had been present.[327] So far as I could tell from the Council minutes, if this amendment had been shown to the Governing Council, it was done *in camera* and there was no resolution. I could find nothing about it on the public record.

Which made me ask: who was the President of U of T at the time?

It was Robert Birgeneau. Thanks to Birgeneau, the University of Toronto's administration was then in turmoil. Its Provost, lured from Michigan to help President Birgeneau make the U of T into a more diverse and research-driven school, had quit in early February, just before President Birgeneau presented his plan to elevate the University to a higher place in the world.[328] The Governing Council replaced the Provost with an interim official, Vivek Goel, and set out to find a new number two.[329] Rumours soon began to circulate that President Birgeneau was seeking a job elsewhere, too. These rumours surfaced in the *San Francisco Chronicle*, the *Varsity*, and then in the *Globe and Mail* in July.[330] By then, President Birgeneau had interviewed for the position of Chancellor of the University of California, Berkeley, though he'd insisted on a seven-year term when he took the job at the U of T in 2000. By the end of July, 2004, Birgeneau had taken that California job. By then, too, both the Chairman of the Governing Council and the Vice-Chairman were about to step down.[331]

The Honourable Frank Iacobucci, who had just retired from the Supreme Court of Canada, and had served as Dean of Law and Provost at the U of T, was appointed interim President at a special meeting of the Governing Council held in August.[332] Iacobucci became Senior Counsel at Torys the following month. He had also just been appointed to the Torstar board. (The following spring it was announced that Iacobucci would replace John Evans as Chairman of the Board of Torstar where Iacobucci's former gold medal law student and good friend, Robert Prichard, was still President and CEO.)[333]

Had Riggall signed this amendment because someone told her to? Who? How could I find out? She had not responded to my attempts to interview her, nor had Felix Chee, John Neale, or Brad Martin. Doug Gibson and Arlene Perly Rae had said they knew nothing about this 'put.' I emailed Iacobucci through his assistant at Torys. I wanted to know if he'd been informed of the decision to move back the 'put' for three years.

A week later, Iacobucci called back. When my associate asked if she could tell me who was calling, he told her to say "Frank." (It's not every day a former Supreme Court Justice calls back using his first name to identify himself.) He told me he certainly knew of Avie Bennett's gift. Like Prichard, he called it "a great act of generosity." I told him I'd seen a legal opinion that referred to the 'put,' and had read the amendment that put it off until 2008. I asked if he had been made aware of that.

He said he had been briefed on the agreements and on the 'put' at some point. But the amendment "never came to me when I was interim President," he said. Then he asked me how I had come to see a legal opinion, since legal opinions are covered by solicitor-client privilege.

Through a FIPPA, I said. Robert Prichard suggested I should file one.

By then I was pretty sure I'd found the pattern of a familiar mind at work. Timing is everything in business: Avie Bennett, a master of business timing, would have understood early in 2004 that upheaval in the University's administration presented an opportunity to arrange matters to suit First Plazas and Random House. Neither would have wanted to pay the U of T $5 million if they could avoid it. Besides, a federal election was coming at the end of June, 2004. If the University called that 'put' on schedule in July 2005, Random House would have had to go to the government to get permission to acquire the U of T's shares, and that permission might have been denied by a new Paul Martin minority government. That Martin would only win a minority had been predicted by pollsters since the Liberal Sponsorship Scandal began to unfurl in front of Mr. Justice Gomery in 2003. Even if Martin wanted to say yes to the sale, it might have been too dangerous politically. And if his government said no, then Bennett would have been forced to spend $5 million himself to buy U of T's shares, while Random House got stuck with unpaid debt. Worst of all, control of M&S would have landed back in Bennett's lap. His exit would become no exit, which would engender huge embarrassment all around.

And so, the amendment had been agreed to more than a year before it was needed, just after Doug Gibson was moved sideways in favour of Doug Pepper, a novice in the affairs of M&S. If there had been a vote on the M&S board about this extension, Bennett and Neale could have tweaked its outcome without difficulty, but since Perly Rae could not remember having heard the word 'put,' ever, it is likely that the amendment was simply agreed to between the shareholders—Neale and Riggall. (If you read this book, Ms. Riggall, please tell me who asked you to sign the amendment for the Governing Council. I'm dying to know.)

But this still left me with the question—why, after agreeing to this extension, had the University still failed to exercise the 'put' in 2008?

I ploughed through the financial documents the U of T had included in the package, hoping to find some answer there. But I was disappointed. First, the University had not given me a single complete financial statement. It had handed me instead one non-consolidated statement of income and retained earnings, one statement of operations and retained earnings (deficit), three statements of operations and deficit, and a draft—labelled number seven—of one financial statement for the year ended December 31, 2005, the most recent information in the envelope. Only one statement carried the imprimatur of an accounting firm—Price Waterhouse Coopers. The rest had no author at all.

I realized after going through these documents that I simply did not understand enough about the publishing business to make sense of them. I needed to show them to experts. But several numbers did jump out. For one thing, in the report detailing revenues for the last half of 2000, net sales had been $8 million, providing net income of $200,000. Oddly, Doug Gibson had thought net sales for the whole year were only about $5 million, yet if these figures were correct, they may have been about three times higher. The other documents showed that for each year after 2000, there were losses. In the draft financial statement for the year ending December 31, 2005, loans made by Random House to M&S had risen to $10,639,928 (a figure not referred to in Helen Choy's write-down memo of the following year. She had referred only to a shareholder deficit of $3 million). Yet Arlene Perly Rae said she had no recollection of deficits or debts in the millions and Gibson had been shocked to hear that the debt reached $16 million by the time Random House took possession of the U of T's shares. Apparently, by October, 2005, these debts had been officially registered and secured by the assets of M&S, includ- ing, among other things, all its contracts and intellectual property— the backlist.[334]

I went downtown and got a copy of that debt registration. I wanted to see if the debt figure registered was the same as the debt actually owed. The registration was dated September 27, 2005, but no dollar amount was listed. When I complained to the clerk, I was told that that information did not need to be filed. Even if it had been filed originally, there was no record of it any longer. The whole file had been erased when the debt registration expired on the 27th of September, 2012.

16

Stoddart's Story

I decided to show the M&S financial documents to someone who would understand them: Jack Stoddart. He was the former owner of General Publishing, Stoddart Publishing, General Distribution Services, Macfarlane, Walter & Ross, not to mention Boston Mills and House of Anansi, etc. He had agreed to meet. I hadn't seen Stoddart for several years, so I wasn't certain that the man who stood in front of the concierge's desk in the appointed place at the appointed time was actually him.

We'd last met about ten years before at a Christmas party given by a mutual friend, a party full of writers and editors for newspapers and magazines and books, people who made their livings by telling Canadian stories. Most in that room were reflexive Canadian nationalists. Most were inclined to believe that the world needs more Canada, and that Canada will not survive if Canadians don't tell our own stories. Most of us had benefited from government support, either from the rules mandating Canadian ownership and control of publishing companies and newspapers, the grants and tax credits meant to encourage such endeavours, or direct grants for our own works.

The party was held not long after Jack Stoddart's publishing and distribution businesses collapsed into receivership/bankruptcy at the behest of his main creditor, Scotiabank (formerly the Bank of Nova Scotia).[335] As Stoddart moved around the room that night, he'd stirred currents of anger, and wavelets of sympathy. Those with royalties outstanding or books that had no home were not kindly disposed. Those unhurt were more sympathetic. He was no longer seen as a hero of Canadian publishing though he, like Bennett (and so many others in this story) had been honoured as an Officer of the Order of Canada, elevated to that status in 1999 for his great contributions. Public failure changes the way people see us and there are few failures more public than bankruptcy. Avie Bennett understood that better than most.

But we all should have been sympathetic because Stoddart had worked hard for the public good with a brave heart for a long time. Stoddart had lost a business started by his father, along with all his personal investment in it. He'd advocated for all the other Canadian independent publishers, serving for three terms as President of the Association of Canadian Publishers. He'd lobbied key players in the federal government (Sheila Copps, Herb Gray, and Paul Martin) to introduce a federal tax credit system like the one that funds the making of movies and television. He'd thought it would encourage Canadians to invest in publishing. He'd distributed large independents and small ones including the small literary outfits banded together as the Literary Press Group. He'd published, or helped publish, or helped finance, many important non-fiction books, which explained us to ourselves. He'd invested in or owned most of the leading independent publishers at one point or another, including Douglas & McIntyre, House of Anansi, Boston Mills, Key Porter, Macleod, Musson, New Press, Macfarlane, Walter & Ross, and Cormorant Books. In some companies, he owned a minority interest and got a board seat. In the case of Macfarlane, Walter & Ross, which he'd financed and distributed for the principals (Jan Walter, Gary Ross and John Macfarlane), he'd owned 51%. At a certain point, his total revenues were about $100 million a year, but at the end, General Distribution Services owed $16,983,460.16 that it was unable to pay to creditors and General Publishing Co. Limited was $20,357,590.94 in the hole. General Distribution Services and General Publishing Co. Ltd's bankruptcies came close to taking down the whole shaky edifice of independent Canadian publishing. The lists of the unsecured creditors covered page after page of small type. The secured creditors included Bank of Nova Scotia, which alone was owed $14 million.[336] When such a thriving industry is ended by the court, it is a scarring, life-altering experience for everyone.

Stoddart got into trouble in that dark period between 2000 and 2002 when Bennett handed off M&S, and Chapters withheld payments to distributors and publishers for up to 160 days and then merged, under the terms ordered by the Competition Tribunal, with Indigo. Distributors had to pay their publisher clients within 60 days, so Stoddart's distribution company needed a $22 million line of credit. He'd found an American bank, Finova, that was willing to lend on receivables instead of the Canadian practice of banking on assets. But then Finova went bankrupt. Berkshire (along with a company called Leucadia)[337] bought its assets and decided to get rid of its Canadian clients. Stoddart had to find another bank fast, but no Canadian bank wanted him. He was over-leveraged and overreliant on a government sanctioned monopsony, the Indigo-Chapters merged entity. In his capacity as President of the ACP, Stoddart had been prevailed upon to support that merger, and the ACP had done so.[338] At a certain point, he told me, he called Heather Reisman to say how bad it would look if Indigo caused his companies to go under. The Bank of Nova Scotia became his banker. But then the Bank took fright as Indigo sent back palette after palette of books. The bank hired Deloitte & Touche Inc. to take a hard look at his business.[339]

As Reisman told the Standing Committee on Canadian Heritage, Chapters' warehouse/distribution/wholesale system, which she took over, was a disaster. This disaster was soon transferred to distributors: returned books came flooding back into the General Distribution warehouse. They had come into it first on consignment, as the property of their publishers: but as soon as Chapters or Indigo had placed an order for them, the books became the booksellers' property—unless returned. Due to Indigo's interpretation of the start date of the Competition Tribunal's mandated Code of Conduct, returns suddenly went up three times higher than normal and this was so badly handled that whole palettes of books were returned to the General Distribution warehouse that had never been distributed by General Distribution. (One such palette contained 40 unopened boxes of Jonathan Franzen's *The Connections*, a HarperCollins book.) Soon, no one was sure what anybody's real receivables were.

After the bank pulled the plug and the receivers took over, the issue of who owned what in the General warehouse made everybody crazy. Various publishers' books that had been distributed by General were stuck in the warehouse[340] for a time, cutting off publishers' cash flows as they argued about whether they owned the books, or someone else did.

The plan of arrangement was overseen by a judge who did things that surprised the very experienced bankruptcy lawyer acting for Stoddart. The court appointed a Monitor, who also acted as trustee. It was the same gang from Deloitte & Touche Inc. who'd first taken a close look at Stoddart's companies on behalf of his lender, the Bank of Nova Scotia, and did not like what they found.[341] The trustee did things that surprised Marc Côté, once an employee of Stoddart Publishing (a subsidiary of General Publishing), then a co-owner of Cormorant Books, with offices in the General Publishing office. Côté was elected as an inspector of the bankruptcy by his fellow creditors. Stoddart and his partner were not asked for help as the trustees tried to sell assets. Instead of being sold as a going concern, General Publishing was bankrupted (Stoddart Publishing died with it), though the group's educational publisher Irwin was sold to Thomson, Cormorant Books was sold to Marc Côté and partners, Boston Mills and Anansi were sold as well.

Stoddart had told me this story in several long phone conversations. As he talked, it had sometimes felt as if the walls were closing in because the Canadian publishing world is so cloistered that it seems as if every part of it has been, at some point, enmeshed with every other part, and each actor has had a role in every other actor's play. His story was like so many other Canadian business stories: it reminded me of what happened to Bennett's Principal Investments. It might have happened to M&S, too, if Bennett hadn't taken it over from Jack McClelland, dealt with the bank, become his own lender, and then handed M&S on to the U of T and Random House just as Canadian publishing went into the tank. Bennett created an exit for himself at exactly the right time thanks to his insight and to good information gleaned from friends in high places. He had gotten himself on the right boards, made himself glamorous, befriended those who made the decisions he had to live with, recognized who could benefit most from his plan, and, as Stoddart put it, hired very able counsel. He saw danger coming long before it arrived. You will not be surprised to learn that Stoddart greatly admires Bennett's intelligence.

I heard the concierge tell Stoddart that I was waiting for him, so I walked up to him, shook his hand. He looked a lot older than I remembered. His white hair still slicked straight back from his forehead, but the hairline itself had moved back farther than before. His eyes behind the aviators were still an arresting blue, but he was heavier and yet more tentative than I recalled. He was not dressed to impress (well why would he be when meeting me?). He was wearing an all-weather jacket, a striped shirt and a blue sweater vest—not the dapper man I remembered from that party.

We took the elevator to the apartment that he and his wife Nancy share with a friend as *pied-à-terre*. Stoddart doesn't come into Toronto often. He mainly lives in Prince Edward County, Ontario's latest wine growing region. He still lives fairly comfortably because he was never required to sign personal guarantees for his business loans—because his track record was good and his business had generally supplied its own capital. This was very unusual in the book business: the lead partner of another publishing company he invested in had been forced to use the family home as security for an operating line. That partner had to hunt for years to find Canadians willing to buy the company. The sigh of relief when an offer finally came in must have been heard from one end of Moore Park to the other. That company was shut down only a few years after the sale.

Stoddart's *pied-à-terre* is in a very ordinary apartment tower in northern Rosedale, so I expected no grandeur within, but when Stoddart opened the door, my mouth fell open because the view was astounding—south over green bowers to the glistening bank towers clustered around CN's great spire, and beyond, to the wide blue of Lake Ontario. I tried not to let the view distract me as we sat at the dining table and waited for his friend and colleague, Marc Côté. Côté is the President, Publisher, Editor and one of three owners of Cormorant Books. He is very smart man with a wicked tongue, so he has made a few enemies in the publishing community. Stoddard thinks his own memory for detail is not what it was, and wanted Côté to help.

Did I give you Michael Wernick's name? Stoddart asked.

He'd been trying to remember the name of the lead bureaucrat at Heritage Canada when, in 1999, the Department denied permission for General to do a joint venture with American-based Ingram, the largest book distributor in the world. Ingram's clients included Amazon. Stoddart said that that deal would have brought to Canada state-of-the-art computer systems, the Amazon database, and access to a worldwide sales and distribution network. Why was his request denied? He was told that the government was concerned that Ingram would have de facto control over the venture because Ingram wanted to appoint its Canadian lawyer to the board as a Canadian director. (The way Doug Pepper, a former Crown and Random House employee, represented the U of T on the M&S board?) The government insisted that since the lawyer's firm had worked for Ingram, Ingram would be able to influence that lawyer. Stoddart said Ingram had pulled out in disgust, calling Canada a third-world country with loosey-goosey rules.

Brazil with snow, I found myself muttering. For my friends, anything: for my enemies, the *Investment Canada Act*.

I told Stoddart I had already found Michael Wernick's name in the correspondence on the M&S gift and sale. He's Clerk of the Privy Council now, I said.

Oh shit, he said. That's why they're all afraid of him. By all, he meant all the publishing people and cultural bureaucrats he'd run into at Jackie Hushion's funeral the previous fall. (Jackie Hushion had once been executive director of the CBPC, the group that represents foreign-owned publishers.)

Côté was late, so I showed Stoddart the M&S financial reports. I had also brought the memo written by Ron Scott on the value of the tax credit receipt that was issued for Bennett's gift of the M&S shares. We were turning pages when Côté knocked on the door and walked in. A tallish man in middle age, with a sharp sense of right and wrong, Côté was the picture of preppiness in a green sweater and chinos.

They both seemed shocked by what I had learned. Though Stoddart had guessed right in 2000 at the size of the tax credit receipt issued by the U of T, had guessed right that Random House got de facto control of the company as the deal closed, he was still surprised at the total value placed on M&S, the size of the debt M&S built up with Random House, and especially that the government had declared the new M&S to be "Canadian" with its eyes wide open. He considered Ron Scott's way to measure the value of a Canadian publishing company at 1.25 times net sales to be plain ridiculous. Why? Canadian English language trade book publishers make almost no profits, he explained. "There was never a trade publisher sold in Canada for anywhere near annual sales. The education business worked that way. In trade publishing, no one would buy it... what did Anna Porter sell her company for? Maybe for debt."

His father's company had begun to make a little money in the 1960s, he said, but things had gotten much better after the government introduced its rules about Canadian ownership of publishers and distributors. Then, they were able to get exclusive distribution rights from major American publishers, such as Simon & Schuster, and British publishers as well. Even so, they still made only about 3% a year on sales. "And 1% was the norm," said Stoddart. "We made almost all of it from foreign book distribution."

A 1% profit on sales of $10 million is $100,000. But corporate taxes in the 1970s and early 1980s were 50%. So a company with sales of $10 million would be left with $50,000. And that's why Stoddart had gone into the business of publishing Canadian non-fiction. First, it sells better than fiction but also "rather than giving the government half of what we made, we invested in important Canadian books instead of paying taxes. We showed minimal profits. But we built the most successful non-fiction list in Canada."

Even so, his Canadian publishing business depended for its life on the distribution of foreign publishers' works. So when Avie Bennett sold off the M&S agency business, while giving control to the U of T, he'd cut off a major revenue generator. Therefore, valuing the company at 1.25 times net sales made no sense at all.

He and Côté started to tell stories about House of Anansi, which Stoddart once owned. Anansi never made any money until they decided to publish the Massey Lectures—which CBC Radio broadcasts across the country—in paperback form. From then on, with the exception of one year, the Massey Lecture profits had funded House of Anansi, rarely selling fewer than 15,000 copies a year, once as many as 100,000. "We sold it to Scott Griffin on the way down," said Stoddart, during the period of reorganization before the bankruptcy.

Griffin was in military equipment, Stoddart said. (Actually, one of his companies made shock absorbers and other parts for military vehicles.)[342] "He wanted to be in something..."

"A glamour business?" I asked.

Griffin also happened to be a good friend of Michael Ondaatje's (went to Bishop's together, said Côté)[343] who told him that if he wanted to do something good, he should buy Anansi. Michael Ondaatje is married to the author, Linda Spalding, whose daughter, Este Spalding, is a poet published by Anansi. Este Spalding also served on Anansi's editorial board and was well known to Martha Sharpe, then Anansi's Publisher. Sharpe knew that Anansi would go down if General went down and by spring of 2002, she knew that General *was* going down. At the first party in honour of the Griffin Poetry Prize, which Scott Griffin created and endowed, she had joked with him that he should also buy Anansi. As things grew desperate at General, she quietly asked around in the community of writers for help.[344] And soon, Griffin had a meeting with Stoddart.

"The dollar figure was pulled out of the air," said Stoddart. "I sat with him in his home. He said $1 million... He said on one condition—that Martha Sharpe went with it [Anansi]. She was to be let go the next week... I swallowed and said, you're sure? He had a CFO with him. The CFO told him he was crazy to do it at all."

Stoddart had sold Macfarlane, Walter & Ross to Bennett for the same amount, $1 million. Stoddart's theory at the time about why Bennett wanted MW&R was that Bennett was paying Doug Gibson an unheard-of salary as Publisher of M&S, and Gibson was not doing as well as Bennett had hoped with non-fiction. Non-fiction was Stoddart's specialty and Macfarlane, Walter & Ross's total focus. But only three years later, M&S shut down Macfarlane, Walter & Ross, and in 2004, amalgamated it with M&S. Stoddart, along with others, had then developed another theory about why it had been closed, a theory I'd checked out. The belief was that M&S wanted to suppress a book in the MW&R pipeline—Stevie Cameron's *Three Amigos*.

No, said Jan Walter, then the Publisher in charge of MW&R's operations, that never happened, there'd been no interference whatsoever from M&S. Walter explained that MW&R had lost a lot of money and had no obvious winners in its pipeline, which was exactly as Doug Gibson had explained his decision to me. Walter had also shared with me that though she and Gary Ross and John Macfarlane owned 49% of Macfarlane, Walter & Ross, they had seen next to nothing of the $1 million Stoddart got for it [because, Stoddart explained, they hadn't put in any investment, he'd financed it all]. And they had only earned bonuses of about $900 for *Boom Bust & Echo*, which sold 300,000 copies.

But never mind theory. The real point Stoddart was trying to get across to me is that losses have value. Even though his companies made money, things had always been arranged so as to never show a profit. One of his companies could show a loss when the other had a big gain: not showing a large profit, which attracted tax, meant money was available for other publishing ventures. The Unanimous Shareholder Agreement defined dividends as that which "will be funded from cash flow remaining after the payment of taxes, principal and interest on any outstanding debt, amortization costs, depreciation and other expenses (including any amounts paid or payable under the Administrative Services and Financial Support Agreement)."[345] Other than in the first half of 2000, no profit had been shown, let alone a dividend paid. The foreign-owned publishers were very adept at this sort of tax avoidance, he said. He'd actually looked into it in the days when government reports still listed in public the taxes paid by foreign-owned entities. His competitors, the foreign-owned publishers, never paid taxes. He'd tried to interest Revenue Canada in his findings. They'd told him they might look into it if he filed a complaint.

Together, we began to parse the financial reports I had brought with me, starting with the report for the last six months of 2000 when the U of T first had possession of the M&S shares. Returns were only 26% of total sales for the period, which was pretty good, because in the spring of 2000, the returns had been awful.

"The cost of sales was $2 million, on sales of $8 million," said Côté as if that meant something important.

So what does cost of sales mean? I asked.

"In the historical sense," said Stoddart, "in Canada, it is the cost of paper, printings, binding and any preproduction expense" but not advances paid to authors, marketing, sales or distribution. "Royalties come out of those sales."

This was the only report in which M&S had shown a profit—in this case retained earnings of $200,000 and a provision for tax of $100,000, which Stoddart took to mean that they had made $300,000. But the company couldn't really have made money for the whole year.

Why not?

"In trade publishing, in the first calendar six months you lose what you won in the last six," said Côté.

As he looked at the next years' reports, Côté became agitated, convinced that a lot of costs were being moved into costs of sales, a category he felt could easily be manipulated. In the first full year, 2001, the fees charged for administrative services had been set by agreement at 25.7% of net sales. [Net sales were defined as gross sales less returns as determined by M&S.] Côté thought that percentage got higher in the years that followed. But when I looked hard at those numbers, I didn't see it that way. Net revenue for 2002 was almost the same as in 2001, though gross sales had improved by about $800,000. But that was because the returns went from 25% to more than 30%. Sales and marketing expenses actually fell by about $600,000 that year, as did all the other expenses except for publishing. However, loss due to a write down of $1,447,990 greatly increased the company's losses from $459,000 in 2001 to $1.8 million in 2002—bringing the deficit to more that $2 million from only $159,452 the year before. Was that write-down due to losses from Macfarlane, Walter & Ross? There was no note attached to this document explaining it. There had been a note in the original document, but it had not been included in the copy given to me.

There was nothing in the report for the year ended 2001 that showed $1 million moving to First Plazas Inc. to pay out its promissory note, or of Random House making a loan to M&S. However, the administrative costs that year were about $1 million higher than in the following year, 2002. This item also had a notation pointing to an explanation that must have appeared in another part of the original document, but it was not included in what was sent to me.

What seemed more important than any possible manipulation of cost was that gross revenue only improved marginally after Random House took over management of M&S. The major argument Bennett had made, and the University had accepted when he sold 25% of M&S to Random House and gave 75% to U of T, was that the M&S business would grow due to Random House's efficiencics, its adoption of digital, its great sales and marketing, etc. But the business soon began to shrink. In 2001, gross revenue for the year ended December 31, was $16,228,000 versus $10,679,139 for the last half of 2000. It went up to $17 million in 2002, but after the shut-down of MW&R, gross revenue fell by almost $2.5 million in 2003, and in 2004 fell again by $1.5 million. That was the year

Doug Pepper took over from Doug Gibson, the year the 'put' was extended until 2008. In the year ended December 31, 2005, gross revenue plunged to $10 million and sales returns climbed to over 30%. Liabilities had come to the point where they equalled assets, almost legal insolvency. By then, the amount due to Random House for financing had also climbed to $10,639,928 and no interest was being paid on debt. In other words, by 2005, M&S was in deep, deep trouble and Random House could have pushed it into bankruptcy then and there, but the cause of the problem was reduced sales and the way unpaid debt accruing interest charges at 6% can become an anvil weighing down a company. As sales plummeted, the costs of sales and marketing stayed even. Order fulfillment and administrative costs actually dropped—but not as fast as sales. And somehow, the cost of publishing went up by $200,000.[346]

We turned to how much revenue came from grants and other income [defined as grants not tied to a specific project] over the five years for which I had reports. Only $153,418 in grants was received in the last half of 2000, but M&S and its subsidiaries got $1.8 million in grants in 2001. This was reduced to $1.2 million in 2002, but rose by $100,000 in 2003 and basically stayed at about $1.3 million in both 2004 and 2005. A note on these grants in the draft financial statement of 2005 said: "amounts received include an annual grant of $43,560 (2004: $39,780) from Ontario Arts Council and $161,200 (2004: $163,700) from Canada Council." Oddly, the Department of Canadian Heritage grants were not mentioned. Later, I calculated the total for the period: for the four and a half years between June, 2000, and the end of December, 2005, M&S took in federal and provincial grants worth $7,309,925. The total figure for the entire 11 years must have been at least double that: the government of Ontario had also introduced its own book fund, not to mention its tax credit.

Stoddart said that when the M&S gift/sale was announced, he had been angry about two things: first, that he thought it broke Canadian law about who can own a Canadian publisher, and second, because Bennett had claimed to have offered him the company when no such thing had occurred. "Avie was not happy with me—but he got his deal done. He got his money back and he got around the Canadian government."

"When I was head of the Association of Canadian Publishers," Stoddart continued, "we lobbied Ottawa for a tax credit system, exactly what the U of T did here [issuing the tax credit receipt to Avie Bennett for his gift]. If you wanted to donate, it would be as if you invested in a cultural industry, but you'd get a tax credit for it, big or small. I saw Herb Gray, saw Sheila [Copps], saw the Minister of Finance then, Paul Martin, with two advisors and their answer was, we have austerity and no tax credits for anyone. That's why the Canadian publishing companies weren't worth anything. We could have done generational transfer if people could invest in return for a tax credit."

As Stoddart talked, Marc Côté burrowed deeper into the statements. He paid close attention to those describing events in 2001 and 2002. They both showed *net* revenues from sales of about $11,600,000.[347]

"That was the last year of General," said Stoddart. "We did $100 million in 2001, so, of all the publishing and distribution of our books, of that, at least $50 million was for Canadian books. The rest of the $50 million was from the ones we licensed as distributors of foreign books. Just for Canada."

"But all of M&S was just this," said Côté.

In other words, the stated value for M&S in 2000, was, in Côté's view, a fiction. Random House had paid $5.3 million for 25% of the shares, a minority position. Ronald Scott had determined that this was a price paid in the open market by a third party at arm's length. Scott had suggested another way to measure value would be to multiply annual net sales by 1.25. But the net sales shown for the last six months of 2000 ($8,047,415), could not just be doubled to get the approximate net sales for the entire year. Net sales in the first half of any bookselling year are much fewer than in the second half. The first half is when returns from the previous Christmas sales season pour back into the publishers' laps. In addition, by the last half of 2000, M&S was a smaller company than the M&S of 1999. Bennett had retained the agency business. That meant the annual sales for 2001 were a better reflection of the true value of the company that Random House invested in.

When I multiplied $11,600,000 (the net sales for 2001) by 1.25, it came to $14,500,000. In other words, by that measure, the whole company was worth less than the value of the tax credit receipt issued to First Plazas by the U of T for 75% of the company. Random House's 25% was therefore worth about $3.6 million, not $5.3 million. It is not possible that the Random House executives who purchased these shares failed to understand the value of what they'd bought. With their eyes wide open, they had paid a very large premium. Why?

It had to be because they knew they were getting de facto control of a competitor, one that would be able to apply for grants and tax credits unavailable to Random House.

The draft financial statement for 2005 showed that M&S had non-capital losses "available for carry forward of approximately $4,351,000 to reduce income taxes payable for years up to 2015." These tax losses had value. When Macfarlane, Walter & Ross was amalgamated with M&S in 2004, its losses became M&S's losses and could be used to offset taxes owing, if ever a profit materialized, even up to ten years in the future. The same applied to Random House: it could get benefit from the loans it had made to M&S through amalgamation. But in order to get permission to absorb M&S, the U of T had to refrain from calling that 'put' until the right political moment. It would be easier to get permission to transfer the University's shares of M&S from a government of the right political persuasion—a Conservative government rather than a Liberal one. After amalgamation, M&S's losses could soak up taxes owing on profits made by one of Random House's other wholly owned entities. M&S had, by my estimate, won at least $14 million in grants from two governments during the 11 years when the University held 75% of its shares. When it became a foreign-owned entity in 2012, Random House could no longer apply for grants, but it was certainly entitled to make use of those losses and reduce taxes accordingly.

In other words, the Canadian taxpayer paid either way.

Côté and Stoddart kept returning to the subject of the Stoddart/General bankruptcy. Who could blame them? Though both M&S and the Stoddart/General companies had ended, their endings had very different effects. For one thing, Avie Bennett remained a hero, and Stoddart did not. For another, the Stoddart/General assets were dispersed and the brands nullified. Because there was no bankruptcy of M&S, but absorption, its brand, its backlist and its losses became useful assets for Penguin Random House and its owner, Bertelsmann.

Just before the bankruptcy, when they were still trying to reorganize, Stoddart told me, he went to Ottawa and asked if he could please sell his companies to foreigners. He went to see Michael Wernick, then still in charge of foreign investment review in the department of Canadian Heritage. As he remembered that meeting, Wernick told him the government could not allow him to do that. "He said it would upset another deal," said Stoddart. That other deal, in Stoddart's view, was Stoddart's sister Susan's sale of Distican to Simon & Schuster. Distican was a paperback company/agency business Susan Stoddart took over when the Stoddart siblings split the family business in 1984 and went their separate ways. Simon & Schuster's works were distributed by Distican in Canada. According to Roy MacSkimming in the *Perilous Trade*, Simon & Schuster threatened federal officials that if Canadian Heritage didn't permit it to buy Distican outright, it would simply stop distributing Simon & Schuster books in Canada. According to MacSkimming, federal officials blinked. The explanation offered to the public for permitting the sale of Distican to a foreign entity was that officials were trying to save 80 jobs. The transaction was announced in November, 2002,[348] about four months after the General bankruptcy proceedings were finished[349] and the fuss over whither Canadian publishing had died down.

"After I was done," said Stoddart.

At that funeral for Jackie Hushion, Stoddart said, he ran into Allan Clarke who had once run the publishing policy section in Canadian Heritage, the same Allan Clarke recommended to me by Sheila Copps. Stoddart asked Clarke who he worked for. Clarke replied, Michael Wernick.

"I asked why he let the M&S deal through," said Stoddart. "He shut down immediately. He said 'you don't want to go there.'"

At that point, I closed my notebook. But later, I had to ask Stoddart: had he ever been involved in politics, was he a known supporter of any party?

He said no.

17

Harlequin

I picked up OpEd page of the *Toronto Star* one morning in late January, 2016, and read the text equivalent of a one-way shouting match. John Honderich, Chairman of Torstar, owner of the *Toronto Star* and many other media properties, blasted away at Paul Godfrey, a well-known supporter of the Conservative Party and the CEO of the very troubled Postmedia Network Inc. Postmedia had been created to buy the Canwest newspapers out of bankruptcy in 2010. Then it bought the Sun chain of newspapers in 2014.[350] Godfrey had been giving speeches to put a better face on his just-announced merger of the newsrooms of Postmedia's formerly "competing" broadsheets with the Sun's tabloid papers in Calgary, Edmonton, Vancouver, and Ottawa.[351] In the process, Postmedia had also let go 90 staffers,[352] including the first female Editor of the *Edmonton Journal*.[353] Godfrey had declared that the remaining staff journalists would write and edit for both papers, somehow employing different *voices*. Godfrey had also tried to position Postmedia as a saviour of Canadian journalism, stating that no other Canadians had made an offer to buy the Canwest assets out of bankruptcy. Had it not been for his group, backed by Golden Tree Asset Management, leader of a group of US hedge funds, those papers would be defunct.[354]

Nonsense, Honderich shot back, Torstar had offered $800 million, which wasn't accepted, and others had offered too.

There was a larger fight behind this one: Godfrey had also been signalling to the brand new federal government that something had to be done to free Canadian newspapers from the *Investment*

Canada Act and the Canadian-advertiser provisions of the *Income Tax Act*. According to Michael Lewis, writing in the *Toronto Star* alongside David Olive on the same subject, two years earlier, Postmedia had hired a lobbyist to press this case in Ottawa, and Godfrey had met with the new Prime Minister to ask personally for changes.[355] The point Honderich made in his OpEd was that Postmedia had handed over "virtual" control of the largest chain of Canadian newspapers to foreign interests due to the huge debt it owed to New York hedge funds. Godfrey acted as their Canadian "front," Honderich said, implying that this should not have been allowed.[356]

Doug Gibson had said the same thing.

Hey, I said to clever husband over breakfast that morning. This Postmedia situation sounds like the M&S deal. But isn't Honderich living in a glass house? Torstar sold Harlequin to HarperCollins for $455 million.[357] How did he get *that* past the *Investment Canada Act*? At least Godfrey could argue that the Canwest was in financial distress when Postmedia borrowed from the hedge funds and bought the assets. That was not the case for Harlequin.

And then I remembered that Prichard had said he'd had something to do with getting the Harlequin sale through Ottawa. At first, I'd thought I misheard him because the sale happened in 2014 and Prichard left Torstar in 2009, and he'd also said something about dealing in Ottawa on behalf of Penguin regarding the merger with Random House. Could he really have argued for three of these deals? And Honderich had not mentioned the *Investment Canada Act* in his OpEd. Why not?

I emailed Honderich and asked for an appointment, telling him what I wanted to discuss. The next day, Honderich said yes.

There was only a thin skiff of snow on the streets, and a few slicks of ice in the shadows as I drove down Bathurst to Queen's Quay and the *Toronto Star* building. I hadn't been to the waterfront in ages: I'd been spending too much time in hospital rooms, enveloped in a surround sound of breaking glass, relentless coughs, and the endless beeping of the machines.

I somehow made the turn too soon, ending up on Fleet Street, which I took as a sign. I went around in a circle and tried again, this time ending up on the portion of Queen's Quay reserved for street-cars. Yikes! I had been distracted by memory, a dangerous form of travel. I once worked in a puppet theatre over on Centre Island and took the ferry there from the terminal on Queen's Quay every day. As I tried to maneuver back to the legal side of the road, my mind fled across the lake in that creaking boat: I smelled the mildewed life jackets, the cool dank water, heard the swans honking at the water's edge, saw the avid hands of children reaching for their tickets at the theatre's box office. I tried to yank myself back into real time by locating the ferry terminal as I drove—it was there, somewhere, but where? Everything seemed so overbuilt, so overblown, so not as it once had been. I was driving through the heart of a brand-new principality, a Monaco of reflective glass, when I spied the *Star* building, which seemed as out of place, as out of time, as me.

It's made of concrete in a modified brutalist style. It was built by the Reichmann's Olympia & York Developments for Beland Honderich, then the Publisher of the *Toronto Star*, and John Honderich's father. The Honderich family owns 14.8 percent of the Voting Trust which owns about 44% of Torstar.[358] Control of the Trust is shared among the other four management families who acquired it after the *Star's* founder died. Though Torstar shares trade publicly, those shares with the right to vote reside almost entirely within the Trust: it controls 94.7% of them. I'd interviewed Beland Honderich years before about the Reichmanns. He'd been open and easy when describing his dealings with them when so many others in town had refused to talk at all. Because: he was Beland Honderich, the Publisher of the *Toronto Star*, and he was afraid of no one.

I parked the car and walked into the main lobby where an ancient linotype machine rears up on a pediment like a post-industrial sculpture. The place felt empty. Torstar, like Postmedia and all the other major media properties in Canada, had not been doing well. Revenues were down 9.9%. It was about to announce a quarterly loss of over $53.5 million, and another $23 million loss would follow in the next quarter. It would slash the dividend twice, too. It had announced the closure of several small newspapers, such as the Guelph *Mercury,* along with its state-of-the-art printing plant up in Vaughan.[359] The *Toronto Star's* Publisher, John Cruickshank, would step down in a few days to be replaced for a short time by the CEO, David Holland, who would then move on to retirement himself.

Newspapers present a great many more Canadian stories to a great many more Canadians than book publishers. These articles may not be so well written or so complex as books, but to understand what is going on in Canadian communities, and in the community called Canada, there have to be communally read publications like the *Toronto Star.* An argument can be made that newspapers invented democracy and vice versa, that the shared experience of reading about current events and personalities creates a public commons of shared knowledge, enabling voters to make choices. This is why there was a rule forbidding the sale of Canadian newspapers to foreign interests long before the *Investment Canada Act* was passed. Yet like leading Canadian book publishers, major newspapers have been dying, and for the same reasons—the Internet, Amazon, Google, online publications, social media platforms, YouTube, free online classified advertising sites like Kijiji. Charts of Torstar's annual revenues over the last decade show a downward trend, along with a few dead cat drops. Yet the *Star* in particular has been vital to public life in this country. Its investigations have launched a vast number of policy debates that resulted in major changes in law and social practice and even in our most basic beliefs about what goodness and fairness mean. Its feature stories have led to all kinds of important careers being raised up or dashed down. I cannot imagine what would happen to Canada if the *Star* was sold to Rupert Murdoch, or if a foreign hedge fund got hold of it by means of high interest debt that grows like kudzu, the situation of Postmedia.

I took the elevator up to the sixth floor where the Torstar executives have their offices. While I waited on a couch in reception, I gazed at the rows of framed cartoons painted for the *Star* by that immensely talented social critic/artist Duncan Macpherson. I'd forgotten how clever he was, what a meat cleaver of a mind he had. There was one image of enduring truthiness that made me laugh out loud: a little Canadian Prime Minister dandled like a baby on the huge, fat knee of a Texan in Stetson and boots and labelled Big Oil.

Honderich appeared and walked me to his office, a nice space with a desk angled to the light and a stunning view of the green / blue lake heaving under an icy skin. A poster from Fritz Lang's *Metropolis* broods on one wall. He looks a little as his father did at the same age—bow tie, grin, straight thick greying hair. He is heavier than when we first met years ago in the *Star's* Ottawa bureau, its tiny rooms half buried in old newspapers. By then, he'd gotten a law degree at the U of T, and then gone into the family business, working first for the competition, the *Ottawa Gazette*, then for the *Star* in Ottawa.[360] At that point I was a freelancer and was staying at the home of his colleague, author and journalist Mary Janigan, because I was working on a story for a magazine that had a limited expense budget. (In the good old days, Canadian magazines still *had* expense budgets.) Janigan lived near the canal in a small house with a slobberingly friendly dog and a constantly ringing telephone because the *Star* was a 24-hour operation and she was always on call. Except when she stashed the phone in the fridge so she couldn't hear it ring.

I'd told Honderich in my email that I was working on the story of how M&S ended up in the hands of a foreign owner, and I needed to know how Torstar managed to sell Harlequin Books to HarperCollins without falling afoul of the *Investment Canada Act*. I'd mentioned that Prichard had said he had something to do with it, and I needed to check facts. So we got right to it.

Anyone who works in newspapers knows there was a civil war for control of Torstar, and the *Star,* between Honderich and Prichard, which Honderich appeared to lose early in 2004. To the dismay of his fellow journalists, it was announced in January of that year that he would step down as Publisher in May. There had been disagreements over cost-cutting versus new investment, about backing John Tory for mayor (Prichard) versus David Miller (Honderich and the *Star*) and over coverage of the Middle East. The new, Prichard-appointed Publisher who took Honderich's place was Michael Goldbloom, formerly of the *Montreal Gazette*, who Prichard had first brought in to the *Star* as Deputy Publisher and strategist. The new Editor was

Giles Gherson.[361] The next year, retired Supreme Court Justice Frank Iacobucci, Prichard's friend and former professor, replaced Evans as Torstar's Chairman.

After he left, Honderich collected an Order of Canada and an Order of Ontario and served on advisory commissions. But eventually he also mounted a palace coup by organizing the families that control the Torstar Voting Trust. In the recession of 2008, the investments Prichard had made in CTVglobemedia and Black Press required major write downs and a dividend cut. By 2009, Honderich was Chairman of the Voting Trust, and then Chairman of the Torstar Board. The Honourable Frank Iacobucci was out, and Prichard was too.[362]

I almost expected Honderich to say that Prichard had nothing to do with selling Harlequin Books to HarperCollins. Instead, he began to praise Prichard for his insight and foresight. To frame this story, he referred to the Baie Comeau Policy, and how Prichard, as early as 2007, had wisely decided that they needed some sort of advance opinion from Ottawa that would allow Torstar to sell Harlequin Books if they had to. And so Prichard went to Ottawa to ask for a Ministerial Letter of Opinion that could not be retracted by subsequent Ministers if the facts remained the same. Sound familiar?

"It was 2007, 2008 when Rob went up and said we know there's this policy...," said Honderich. That was seven years after Prichard and Bennett went to Ottawa to make the case about the gift/sale of M&S. And the timing was right: there had been a change in government in Ottawa. Harper's Conservatives had a minority and little obvious interest in cultural policy.

As Honderich explained it, for the Harlequin Letter, Prichard had developed a rationale quite unlike the one used to get a Letter from the Minister declaring the new M&S to be Canadian. To advance the M&S handover, Bennett had claimed in public that the U of T would have control, while Prichard secretly promised that the U of T would never claim to be a crown agent and sell its M&S shares to a foreigner. Instead of showing how the Harlequin sale to a foreigner could be made to fit Policy, Prichard argued that the Policy had never been meant to apply to Harlequin.

Harlequin had been purchased by Torstar during Beland Honderich's day as a hedge against downturns in the newspaper business. Prichard had argued it was not *really* the sort of Canadian book publisher that the Baie Comeau Policy (and the *Investment Canada Act)* were meant to protect. Only three percent of Harlequin's business is Canadian, Honderich explained to me. While there were a number of Harlequin jobs in Canada at its head office in Toronto, mainly Harlequin had become an international operation based in the US, using American authors, using American distribution out of Kentucky, and selling its stories in translation from offices all around the world. Harlequin was certainly publishing stories, but they weren't *Canadian* stories.

"There's a subsidiary office in New York as well as in France, Spain," said Honderich. There were offices as well in Germany, Poland, India, Japan, etc. "I thought Baie Comeau was developed to protect companies here from being taken over by US publishers, like Bertelsmann and Hachette. I saw Baie Comeau as [something] to protect those [companies] promoting Canadian talent. I'm not sure that policy is designed to protect a worldwide publishing [company]."

That, in a nutshell, had been Prichard's argument. Honderich repeated it to me several times. He agreed with it.

But Harlequin wasn't losing money, I said, and it wasn't offered to a Canadian either, right? Those are the requirements for Canadian publishers seeking an exemption from the *Investment Canada Act* under the Policy. Had someone made you an offer? Were you looking for one?

Honderich placed his leg over his knee. "We were not looking for a sale, Rob Prichard made the decision that should an offer come up, we should be in a position to accept it."

It sounded as if Prichard had taken lessons on how to manage bureaucrats—first come up with a good story—from Avie Bennett. Or was it the other way around? Bennett had been on the Governing Council of the U of T, and then on its Business Board, when Prichard was law school Dean, and then President. Bennett had helped make him President. They'd known each other for a long time, long before the M&S gift/sale idea was hatched. Maybe it was shared habits of mind that commended each to the other in the first place.

"When we did sell," said Honderich, "we still had to undergo the same test, the high bar of the Baie Comeau was in place."

That of course was a matter of debate. Those lawyers at Stikeman Elliott, Doug Gibson, and my first informant certainly had not seen it that way.

So what happened?

"We ended up with a letter from Industry Canada saying in effect that the polices did not apply if… a third-party offer came forward… But we couldn't go out and shop it. Not allowed."

I was pretty sure he meant Heritage Canada, specifically the Minister of Canadian Heritage, not Industry Canada, but I didn't challenge him. When did you get that letter? I asked.

"I think in 2009 we got the letter. I was on the board as a board member."

The letter, as he remembered it, had set out the government's terms. The government said it would accept the sale of Harlequin Books to a foreign entity if Torstar could show that the offer was independently made (in other words, that Torstar had not sought it out) and that this was not contrived. When HarperCollins came calling, it was because of Harlequin's international network. Under the direction of Donna Hayes, the Harlequin CEO, the company had moved into a whole new series of genres, including Christian evangelical love stories, that found a large audience, and it had set up translation staff in offices around the world to get the books out in as many languages as possible. "That's why we got the big bucks," Honderich said, with a huge grin.

Did they arrive with the big offer in hand?

They came in November, 2013, and the deal was negotiated, he said. "It was a New York guy, can't remember his name, an investment banker who came first."

So the offer changed?

"Yes, the offer changed," he said, and laughed again. "That's what we're here for. We felt we came out with an excellent price."

How did you work out the value? I asked, thinking of the rules of thumb for valuing a book publisher as described by Ron Scott in his opinion letter. Was it based on net sales? I asked.

"It was more how did HarperCollins value it," he said. "Back revenue or forward revenue? In this case, no question, Harlequin was under threat, the revenues were decreasing... In terms of the valuation, they put a huge strategic value on its international assets, the humans in offices with skill sets. Excellent people, operations in Japan, Australia, top level, incredible partners of huge value to them. The backlist has a valuation but [it] was more how they valued that. We had a sense of what we could get... but they surprised us with how high they were willing to go."

So Robert Prichard did this, I said.

"I'm here to say I fully support what Rob did—he showed foresight that served the company very well."

It had occurred to me that Honderich and Prichard are about the same age and may have known each other at the U of T law school, so I asked when they'd first met.

"Rob and I go back to childhood," he said. "Same neighbourhood."

Of course. Everybody in this story was cross-linked to everybody else.

Are you still a cultural nationalist? I asked. Or have you changed your mind? What do you think of the Policy and the *Act*?

Well, he said, outside of the way it shrinks value for companies because it imposes constraints on sales, he thought the CRTC with its regulations on airplay for Canadian songs, etc., had been important. "We had to have mandated slots. Now the view is, let Canadians go and compete in the world and we do well. Drake, The Weeknd, Bieber, you have a sense we don't need the protection anymore, let Canadians thrive in competition."

In 2009, did you believe that? I asked.

"I've evolved in my thinking. Harlequin was worldwide. The brand was strong, even among Christian evangelical lines," he said with a grin. "But along comes Amazon. They sold Harlequin books, but who had the customer name and the credit card? Amazon. That's the world we're now dealing with. The competitive environment changed dramatically. The niche [was] no longer protected. So it came down to single title successes like every other publisher. [You] try your best but you're up against giants. It lost its niche, became another publisher, a smaller one, a metaphor for how other things have gone today. We saw the dramatic declines in revenue—30% in one year… and [we were] mainly in the US market. Prichard took the initiative—[an] extensive period of meeting with officials. It was the Stephen Harper government, not prone to do favours for the *Toronto Star*. The officials saw it as a worldwide company located in Canada. Is that what the *Act* [was] meant to protect?"

It was Prichard who saw the bad times coming, he reiterated, Prichard who was prescient enough to act. The heyday of Harlequin had been in the late 90s. Owning Harlequin had buoyed the *Toronto Star* then: the difference in value between Canadian and US dollars had translated into $100 million a year in revenue for Torstar from Harlequin's US sales. Donna Hayes had further advanced Harlequin by extending its genres and expanding heavily into world markets. (She left the company before the sale to HarperCollins was finalized.)

When Honderich mentioned her name again, I remembered that Donna Hayes is married to Brad Martin, CEO of Penguin Random House.[363]

When the offer came from HarperCollins, thanks to Prichard's fore-sight (and his experience with M&S, I muttered over my notes) it was not necessary for Torstar to go to Ottawa and try to make a spurious argument about how Harlequin was in awful trouble (it wasn't) and no Canadian had stepped forward to buy it (it wasn't on the block). The Minister's letter was already in Torstar's pocket, a letter, according to Honderich, that bound any future government, just as Sheila Copps' let-ter had bound future governments to her definition of M&S as Canadian in spite of Random House acquiring de facto control along with its 25%.

"We had a signed document" said Honderich. "We had to show it was an independent third party offer and that was easy to show. We had evidence of that. There were meetings in Ottawa."

With?

He said he thought it was Investment Canada.

Wouldn't it have been Heritage Canada? I asked. Was the man's name Harold Boies?

Boies administers the *Investment Canada Act* issues within Canadian Heritage. I knew that because we'd emailed back and forth. He'd told me nothing at all about the M&S transaction, pleading that the *Investment Canada Act* precludes him from offering any information.

"That does ring a bell," said Honderich. "I know there were meetings in Ottawa with the Heritage people. Most of the discussions were about guarantees of jobs in Don Mills (where Harlequin has its headquarters) and the head of the company staying here." These promises, made by HarperCollins, "did have a time horizon."

And no one asked if you were going broke or if you'd offered Harlequin first to Canadians?

"This is what Prichard did," Honderich replied. By which he meant, Prichard's it's-not-really-Canadian argument had somehow successfully neutered the requirements of the *Act*. And so: Torstar got $455 million from HarperCollins, which it used to pay down debt as it invested heavily in a tablet version of the *Toronto Star*. It was still reporting losses, big losses, but how much worse would things have been if Torstar hadn't been able to sell Harlequin?

What do you think about the Policy now John? I asked, almost dreading what he would say. You say you're a nationalist, but what about that?

"I'm the Chairman of Torstar. We feel we made a strategic decision to exit at a time when threatened. I *am* a nationalist. I never felt this violated the spirit or the intent of Baie Comeau."

But it violated the intent of the law, not just a policy, I found myself thinking. Okay, I said, look what happened with M&S. Now it's just a brand among brands owned by Bertelsmann.

"M&S' whole business was doing Canadian books, by Canadian authors. Harlequin did none of that. All the big writers and titles were American. The essence of the company was American. The distribution was out of Kentucky."

Should the Policy remain?

"When I talk [about] economic conditions, conditions have changed… The economic realities of the world, open [borders] the digital revolution plus Amazon, make it much more challenging for small Canadian publishers to survive. If—what we experienced is it's much more difficult to survive today, the Policy may no longer fit the times."

I reminded him of what Prime Minister Justin Trudeau told the *New York Times Magazine* just after the election. He'd said: "There is no core identity, no mainstream in Canada. There are shared values—openness, respect, compassion, willingness to work hard, to be there for each other, to search for equality and justice. Those qualities are what make us the first post-national state."[364] I pointed out that Mélanie Joly, the Minister of Canadian Heritage (who once referred to herself as the Minister of Symbols) had said that all of cultural policies were up for review, everything is on the table. So, what about newspapers? I asked. Should Canadian newspapers be on the table?

"In terms of right now, there's a great debate presented by Godfrey to get rid of the restrictions on foreign ownership of Canadian newspapers. We are all alone in that area that the rules should be maintained. In book publishing, you cannot overestimate the impact of Amazon. You cannot overestimate the impact. They have all the information on you. They make great use of it."

And the Internet's impact on newspapers had also been dreadful. "We once had 60 pages of classified ads which paid for a lot of reporting," he said. "Now it's Kijiji for free." He still saw the value of keeping Canadian newspapers in Canadian hands "but I understand the economic conditions. It's a Postmedia world. Yet the recording industry and the film industry are not doing too bad."[365]

Well, thanks to the handover of M&S and the merger permitted between Penguin and Random House, a third of Canadian book publishing is mostly in the hands of Penguin Random House, I said. And at Penguin Random House two people have the last word on what's going to be published. How does that serve us?

"Yet the viability of the publishers is very much in question," he said. "The economics don't lie in that respect."

In effect, you're saying—keep the rules intact for the newspaper business, but not for the other cultural industries, I said.

He said he took the point. No, he did not know whether the *Star* would give testimony at hearings into the demise of local news. They had just begun, led by the new chairwoman of the Standing Committee on Canadian Heritage, Hedy Fry, in response to the Postmedia mergers and the *Star*'s closure of smaller papers. He said the *Star* had not yet been invited. (He did testify later in the fall.) But he said he was delighted that the conversation had at least begun, because the questions, the economic realities, were very real. The important issue, he said, is: "What will it mean for our democracy?"

When I got home, I emailed Robert Prichard at Torys. I asked if I could interview him on how he'd framed the Harlequin argument for the bureaucrats in Ottawa. He'd been involved in three success-ful maneuvers that had resulted in permissions from the Minister of Canadian Heritage. He'd helped argue successfully for permitting the merger of Penguin Canada with Random House of Canada, which created a publishing oligopsony. He'd argued successfully that the U of T would have control over M&S in spite of what the agree-ments said. He'd argued successfully that the sale of Harlequin to a foreigner should be allowed because Harlequin—started in Canada, head office in Canada, controlled by a Canadian entity—should be considered as more foreign than Canadian. This gave new meaning to the word flexible.

I told him that John Honderich had said very nice things about his insight and foresight in getting officials to see things his way. I said it was clear he is the best lawyer in Canada. Would he give me an interview to explain his argument and discuss the letter permitting the Harlequin sale?

He would not. It was his opinion that only the current offi-cers of Torstar should speak on Torstar business, specifically John Honderich, the Chairman, and David Holland, its CEO. Since they had all operated together as a team, they were well placed to explain. On the subject of him being the best lawyer in Canada, I had been "misinformed." Since he had only been practising law for five years, he couldn't even claim competence, let alone accomplishment.

I took Prichard's advice once more and asked for an interview with David Holland, then still the CEO of Torstar. Holland gave me 15 minutes on the phone. I confirmed with him the basic facts gleaned from Honderich, though Holland was reluctant even to do that. I asked for the name of the American investment banker who had come to see him. He said the whole business of getting permission to sell Harlequin had been a confidential matter between Torstar and the federal government. Yes, there had been a net benefit test. No, he could not recall if the requirement of the government was that Torstar could not shop Harlequin, but could sell it if an independent third party came to them. This was all done in confidence, he reiterated.

But the *Investment Canada Act* does not prevent companies from saying whatever they want to about these matters, I said. Would it be possible to show me the letter the government issued?

He stuck to his position. And he refused to show me the letter.

I asked if his views on the policy requiring Canadians to own Canadian newspapers had changed.

"I learned a long time ago to never say never, but... As of today we think they should remain in Canadian hands," he said.

As of today? It's all confidential, even when it doesn't have to be? If even Torstar was no longer sure of the virtue of the *Investment Canada Act* and its protection of Canadian ownership of Canadian newspapers, the whole cultural nationalism game was well and truly over.

Pierced in secret, left to bleed, smothered by silence.

18

Endings and Beginnings

Ellen Seligman, McClelland & Stewart's legendary fiction editor/ publisher, died in the spring of 2016. When her obituary appeared in the newspaper, it was a sad surprise. Unlike the way most information moves through the CanLit community—like the unmentionable through a Canada goose—almost no one, not even a writer whose novel she was editing, realized that she was ill, never mind that it was terminal.[366] She had worked with all the usual suspects, Margaret Atwood, Jane Urquhart, Michael Ondaatje, Anne Michaels, Rohinton Mistry, Leonard Cohen, stretching the normal practice of editing far beyond offering structural suggestions or rearranging sentence order. One writer, Patrick Lane, said she had "inhabited" his manuscript.

She was an American, born and bred in New York City, a graduate of the University of Wisconsin. Her private life was just that, though there were the usual rumours. One publishing person insisted that she was a descendant of the famous Seligman banking family, their business founded in the middle of the 19th Century by Joseph Seligman and his brothers, with offices in Frankfurt, London, and New York, and that she was connected by marriage to the Guggenheims.[367] Was this true, or a good story? She told the *Canadian Jewish News* in 2001,[368] just after her elevation to Vice-President and Fiction Publisher at M&S, that she came to Canada for romantic reasons. Whoever that romantic reason was, the man who became her lifelong partner was James Polk, the former husband of Margaret Atwood, whose life partner by then was the novelist and political activist Graeme Gibson. For years Polk was the editorial director of the House of Anansi where he, too, worked with the great and about-to-be great of CanLit. He too was an American who[369] found his way to Canada after doing his doctorate at Harvard. He served on the RBC Taylor Prize jury in 2014, so a short biography of Polk can be found on its website. It mentions that when Polk was an advisor to the Ontario Ministry of Culture, he developed the Ontario Book Publishing tax credit, only available to Canadian-owned and controlled companies. The officials of the Ontario Media Development Corporation had told me that "Canadian controlled" is in part defined for the tax credit's purposes by reference to the federal *Income Tax Act*. But when I looked for the *Income Tax Act's* definition of control, I learned that it is not defined in that statute, but it has instead been interpreted in various ways through various court decisions. Usually, control means 51% ownership of the voting equity of a company, but the courts have ruled that non-arm's length relationships can transform even 25% ownership into control, as can significant levels of debt.[370] Had Polk discussed with the Ministry of Culture that its book tax credit rules might not accommodate the ambiguities of McClelland & Stewart, when it was de facto controlled by Random House, though 75% of its shares were held by the U of T? Had his partner, a leading figure at M&S, made these complexities known to him? I can't answer these questions because neither Seligman nor Polk responded to my emails requesting an interview. The one I sent to Polk was forwarded to him by Martha Sharpe, a former Publisher of Anansi and a friend of Ellen Seligman's.

Seligman had a private funeral, but her former employer, Penguin Random House Canada, announced it would hold a memorial in her honour. Normally, memorials for celebrated persons are open to the public. This one was by invitation. The invitations were sent out by email with instructions to RSVP to Canada@penguin-randomhouse.ca. I did not get one, but a source who did sent me his. I decided I wanted to go.

Once, years ago, I called Seligman at the recommendation of another editor when I was starting to write fiction. I asked if I could show it to her. She'd responded in that nasal, monotone-yet-droll voice of hers, neither encouraging nor discouraging, neither enthusiastic nor the opposite: well, I guess, maybe, she'd said. Nowadays, no one in her position would take such a call let alone be open to reading the work of a stranger with no track record. But that wasn't why I wanted to attend the memorial. In my mind, her death was entangled with the end of McClelland & Stewart. Her passing marked its termination more profoundly than any merger document or Minister's decision upon review. It also marked the end of something more important than the absorption of one business by another, and that is the disappearance of the political belief, expressed in law and policy, that Canadian words will build this country. Does anyone in government still hold that there is a Canadian identity greater than the sum of us all which must be reflected in print in order to keep Canada becoming itself?

How strange, yet Canadian, that some of those most responsible for delivering our vital stories into the world were born and raised in the United States of America. Our cultural protectionism was supposed to save us from the overwhelming cultural energy of our Neighbour to the South, yet some of those imbued with it helped us become who we are—whoever that is.

So I thought of the memorial as a coda. Every book needs one.

Besides: in the middle of July, an announcement was sent around the email chain that Penguin Random House Canada had hired Jared Bland in "the newly created role of Publisher" of M&S, which entailed oversight of its profitability as well as taking charge of the in-house magazine, *Hazlitt*.[371] No mention was made of former M&S Publisher and President Doug Pepper in the cover note, but the full announcement said Pepper had been assigned to run Signal, a non-fiction imprint, reporting to Bland. This was odd because Bland has a much shorter publishing resume than Pepper. Bland's previous job was as the Arts Editor at the *Globe and Mail*. Born in Springfield, Illinois, Bland studied English literature at the University of Toronto and did graduate work there on Canadian poet Al Purdy. After interning at *Walrus*, Bland became its managing editor. Then there was a short stint as an editor at House of Anansi after which he joined the

Globe.[372] Pepper, by contrast, had been editing and publishing books for three decades. Bland had been made a Vice-President, thus no one could accuse Penguin Random House of sloughing another undertaking. It had promised the Minister of Canadian Heritage that those managing the remains of M&S would have the same level of autonomy as the leaders of Doubleday, Knopf, and Random House: those undertakings remained in force until December, 2016.[373]

The announcement tried very hard to purvey the notion that M&S still exists. It devoted several paragraphs to its great importance at Penguin Random House Canada. Apparently, it was even assigned a new Editor-in-Chief—the same woman who performs the same duties at Doubleday.[374] So I was curious as to how M&S would be portrayed at Seligman's memorial: alive or dead?

I sent a query to the RSVP address saying I would like to come to the memorial: would that be okay? No response. No matter, go anyway, I thought. Bearing witness is one of the things reporters must do, though witness is a fancy word for the reality. The reality is that at important events, invited or not, we lurk. This isn't as bad as it sounds. Reporters today are much better behaved than they used to be. My elders, at *Maclean's,* used to regale me with stories of the good old days when they worked for Canada's great newspapers. They were often sent out to get photos of a newsworthy person who had just died. If need be, they were expected to break into that person's house and steal a picture right off the wall so it could appear in the paper. Some of them got really good at it.

Seligman's memorial was held on the last day of summer, 2016. The morning started out grey. I listened to the radio news in a state of free-floating anxiety that soon affixed itself to an item about the vicious bombing of Red Crescent relief trucks carrying food and medicine to the starving and the wounded near Aleppo, Syria. Our Prime Minister, Mr. Sunny Ways, had been to China and had agreed to consider an extradition treaty with China. To show its gratitude, the Chinese had at last deported home a Canadian missionary who they'd jailed as a spy.[375] There was also talk of a free trade deal between Canada and China. The civil rights folks were nervous about the proposed extradition treaty, and the trade people were edgy about a free trade deal.

I got in the car and drove downtown feeling thoroughly unsettled, though the sun had come out and the heat was rising and that sort of weather usually makes me happy. I figured out in the parking lot that I was nervous about going to this event, so nervous it was as if I had never before gone somewhere uninvited with my notebook and pen in hand. What was there to be afraid of? I reminded myself that we in Canada are almost immune to the horrors destroying lives elsewhere in the world. I told myself that I should be grateful for the fact that I live in a country of laws, though this M&S story demonstrated that our laws are played by lawyers the way Rostropovich handles a cello, and if you have friends on the Hill, things turn out better than if you don't. I told myself I should weep with joy that we consider that sort of thing to be a problem.

I told myself I should keep things in proper perspective. So what if I got thrown out?

Koerner Hall is reached through a spectacular structure of glass and steel affixed to two 19th Century buildings housing the Royal Conservatory of Music. Once upon a time, I took my children there for their piano lessons. Back then, the rooms were dowdy and the floors were as brittle as dried bird bones: there was an awful little snack bar full of sugary things my children wanted to eat right by the parking lot door. But there was music everywhere, a mad symphony of glorious (and inglorious) sound pouring from this studio and that one, and especially from the master classrooms where the finer points of performance were taught. Just to sit and wait as a child took her lesson was to be lifted up.

The new entryway has an echo, but no music could be heard. The snack bar has disappeared. A ramp goes down to an elegant food court and up to the Hall. Young women in chic dresses guarded the ramp going up. But they didn't ask if I had been invited, they just waved me on my way.

Upstairs, outside the hall's main doors, my past and present were enjoying a conversation. Julian Porter, Q.C., who guided me and

Toronto Life through the Reichmann libel case, was talking to Arlene Perly Rae, former director of M&S. She was leaning on a cane. She seemed to have forgotten our phone conversation. She explained to me, as if I didn't know, that she had once served on the M&S board. Brad Martin, standing off to the side, gave me a funny look. I scurried inside and found a seat before someone called security.

Koerner Hall has velvet-draped walls and an intricate, wooden, acoustically tunable ceiling. It seats 1,135 people. There is a stage that is neither large nor small, which sported two large displays of flowers and two lecterns where people would speak. An agent friend sat down beside me. I had grabbed an aisle seat, the better to see people coming in. Two writers walked down the opposite aisle and leaned in to graze cheeks. They both looked stricken. I knew this was not about Seligman's death, because that was old news, but about the demise of another writer and friend who had died suddenly only two days before. John Bentley Mays was an art and architecture critic of very wide intellect and insatiable curiosity, yet another former American who helped us discover ourselves.

I waited for the music to begin, but there was none. (At Bentley Mays' memorial Mass, by contrast, the music would be so beautiful.) This memorial began instead with a speech given by a young colleague of Seligman's who cried as she recounted what it was like to work for her, to be mentored by her. She provided a long list of Seligman's quirks, peculiarities, oddities, which were attested to over and over by the other speakers who followed her. Seligman was a fanatic about temperature control in the office, she wore elegant clothes, she was absolutely relentless in her quest for perfection, all forms of perfection, she was fun, she was funny, she was fierce, she was girly, she was everyone's Dear Reader. The books she'd edited had won an inordinate number of big prizes. Anne Michaels, Michael Helm, Michael Ondaatje, Jane Urquhart, Elizabeth Hay, Linda Spalding all told similar stories about working with her. (Rohinton Mistry read from Tagore.) They described the joys and the terrors, even the horror, as one writer expressed it, of realizing that Seligman's evisceration of her novel, one that she had been so sure was wonderful, was warranted. When Seligman asked how she was feeling, she'd replied that she was in a panic. Seligman had said that was good, an arrogant writer is a poor writer. Michael Helm told the story of how she called him to say she had acquired his novel, that it was spectacularly good, a gift to literature, and how he then spent month upon month upon month in endless conversations with her that led him to change just about everything in it (except its sense and meaning).

Yet the most affecting description of this editing process was the one Steven Price described in various other places (the *Globe and Mail*, the *Literary Review of Canada*, *Hazlitt*) before or just after this event. His was the last book Seligman edited.

She never told him she was dying. She never told him she was ill. She called him almost every day, spending hours on the phone working through his novel from beginning to end, hour after hour of intense conversation as she made suggestions, and he considered them, and made some back. She listened to him type while he made changes on his computer, and read them aloud to her, hour after hour after hour of thinking about character, dialogue, setting, motivation, language, always hunting for the precise word, day after day, week after week. This is why the phrase 'Ellen Seligman is on the phone' filled her writers with dread and dismay, joy and exhilaration. Seven days before she died, she called and left him a message. It was clear she thought it was Friday, and only belatedly realized it was in fact Saturday and not a workday for most people, and said she'd call again on Monday. After she died, Price and his wife replayed the message over and over.

Having never worked with her, I had no idea she'd worked this way. I had not met anyone in the book business who worked this way. (My editor scrawled "Oh, yeah?" beside that sentence.) One speaker said she was sometimes called Canada's Maxwell Perkins, after the legendary American editor who pulled wonderful works from his artists through a similarly laborious process. But in fact, she was the one and only Ellen Seligman. Though she'd had many offers to go and work at larger publishing houses in London or New York, she told those who asked that she stayed at M&S because of its independence.

The last speaker was Kristin Cochrane, Penguin Random House Canada's President. She made it clear that this event had been brought to us by Seligman's employer, that business was afoot here, as well as memory. She praised Seligman as a businesswoman, along with pointing out, yet again, her quirks and oddities. I couldn't help but think that this was an attempt to rewrite Seligman's work life, or life's work, so that it made some sort of business sense. Because nothing described in this memorial made any sort of business sense. No publishing company can afford to employ as publisher, an editor who lavishes months and years of her own effort on one or two books. That behaviour is the antithesis of business, it is the behaviour of an artist whose medium is the writer. A rumour had reached my ears that Seligman kept her illness under wraps because she feared her employers would use it as an excuse to be rid of her. I discounted it from the moment her former junior began to speak of her with such passionate love and respect. Yet that rumour spoke another sort of truth, one in keeping with the economic reality of Canadian publishing: Seligman must have driven the bean counters at Bertelsmann to distraction because she didn't work according to a normal schedule, yet they couldn't remake her, and they couldn't do without her either.

But now she is gone.

The Minister of Canadian Heritage, Mélanie Joly, is a very photogenic person. Blond, beautiful, her feelings show on her face and her body as she moves. The camera loves her. She seems the very embodiment of openness. As I would later learn, a Quebec publisher had brought out a book by Joly propounding her ideas on changing the rules of the political game just after the last federal election.[376] Yet I had been trying for some time without success to find out more about her intention to reinvent the way Canadian culture is supported by the federal government, specifically publishing. On the one hand, as one of its first budget initiatives, the new Liberal government had offered $75 million more to the CBC, to be followed by $180 million every year for five years, and $40 million more to the Canada Council, with $150 million to come in 2020 (which is the next best thing to maybe).[377] Yet, on the other hand, that phrase of hers, everything is on the table, sounded like surgery coming. Get ready.

In the summer of 2016, Canadian Heritage's website invited Canadians to take part in an online/social media consultation process concerning what they called Canadian content in a digital world. This apparently was what was meant by everything is on the table. Many of the arts are now transmitted in digital form, according to Minister Joly and her Department, and Canada should aim to export its cultural content to a global audience. This is not the same aim as reflecting Canadians to themselves. This online consultation process, according to the website, had unearthed several themes for the Department and the Minister to consider, including the idea that cultural content producers should aim at the export of democracy.

That seemed to me to be a dubious aspiration for those who write novels or poetry, or for those who are trying to report on the world through books and magazines and newspapers, but I tried to keep an open mind. I also worked hard to ignore the use of the word "content" to describe cultural endeavours. This is the information technologists' notation for what artists create. It is an insulting word, an empty bag of a word for the always changing, always surprising gifts of human minds and hearts. It reflects the point of view of those who control the means of digital distribution.

The website referred to a series of "in-person" consultations to be led by the Minister, a process to be announced at the end of the summer. I thought I should attend the event scheduled for Toronto, the home of most of Canada's English language cultural workers and many of its leading cultural institutions, as well as most of its English language publishers, because this consultation process was aimed at new beginnings, at a new policy for a new age. Perhaps it would lead to an answer about whether or not Canada should still protect publishers from foreign ownership, whether it should continue to support the reflection business at all, and if so, how.

Beginnings are always interesting. As Doug Gibson had put it when Bennett handed over M&S to Random House and the U of T, "the King is dead, long live the King."

I filled out the online questionnaire and followed the instructions to check in with that website every now and again to see when the in-person events would be held.

Nothing new on this subject appeared there, except the announcement of the formation of an advisory group appointed by the Minister to help her figure out what the future should look like. No book publishers or book editors were in that group, although a magazine person was.

The literary agents were nervous about what was afoot. They held meetings, and according to the minutes of one of them, planned to make representations to the Minister. One publisher told me that one of his competitors had gone to Ottawa for a consultation and had expressed his concern about this everything-is-on-the-table business. He'd been told by officials not to worry; book publishing represents such a tiny fraction of the Departmental budget ($1.9 billion) that no attention would be paid to it at all.

Was that Good? Or Bad?

In mid-September, the Canadian Heritage website said the government was organizing five in-person events across the country at which the Minister would appear. The one for Toronto, the cultural capitol of English Canada, home of the largest segments of the film and television industry, music industry, games industry, publishing industry, dance, opera, theatre, what have you (close to 45% of all Canada's cultural industry jobs are in Ontario), was scheduled for October 12.

I was annoyed that no one had sent me a press release about these meetings, though I had been trying to get my name added to the Department's media list for some time. Apparently my requests, including my request to interview the Minister, had fallen in some deep hole.

But I was shocked when I realized that October 12, 2016, was Yom Kippur, the most significant day in the Jewish calendar. Wow, I thought, that's got to be a mistake, who would brag about diversity as our strength, as Canadian Heritage always does, and then hold a public consultation event on the arts, culture, publishing, television, etc. on Yom Kippur? There are a few Jews involved in these industries (such as me). I was told, later, that October 12 had been chosen because the House of Commons was not sitting that week.

Though I now had a date, a very inconvenient date, the website did not announce a place or time for any of the events listed, not in Vancouver, Montreal, Halifax, Edmonton, or Toronto.

There was a note on the website that a company called Ipsos was in charge of organizing these events. Ipsos, I soon learned, is foreign-owned: its head office is in Paris, France. I spoke to Marc Beaudoin in Ipsos' Ottawa office, asking for the time and place of the Toronto in-person event. I also asked to attend. He said these in-person consultations were by invitation only, but there would be tweeting and live-streaming. I said that was nice, but no one following on social media would be able to ask the Minister a direct question. I understand your concerns, he said. Please tell the Department.

Who *is* invited? I asked.

That too is up to the Department, not his territory, he said. He gave me the name and number of the man in charge of the who, the where, and the when—Scott Shortliffe, a Director General at Canadian Heritage.

Shortliffe returned my call the next day. He explained that these events were working sessions, that's why it was by invitation only, space was limited. Why would space be limited? I asked. Rent a bigger space. Who is invited?

No answer.

I asked to be invited as media to cover the event. I asked to be sent the invitation list. I was told my name and information would be passed on to the right people.

About two weeks before the Toronto event, I phoned the Department of Canadian Heritage, the Minister's office, and the Ipsos folks again asking for the time and the place of the Toronto consultation. No replies. At that point, I realized I needed to haul out my investigative reporter tool kit. The Department of Canadian Heritage seemed to be treating the time and place for public consultation on the future of Canadian content in a digital world as a secret.

I emailed people in the Toronto cultural community who I thought might have been invited. I started with Elaine Waisglas, artist, photographer, and partner of Michael Hirsh, co-founder of Nelvana, a major animation company specializing in the adaptation of children's literature. Hirsh had eventually sold Nelvana to Corus, and then had founded more companies selling stories around the world. Waisglas said neither of them had been invited and said she didn't realize that everything was on the table.

You and Michael should be there, I said.

Waisglas contacted Gail Dexter Lord, a world-renowned museum consultant based in Toronto, to find out if she had been invited. No, not invited either. Later I would ask Rita Davies, Chairwoman of the Ontario Arts Council, formerly the transformative executive director of the Culture Division for the City of Toronto, and before that leader of the Toronto Arts Council, if she was invited to attend. No, she had not received an invitation either.

I studied the advisory group list to see if there was anyone on it who I could contact to find out where and when the event would be held. The list included: a producer of CBC's Republic of Doyle; an actress/writer with a web series running on Hulu; the President of CPAC; the chief digital officer of the Film Board; the CEO of TVO; Dean of Communications and Design at Ryerson; the President of the Society of Graphic Designers in Quebec; the CEO of APTN; the founder of the Society for Arts and Technology in Montreal; the President of Secret Records of Montreal; the Executive Vice-President of Public Policy at Rogers Communications (Ken Whyte is also a director of Munk's Aurea Foundation); the Chairman of DHX. Someone must have raised a concern that this group was heavy on executives, light on "content" makers.[378] Three women were added after the Vancouver consultation—two writers and a dancer. There were no book publishers at all, nobody currently in the newspaper business or directly in the magazine business, and no leading authors. Meanwhile, Elaine Waisglas and Michael Hirsh put a PR firm on the case and they soon got an invitation. Elaine sent me an email with the time and place: Art Gallery of Ontario, in the Baillie Court, at 12:30 p.m. on Yom Kippur.

I got to the museum in plenty of time. The Baillie Court is on the third floor, accessible only by the AGO Members' elevator at the back of the building, or, by the fabulous circular staircase that arrived with the Gehry rewrite of the AGO. There was one small stanchion beside that elevator carrying one small sign advertising the Canadian content in a digital world event. It was the only such sign in the building.

I sat on a bench opposite and waited to see who showed up.

People came in small groups. No familiar faces. Then there was a gang of four with phones in their hands muttering about messaging the Minister. Shortly thereafter, the Minister herself appeared, resplendent in over-the-knee leather boots and a charming cornflower-patterned blue jacket. She disappeared with her retinue into a side room. Elaine Waisglas came in after that, went upstairs, and came right back down. There's a press table up there, she said. Just go up and sign in.

So, I went up. There was a press table. There was a sheet of paper where media persons were supposed to sign in. There were a couple of names on it, which meant that at least some other media had been informed. Why not me? I told the woman at the table that I was not on her list but would like to attend. Is that a problem? No problem, she said, just sign in, there's a scrum later with the Minister. At this point my ears got hot because I was very annoyed. Investigative tools should not be necessary when there's a press table and any journalist can enter just by signing their name to a piece of paper.

You know I've been trying to get information about this event for quite some time, I said to her. I asked to be on the press list, no one got back to me.

Oh, you should speak to the Press Secretary for the Minister, she said.

We were in an open space off the main room. People were milling about. I spotted a youngish man who I had seen before walking with the Minister. Pierre-Olivier Herbert, said his name tag. That is the name of the Minister's Press Secretary, the same person I'd left messages for. I went over to meet him. I expressed my annoyance. He didn't seem to understand why I was annoyed. I explained I had left messages for him, and for his assistant, which had not been returned, asking to be included on the press list. Now he remembered that he'd handed off my email to his assistant, so it was her fault if I never heard back. I said I had also asked for the list of all the invitees to these events.

Oh, can't do that at this time, he said.

Why not? I said, people are here, they've been invited, you sent out the invitations a while back.

Well there's still Montreal to come, he said, meaning refusals were still coming in and invitations still going out.

When will you have the list of invitees? I asked.

In due course, he said.

Are there any publishing people on it?

He said there were.

Anyone here today who is in publishing?

I can't give you the name at the moment, he said, backing away.

At this point a policy person with the Department came forward because she had heard me mention that I was working on a book on publishing. She asked me for my card. Don't have one, I said, I'll write my email on this piece of paper for you. She rummaged in her purse for her card. She wanted me to contact her, she said. She assured me she would reply right away. So I took her card and explained what I was writing about and that I wanted the list of invitees to this event, especially in publishing. Is there anybody here today who is in publishing? I asked. She thought there was. Can I have the name? I asked. You should speak to the Press Secretary, she said. At which point my ears got hot again. I had begun to figure out that this absurdly evasive behaviour was not aimed at me. There was no aim here at all except to pretend to listen to a few well-chosen people of known views, and then write whatever policy the Minister or her Department had in mind from the start. Perhaps this moment of realization is when my whole face went red. Perhaps my face going red frightened the policy person.

"Oh," she said with that look of concern: "are you okay?"

"Perfectly fine," I said through gritted teeth. "Just pissed off."

I told her I would write her later that day and walked into the main hall. There were eight tables of ten with place cards for the invited. So, I thought, 80 people invited. That's a pretty small number to represent the views of the English language cultural centre of Canada. But then I realized that each table also had an Ipsos facilitator, so the real number of invitees was 72. Later we would be told that five local area MPs had come to this event as well, so the number of invited cultural folk dipped down to 67. I spotted no one representing Unifor, a union that represents journalists and other writers, which had published an ad in the morning paper trying to get the Minister's attention on the subject of its members losing their jobs at newspapers and in other media.

There was a journalist standing beside me from the *National Post*. How did you hear about this? I asked him.

There was a press release, he said.

To you? I asked.

No, just to the paper, he said. He thought it had come three days earlier.

Do you know who's invited? I asked. No, he said, I'm just gonna take pictures of the name cards on my phone. Which he did.

The actor, Paul Gross, made a speech and introduced the Minister. The way he told it, things are tough in the world of Canadian content. "Consolidation has not helped us," he said. No kidding, I muttered. "We're ten years behind, the failure of SHOMI gives a good indication of where we're failing," he said. But since the new government and the Minister had taken an interest, he advised all assembled to take advantage of that and move forward. As to the Minister, he said, she is a thief and she doesn't apologize. Apparently, he had appeared at TIFF with the Minister and at a shared meal she took over his fruit cup.

The Minister told a different story. First, she thanked the Mississaugas of the New Credit First Nation for allowing us to be on their former lands. Then she mentioned that former councillor and MP Adam Vaughan was in the room as a guest and she named as well each of the other MPs, plus Ken Whyte of Rogers. She wanted everyone to know that "we come at this from a position of strength" that we have all this talent, that we are "number one in virtual reality due to the National Film Board. Our authors are celebrated around the world so that is why we are the guest of honour at the Frankfurt Book Fair in 2020!"

But, she said, she still really needed help and so she was here to listen. There was an 8.9 % growth in the creative sector in the UK last year, pushed by that government, and she wanted the same for Canada. (Canada had an overall growth in GDP of 1.2% in 2016, which might climb all the way to 2% in 2017. Statistics Canada reports that cultural industries contribute about 3% to Canada's GDP, and that this sector grew by 2.8% between 2010 and 2014, about half the growth was in audio-visual and interactive media.[379]) The invitees in the room, she said, represented "the present and the future of our country's culture, the world is watching us, and is wide open to the stories we have to tell. Diversity is our strength..."

At this point she launched into a speech that Ontario Arts Council Chairwoman Rita Davies would have made better—if she'd been invited—the one about the economic value of culture, the number of jobs it generates, the percentage of GDP it represents. For some reason this roused a man who was leaning against a wall to burst into hoots and hollers and a fit of handclapping as if she'd done a quadruple toe loop. "Think big for today and tomorrow," she concluded. At which point she introduced Scott Shortliffe, Deputy Director General Broadcasting and Digital Communications, Canadian Heritage, to "frame the questions."

Shortliffe, a chubby fellow in a sweater, gave a talk about the culture ecosystem and the federal tool kit available to tinker with it. Apparently, no one in the Department of Canadian Heritage worries about mixing metaphors.

Finally, a man from Ipsos named some of the other important people in the room—a person named Corey Vidal who has 71 million YouTube views, someone from Vice Media, someone else from Twitter, and, oh yes, the brand-new Vice-chairwoman of TVO, Ms. Trina McQueen. Everyone was asked to tweet as they worked, this tweeting was very important. "This is a working session," he said enthusiastically. "You guys get to do the heavy lifting. As the Minister said, be bold."

The event was live-streamed on Facebook. Most comments I read later were complaints that the audio wasn't good, that the social media participants couldn't hear what was being said by the people in the room. My stomach began to growl because I was fasting, October 12 being Yom Kippur. I fast on Yom Kippur (though I also work on Yom Kippur, which makes no sense at all from a religious point of view, but then religion makes no sense from any point of view). I did not stay for the remainder of the in-person event, nor did I stay for the Minister's scrum. I went home.

I pulled out the policy person's card and emailed her as she'd asked me to do. Who was invited to these events? I asked. What are their affiliations? Were there any publishers in the room? Names please?

No response.

I found that sufficiently annoying that I filed one more Access to Information application on October 17, 2016, with the Department of Canadian Heritage. I asked for a list of the names and affiliations of all those invited to participate in the in-person events on Canadian content in a digital world. I asked for a list of all those who attended, and in particular, I asked for the names of any book publishers or newspaper or periodical publishers, and the names of any writers who attended. I also asked for the names of the five Members of Parliament who attended in Toronto, and their constituencies.

Please note: I used the word "list" twice.

Remember that word.

I placed a bet with myself: they will answer on time, but they will withhold most of what you want to know. I wagered fifty cents.

The federal government gives itself thirty days to respond to Access to Information requests. It must do so either by sending out the documents requested, or, by giving itself more time to get permissions from third parties or to extend the search to other departments. I filed my request online. The response arrived several days after the date stamped on its cover letter—November 16, 2016—29 days after I filed. The Department had made it just under the wire, if you consider stamping a date on a letter the same thing as delivering it on time.

The response included a CD-ROM. I opened it and printed the contents out. It consisted of a few unlabelled pages that seemed to be a list of those who attended the Toronto event—I knew that because Paul Gross's name was there and so was the name of one person—one!—from the book publishing community. Barbara Howson was listed as representing "Anansi Press and Groundwood Books." House of Anansi Press owns Groundwood Books. (Stoddart used to own House of Anansi. Now, Scott Griffin does.) Though Barbara Howson's title was not on this sheet, I can tell you that she is the Vice-President for Sales and Licensing. No other book publishers' names appeared.

A member of the Prime Minister's Youth Council was on the list. Names, affiliations and "justifications" were given for some names, but not for others. I found Elaine Waisglas's name, but she was not identified in any way. Michael Hirsh wasn't identified either, nor was Trina McQueen, the new Vice-Chairwoman of TVO. Email addresses, twitter handles, whether the person was under the age of 40, Aboriginal, etc., were withheld.

The covering letter directed me to an attendees list for all five cities involved, which had been posted to the Department's website. The information regarding the Toronto attendees as posted on the website differed from the list sent to me on the CD-ROM. Though I scoured all the lists, I found only one other book publisher person: she worked for an English language trade book publishers' association in BC, and had attended the Vancouver event. She had formerly worked for Toronto's Coach House Press. There was a scattering of representatives from newspaper publishers' associations represented at the events in the West. But there were four times as many representatives from Telus as from book publishers.

No MPs' names appeared on any of the lists.

The cover letter said: "Please note that information is withheld under subsection 19(1) [personal information] and paragraph 21(1) (a) [advice or recommendations.]

Attached to the letter were these sections of the *Access to Information Act*. A section also relied on from the *Privacy Act* was not enclosed. I reproduce these sections here as an endnote for anyone interested enough to read them.[380]

Privacy was claimed for almost all of the blackouts, except for a curious one beside what appeared to be a short biographical note on a woman described there as a poet. This note was deemed to be exempt under section 21.1(a) of the *Access to Information Act,* which deals with advice.

The last page said that pages 9 to 14 of this unnamed document "are withheld pursuant to section 19(1) of the *Access to Information Act."*

I got in touch with Barbara Howson to ask her how she came to be the only publisher invited. She explained it was probably because she had previously been invited to an advisory session organized by the Department of Canadian Heritage, the Canada Council, and Global Affairs Canada. [Global Affairs is the new name for the Department of Foreign Affairs which was originally called External Affairs: apparently, nothing is foreign or external to us now.] That meeting had been about the budget commitment to promote "and export Canadian artists and cultural industries" abroad. Howson explained that her name had been put forward to contribute to that policy-making exercise because she has been active with the Canadian Publishers Association, along with other groups, and Anansi is a leading Canadian publisher.

So what happened at the in-person event? I asked. What did you talk about? Was there any discussion about doing away with the law protecting Canadian publishers from foreign owners?

She described the event as being "broader in scope." They did not seem to understand, she said, that "digital for publishing is a very different concept than digital in dance, music, film, interactive or gaming. All these areas were represented."

She had tried to raise publishing issues such as the recent changes to the *Copyright Act.* The *Act's* "educational exemption" allows schools to copy and distribute published works without payment of royalties. She also tried to talk about "having a healthy Canadian-owned ecosystem—author, publishers, distributors, wholesalers, retailers, online and bricks and mortar."

She didn't get far, being the only one in the room with a direct interest in these subjects. So, apparently everything had *not* been on the table. The Canadian ownership of Canadian publishers as dictated by the *Investment Canada Act* and the Book Policy had not come up.

On the cover letter to the Department's response to my Access to Information request I found the name and number of a person to call if I had any questions. I had questions. I wanted to know why the names of the MPs who attended the Toronto event did not appear in the CD-ROM, which apparently listed attendees, nor on the published list of attendees on the Department's website. I also wanted to know why some seemingly innocuous and publishable information had been blacked out.

Louise Bertrand explained that certain things were blacked out because some of those who attended gave their permission to reveal it, but some did not.

Well yes, I said, but I asked for the names of the MPs who attended in Toronto and their names were not included.

She said she had no knowledge of any MPs.

I told her the Minister had named them in her speech which was live-streamed, but inaudible, so I could not get them from that source and they were not listed on the website. I asked if she could please get me those names.

She reiterated she knew nothing about any MPs.

But they were there, I said, and they are not on the lists you have provided. Please go back and ask for the names.

She said the names did not appear anywhere, and that was that.

I began to shout. There must have been emails sent out to invite them, I said.

Nothing in the Department, she said.

But then the Minister's Press Secretary will have them, please go and ask because there has to be a list, there had to be emails, they were there.

She became unhappy with my tone. She said that there were many others making requests and my request could go to the back of the line if I continued to speak in that fashion.

I said: are you threatening me? Then I said that I'd asked for the list of invitees: but no list sent to me showed who had been invited, only who attended.

She said that is private.

It was a public series of events, I said. (I confess: by then I was yelling again.) It was live-streamed. You have a public duty to release that information.

She said I could make a complaint.

It might have been wise, and it would have been better for my blood pressure, if I had just stopped there, accepted what they sent me and left it at that. But I was beyond hopping mad. Because: I felt as if the whole exercise of asking people for their advice, of holding in-person events, of holding nation-wide online consultations concerning the cultural future—which surely should have included the future of Canadian publishing because hey, we're invited to be the honoured guest at the Frankfurt Book Fair in 2020!—had been a put-up job. This Minister, this government, had no intention of grabbing hold of the third rail of Canadian politics. While this Minister had said everything is on the table, she did not intend to risk her political neck with a public debate over whether the government should continue to protect Canadian publishers from foreign ownership. She intended to leave the *Investment Canada Act* provisions and the Policy as is—likely until there are no Canadian publishers left standing.

How did I know that? You don't invite only one actual representative of English-language publishing to a public consultation in Toronto on Yom Kippur, the same one you already consulted in private, if you really want such issues to be publicly addressed. That's what you do if you want to shove those issues under the table while maintaining you've been exhaustive in pursuit of a shiny new policy. When it is pointed out that there is nothing in that policy that pertains to the Canadian ownership of Canadian publishers, you will be able to say that's not the government's fault, publishers were represented, let's move on.

Did the Canadian government still believe that Canadian-owned publishers are necessary to defend Canada's national sovereignty? I did not think so. The Prime Minister had said there is no core Canadian identity. The Prime Minister is a globalist, not a nationalist. But that didn't mean that his government intended to take the so-called publishing "ecosystem" in hand and reshape it, either. It seemed quite clear that this government intended to do what the Harper and Martin and Chrétien governments did before: keep the elected out of the line of fire as the bureaucrats help friends and treat troublemakers or neutral parties to a sharp dose of the law.

I was angry at myself more than at the bureaucrats in the Department. I had made the mistake of taking this exercise seriously, because I do that, and because I expect my political representatives to do that. But they have other ideas.

Personal insight notwithstanding, I couldn't leave well enough alone.

I followed up with a call to Jaye Jarvis, the Director of Access in the Department of Canadian Heritage. I left a message stating the file number, demanding an explanation.

When we spoke on the phone, I was still simmering. I mean come on, what is simpler and less invasive of privacy than providing a list of names of people already mentioned as attendees in a public speech by the Minister?

Ms. Jarvis was very friendly. She had looked at the file, she saw what I'd asked for and what was sent. The *Act* requires the Department to follow it strictly, she said. (Wrong again, I wanted to shout, you've got more room to move than the average elephant, but for a change I held my tongue.) The Department can only provide what is in the control of the Department, not something within the office of the Minister.

What do you mean you can't give me stuff from the office of the Minister? I shouted. Yes, I admit it, I shouted, because I had already received material given to the Minister, and therefore held in the office of the Minister, in response to my last Access to Information request. Everything I had been sent then could have been classified as advice to the Minister and withheld under section 21 of the *Act*. Instead, someone had decided to show me what the Minister was told to say in response to questions in the House or from reporters about the transfer of McClelland & Stewart by the U of T to Random House in 2011. And they sent me stuff I didn't ask for—as had the U of T.

Well, she said, there was a Supreme Court of Canada ruling in a suit brought by the Information Commissioner versus the Privy

Council Office. It was determined that anything in the Minister's office must be withheld. The case had something to do with agendas. "The Minister's office is not subject to the *Act,*" she said.

I'd like that citation please, I said.

She said she would send it. I could say I'm still waiting for it, but that would not be true, not because she sent it, she did not, but because I searched it myself. She was right. The Supreme Court found in 2011, after various cases and appeals of those cases had worked their way up to that august bench, that a Minister or the Prime Minister is not an employee of a government institution, and so the Minister's offices are not adjuncts of the Departments they oversee, and so the information in their offices (such as the Prime Minister's agendas, which is what the Information Commissioner was trying to disclose) are outside the reach of the *Access to Information Act.*[381]

But the real problem with my request, she told me, was that I had asked for lists. "We responded to the request," she said. "We cannot give records that don't exist. We gave you the list that was available. There is no list of Members of Parliament who attended..."

But they were there, I said. The Minister named them in her speech which was live-streamed on Facebook, so someone invited them, which means there are emails...

"That they attended, I have no doubt," she said, "we cannot create lists after the fact."

There is nothing in the *Act* that says that, I said. I asked once again for a court citation. We are entitled to this information, I said to her, no, yelled at her. The Ministers all have mandates from the Prime Minister to be transparent and open. Yet your Department has even withheld Twitter handles for people asked to tweet at the event, which means the event was public, so their handles are public, you understand that, right?

Twitter (handles) are withheld under section 19(1), personal information, she said. Twitter handles and bios.

Except bios appear alongside some of the names in the document you sent. Did your people ask people whose bio sections are blank if they wanted their Twitter handles and bios withheld as personal information?

Well, she said, it would have taken more time.

But the Department did not ask for an extension, I said.

No response.

I want the names of the MPs, I said, once again in a fury. I intend to publish this, which is going to be very embarrassing for you. For goodness sake, you can't give me the names of five MPs named by the Minister in her unfortunately inaudible speech at a live-streamed event? Five names?

We don't make lists, she said.

And that was the end of the beginning.

The Wrap Up—Useful for Fish

When I set out on this journey, one of my informants asked me these questions: who are you? What do you want? Later, the accountant, Ron Scott, asked: why do you care?

You would think I could spit out the answers after so much time spent asking other people questions. But I am still unsure how to describe who I am, or what it is I want. And perhaps that is because I am still uncertain about the virtues of cultural nationalism, the government policies and law that enabled it, and the bureaucrats who let the whole thing die.

I do know this: Canada has come to the end of a political cycle that erupted with the October Crisis in 1970, was further galvanized by the Nixon Shock, the grinding horror of the Vietnam War, and other egregious behaviours of our southern neighbour. These factors led to the first articulation by the elder Trudeau of a new kind of Canada, one where everyone would be welcome, where all ethnicities have equal place. Trudeau employed nationalist/protectionist policies the way a fisherman casts a lure, to hook unhappy boomer voters and drag us back onside. But he wasn't committed to them. And subsequent Prime Ministers behaved as if Canadian economic nationalism was a major mistake for any trading nation, especially this one, a mistake that had to be rectified, but very, very carefully. Cultural nationalism was employed to placate wary boomers so they could get that job done.

Now, Canada's Prime Minister propounds a globalist policy.

But the rest of the world is just entering a phase that Canada has apparently left behind, a nationalist/protectionist cycle marked by familiar milestones: murderous bombs in the streets; threats of exits from federations; arguments over defending national boundaries; the rekindling of ancient, ethnic animosities. Splintering is its own reward: the UK's vote to leave the European Union reinvigorated Scottish nationalists in their determination to leave the UK. Marine Le Pen's run for the Presidency of France included a call to reinstate France's borders, to permit the French to be French. Nationalist parties began to attract big blocks of votes in Germany, the Netherlands, Italy, and Greece because the economies of northern and southern Europe are at sixes and sevens, but also because too many dark-skinned refugees who pray facing East have fled to these havens to escape bombs and dictators and thugs. The appearance in northern towns of brown men, and women wearing head scarves or veils, is seen by some as an assault on the culture of white Europeans. And so the pillars of the European Union—that vast federation meant to be a peaceful and alluring market for multinational corporations—shake like the limbs of an addict hunting his next fix.

And then there is the reality show unfolding next door. Watching the nationalist brouhaha in the US over: the wall to keep the Mexicans out; the old, white, male billionaires, investment bankers, and that oilman appointed to the Cabinet so Trump can make America Great (First) Again; the retraction of visas and the slamming of doors in the faces of desperate refugees who had the bad taste to be born in the wrong countries; the bizarre utterances of Stephen Bannon (the éminence grise in President Trump's backroom) who has compared himself to Lenin while also calling himself an American sovereigntist, is enough to put anyone off protectionism, economic or cultural.

In fact, all of this, but especially the murders of six Muslim men in a Quebec City mosque (who had to be buried elsewhere because the Quebec City Council had not yet seen fit to permit Muslims their own cemetery), induces appreciation for globalist ideals. The dream of One World is so strong that some people think that such a global order (to which we all will belong by definition) is already a political fact. A few years back, I crossed the border to the US on a bus. A drunk climbed aboard in Windsor, only to be hauled off in Detroit as the dogs sniffed our bags for drugs. He had no papers to prove his identity and nationality, nothing to show where he belonged.

"Hey," he cried as they dragged him from his seat and into the customs shed, "you can't do that, I'm a Citizen of the World!"

And yet there is something about cultural nationalism as practiced here that still appeals to me: to quote that great Canadian poet, Joni Mitchell, whose songs are known around the globe, but who first found fame in the US:

"Don't it always seem to go
that you don't know what you've got
till it's gone…"

Cultural nationalism forged a different Canada from the one I was born to. The Canada I was born to could not hear itself think, and served as a treasure house for two competing empires, its economy managed in their interests. Those empires did not care to hear from us, were not interested in our stories unless they could smell profits in them, or they could have been written by one of their own. Cultural nationalism, enforced by law and policy, allowed us to see ourselves, to hear ourselves, but most of all, to acquire a sense of Us and to see what We have accomplished, the good as well as the awful. That's how our national community grew strong enough to acknowledge the wrongs we did to those whose lands we stole by decree and treaty, by trickery and deceit, and whose children we destroyed through 'education' designed to wipe out their group identities.

This brings me to the issue of identity. According to the Prime Minister, Canadians do not have a national identity and do not need one. Yet there is a need, a hunger, in most of us that globalism can never fulfill, a longing that ethnic nationalism or tribalism or religious fundamentalism or racism or criminal gangsterism is sometimes able to satisfy. Humans must, by necessity, belong to intimate groups. Don't believe the 19th Century nonsense about rugged individuals dragging themselves up by their bootstraps and succeeding on their own. No one *survives*, let alone succeeds, on her own. We construct our individual identities from our interactions in small groups. Group identities are shaped by shared history. Shared history creates a framework for our personal narratives: it anchors us, even as the ground shifts under our feet. Group identity is a pacifier we suck on in the face of all kinds of terrors: it helps obscure the scary truth that all truths will be rewritten, that nothing is stable, that change is inevitable. We use our shared stories to hang on to each other even as we are being torn apart.

Example: I fast on Yom Kippur, though I also work that day if I have to, in spite of the fact that work is forbidden to Jews on High Holidays. I fast: yet I am as religious as a sock. Why? To satisfy that longing. On Yom Kippur, when I fast, there is a group to which I clearly belong.

The Prime Minister of Canada had the awful task of speaking at a funeral service in Montreal for those shot in the mosque in Quebec City. Globalists have trouble speaking to identity, but human communities require that their leaders do so. He had to assert his father's idea of Canada—inclusive, pluralist, a mosaic—over a narrower form of identity, an ethnic or racist one that is violently exclusive. Trudeau said: "It is with a heavy heart that we come together this afternoon to grieve the loss of these innocent lives. But as a community and as a country, together we will rise from this darkness stronger and more unified than ever before—that is who we are."[382]

Note: he acknowledged there is a Canadian We, but he did not describe who we are, he only referred to what we must do, as if group action is the same as identity. But identity is not just a function of action. Though the globalist idea is rational and seems utterly obvious (of *course* all human beings everywhere are equal, of *course* the world belongs to us all) reason has little to do with identity, the need for which arises out of physical vulnerability. Countries are not intimate groups, even when they're very small, yet they are much more intimate than the entire world. So it's not a question of whether globalism makes sense or whether we are or are not past the need for nationalist policies, it's more a question of whether human beings can live meaningful lives in a globalized world. Globalism raises these questions: who governs, who decides, and how? Currently, the globalist agenda mainly benefits billionaires who try to manipulate political decisions that affect their interests. How do the rest of us get a vote?

So: what do I want? Here's one answer. I want to belong to an open, pluralist society that respects all its members, expects me to participate in making its choices, and helps me tell its stories. (I want to be young again, too.)

Why do I care? Do I still care?

Maybe I pursued this story not because I care, but just to get to the bottom of it, because it was hard, because I discovered bottomless cleverness at work and I have always been fascinated by cleverness (thus, clever husband). And really: when I did get to the bottom of it, what did I discover? Yes, the law and policy meant to advance Canadian literature through the protection of Canadian publishers was followed, but in a way that gutted the law's spirit and turned the meaning of the policy inside out. But was anyone unjustly enriched? Jack Stoddart thinks Avie Bennett probably got back the total investment he made in M&S over the fifteen years in which he owned it, thanks to the tax credit receipt and the sale to Random House. Bennett was certainly entitled to strive for repayment, but why did civil servants look the other way while the law and the policy on de facto control were twisted like licorice Twizzlers?[383] No doubt they consoled themselves by arguing that they'd at least saved jobs in the book business, and protected their Minister from a hue and cry over cultural nationalism. Yes, clever professionals and a brilliant businessman exploited tax law, the rules of bankruptcy, and the *Investment Canada Act*, turning them one way, and then the opposite way, to get to a desired end. But isn't that kind of flexibility exactly what an efficient economic system requires? Isn't lack of flexibility the grievous flaw that brings down planned economies? The transfer of 75% of the shares of our most important publishing house for $1 may not have been the end point sought by Canadians who write, edit, and make books, but that does not make it wrong.

Maybe the notion that a national literature is vital to national sovereignty is wrong. Or maybe it was right once, but is wrong now. Once, in the second decade of the last century, Canadian book publishing was a thriving business without government support or protectionist rules necessary—back when information was shared in one direction, back before radio and television provided competing means to tell stories. Profits could be made then from the creation and distribution of stories printed on paper. Nowadays, mountains of money are made from the hardware and software which permit stories to be reduced to digits and shared everywhere. Clever machines enable everyone and anyone to be publisher, author, videographer, citizen reporter, stand-up comic, 3-D machinist, controller of robots, nanosecond star, group organizer and rabble rouser. These machines have enabled the birth of an infinite array of information commons, virtual communal places where everything and anything can be made, shared, discussed, distorted, described, misdescribed, faked, all open to everyone in any country that does not censor the Internet. These information commons are utterly different from the kind created by the makers of books, newspapers, and magazines.

The old information commons—books, magazines, newspapers—are the provinces of their gatekeepers. Their precincts are defended by legal and territorial boundaries. I was one of those gatekeepers when I was young. We were so arrogant: we assumed we knew what people wanted to know, and worse, what people needed to know, and worst, who among us had the talent to engage with the audiences who paid to enter our paper communities. But as the new means to distribute storytelling became available, as the young began to connect with each other on Facebook, YouTube, Hulu, advertisers and consumers abandoned the old commons in favour of these multi-directional new ones. Mountain ranges of money accrued to the enablers of every-which-way sharing platforms, rather than to those who create what is shared. Book publishers' revenues have been shrinking and shrinking, because free offerings delivered via these new platforms attract people who can't be bothered to go to a bookstore and hand over money for entertainment or enlightenment.

Advertisers go where the greatest number of eyes can be found. As television audiences also fractured, because there are so many new ways and places to share visual stories, those revenues dived, too. If you want to see really interesting drama and comedy you have likely disconnected your cable and have a cheap subscription to Netflix, which is not regulated or taxed by the government of Canada, and does not care about reflecting Canadians to themselves, or building Canada word by word.

Protectionist laws applied to cultural industries may have been politically necessary and enforceable when I was young, but in a time when information knows no boundaries, some of them have become unenforceable, and therefore economically stupid. My publisher insists that economic inefficiency is beside the point. He argues that some things are worth doing though they have no economic purpose, that creating literature is one of those things, and people do it because they want to, or have to, and not to earn a living. He does not need to remind me: I know I write because I need to, not as a way to be wealthy, but to try to understand myself and the world I live in. That's why I will continue to write though my bank account is a disgrace. But do we really want a public policy that depends on publishers being willing to forgo even the possibility of an upside? Grants have led to the proliferation of many small book publishers who will never earn significant profits, will never be big enough to compete with foreign-owned multinationals for talent, and will find no Canadian buyers for their companies when they are old and grey. The mere existence of the law and the policy depress the value of the companies they build, even though our national cultural commons has not really been protected from foreign buyers for the past 18 years. As Canadian Heritage bureaucrat Jean-Pierre Blais told the Standing Committee on Canadian Heritage in June, 2010, since 1999, more than 90 percent of applications for the sale of Canadian cultural industries to foreign owners were approved. In all that time only three were denied.[384] But our publishers' investments are discounted anyway, just because the *Act* and the Policy exist, just because a bureaucrat and a politician might decide to say no to an application in the future.

Rules are supposed to be enforced, otherwise why have them? In the beginning, these protectionist rules created a mini-economy that allowed me my life as a writer. But later, their creative interpretations by politicians and bureaucrats created something very unhealthy. Instead of a thriving book publishing ecosystem, we have ended up with an endangered one dominated by one foreign book publisher and one Canadian bookseller. The situation for newspapers and magazines is, if anything, worse.

Now it is probably true that writers in midlist (writers who have published a few books, won a few prizes, found a smallish audience, writers like me), never mattered much to the life of this nation. But on the other hand, if Canadians don't tell Canadian stories to each other, what then? How much ignorance of our evolving nature can this nation—any nation—endure and still function as a democracy? Investigating and then telling this story has made clear to me so many things about the way Canada really works, about the intimate ways in which our decision makers and business leaders intersect, interlink, help and hurt each other. I have met many lawyers in my time as a journalist, but pursuing this story convinced me that Canadian lawyers are a special breed. They are hard-nosed, objective, and can turn any argument inside out and upside down and still make it work. These are the kinds of things Canadian readers and voters need to know, that Canadian writers and reporters need to dig into. Would Rupert Murdoch's publishing machine print them? If I had only been able to publish this story on my blog, would you have read it?

And getting back to why I care: not doing wrong is not the same as doing right and not even the citizens of a post national state should delude themselves about that, though we often do. Millions in grants were paid out to McClelland & Stewart, Macfarlane, Walter & Ross, and Tundra as if they were controlled by a Canadian entity, when in fact they were not. Thanks to Copps' Letter of Opinion, this was not legally wrong, because Copps' Letter blessed M&S as "Canadian," regardless of Random House of Canada's de facto control. But it clearly wasn't right, either. There was all that public posturing, and all that praise of the deviser-in-chief, not to mention his elevation to the highest level of the Order of Canada. While Bennett deserves all kinds of praise for his intelligence, his foresight, his planning, and for carefully shepherding M&S at his own expense for 15 years, and then keeping his watchful eye on the place for 11 years more, it is not right that he is praised for what he did not do. He did not keep M&S Canadian. He handed it over.

And what about our leading institution of higher learning, a place devoted to the search for truth, publicly pretending to be in control of M&S while its accountants said the opposite in private? Did that private declaration constitute a new material fact that could have overturned Copps' Opinion, the one pronouncing the new M&S to be Canadian? I am pretty sure lawyers would say no, the material facts had *not* changed, just their interpretation, so the government could not withdraw its blessing from this gift/sale because the government had been made aware of *all* the material facts at the time of the transaction. The Minister and her officials made a Brazilian (for-my-friends-anything-for-my-enemies-the-law) ruling that no matter what the contracts said, the new M&S would be "Canadian." Her officials would have understood and explained that Random House would inevitably end up with 100% of the M&S shares if Copps issued her letter of Opinion. Nevertheless, she issued it. Neither Copps nor her officials can argue that they were misinformed.

Also, I have to say: the sheer size of First Plazas Inc.'s charitable tax credit receipt still sticks in my craw. As I know from reading the testimony given to the Standing Committee on Canadian Heritage in 2000 (and as that mysterious Q. and A. in my Canadian Heritage *Access to Information* file made clear), $15,900,000 amounted to almost half the dollars dispensed annually to Canadian publishers by the Canadian Heritage book fund then, and now. By the time the correct tax formula was applied, Bennett may have realized much less than that amount as cash, but still, the government might have been able to use that money to help others. In 2000, 10,000 books were produced by Canadian publishers, half by Canadians. As the law was ignored and the policy upended, the number of books originated annually in Canada declined to about 6500—a drop of almost 40%—and the number authored by Canadians fell to 4,000.[385] What if $15,900,000 had been used to support an investment tax credit for the Canadian publishing industry? Would Key Porter Books, or McArthur & Company, or General Publishing, or Stoddart Publishing, to name a few extinct Canadian companies, still be in business?

What should we do?

I'm just a reporter. I find stories and tell them. I don't hold myself out as a person able to invent great public policy. On the other hand, I no longer expect good policy to come from the Department of Canadian Heritage. Maybe the Department agrees with me. The Department contracted the Public Policy Forum in 2016 to generate recommendations on what to do about dead and dying Canadian newspapers and the disappearance of local TV news. The Public Policy Forum is directed by people who work for large interests with global aspirations—BCE, the Royal Bank, Ernst & Young, the Munk School of Global Affairs, etc.—as well as by bureaucrats running governments. As the Deputy Clerk of the Privy Council sits on its board, along with the Deputy Minister of Citizenship and Immigration, and the Secretary to the Ontario Cabinet, the Public Policy Forum cannot be considered an *independent* think tank, though it might appear that way to some. It's more like a cheerleader for policies the government wants to promote, or, a test bed for policies that bureaucrats would like to expose in public so that political costs may be estimated in advance of commitments.

The Forum published its report in January, 2017.[386] "The Shattered Mirror: News, Democracy and Trust in the Digital Age" was written by the Forum's CEO, Edward Greenspon, a former Editor-in-Chief of the *Globe and Mail*, a former strategist for Torstar, and not so long ago a journalist for *Bloomberg News*. It called for drastic measures to support Canadian journalism in order to defend democracy, defeat the rise of "fake news," and reverse the disastrous consequences of the terrible, galloping decline of Canadian print and television news operations. The recommendations were intricate yet sweeping. Significantly, the report did not call for Canadian ownership rules to be enforced. It called for, among other things, changes to tax law and the CRA's charity rules to grab back some of the profits siphoned from the Canadian market by the likes of Netflix, Google and Facebook, and to redirect them to fund "civic" journalism by Canadian reporters and editors working for whoever owns their publishing companies.

The government is clearly no longer interested in protecting Canadian publishers from foreign buyers. Yet who owns what does matter, especially when it comes to newspapers. It took Jeff Bezos, the founder of Amazon, to haul the *Washington Post* back from the brink: he did it in part through the use of Artificial Intelligence which wrote some of the *Post's* coverage of the 2016 US federal election (which doesn't bode well for the future of human journalists). Apparently, he wanted to save the *Post* because the *Post's* journalism is necessary to American democracy and he's an American. The Sulzberger family, which owns the *New York Times,* is also engaged in a desperate struggle to keep that newspaper alive as it transforms itself to fit our digital age.[387] Would either of them fight so hard to support the *Toronto Star* if they were its foreign owners? Do Americans care as much as Canadians about Canadian democracy?

I don't know if Prime Minister Justin Trudeau is right when he asserts that Canada has arrived at a place no country has even tried to get to before, a place beyond nationhood. I don't know if Canadian literature has actually become a Literature of the World. I do know that we didn't create a protectionist publishing policy in order to make a Literature of the World: we did it to reflect ourselves to ourselves. And the need to see ourselves so we can govern ourselves will never disappear.

While I don't have any better suggestions than those offered by the Public Policy Forum, I think that finding the right ones may matter much more now, in this globalized yet splintering world, than when I was young, when opportunity was created by governments for writers like me to tell Canadian stories.

Just because I don't know what to do, doesn't mean I don't care.

I do care. And I demand that you care.

Because: we're Canadian.

Acknowledgements

I would like to thank the Government of Ontario for giving me a grant from the Writers' Reserve program. I would also like to thank the friends knowledgeable about the publishing business who spoke to me informally and provided very valuable insights. While I cannot name you, I can, and do, thank you for trusting me.

Several friends and colleagues took the time to read various versions of this manuscript and comment on them. I never know if my work is readable until the people I really write for, my friends and relatives, have given me their opinions. Philip Turner, a former US bookseller and then publishing executive and now editor, agent, blogger and writer, who is the next best thing to an honourary Canadian, edited my last book, *Smarts*. He agreed to read an early version of this manuscript when it was still lumpy and disagreeable and no fun to read at all. His positive response gave me the courage to finish. Charles Greene, who has been my dear friend, and my husband Stephen's dear friend and business partner, since 1971, also read the manuscript. He had many, many changes to suggest, because he read with great attention, and all of his suggestions were helpful. Stephen, my husband and partner and collaborator-in-chief, read the manuscript in its early form when I was quite sure I should just forget the whole thing, and said keep going, it's worth the trouble. Thank you, Stephen: if it doesn't work out well, I'll blame you, as usual. My good friend, the journalist, video producer and former magazine editor, Dawn Deme, read the manuscript when I thought I was done. She was able to show me that I was not. Dawn gave me some of my most interesting journalism assignments when she was the Editor of

City Woman magazine. Those long form pieces prepared me to tackle books, so in many ways, I owe my career as an author to her, but her friendship matters more. The thing about forever friends like Dawn and Chuck, and the love of my life, Stephen, is that we always seem to be interested by the same phenomena, but each from a different perspective. Our conversations have been going on now for more than forty years without any diminution of interest.

Finding a Canadian independent publisher who would consider taking on this book was the unhappy task of my agent, Sam Hiyate, of The Rights Factory. Because he could not offer it to foreign-owned publishers, he could not hope to have anything like fair recompense for his work, but he did it anyway. Thank you, Sam, for all your efforts, and for helping me find Dan Wells, publisher of Biblioasis, who was willing to stick his neck out. After all, another Canadian independent publisher turned this project down because it might upset friends working for foreign-owned publishers.

Dan and his associate, the very able editor John Metcalf—a Member of the Order of Canada for his long service to Canadian literature—worked this book over from end to end. John does not use a computer, and so he does not use email. One communicates with him on the telephone or on paper, which is sent through snail mail in an envelope with an actual stamp, a technology stretching far back into the most distant haze of time. He writes his notes on a physical copy of the manuscript by hand. John argued with me that this book should be treated seriously, that I was too flip, that the personal stories went on far too long. He labelled them char for character and drew lines through them indicating that they belonged in the trash. I love telling stories, human stories, my own stories, so I was inclined at first to throw John in the trash, but gradually his point of view acquired merit. So I strove to find a better balance between char and straight reportage. While some char has been retained (because this is a story and stories need characters, and this story, being a business story, needed a lot of character to get readers past legal jargon and the numbers), his comments turned out to be really helpful.

Dan Wells is young, but is nevertheless an old-school publisher who actually reads and rereads and rereads again the entire manuscript he has decided to bring out and keeps coming back at his writers on all points that he is concerned about, that he believes could be improved. He invariably pointed to real weaknesses in my argument or in my storytelling and often had ideas about how to strengthen the argument with more end notes or how to tighten the stories and pace them better. Dan provided the kind of editorial experience that I so prized when working with Marq de Villiers as he edited *Toronto Life* or with Dawn Macdonald when she ran *City Woman*. He took extraordinary care, as they did, to bring to readers the very best work he could induce a writer to produce.

Working with Dan and John was heartening: I was relieved to find that careful attention is still brought to bear in Canadian publishing. Artists who use words need editors and publishers who will help wring the very best from them. Do you hear that Canada Council and Department of Canadian Heritage? It's important to fund the artists, but don't forget to send Canadian publishers more money!

This story presented a number of difficulties in the telling. Stuart Robertson, for many years a leading lawyer advising writers and publishers on the laws relating to publishing, is an expert on how to look those difficulties in the eye and to find a way to appropriately frame a story (fingers crossed!) so it can be told fairly. He is subtle, careful, can imagine how words may be misconstrued, and always draws a bead on confused or ill-considered prose. He improved this book in every way. Thank you, Stuart for your care and kindness.

All the people who helped produce and market this book—thank you. Natalie Hamilton and Casey Plett took charge of publicity. Chris Andrechek designed and with Ellie Hastings managed the production. Copy-editing and Indexing were done by Allana Amlin. And the cover design is by Michel Vrana.

All those who permitted me to interview them but insisted that their names be withheld, thank you for your time and your information, and I hope that you can live with the result. I am in debt to all those who allowed me to interview them and permitted their names to stand. Jack Stoddart and Marc Côté were especially helpful and gave me a lot of their time. Robert Prichard pointed me in the right direction: this book would not have been possible without his suggestions. Avie Bennett was good enough to give me an interview, for which I am most grateful. Doug Gibson gave me two, and suffered many questions which were discomfiting, so thank you Doug. John Honderich was open, helpful, and focused on what really matters, as always: thank you, John. The University of Toronto's office of Freedom of Information and Protection of Privacy was extremely helpful, and in the end, University of Toronto was as open and transparent as it could be. A special thanks to Elaine Waisglas and Michael Hirsh for getting me into that in-person event in Toronto when the Department of Canadian Heritage was trying to keep me out.

All errors that remain after fact checking and Googling and endless arguments about what things might mean with clever husband, are of course my own.

End Notes

1   Attributed to Getulio Vargas, both an elected President of Brazil, and later, its dictator.

2   "Giving Away the Store," Brian Bethune, *Maclean's*, July 10, 2000.

3   See: Jason McBride, "It's Alive: Canadian book publishing stirs" Canadianbusiness. com, August 20, 2013.

4   Figures for Ontario, where about 80 percent of English language publishing takes place, are provided by the Ontario Media Development Corporation. In 2010, Ontario-based book publishers had operating revenue of $1.286 billion reduced to $1.23 billion in 2012, a 6% decline. Operating profits also decreased from $144,771 million to $115,036 million. See: "Industry Profiles, Book Publishing" at omdc.on.ca/collaboration/research and industry information. Federal figures are available from Statistics Canada in the Daily under the title Book Publishers. The report of May 6, 2016, describes book publishing in Canada for the year 2014. Total operating revenue for all Canadian publishing was only $1.7 billion on total sales, of $1.4 billion of which 81% were domestic, 18% foreign. Trade books accounted for $331 million of those sales, whereas educational publishing took in revenues of $366 million. Due to the bankruptcy or shutdown of several Canadian independents and the government- permitted sale of Canadian companies to foreign owners, such as Penguin Random House Canada, $472 million of foreign-owned companies' titles were sold in Canada that year, versus $335.4 million that were originated by Canadian-owned companies. Foreign authors sold $683 million worth of books in Canada, whereas Canadian authors sold fewer—$681 million. Ebook sales amounted to only 13% of total sales. Total number of new published titles (all forms including educational and trade) were 14,218, of which 10,433 were Canadian. See: Book Publishing Industry 2014, at statscan.gc.ca.

5   Newspaper publishing has declined radically. In 2015, total Canadian newspaper revenues fell to $1.4 billion, down 12.6% from 2014. National advertising income fell 24.2%, half of what it had been in 2012. See: "Canada newspaper ad revenue slumped in 2015: industry group" by Alistair Sharp, Reuters.com, May 13, 2016.

6   See: "North Star," by Guy Lawson, *New York Times Magazine*," December 13, 2015.

7   See: "Language of Nazism revived in Germany: long-taboo terms defended under guise of free speech as nationalist feelings surge," by Anthony Faiola and Stephanie Kirchner, *The Washington Post*, as published in *Toronto Star*, December 11, 2016.
8   See: StatsCan Publication 2012, 87F004X—Publishers and also *The Perilous Trade*, Roy MacSkimming, page 4.
9   See: "Indigo Reports Q1 Results: Strong revenue growth continues same store sales growth 7.7%," August 9, 2016, attributes double digit growth to general merchandise category.
10 See: Book Publishing in Canada: Market Research Report, January 2016, at Ibisworld.ca/industry/book_publishing.html. See also: "It's Alive: Canadian book publishing stirs," by Jason McBride, *Canadianbusiness.com*, August 20, 2013.
11 See: 2013 Salary Survey, *Quill & Quire*, at: quillandquire.com/wp-content/uploads/QQ-salary-survey-2013.pdf.
12 See: Book Publishing in Canada: Market Research Report, January 2016, by Ibisworld. Book industry revenues and unit sales have been declining steadily since 2009, and this trend is expected to continue through 2020. Book publishing's contribution to Canada's GDP has been declining at about 1.8% per year and that trend too is expected to continue though 2020 while Canadian GDP grows at the rate of about 2.1% per year over the same period. See: Ibisworld.ca/industry/book_publishing.html.
13 The leaders and main decision makers of Penguin Random House Canada are Kristin Cochrane, President, and Brad Martin, CEO.
14 See: "Book Publishing in Canada: Market Research Report," January 2016, Ibisworld, at ibisworld.ca/industry/book publishing.html.
15 The joke goes like this: the man's family looked for him here, there, and everywhere for years and years. They hired private detectives, they scoured the obituaries of faraway newspapers, but he'd vanished without a trace. Finally, one of the man's brothers heard he was working in a travelling circus, a circus coming soon to their town. When it arrived, the whole family went to see the show under the Big Top hoping to catch sight of him. No luck. Disappointed, downcast, they had just about given up when they finally spotted him, dressed in a clown suit, sweeping up the piles of fresh poop left in the sand by the elephants and the big cats. They ran to him, grabbed him, hugged him.
    All is forgiven, they said, please, please leave this sordid life you're living and come home with us.
    What? he replied with total disdain. And give up show business?
16 Ibid, Daily, Book Industry, Statistics Canada, May, 2016.
17 StatsCan survey of Canadian publishing 2012, 87F004X-Book Publishers
18 See: "Devaluing Creators: Endangering Creativity" 2015, the report of an income survey by The Writers Union of Canada along with *Quill & Quire* at www.writersunionon.ca/sites/all/files.

19 *The Perilous Trade: Book Publishing in Canada 1946–2000,* by Roy MacSkimming, McClelland & Stewart, trade paperback edition 2007.

20 See: Petroleum Industries, *The Canadian Encyclopedia,* www.canadianencylopedia.ca

21 *Who Has Seen the Wind,* W.O. Mitchell, Macmillan, 1947; *People of the Deer,* Farley Mowat, Little Brown, 1952; *The Golden Trail,* Pierre Berton, Macmillan, 1952.

22 "Rhetoric and the Trajectory of Multicultural Policy in Canada and the United Kingdom," by Anna Dewar, unpublished MRes Thesis in Public Policy and Management, School of Politics and Sociology, Birkbeck College, University of London, 2007.

23 See: *The Perilous Trade* by Roy MacSkimming, McClelland & Stewart, 2007, p. 30.

24 Ibid, MacSkimming, p. 31

25 Ibid, MacSkimming, p. 24.

26 Ibid, MacSkimming, p. 23.

27 Ibid, MacSkimming, p.154.

28 Ibid, MacSkimming, p. 141-147

29 Ibid, MacSkimming, p. 147-148.

30 http://http://www.thecanadianencyclopedia.ca/en/article/committee-for-an-independent-canada.

31 Ibid, MacSkimming, pp. 147–149.

32 For all this material on the Waffle within the NDP I am indebted to Cameron Smith's remarkable history of the Lewis family. *Unfinished Journey: The Lewis Family,* Summerhill Press, 1989. See page 451.

33 Ibid, Cameron Smith, p. 438.

34 Ibid, Cameron Smith, pp. 440–450.

35 See: "Nationalism Versus Continentalism: Ideology in the Mirror of the MacDonald Royal Commission," Ph.D. thesis of Gregory Inwood, 1997, University of Toronto.

36 See: "Canadian Culture/Trade Quandary and the Magazine Case" by Dennis Browne, *Canadian Parliamentary Review,* February 20, 1998.

37 See: Office of the Historian at https://history.state.gov/milestones/1969-1976.

38 See: "The Cold Facts" by John Aitken, *Maclean's,* February 1, 1974.

39 We presumed and we were right: see Chile and the United States: Declassified Documents Relating to the Military Coup, September 11, 1973, Peter Kornbluh, National Security Archive Electronic Briefing Book No. 8.

40 See: "Inside the Watergate Hearings," by John S. Leopold, *Maclean's,* December 1, 1973.

41 See: *Cloak of Green,* by Elaine Dewar, chapter 16, endnote 2 on the role of MA Hanna and John J. McCloy in the 1964 coup.

42 Ibid, MacSkimming, p. 214.

43 See: "Canadian Foreign Investment Review Act Revisited" by Barry J. O'Sullivan, *Fordham International Law Journal,* Article 8, Vol. 4, Issue 1, 1980. See also how

Bantam was taken over by M&S, and Simon & Schuster was forced to partner with General Publishing, as described by MacSkimming in *The Perilous Trade*, p. 328.

44 See: "Canada. Hanging Out the Welcome Sign," by Jamie Murphy, *Time Magazine*, Dec. 24, 1984.

45 See: "Mister Right" by Michael Posner, *The Walrus*, September 12, 2012. See also bio of Charles McMillan, Shulich School, York University.

46 See: The Investment Canada Act: Thresholds for Review, at www.ic.gc.ca/iec/site/ica-lc.nf/eng/h.

47 Ibid, *Investment Canada Act*, Section 14.

48 See: a careful explanation of the origin of the policy in *Yankee Doodle Dandy: Brian Mulroney* , by Marci McDonald, p. 162–163.

49 The popular vote was 5,667,543 for the Progressive Conservative; 4,205,072 for the Liberals; 2,685,263 for the NDP. The PCs and Liberals won almost the same number of seats in Ontario: the Conservatives won the election due to the number of seats won in Quebec and Alberta.

50 See: The Daily, Book Publishing 2014, Statistics Canada, May 2016.

51 According to Statistics Canada, only 22.6% of households had a computer in 1999.

52 The first blogging software was made available in 1999, but came into its own after September 11, 2001, when major news media could not keep up with events. See *Blogging: How Our Private Thoughts Went Public*, by Kristin Roeschenthaler Wolfe, p. 9.

53 YouTube was founded by three PayPal employees in 2005, and bought by Google in 2006.

54 See: Evidence, Standing Committee on Canadian Heritage, testimony of Michael Wernick, May 9, 2000.

55 See: Copps' Letter of Opinion June 23, 2000, copy in possession of the author.

56 See: "Giving Away the Store: Avie Bennett's unprecedented donation of industry icon McClelland & Stewart brings praise—and a storm of criticism," by Brian Bethune, *Maclean's*, July 10, 2000.

57 See: "Has the Canadian Government Turned the Page on Its Book Policy? An Opportunity for Foreign Investors to Consider Investments in the Canadian Book Industry," by Shawn C.D. Neylan, Michael Kilby, John Leopold, Michael Gelinas of Stikeman Elliott LLP, June, 2014.

58 My entanglements with both the foreign-owned and the Canadian-owned side of Canadian publishing, and with several other entities involved in this story, include the following:

James Lorimer, a Canadian publisher and diehard evangelist for a nationalist Canadian publishing policy, saved the second book I wrote, *Cloak of Green*, from oblivion. It had been sold originally to the Canadian "controlled" subsidiary of a foreign entity (meaning the Canadian company was owned 51% by Canadians who theoretically controlled it, and 49% by the foreign entity that actually did). The Canadian owners were my former agents. They had bought my book at the proposal stage from my new agent, who had bought their agency from them when they became publishers. When they were pushed out of the publishing company by the higher ups in New York (how's that for "control"?), the next group of Canadian owners rejected my book (as well as many others bought by their predecessors) at first draft stage. I had researched it over the course of six years. Their consultant sent me a one page kiss-off note suggesting I go back to English 101. James Lorimer took over the project, published it, promoted it, and it is still in print both in English and in Portuguese translation. (And unfortunately for Lorimer it is also available on the Internet for anyone who wants to read it for free.) Needless to say, years of work would have been wasted, but for a Canadian owned and publicly supported publisher willing to take a big risk.

Penguin Canada was supposed to publish my most recent book, *SMARTS*, in Canada. Penguin backed out after it merged with Random House of Canada to become Penguin Random House due to the worldwide merger of the parent companies. The union of the Canadian subsidiaries was permitted by the Minister of Canadian Heritage, James Moore. With the help of friends with bookmaking skills, I published *SMARTS* myself through the createspace/Amazon system. The book is available in English everywhere except Canada. Chinese and Thai publishers bought translation rights. Was I annoyed at Penguin? Yes and no. I would never have been able to do the research to write the book without Penguin's advance. It was hard work to get the book produced and available for sale on the Amazon system, annoying work. But for the first time, I published without having to please anyone but myself, and that was exhilarating.

I have a history with Torys LLP dating back to that first book I wrote, which was not published, the one that stirred great controversy and cost Random House a pile of money. Under its former name, Tory, Tory, DesLauriers and Binnington, it acted for the developers who sued me and *Toronto Life* Magazine over our story about them. Torys LLP was also involved in one of two class-action lawsuits that I helped bring against various publishers concerning electronic rights to freelancers' articles. Torys represented the opposite side in one of those cases.

59 Ibid. Stikeman Elliott.
60 See: "Everything's on the table" by Daniel Leblanc, *Globe and Mail*, April 25, 2016.
61 See: "Has the Canadian Government Turned the Page on Its Book Policy? An Opportunity for Foreign Investors to Consider Investment in the Canadian Book Industry," by Shawn Neylan, John Leopold, Michael Gelinas, Stikeman Elliott, 2014.
62 See: Section 36(1) *Investment Canada Act*.
63 See: Simon & Schuster Canada website, Kevin Hanson appointment as publisher in 2013 + Stikeman Elliott blog re: publishing and foreign ownership, 2014.

64 See: *A Great Game,* by Stephen Harper, Simon & Schuster Canada, 2013.
65 "HarperCollins Canada gets out of distribution, CEO David Kent to leave." Deborah Dundas, *Toronto Star,* November 4, 2014. See also Mark Medley, *Globe and Mail,* same day
66 See: "Jared Bland named M&S publisher" *Quill & Quire,* July 18, 2016.
67 Chapters had 65% of the market according to evidence given by Competition Bureau officials to MP Inky Mark in a hearing of the Standing Committee on Canadian Heritage. See: Evidence of March 20, 2000.
68 See: admission of Chris Busutil to MP Mauril Belanger re: Chapters' share of the market in evidence, March 30, 2000. See Firefly complaint as cited by MP Mauril Belanger in Evidence of same day.
69 See: "Chapters Struggles to Survive" by Jane O'Hara, *Maclean's,* August 14, 2000, as reproduced in the Canadian Encyclopedia at: www.thecanadianencylopedia.ca/en/arictle/chatpers-struggles-to-survive.
70 See: MP Mauril Belanger's interrogation of Competition Bureau staff who appeared before the Standing Committee on Canadian Heritage, Evidence: March 30, 2000.
71 See: "The Challenge of Change: A Consideration of the Canadian Book Industry," Clifford Lincoln MP Chair, Standing Committee on Canadian Heritage, June 2000.
72 See: U of T Bulletin story by Jane Stirling, June 26, 2000.
73 See: Minutes of U of T Governing Council June 29, 2000. See also minutes of Governing Council, August 22, 2007 re: office of the Governing Council Memorandum on the Authority. Under: Memo to Members of Committee on Academic Policy and Programs, Item 4.
74 See: Brian Bethune, "Giving Away the Store," *Maclean's,* July 10, 2000.
75 Email of Erin Lemon, Executive director, News & Media, the University of Toronto, to author.
76 Those in attendance at the June 29, 2000, meeting included: Wendy M. Cecil-Cockwell (chair), Mary Ann V. Chambers, the Honourable Henry N.R. Jackman, Chancellor, Professor J. Robert S. Prichard, President, Professor Mary Beattie, Dr. Robert Bennett, Brian C. Burchell, Professor Jack Carr, Professor John R.G. Challis, Professor W. Raymond Cummins, Dr. Shari Graham Fell, Professor Vivek Goel, Dr. Anne Golden, Dr. Robert J. Kyle, Mr. Gerald A. Lokash, Professor John. T. Mayhall, Professor Ian R. McDonald, Ahmed Rafi Mian, Professor Heather Munroe-Blum, Dr. John P. Nestor, Elan Ohayon, Rose M. Patten, the Honourable David R. Peterson, Kashif S. Pirzada, The Honourable Robert K. Rae, Professor Wendy Rolph, Dr. Joseph L. Rotman, Susan M. Scace, Professor Adel S. Sedra, Professor Kenneth Sevcik, Amir Shalaby, Robert G. Spencer, Terrence L. Stephen, Wendy Talfourd-Jones, John H. Tory, Professor Ronald D. Venter, Nancy L. Watson, Dr. Alexander R. Waugh, Judith Wilson, Vilko Zbogar, Louis R. Charpentier, (Neil Dobbs, Margaret McKone). Those absent included: The Honourable William G.

Davis, Shruti Dev-Vayyar, Wanda M. Dorosz, Ljupco Gjorgjinski, Paul V. Godfrey, Peter A. Herrndorf, Brian Langille, Jacquiline C. Orange, Professor Emmet I. Robbins, and staff, including: Professor David Cook, Vice-Provost, Dr. Jon S. Dellandrea, Vice-President and Chief Development Officer, Professor Michael G. Finlayson, Vice-President, Administration and Human Resources, Professor Derek McCammond, Vice Provost, planning and Budget, Professor Ian Orchard Vice-Provost, Students, Professor Caroly Tuohy, Deputy Provost, Robert G. White, Chief Financial Officer, Professor Carl Armhein, Dean, Faculty of Arts and Science, Susan Bloch-Nevitte, Director, Public Affairs, W.G. Tad Brown, Finance and Development Counsel, Professor Ian Clark, President, Council of Ontario Universities, Matthew Cockburn, Torys, Brian Davis, Torys, Mr. Martin England, Assistant Vice-Provost, Planning and Budget, Dr. Beata FitzPatrick, Assistant Provost, Rivi Frankle, Director of Alumni and Development, Manon LePaven, President, Association of Part-time Undergraduate Students, Professor Judith Globerman, Status of Women Officer, Cathy McCauley, Executive Assistant to the President, Director of Special Events and Associate Campaign Director, Dr. Peter Munsche, Assistant Vice-president, Technology Transfer, Christine Oke, Assistant Vice-Provost, Professional Factulties, Janice Oliver, Assistant Vice-President, Operations and Services, Kasi Rao, Director of the Office of the President and Director of Government Relations, Maureen Somerville, Chair, College of Electors, Jorge Sousa, President, Graduate Students' Union.

77 See: "McClelland & Stewart Owner Donates Canadian Publishing House to University of Toronto," University of Toronto News and McClelland & Stewart, press release, June 26, 2000.

78 Ibid, Bethune, July 10, 2000.

79 See: Schedule attached to Unanimous Shareholder Agreement between McClelland & Stewart, the University of Toronto, Random House of Canada, First Plaza Inc., July 1, 2000.

80 See: David Foot website.

81 Ibid, MacSkimming, p. 374.

82 See: "Avie Bennett's Master Stroke" by Scott Anderson, *Quill & Quire*, August 2000, and see also:

"Giving Away the Store: Avie Bennett's unprecedented donation of industry icon McClelland & Stewart brings praise—and a storm of criticism" by Brian Bethune, *Maclean's* , July 10, 2000.

83 Ibid. Brian Bethune.

84 Ibid. Brian Bethune.

85 See: U of T Bulletin, Jane Stirling, June 26, 2000.

86 See: Canada Council site eligibility requirements for literary publishers at https://apply.canadacouncil.ca/AreYouEligible.aspx and see also: Canada. pch.gc.ca/eng, Canada Book Fund Support for Publishers. Date last modified, 2016–04–21.

87 Ibid, Bethune.

88 Ibid, Bethune.

89 Ibid, Bethune.

90 Ibid, Bethune.

91 Ibid, Bethune.

92 Ibid, MacSkimming, p. 374.

93 Ibid, Bethune.

94 See: "Black out: Canwest to buy 100% of National Post," CBC News/Business, August 24, 2001, cbc.ca.

95 See: "The Good, the Bad and Ugly: Financial Markets and the Demise of Canada's Southam Newspapers," by Marc Edge, Nanyang Technological University of Singapore; and also: "Does Ownership Matter? The Effects of Ownership on the Coverage of Political Scandal in Hollinger and Canwest Newspapers," by Lydia Miljan and Christina Howoran, paper for Canadian Political Science Association Meeting, Halifax, June 1, 2003, and see also "The Rise and Fall of Conrad Black, a Timeline," by David Olive, *Toronto Star*, March 11, 2007. Black sold the remaining 50% of the National Post to Canwest in August, 2001.

96 The allegation was that the Prime Minister had improperly used his position to influence a federal development bank regarding a property in his riding in which he once owned an interest.

97 See: "Monopsony and Predatory Buying: The Canadian Landscape Is Wide Open," by John F. Clifford and Sorcha O'Carroll, Competition Law Group, McMillan LLP.

98 See: "In the Matter of the Securities Act R.S.O. 1990, c.S.5, as amended, and In the Matter of Chapters Inc. and Trilogy Retail Enterprises LP, Reason for Decision" Howard Wetson, the Ontario Securities Commission, February 9, 2001.

99 See: *Titans: How the New Canadian Establishment Seized Power,* by Peter C. Newman, Penguin Books Canada Limited, 1998, pp. 235–237.

100 Indigo proxy circular of 2004, states Wright is an officer of controlling shareholder of Indigo, Trilogy.

101 "The Heather and Gerry Show," by Marci McDonald, *Toronto Life*, June 2005.

102 Ibid, *Titans*, Peter C. Newman, pp. 236–237 and also *Fireworks: The Investment of a Lifetime*, by Andy Sarlos, pp. 142–148.

103 Pencer started in business running vending machines, then got into catering in Montreal. His friend, William Obront, was a butcher. The Cliche Commission, (Brian Mulroney was one of the Commissioners) inquiring into organized crime in Quebec, heard testimony that Obront had supplied Expo 67 events with tainted meat. Apparently, Obront met his mob friends in one of Pencer's establishments, and Pencer bought Obront's meat business out of bankruptcy. In the late 1970s, Pencer moved West, got involved with meat packer Burns Foods, which later sued him and won $600,000 as a settlement. Pencer bought real estate and car dealerships in Alberta, and in 1981 bought the ailing Financial

Trust in Toronto. As Peter Newman recounts in *Titans,* Pencer issued to himself about $100 million worth of what became Financial Trustco's worthless paper before the company was sold.

104 Ibid, Marci McDonald, *Toronto Life,* and Peter C. Newman, *Titans,* p.236–237.

105 Ibid, Andy Sarlos, p. 151.

106 See: "Publishers worry that Ottawa will allow more access to foreign firms" Kate Taylor, *Globe and Mail,* Dec. 31, 2000.

107 Ibid. Newman, *Titans,* p. 235.

108 Ibid. Newman, *Titans,* pp. 218–233.

109 Onex, Switzerland is a town just outside Geneva where numerous numbered companies are registered for the purpose of parking assets far from nosy tax officials. I called Onex to find out if the company was named after the town. There are no PR people working at Onex, so I was passed on to a woman who undertook to find out. I said I wondered if it had been named for Onex as Schwartz had spent an interesting summer there many years ago. No, said the woman, after checking, the company was not named for Onex, Switzerland, it was just a name that the founder, Gerry Schwartz, happened to like.

110 If ever you want to read a truly fascinating description of the business aims of the leveraged buyout operators of the 1980s, read Onex's private placement offering of 1986. You'll have to go to a business library with a microfiche reader to find it, but it's worth the trip. Schwartz, who signed the offering, states that Onex hoped for annualized returns of 36%. A good return from a manufacturing company then was about 15%. The document invites new investors to consider directly purchasing shares of companies Onex is interested in acquiring—in other words, to act in concert with Onex as it works to buy control of companies. The document explains that Mr. Schwartz and his managers would be paid fees for their services and Onex managers would be loaned money, interest free, to buy and hold 20% of Onex shares, loans repayable in 20 years. The document also declares that Schwartz, or the Schwartz family group, would have to be bought out at a great premium if ever the Onex board decided to part ways with Schwartz, or if he died or became incapacitated. Why? Onex's success would hinge on Schwartz's training and his seven years working on Wall Street. The document explains that he had many personal contacts with the then leading players among Wall Street investment banks, especially: Lazard Frères; Drexel Burnham Lambert; Lehman Brothers; Bear Stearns. Such contacts, said the offering, would be absolutely essential for a successful business. Why? In order to gain control of a company with the minimum outlay of Onex's capital, Onex would arrange loans from these institutions guaranteed not by Onex (no recourse to Onex, is how the document puts it), but by target companies' shares and target companies' cash flows. The document suggests that Onex's management had found very innovative ways to avoid tax, and a means to trade Onex units privately, though a public offering at some point was contemplated.

In fact, Onex went public a little over a year later, just before Black Monday of November 1987 when stock markets crashed everywhere. The share price dived, but according to Andy Sarlos in *Fireworks,* Schwartz did extremely well anyway.

111 See: Onex website.

112 See: Onex management information circular of 2015.

113 See: Onex website and its paragraph on alignment.

114 See: "Canada's Top 100 Highest-Paid CEOs" by Graham Scott, Canadian Business, Jan.20, 2015 at http://www.canadianbusiness.com.

115 See: http://www.onex.com

116 161 Bay Street 49th floor for both See Trilogy Retail LP and Onex, Indigo Management Information Circular of February 2016.

117 According to the Indigo Management Information Circular of February 2016, Heather Reisman owned 98,000 shares, Gerry Schwartz owned or controlled 15 million plus.

118 See: testimony of Larry Stevenson to Standing Committee on Canadian Heritage, April 13, 2000.

119 Ibid, Ontario Securities Commission, February, 2001.

120 See: "Government Approves Chapters-Indigo Merger," by Leah Eichler, *Publishers Weekly*, June 18, 2001.

121 See: "Monopsony and Predatory Buying: The Canadian Landscape Is Wide Open," by John F. Clifford and Sorch O'Carroll McMillan LLP.

122 See: Federal Court of Canada website, Mr. Justice Marc Nadon's official bio, at www.fca.caf.gc.ca.

123 Ibid, Peter C. Newman, *Titans*, pp.231–232.

124 See: Indigo Books & Music Annual Information Form, July 29, 2003.

125 See: "The Heather and Gerry Show," Marci McDonald, *Toronto Life,* June 2005.

126 See: "Martin's family's theatre faces wrecking ball," by Charlie Smith, *the Georgia Strait*, July 28, 2005. See also: *Cloak of Green,* by Elaine Dewar, p. 280.

127 See: Report of the Competition Commissioner, 2005.

128 See: Indigo Books & Music Management Information Circular of May 12, 2006.

129 "Here Is the First Book Ever Ordered on Amazon," by Megan Garber, www.theatlantic.om/technology/archive/2012.

130 See: Testimony of Heather Reisman before Standing Committee on Canadian Heritage, March 12 and March 13, 2001.

131 Ibid, Testimony of Heather Reisman

132 See: "Indigo Sells Kobo: A Q and A with Heather Reisman," *Canadian Business,* November 9, 2011.

133 See: Press release of Trilogy titled "Retail Enterprises LP Agrees to Sell Two Million Indigo Shares" Jan. 29, 2010.

134 "Booksellers take on Ottawa over Amazon's distribution plans," Marina Strauss and Omar El Akkad, *Globe and Mail* March 8, 2010.

135 See: "Mr. Right," by Michael Posner, *The Walrus*, September 12, 2012.

136 See: "Amazon given green light to set up shop in Canada," by Omar El Akkad and Marina Strauss, *Globe and Mail*, April 12, 2010.

137 See: "Industry Canada Launches Review of Investment Policy in Book Publishing and Distribution," which appeared in the law firm Fasken & Martineau's Antitrust/Competition & Marketing Bulletin. As the first paragraph made clear, the title was in error. It was the Minister of Canadian Heritage who announced this review and carried it forward with a discussion paper produced by the Department along with requests for submissions. www.fasken.com/investing-in-the-future-of-Canadian-books. The discussion paper is called "Investing in the Future of Canadian Books: Review of the Revised Foreign Investment Policy in Book Publishing and Distribution." Discussion Paper of July 10, 2010.

138 See: July 2, 2010 Aleksandra Sagan for Canadian Press. "Debt is in tiers." See Thestar.com "Canwest newspapers to be called Postmedia Network, Paul Godfrey says," and see Alexandra Sagan for Canadian Press. Debt is in tiers, first group is $685 million, $950 million to pay off bank creditors owed $925 million. Thestar.com July 7, 2010.

139 See: theStar.com. "The US hedge fund manager backing a major newspaper merger," by Dana Flavelle, Business. October 24, 2010.

140 See: Evidence, Standing Committee on Access to Information, Privacy and Ethics, November 2, 2010.

141 See: Evidence, Standing Committee on Access to Information, Privacy and Ethics, Testimony of Nigel Wright, November 2, 2010.

142 Ibid, Evidence, November 2, 2010.

143 See: Indigo Books & Music Annual Information Form for the Year ended April 2, 2011.

144 See: "Reisman Sells Kobo" *Canadian Business*, November 9, 2011.

145 See: "Has the Canadian Government Turned the Page on Its Book Policy?" by Shawn C.D. Neylan, Michael Kilby, John Leopold, Michael Gelinas for Stikeman Elliott LLP, June 2014.

146 In the UK it is also about 30%, but starting to slip. See Guardian.com Feb 3, 2016 "Ebook sales falling for first time."

147 See: David Hume, *The Life of David Hume, Esq. Written by Himself,* reproduced in *Dialogues Concerning Natural Religion, David Hume,* The Library of Liberal Arts, Thomas Nelson & Sons Ltd., 1947, p. 234.

148 Avie Bennett's biography on the *Historica Canada* website, an organization whose Foundation he was chairman of from 2003 to 2011, confirms this claim: "With no Canadian company interested in taking it over, and prohibited by federal legislation from selling majority control to a foreign firm, Bennett structured an innovative deal that ensured the integrity of McClelland & Stewart while raising necessary funds for continued investment."

149 See: "Bertelsmann's Nazi Past," by John S. Friedman and Hersch Fischler, *The Nation*, December 29, 1998.

150 See: "Hitler's Revisionist," by John S. Friedman and Hersch Fischler, *The Nation*, October 21, 1999.

151 While Friedlander's group went to work, another Canadian connection with Bertelsmann emerged at the same time as Random House of Canada began to manage M&S. Groupe Bruxelles Lambert is partly owned by Power Corporation of Montreal. The Groupe bought 25% of Bertelsmann AG and Andre Desmarais joined the Bertelsmann board to watch over this interest. He stayed on that board until 2006 when Bertelsmann bought the stake back from Groupe Bruxelles Lambert.

152 BBC News World Edition, October 8, 2002. "Bertelsmann admits Nazi Past." See also *Telegraph*.co.uk. October 10, 2002,

153 See: "German media giant admits it backed Hitler," Hannah Cleaver, *Telegraph*, October 10, 2002.

154 As proof, my informant offered me a scan of a 2003 Canada Council document listing titles published by McClelland & Stewart in 2002, which had qualified for support under its Block Grants Book Publishing support program. Books are categorized as new, as reprints, as fiction (novels or short stories) or as non-fiction, and different levels of support were available according to those categories. The document clearly shows that *Canada: A People's History Volume Two* was classified as a novel, when it is non-fiction. Mavis Gallant's *Paris Stories* and *Pegnitz Junction* are characterized as new short story collections, not reprints, though they are both reprints, so they were funded at 100% not 50%. See document dated 2003/05/07. He also showed me his correspondence. The Council claimed that these must be inputting errors.

155 And he followed up that allegation with an email, later. The tax credit offered to publishers in Ontario is calculated at 30% of eligible expenditures by Canadian owned and controlled publishers producing and marketing works by Canadian authors. The publisher must file a tax return in Ontario. The tax credit caps out at $30,000 per book for qualifying applicants. Assuming M&S got the maximum credit for an average of about 40 books published per year, its Ontario tax credit would have been about $1.2 million a year in the years from 2007 until 2011. Ontario does not publish information about who gets this tax credit or how much, it only lists the total value of applications made and the total amount of certificates given each year under its program. The totals given amount to about $3 million a year, with about two thirds of applications earning certificates. See also: email from OMDC spokesperson, George McNeillie, to author, September 30, 2015.

156 The executive, Ken Thomson, has a LinkedIn Bio.

157 See: "Stewart House in Bankruptcy," by Judith Rosen, *Publishers Weekly*, February 10, 2003. The previous year, an Ontario court issued a judgement regarding a financial dispute between Stewart House and a game company that it acted as the distributor for. This ended in a large monetary award against Stewart House.

158 See: Minutes of the Governing Council, University of Toronto, June 29, 2000.

159 See: Minutes of the Business Board, University of Toronto, October 2, 2000.

160 See: "Internationally renowned leader to head Foundation," January 16, 2012 at www.sunnybrook.ca/foundaton/media/item.

161 See: "Investing in the Future of Canadian Books: Review of the Revised Foreign Investment Policy in Book Publishing and Distribution," Department of Canadian Heritage, July 2010.

162 See: email from Catherine Montgomery, Program Officer, Canada Council for the Arts, October 1,2015.

163 See: "Disclosure of Grants Contributions an Awards over $25,000 at www.pch. gc.ca/pc-ch/dp-pd/list-eng.cfm?s.

164 Decisions October-November-December 2011, Canadian Heritage website at: pcb gc.ca/eng/1359562637714/1359562712317.

165 See: Investment Canada Act, section 28(4).

166 Emails of Derek Mellon, Media Relations Industry Canada, August 26, 2015.

167 Another example is the story of Sino-Forest Corporation, trading on the Toronto Stock Exchange, offices in Hong Kong and Mississauga, Ontario, though its forests were in mainland China. These forests were not as publicly described, which was discovered by Muddy Waters Research. This led to a cease trade order by the Ontario Securities Commission and an order that the executives step down immediately. The order had to be rescinded immediately because the OSC has no power to make such an order. See: "Sino-Forest Halted as Regulator Rescinds order on Executives" by Christopher Donville, in www. Bloomberg.com/news/articles/2011-08-26/sino-forest-executives-ordered-to-resign. The company went into receivership and as it did so issued a libel suit against Muddy Waters in Ontario. The company is defunct.

168 See: In the Mater of the Securities Act RSO 1990, c.s.5, As Amended, and YBM Magnex International and Harry W Antes, Jacob B. Bogatin, Kenneth E. Davies, Igor Fisherman, Daniel E. Gatti, Frank S. Greenwald, R. Owen Mitchell, David R. Peterson, Michael D. Schmidt, Lawrence Wilder, Griffith McBurney & Partners, National Bank Finance Corp. at: www.osc,gov.on/en. See also Wiki on Semion Mogilevich, Don of Russian mafiyah dons.

169 See: Josef Sigalov's gifts through his companies to Paul Martin's re-election campaign, as well as to the campaigns of other Liberal candidates in 1993, as well as to the federal Liberal Party and the federal Progressive Conservative Party. Sigalov was the Canadian associate of the leader of the Russian Mafiya in New York, and their business discussions involving extortion, etc. had been wiretapped by the FBI. These matters were published in "Democracy Inc." Elaine Dewar, *Toronto Life*, in 1997. (The story can be read online at: http://groups-google.com/forum/#1topic/soc.culture.urainian/1wfvNSODXxE). A lawyer working for the Liberal Party called this reporter to ask how they could return these contributions made to candidates. I had to explain that Sigalov had also

made contributions to the Liberal Party of Canada, but as to how to find him, good luck, he was reported to have died of a brain tumour in Moscow and been buried in a cemetery in Toronto, though no one was able to tell me that they had actually seen the body.

170 See: "Toronto Journal; Russians Are Coming, but for Money," Clyde H. Farnsworth, *New York Times*, October 2, 1993 and "Where Fools Russia; from the Kremlin to Toronto's posh Bridle Path; smooth-talking Dmitri Yakubovsky rode the collapse of the Soviet Union," *Saturday Night Magazine*, December, 1995.

171 See: Confidential Private Offering Memorandum Onex Capital Corporation and Oncap Holdings Corporation offering approximately $75,000,000 in New Units. February 3, 1986.

172 See: "The Collapse of Drexel Burnham Lambert," *New York Times*, Business Day, February 14, 1990.

173 Ibid. *Cloak of Green*, Dewar, p. 289.

174 See: *Titans*, Peter C. Newman, p. 177–179.

175 I am indebted to my friend Marci McDonald who dug this out and wrote about it beautifully in *Yankee Doodle Dandy: Brian Mulroney and the American Agenda*.

176 Ibid., Marci McDonald, pp. 271–273.

177 Ibid. *Cloak of Green*, Dewar, p. 286–287.

178 Connacher and his people drank hard, played harder, and made a lot of money very fast. One of his former associates bought a great big house in a privately owned park and let the family dogs poop on its ballroom floor rather than fence the great big lawn. There were great big parties on the great big lawn, but in the end, the house was seized by the bank as the owner left the country under a cloud. (The precise nature of that cloud is not known to me.)

179 See: *Barbarians at the Gate: The Fall of RJR Nabisco*, by Bryan Burroughs, HarperCollins, 1991.

180 See: *On the Take: Crime, Corruption and Greed in the Mulroney Years*, by Stevie Cameron, pp. 390–413.

181 See: *The Perilous Trade*, Roy MacSkimming, p. 162.

182 There was quite a fuss when it was reported that Paul Martin Sr. (then government leader in the Senate), Jack Austin (then principal secretary to Prime Minister Pierre Trudeau), Bill Teron (then head of the government's housing agency, the CMHC), and Maurice Strong (the founding chairman of Petro-Canada plus various other government appointed roles), owned chunks of this company while they held public office. Jack Austin in particular was accused of conflicts of interest, and the fuss led to new rules about what public officers had to do to keep their skirts clean.

183 See: "Takeover Part I" and "Takeover Part II," by Elaine Dewar, *Canadian Business*, 1985, November and December respectively.

184 See: "Canada's Richest People," Staff, *Canadian Business*, December, 24, 2015.

185 Ibid, Dewar, *"Takeover Part II."*

186 Ibid, Dewar, *"Takeover Part II."*

187 "They're all Jews together," one WASP Bay Streeter hissed at me when I came to interview him about the takeover, not realizing that I'm Jewish. He was deceived by my last name.

"Tell me something, sir," I said to him trying to hold my rage in check. "Is it the fact that Mann is Jewish that you object to, or his business practices?"

"The business practices of course," he'd said, smugly.

188 Like the M&S deal, official institutions only appeared to be in control of events. The OEB gave its imprimatur to a deal that had already been made and could not legally be stopped only after Unicorp made several public undertakings. It was supposed to hold onto control of Union Enterprises, and therefore Union Gas, for many years. Nevertheless, in 1992, Unicorp, in trouble, sold control of Union to Westcoast Energy, which was later sold to US based Duke Energy, which spun Union into a US company called Spectra out of Houston. That's how one of the largest natural gas utilities in eastern Canada ended up in the hands of a foreign owner—until Spectra was resold this year to Canadian-based Enbridge in a $37 billion deal. See: "Enbridge to buy Spectra Energy in $37 bil-lion deal" by Kelly Cryderman, *Globe and Mail* September 6, 2016.

189 See: *The Perilous Trade*, by Roy MacSkimming, pp. 303–308.

190 O&Y and the Reichmann family were represented by Nigel Wright's firm, Davies Ward & Beck, and Trevor Eyton's former law firm, Tory, Tory DesLauriers and Binnington.

191 *The Reichmanns: Family, Faith, Fortune and the Empire of Olympia & York*, by Anthony Bianco, pp. 226, 312–320.

192 See: *Titans*, Peter C. Newman, pp 204–205.

193 Ibid, MacSkimming, pp. 65–67 and 319.

194 Ibid, MacSkimming, p. 66.

195 Ibid, MacSkimming, p. 321.

196 See: Douglasgibsonbooks.com.

197 See: Avie Bennett's Companion citation, Order of Canada website.

198 "Sondra Gotlieb's Slap Flap" by Elizabeth Kastor and Washington Post Staff, *The Washington Post*, March 21, 1986.

199 Later, I thought we must have spoken about the electronic rights class action law suits.

They began after journalist and author Heather Robertson and I attended a public meeting at the Ryerson School of Journalism in the mid 1990s. It was organized by our former *Maclean's* colleague and the School's Director, Don Obe. The Internet as a publishing platform was still mainly science fiction, but electronic publishing on CD-ROMs and in full text databases had become a shiny new business. Some newspapers and magazines were putting their articles into full text databases and selling subscriptions to them, or, were trying to sell single articles as downloads. The *Globe and Mail,* owned by the Thomson Corporation, had gone into digital publishing long before anybody else and had apparently included freelancers' stories in its databases without asking for permission or negotiating payments. While most freelancers hadn't noticed, someone at the *Globe* must have worried that this practice might infringe copyright. Under copyright law, freelancers retain all rights to their stories except those they sell or give away by written agreement. At that time there were no written agreements between freelancers and newspaper editors, just brusque orders about the number of words wanted and the deadline and the fee. The understanding in the business then was that newspapers and magazines bought the rights to print a freelance story in one day's versions of the newspaper, or in one issue of a magazine. These rights were for sale in Canada, only, but the Internet was beginning to destroy publishing territories.

In January, 1996, Obe called a meeting of the writing community because the *Globe* had begun to insist that all its freelancers must sign contracts giving the *Globe* non-exclusive worldwide electronic rights to their stories forever and for nothing. The more we heard, the more it sounded as if freelancers were getting hosed. Yet the Writers' Union lawyer who attended that meeting said little could be done because no freelance writer could afford to sue the *Globe.* The same lawyer dismissed it as ridiculous that freelance journalists might consider suing as a class.

After the meeting, I spoke to a lawyer friend who thought a class-action *was* worth investigating. He advised us to go see Michael McGowan who had set up a class action practice. Along with journalist/activist June Callwood and freelancer/union organizer Michael O'Reilly, Heather Robertson and I asked McGowan to consider taking the case. He asked us to find out which of our works, if any, were being offered on *Globe* databases. We found plenty, but most usefully, we found an excerpt of Heather's book, *Driving Force,* published by McClelland & Stewart in 1995, which had appeared in the paper version of the *Globe.* Ha, said McGowan, McClelland & Stewart will have had a contract with the *Globe* selling the right to use that excerpt. Let's see if that contract transferred electronic rights. So Heather checked with the rights manager at M&S, Jennifer Shepherd. The contract did *not* convey electronic rights.

Shepherd wrote a letter to the *Globe* asking that the electronic version of the excerpt be paid for or be removed from the database. The *Globe's* in-house lawyer responded with a piss-off-and-die note saying, in essence, that Heather Robertson should be grateful to be published by the *Globe* at all.

So we asked Jennifer to ask Avie Bennett if he wanted to sue the *Globe.*

Did we have a conversation with Bennett? Or did Jen Shepherd convey his answer to us? However we communicated, his reply was: why would I sue the *Globe and Mail?* At first, I was outraged. But then I saw that by not suing, he protected M&S from the huge legal fees it would have incurred to recover a tiny sum by going after a company as big as Thomson, owner of the *Globe and Mail.* And his answer turned out to be the right answer for freelancers too. Michael McGowan launched two class actions with the aid of copyright and patent expert Ron Dimock and his colleague Sangeetha Punniyamoorthiy. Both actions were later led by class action litigators Kirk Baert and Celeste Poltak of Koskie Minsky. The actions became known as Robertson 1 and Robertson II. Robertson II sued the other publishers in the country who had copied what the *Globe* was doing. More than ten years after Obe called that meeting, the Supreme Court of Canada found in a 5-4 decision that by removing freelancers' articles from their context—the original newspaper—and offering them individually for sale, the *Globe*'s copyright on the physical arrangement of the newspaper ceased to apply. In other words: we won on the crucial issue. The remaining issues in both actions were settled out of court. Millions of dollars were paid out to Canada's freelancers. None of that would have happened if Avie Bennett had sued the *Globe*.

200 See: "Anatomy of a Merger," by Mark Medley, *Globe and Mail*, Arts, June 27, 2015.

201 See: "Doubleday Canada and McClelland & Stewart merge into new publishing group," Mark Medley, the *National Post*, June 20, 2012.

202 Penguin Random House produced 20% of Bertelsmann's earnings, and was third on the list. See Bertelsmann 2014 annual report.

203 See: Bertelsmann Report, 2013.

204 See: p. 89, Bertelsmann Report, 2014.

205 Oddly, on Martin's LinkedIn Page I spied a fragment of a financial statement, untitled, undated and without any zeros to show whether the numbers listed represent millions, thousands or just hundreds.

206 See: "Fundamentals of Reviewable Matters Under the Competition Act," by John F. Clifford, McMillan Binch, paper for Canadian Bar Association Annual Conference on Competition Law, Fall, 2002. "Market share above 35%... will normally prompt further examination."

207 See: Schedule A, Unanimous Shareholder Agreement, July 1, 2000.

208 See: "A primer on Competition Investigations in Canada," Andrew D. Little, February 9, 2016, Bennettjones.com/publications/updates/a_primer_on_competition_investigations_in_Canada. See also Section 29(1) Competition Act at www.competitionbureau.gc.ca.

209 On the east side of University Avenue, on the south end of Toronto General Hospital, large letters spelled out Peter Munk Cardiac Care Centre. Munk's name is also attached to the Munk School of Global Affairs, a building northwest of Queen's Park Circle on the University of Toronto campus. Munk is said to have put up $35 million for naming rights for which he got a $16 million tax credit, which caused a campus ruckus. Barrick Gold's mining operations are not beloved by environmentalists and social activists, and yet Munk is said to have gotten some say in the School's academic decision-making, which is usually not tolerated by finer institutions of higher learning. The President of University

of Toronto at the time of that gift was David Naylor: he was also the President when U of T's M&S shares were offloaded to Random House for $1. Naylor was appointed to the board of Barrick Gold as an independent, but soon left. Rob Prichard was appointed to Barrick's board in 2015.

The Munk Debates are funded by Munk's Aurea Foundation upon whose board Nigel Wright sat—yes, that Nigel Wright—until he went to work for Prime Minister Harper in 2011. Wright eventually re-joined Aurea after he was "fired" by the Prime Minister for writing a cheque to Senator Mike Duffy so as to give the public the impression that Senator Mike Duffy was paying back the Senate for expenses he'd claimed. (It turned out that he was entitled to claim them, or at least that claiming them was no criminal offense.) Wright volunteered at a homeless shelter in Ottawa while the RCMP sniffed at his $90,000 payment to Duffy to determine whether or not it was a bribe. They alleged that it was a bribe when Duffy received it, but not when Wright gave it. When no charges were laid against him, Wright returned to Aurea and went back to work for Onex out of its London office. Duffy, after an arduous trial, was found not guilty of accepting a bribe.

Wright's story bleeds into the stories of the others named here who have reshaped Canada's book publishing policy—reshaped Canada, really. Wright was active in politics from his first year at University of Toronto. As a student Progressive Conservative, he worked to dump Joe Clark and elect Brian Mulroney as leader of the Party. Wright entered University of Toronto Law School when Robert Prichard was its Dean. Prichard seems to have marked him as one of the brightest students in his year, although Wright had only graduated from U of T's Trinity *magna cum laude,* not *summa.*

Wright was a good friend of several political operatives who would go on to drive the Common Sense revolution in Ontario, helping bring Mike Harris to power in 1995. In 1997, after providing legal advice to Onex on an important deal, Wright was recommended as a prospective manager to Gerry Schwartz by Anthony Munk, the son of Peter Munk (of Barrick Gold) and one of the early members of the Onex team. Schwartz hired Wright away from Davies Ward & Beck where he had articled and become a partner in record time. He has been at Onex ever since. Wright is godfather to Anthony Munk's son.

Wright apparently spotted Stephen Harper as a person who could unite the fractious right. According to John Ibbitson, who wrote a recent biography of Harper, Wright helped talk Harper into running for the leadership of the Canadian Alliance Party to replace Stockwell Day after the November, 2000 election. Again according to Ibbitson, Wright helped raise money for Harper's successful race. Wright also helped execute the Alliance merger with the Progressive Conservative Party. Along with Irving Gerstein (later Senator Gerstein), Wright founded and directed the Conservative Fund which raises and distributes the Party's money. All sorts of political candidates have been, are, and will be, beholden to that Fund for support at election time.

Robert Prichard also serves on the Aurea board. Aurea gives money to think tanks that are generally considered to be on the right politically, though perhaps libertarian is a fairer characterization, and libertarian is neither right nor left, it's more along the lines of shrink the State back to bare bones and let liberty ring. Some argue that the Munk Debates are aimed at injecting such views into the global marketplace of ideas.

Avie Bennett gave away control of M&S just as Heather Reisman and her husband won control of Chapters and stepped forward to push ideas into the world in another way. Reisman became a program organizer for the Bilderberg group in 2000. Bilderberg is a place where very successful people go to hear each other talk. Like the Rockefeller Foundation, and the Trilateral Commission, it is an organization that provides constant fodder for conspiracy theorists. Some think the Rockefellers want to control everything and it is certainly true that the Rockefellers have spent blood, sweat, and many millions of dollars trying to shape the marketplace of ideas, but they don't control *everything*. Bilderberg was founded in 1954 with the aid of Prince Bernhard of the Netherlands (forced to quit the organization when he was accused of funny business on behalf of Lockheed) plus a little help from the head of the CIA and a grant from the Ford Foundation (which used to aid the CIA in many ways, as did Rockefeller Foundation). Bilderberg's initial purpose was to foster good relations between Europe and the US under a rubric known as Atlanticism as the Cold War reached a peak. Its participants have long been interested in world governance of one variety or another, and in the spread of capitalism: in other words, in the globalization process.

Rob Prichard, on the Onex board since 1994, attended at least one Bilderberg group meeting (which is by invitation only) as did Nigel Wright when he worked for the Prime Minister. Though Gerald Schwartz's business is heavily reliant on free trade in financial services, and benefits from a world in which money can move easily across borders, his name and his company's name do not appear on Bilderberg invitee lists. I suppose that since his spouse is on the Onex board, the Onex presence is implicit.

210 See: "Decade of the Dynamo," by Jack Batten, *University of Toronto Magazine*, Summer 2000.
211 See: public information returns of the Bennett Family Foundation, available on the CRA website under registered charities.
212 See: "Canadian business legend Gerry Schwartz receives honorary Doctor of Laws Today," by Jennifer Robinson and Lucianna Ciccocioppo, www.law.uto-ronto.ca/news/Canadian-business-legend-Gerry-Schwartz-receives-honorary-doctor-of-laws-today.
213 See: Ed Iacobucci at http://www.law.utontonto.ca/faculty-staff/full-time-faculty/Edward/Iacobucci. See also at http:// www.law.utoronto.ca/documents/alumni/Nexus_spring04.pdf.

214 See: Mount Sinai Hospital press release, Dec. 5, 2013 at www.mountsinai.on.ca/about_us/news/2–13.

215 See: bio, Robert Prichard, Chairman of the Board, Bank of Montreal,at www.bmo.com/home/about/banking/comporat-information/executive-bios/robert-prichard.

216 See: obit of Alison Gordon by Brendan Kennedy at thestar.com, February 12, 2015.

217 See: CIBC Historical Effective Prime Rate for June 25th. It rose one percentage point by the next month. http://www.fin.gov.bc.ca.

218 See: *The Perilous Trade*, by Roy MacSkimmingpp. 161–162.

219 See: *Quill & Quire*, Hamish Cameron, February 1986. See also *The Perilous Trade*, pp.161–162.

220 Ibid, MacSkimming, p. 162.

221 See: CRA website: Bennett Family Foundation, founded 1983, directors from 1983 are Avie Bennett, Beverly Bennett and W. Norman Ross.

222 See: biography of N. William Ross, WeirFoulds LLP, on the Canadian Mint website.

223 See: CRA, information return, Bennett Family Foundation, 2015.

224 Returns of the Bennett Family Foundation: CD-ROM providing scans of annual returns from 2005 until 2013, in author's possession. Other returns available on CRA website.

225 See: "Good Reviews" by David Olive, *Toronto Life*, June 1988.

226 Ibid, MacSkimming, p. 142.

227 Ibid, MacSkimming, p.142–143.

228 "Good Reviews" David Olive, *Toronto Life*, June 1988

229 Ibid, Olive.

230 Ibid, Olive.

231 Ibid, MacSkimming, p. 164.

232 Ibid, Olive, *Toronto Life*, June 1988, plus author interview with Avie Bennett.

233 See: *The Reichmanns: Family, Faith, Fortune and the Empire of Olympia & York*, by Anthony Bianco, p. 531.

234 Ibid, Bianco, p. 532.

235 See: "Defenders of the Pen," by Stevie Cameron, National Magazine, Canadian Bar Association, May 1993, at julianporterqc.com/press.

236 "Black's Legal Jousts Continue," by Charlie Smith, *Georgia Strait*, November 18, 2004."US Securities settlement with Conrad Black could be used against OSC," *Maclean's*, Canadian Press, Aug. 15, 2013. See also: "Garth Drabinsky's Fatal Flaw," by Anne Kingstone, *Maclean's*, April 9, 2009.

237 And so, some journalists who had been sued, or threatened with a lawsuit, began to investigate the libel law of Ontario, asking why plaintiffs who resided elsewhere preferred to sue in Ontario. It turned out Ontario had become well known as a plaintiff-friendly venue in libel suits. We put

together a brief about how this had resulted in important stories being killed by major newspapers afraid of the costs of libel suits, or never even started. We wrote that Ontario libel law represents a danger to a vibrant economy and a healthy democracy, and we tried to interest the Ontario government in reform of the law. That's when we discovered that the government had been hard at work on a policy review which would have led to the law becoming even more draconian if certain interests had had their way. We were given a policy paper that had been written by government lawyers without taking soundings from journalists, but after paying close attention to the concerns of leading plaintiffs' lawyers. One of the changes under consideration was to permit dead people to sue. When we at last won a meeting with a Deputy Minister, who, we were told, could make the government listen to reason, she told us she had no sympathy for our concerns as there was a journalist in town who had reported on her work who *she* wanted to sue. When we finally got a meeting with the Attorney General, Howard Hampton, after the NDP won the 1990 election, he listened impatiently as John Ralston Saul (best-selling author, former assistant to Maurice Strong at Petro-Canada, partner of Adrienne Clarkson and later the head of PEN International), explained about the danger of libel chill by reference to the Dreyfus trials and Émile Zola. After about five minutes, Hampton told us there would be no change to the law and left the room.

238 Ibid, Olive.

239 Erin Lemon, the U of T, email to author of July 27, 2015.

240 See: citation for Avie Bennett, Member, Order of Canada, 1991 www.gg.ca/honour.

241 Ibid, Olive.

242 See: "Word for Word: Bennett on Books," *Maclean's*, Sept. 27, 1999.

243 As Marci McDonald recounted in her excellent 2005 story for *Toronto Life* called "The Heather & Gerry Show," Reisman, Schwartz and Prichard had all helped Peterson and his Party. Schwartz raised money for Peterson and for the federal Liberals. Reisman acted as an advisor. Prichard helped the Peterson government with the transition to power (he would do the same for the NDP and then the Conservatives). Apparently, the Reisman/Schwartzs and the Prichards became good friends in this process, together with historian Irving Abella (author of *None Is Too Many*) and his wife Rosalie Abella (then a judge of the Ontario Court of Justice, appointed to the Supreme Court in 2004 by Schwartz/Reisman's good friend, Prime Minister Paul Martin). Thanks in part to Gerald Schwartz, there is now a Rosalie Silberman Abella Moot Court room at U of T Law School. See report of the U of T Alumnae.

244 See: c.v. of David Peterson as posted on University of Toronto website as of 2009 in Governing Council members' biographies. See also: David Peterson bio at Bloomberg.com.

245 See: "Penguin Sets up Canadian Board, with Rob Prichard at its head." By John Barber, *Globe and Mail*, September 21, 2010.

246 See: "Shakeup at Torstar," by Grant Robertson and Gordon Pitts, Globeinvestor. com

247 See: *Titans*, Peter C. Newman, p. 131.

248 See: "Mr. Premier Returns Home," Torys LLP website.

249 I've been on the opposite side of Torys twice. The first time, I said several bad words to one of their lawyers and was tempted to swear at another. The second time, I grew to like them. If you're thinking it's because that second time was the electronic rights class action, when we succeeded at the Supreme Court of Canada against Thomson, you're right, but also wrong. Thomson was represented in that action by two of Torys' smartest advocates and it was a pleasure to deal with them.

250 Ibid, *Titans*, Newman, pp. 55–58.

251 For history of Torys LLP, consult "Our Story" at www.torys.com.

252 See: biography of Robert Prichard at www.torys.com.

253 See: Interview with Robert Prichard, "Prichard the Third" by Thomas Watson, *Canadian Business*, www.CanadianBusiness.com, April 8, 2011.

254 See: www.casselsbrock.com/people, Marshall Cohen, and see also *Titans*, Newman, pp. 34–35.

255 See: Ibid, Anthony Bianco, p. 465

256 See: Cadillac Fairview history at. www.cadillacfairview.com/en_CA/About-us.

257 See: *Canadian Architect*, June 2001, by Leslie Jen.

258 His involvement with Penguin Canada was listed in various bios posted on the websites of organizations he is associated with, including his Torys bio. But recently, it disappeared.

259 Ibid, John Barber, *Globe and Mail*, September 21, 2010.

260 See: Section 118.1 *Income Tax Act* (RSC 1985 5th supplement), and section 13 and subsection (19) (26) (27). And: sections dealing with the meaning of arm's length from Canada Revenue Agency Income Tax Form, S1 F5, c 1 Related Persons and dealing at Arm's Length.

261 See: 1.38 from Canada Revenue Agency Tax Form S1-F5-C1: Related Person and dealing at arm's length.

262 See: Testimony of Jeffrey Richstone to the Standing Committee on Canadian Heritage, March 28, 2000. Richstone described the Department's de facto control test as follows: "…in the de facto control test you look at a host of different factors, including supply arrangements, financing arrangements, all those kinds of things. Under the act, you're allowed full discretion to really fully explore those issues. It's often very much a weighing factor. You weigh all the factors on one side and weigh all the factors on the other and the minister decides finally whether there is a control factor."

263 See: *Onex Information circular*, May, 2016.

264 See: Governor General of Canada's Order of Canada website.

265 Letter of Catherine Riggall to Missy Marston-Shmelzer, July 4, 2011.

266 See: Order of Canada citation for Jon Dellandrea at Governor General of Canada's Order of Canada website.

267 See: "Chee: Building an economic bridge to China" by Jacquie McNish, *Globe and Mail*, March 25, 2011.

268 See: biography of Trina McQueen at http://www.Shulich.yourku.ca/faculty/trina-mcqueen.

269 See: www.ontario.ca/laws/statute/90f31#BK3.

270 See: *Freedom of Information and Protection of Privacy Act* of Ontario, Third Party Information, section 17(2).

271 anatomy.utoronto.ca/about/history htm.

272 Ibid, Evidence, Standing Committee on Canadian Heritage, May 9, 2000.

273 The use of the proceeds from the sale of the shares, or from any profits accruing to the University from the operations of M&S, were laid out in an Agreement between First Plazas and University of Toronto dated June 30, 2000 and signed by Robert Prichard for the Governing Council of University of Toronto, and Avie Bennett for First Plazas Inc. An endowment was to be created by the University to be used for the advancement of Canadian culture under the management of the University through something called the Bennett Committee comprising seven individuals appointed by the President of U of T, normally including one of its nominated directors on the M&S board, three faculty etc. The Committee would decide whether income from its shares of M&S would be put in the endowment, or "expendable," though any income resulting from the sale of shares had to be endowed.

274 See: Section 3.3(a) Administrative Services and Financial Support Agreement, between McClelland & Stewart Ltd. and Random House of Canada, July 1, 2000.

275 See: *Investment Canada Act*, Section 37(4).

276 See: University of Toronto News; McClelland & Stewart, press release of June 26, 2000.

277 See: Share Purchase Agreement between First Plazas Inc. Vendor, and Random House of Canada, Purchaser, 6:00 a.m. July 1, 2000, Article 2.3.

278 See: Administrative Services and Financial Support Agreement, between McClelland & Stewart Ltd., and Random House of Canada Ltd. July 1, 2000 Articles 2.1, 2.2, 5.1, 3.3 (s) and (c).

279 Ibid, Administrative Services and Financial Support Agreement, Article 3.3

280 Ibid, Administrative Services and Financial Support Agreement, Article 2.3

281 See: Schedule A, Administrative Services and Financial Support Agreement, Article 2.

282 Ibid, Schedule A, Article 3.

283 Ibid, Schedule A, Article 7.

284 Ibid, Schedule A, Article 8.

285 Ibid, Schedule A, Article 9.

286 See: Unanimous Shareholder Agreement, Section 2.

287 Ibid, Unanimous Shareholder Agreement, Section 2.7.

288 Ibid, Unanimous Shareholder Agreement, Section 2.8.

289 Ibid, Unanimous Shareholder Agreement, Section 4.

290 Ibid, Unanimous Shareholder Agreement, Section 5.6(5).

291 Ibid, Unanimous Shareholder Agreement, Section 5.4.

292 Ibid, Unanimous Shareholder Agreement, Section 5.5.

293 Ibid, Unanimous Shareholder Agreement, Section 5.6(1).

294 Ibid, Unanimous Shareholder Agreement, Section 5/6 F(2)(c).

295 See: "Re: Fair Market Value of Shares of McClelland & Stewart Ltd. Donated to the University of Toronto," Ernst & Young Corporate Finance Inc., August 4, 2000.

296 Ibid, Ernst & Young Corporate Finance Inc., August 4, 2000.

297 See: Letter of Tad Brown to Avie Bennett, September 26, 2000.

298 See: Memo from Helen Choy to Pierre Piché, April 28, 2006.

299 Ibid, Memo from Choy.

300 See: "Canadian writing enjoys a golden age despite takeover of McClelland & Stewart" Editorial, Toronto Star, Jan.13, 2012. Also see: "Bennett's efforts deserve praise," Letter to the Editor of David Naylor, President, University of Toronto, January 14, 2012.

301 See: Asset Purchase Agreement between First Plazas and McClelland & Stewart Ltd., 12:01 a.m., July 1, 2000. Though a transitional services agreement is referred to, it was not attached.

302 Asset Purchase Agreement at section 2.2.

303 See: Share Purchase Agreement, between Random House of Canada; The Governing Council of the University of Toronto and McClelland & Stewart Ltd., December 30, 2011, article E.

304 Ibid, Share Purchase Agreement, Section F.

305 Ibid, Share Purchase Agreement, Section G.

306 See: "Random House of Canada merges M&S and Doubleday Canada," by Leigh Ann Williams, *Publishers Weekly*, June 21, 2012; and also "Doubleday Canada and McClelland & Stewart merge into new publishing group," by Mark Medley, *National Post*, June 20, 2012.

307 See: Letter of David Naylor to Judith Wolfson and Cathy Riggall, September 1, 2011.

308 See: letter of Cathy Riggall to David Naylor and Judith Wolfson, September 6, 2011.

309 See: letter of David Naylor to Cathy Riggall and Judith Wolfson, September 7, 2011.

310 See: letter of Cathy Riggall to David Naylor and Judith Wolfson, September 7, 2011.

311 See: letter of David Naylor to Cathy Riggall and Judith Wolfson, September 7, 2011.

312 See: letter of David Naylor to Brad Martin, September 26, 2011.

313 See: letter of Brad Martin to David Naylor, September 26, 2011.

314 See: letter of Howard Jones to Elaine Dewar, January 13, 2016.

315 See: Advice to Minister Moore, Random House of Canada Announcement Regarding its acquisition of McClelland & Stewart, January 20, 2012.

316 See: Advice/Recommendation to Minister Moore, dated June 20, 2012.

317 See: Access to Information response, Department of Canadian Heritage, February 24, 2016. Section 14(1) under which these pages were withheld falls under statutory prohibitions against disclosure. "24.(1) The head of a government institutions shall refuse to disclose any record requested under this Act that contains information the disclosure of which is restricted by or pursuant to any provision set out in Schedule II." Schedule II was not attached.

318 See: Letter of Rafael Eskenazi for Howard Jones, Freedom of Information and Privacy Coordinator, University of Toronto, to Elaine Dewar, February 22, 2016.

319 See: Memo from Tad Brown, Finance and Development Council, University of Toronto, to Felix Chee, November 18, 2003.

320 See: Schedule of meetings of Business Board and Governing Council of University of Toronto available online under University of Toronto Business Board meeting schedule.

321 See: Amendment No. 1 Unanimous Shareholder Agreement between University of Toronto and Random House of Canada Ltd. and McClelland & Stewart Ltd. and First Plazas Inc., April 1, 2004.

322 See: Certificate of Articles of Amalgamation, July 1, 2004, McClelland & Stewart Ltd. and Macfarlane, Walter & Ross.

323 See: McClelland & Stewart Ltd. Bylaw No. 2. A bylaw relating generally to the conduct of the business and affairs of McClelland & Stewart Ltd. adopted on amalgamation on July 1, 2004.

324 See: bio of Felix Chee from Teck Resources site as of 06/9/15.

325 See: Minutes of Governing Council University of Toronto, February 11, 2004, appointment for Riggall to begin February 12, and for Vivek Goel to begin on February 12 to replace Provost Shirley Neuman who resigned on February 4. Riggall's appointment was for no more than one year.

326 See: minutes of Governing Council meetings of March 12, 2004 and March 29, 2004.

327 See: minutes of Governing Council Meeting March 29, 2004.

328 See: minutes of March 12, 2004, the U of T Governing Council. See also story of James Hughes, the *Varsity*, July 19, 2004.

329 See: Minutes of Governing Council, March 12, 2004.

330 See: "University of California expected to name Birgeneau to Berkeley," by Caroline Alphonso, *Globe and Mail*, July 26, 2004. Ibid, James Hughes, the *Varsity*, July 19, 2004.

331 See: bios: Governing Council 2003–2004 Chairman is Simpson, Vice-Chairman is Patten. 2004–2005 Chairman is Patten, Vice-Chairman is Jack Petch.

332 See: minutes of Governing Council meeting of August 16, 2004. Iacobucci's appointment was the only business.

333 See: "Torstar names Iacobucci Chairman," by Richard Blackwell, *Toronto Star* March 30, 2005.

334 See: Note 2 to draft Non Consolidated Financial Statement for year ended December 31, 2005.

335 See: Ontario Superior Court of Justice Commercial List, the Honourable Justice Ground, Tuesday 30th of April, 2002. In the matter of a Plan of Compromise or Arrangement of General Publishing Co. Limited, General Distribution Services Limited, Stoddart Publishing Co. Limited, the Boston Mills Press Ltd. And House of Anansi Press Limited.

336 See: Statement of Affairs General Distribution Services, August 19, 2002.

337 See: bershirehathaway.com/news/feb2701.html.

338 See: "Government Approves Chapters-Indigo Merger" by Leah Eichler, *Publishers Weekly*, June 18, 2001.

339 Interview with Robert Biehler, Deloitte, August, 2016.

340 Ibid, Biehler interview.

341 See: In the matter of an application under the Companies' Creditors Ontario Superior Court of Justice Commercial List, Initial Order of Justice Ground, April 30, 2002. Also: Ibid, Biehler.

342 The company is called General Kinetics, of Brampton.

343 See: video of Launch of Griffin Poetry Prize, online, where his bio is outlined and he also speaks.

344 Interview with Marthe Sharpe, August 30, 2016.

345 See: Unanimous Shareholder Agreement, Section 2.8.

346 See: Non-Consolidated Financial Statements of McClelland & Stewart Ltd., Year ended December 31, 2005. Draft #7, April 4, 2006.

347 See: McClelland & Stewart Ltd. Non-consolidated statement of Operations and Deficit, year ended December 31, 2002.

348 Ibid, MacSkimming, p. 388.

349 See: "Simon & Schuster buying Canadian Company" from *New York Times* as reproduced by *Bloomberg News*, November 20, 2002.

350 See: "Get Your Facts Straight Paul," by John Honderich, *Toronto Star,* January 27, 2016.

351 See: "As long as it continues to live, Postmedia is a blight to readers," by David Olive, *Toronto Star,* Business, January 30, 2016.

352 Ibid, John Honderich.

353 See: "Above the Fold" by Margo Goodhand, *The Walrus,* February 4, 2016.

354 Ibid, Honderich; Ibid, Olive.

355 See: "Paul Godfrey wants more foreign ownership," Michael Lewis, *Toronto Star,* January 30, 2016.

356 Ibid, Honderich.

357 See: Torstar Information Form, 2015, p. 26.

358 See: Torstar Information Circular, 2015, p. 1.

359 See: "Torstar slashes dividend for the second time this year," by Sean Craig, *Financial Post*, July 27, 2016. See also: "Guelph Mercury newspaper to close amid financial pressures," by Tim Shufelt and Christin Dobby, *Globe and Mail*, January 25, 2016.

360 See: John Honderich bio, Ryerson School of Journalism at www.Rsj.journalism. ryerson.ca/team/john-honderich.

361 See: "Honderich quitting *Toronto Star*," by Katherine Harding, *Globe and Mail*, January 26, 2004.

362 See: Torstar annual report for 2009.

363 See: "The Lunch: Penguin Random House CEO Brad Martin loves a good read," Mark Medley, *Globe and Mail*, June 5, 2015.

364 See: "North Star," by Guy Lawson. *New York Times Magazine*, December 13, 2015.

365 Some are successful enough to become foreign takeover targets. In June, 2010, the Standing Committee on Canadian Heritage heard testimony on the proposed takeover of film and television production and distribution company, Lions Gate, by the corporate raider Carl Icahn. Lions Gate was founded in BC, was listed on the Vancouver Stock Exchange, produced movies and series television in Canada worth about $800 million a year, owned a Canadian distributor called Maple, but was managed from Hollywood by Americans and only 4% owned by Canadians. Apparently, Lions Gate maintained its Canadian status because two thirds of its directors were Canadian. The then assistant Deputy Minister of Canadian Heritage, Jean-Pierre Blais, would not answer questions from Committee members on whether or not Lions Gate got tax credits for its investments in "Canadian" productions. But he did make it clear that the *Investment Canada Act* had been no real impediment to foreign purchases of cultural businesses. He and his deputy, Missy Marston-Shmelzer, testified that Canadian Heritage gets about 12 applications for such transactions every year, and since 1999 only three had been denied. When asked what constitutes a Canadian company, while acknowledging that in general the *Act* defines it as Canadians owning 50% plus one of a company's shares, Blais also made it clear that the *Act* concerns itself as well with definitions of de facto control which complicate matters. He said, "I think we would run out of time if I were to answer that, since there are only a few minutes left." Blais also said there is no explicit written policy that can be applied to foreign takeovers of Canadian newspapers—there are only implicit rules under the *Income Tax Act*. See: testimony of Jean-Pierre Blais, Standing Committee on Canadian Heritage, June 1, 2010.

366 See: "Last Words," by Steven Price, *Literary Review of Canada*, September 2016. See also: "Celebrated editor Ellen Seligman dies" by Mark Medley, *Globe and Mail*, March 25, 2016.

367 See: Joseph Seligman, Wikipedia.

368 Ibid, Mark Medley, March 25, 2016.

369 See: "Light in the wilderness," by Robert Potts, *theguardian.com*, April 26, 2003.

370 See: "Corporation Control: An Evolving Concept" by Jack Bernstein, Canadian Tax Foundation, 1995 at wwwctf.ca/ctfweb/Documents/PDF/1995, and Income Tax Folio, S1-F5-C1 "Related Persons and Dealing at Arm's Length, referring to Section 251 and 252 of the *Income Tax Act*, last modified 24 November, 2015.

371 See: announcement email of Tracy Turriff of Penguin Random House of July 18, 2016.

372 See: *Globe and Mail* hires Jared Bland as books editor, by Sue Carter, *Quill & Quire*, February 12, 2013.

373 See: undertakings 3 and 7 in Schedule A to Share Purchase Agreement between U of T and Random House dated December 30, 2011. Term of five years is in the preamble.

374 See: "Jared Bland named M&S publisher," by Conan Tobias, *Quill & Quire* July 18, 2016.

375 September 15, 2016, see CTV News, *Toronto Star*, *Vancouver Sun*, etc.

376 The book is called *Changer les règles du Jeu* and can be found on Amazon.ca.

377 See: "Liberal Budget Follows Through on Promise to Restore CBC Funding," by Stephanie Levitz, *Canadian Press*, March 22, 2016.

378 See: Canadian Heritage website with listing of Minister's expert advisory group. Three more names added on October 7, 2016.

379 See: Canadian independent music industry magazine *Cima*, report on cultural industries published at cimamusic.ca/9288.2.

380 "Personal Information

19(1) Subject to subsection (2), the head of a government institution shall refuse to disclose any record requested under this Act that contains personal information as defined in section 3 of the Privacy Act.

Advice, etc.

21(1) The head of a government institution may refuse to disclose any record requested under this Act that contains

(d) advice or recommendations developed by or for a government institution or a minister of the Crown,

(e) an account of consultations or deliberations in which directors, officers or employees of a government institution, a minister of the Crown or the staff of a minister participate,

(f) positions or plans developed for the purpose of negotiations carried on or to be carried on by or on behalf of the Government of Canada and considerations relating thereto, or

(g) plans relating to the management of personnel or the administration of a government institution that have not yet been put into operation, if the record came into existence less than twenty years prior to the request."

So I went to section 3 of the *Privacy Act* at laws-lois.Justice.gc.ca/eng/acts/p-21/page-1.html.

Section 3 is the definitions section of the *Act* that sets out what personal information under the *Act* is, and whether and in what circumstances it may be handed over to the public. Nothing in section 3 other than perhaps subsection c, applies to what I asked for, which was: the names of persons invited by the government to attend a public event, and the names of persons who actually attended along with their positions in particular cultural industries. Their phone numbers or addresses could be withheld under subsection c which demands the government protect the privacy of any "identifying number, symbol or other particulars assigned to the individual." But I ask you: does this include names, titles and Twitter handles of persons invited to Twitter at a live-streamed event? I don't think so.

Besides, section 8(1) says personal information under the control of that institution "shall not be disclosed by the institution except in accordance with this section…" (what follows are exemptions to the shall not which transform shall not into may)

> "(m) for any purpose where in the opinion of the head of the institution
>
> > (i) the public interest in disclosure clearly outweighs any invasion of privacy that could result from the disclosure, or
> >
> > (ii) Disclosure could clearly benefit the individual to whom it relates."

In other words, in the event that the information is already public (live-streamed on Facebook) the head of the institution was fully entitled to give the same information to a journalist.

381 See: MLB-Slaw. Selected Case Summaries: Information Commissioner (Can) v. Canada (Minister of National Defence…) 2011 SCC 25.

382 See: "Together we will rise from this darkness," by Sidhartha Banerjee, The Canadian Press as published in *Toronto Star,* February 3, 2017, p. A3.

383 I can't tell you what Michael Wernick, (a graduate of the U of T, I must point out), was thinking when he reviewed the gift/sale for approval by the Minister because he would not respond to requests for an interview. I made them through the Privy Council Office. I insisted that he must be given a chance to respond, but his media officials insisted no such interview would be granted. When I asked if anyone had put this request in front of Mr. Wernick personally, I was assured that all appropriate steps had been taken. Whatever that means.

384 Testimony of Jean-Pierre Blais, Standing Committee on Canadian Heritage, June 1, 2010.

385 Those figures are Statistics Canada's. Canadian Heritage puts forward different numbers. In it's Cultural Industries November 2015 document, available on its website, it says that in 2014–2015 the Book Fund "supported 6,349 new Canadian

authored titles by 247 Canadian-owned publishers" and that Fund recipients produced 7554 ebooks, an 85% increase over a five year period.

386 Please go to: http://www.ppforum.ca/publications/shattered-mirror-news-
democracy-and-trust-digital-age.

387 See: "Keeping Up with the Times," by Gabriel Snyder; "Robots Wrote this Story,"
by Joe Keohane, "Fake News Factory to the World," by Samanth Subramanian,
Wired, March, 2017.

Bibliography

Books

Bianco, Anthony. *The Reichmanns: Family, Faith, Fortune and the Empire of Olympia and York*. Toronto: Random House of Canada, 1997.

Cameron, Stevie. *On the Take: Crime, Corruption and Greed in the Mulroney Years*. Toronto: Macfarlane Walter & Ross, 1994.

Cameron, Stevie and Harvey Cashore. *The Last Amigo: Karlheinz Schreiber and the Anatomy of a Scandal*. Toronto: Macfarlane Walter & Ross, 2001.

Clarkson, Stephen and Christina McCall. *Trudeau and Our Times: Volume 1 The Magnificent Obsession*. Toronto: McClelland and Stewart Inc. 1990.

Dewar, Elaine. *Cloak of Green*. Toronto: James Lorimer & Company, Publishers, 1995.

Ibbitson, John. *Stephen Harper*. Toronto and New York: Signal/McClelland & Stewart, Penguin Random House, 2015.

MacSkimming, Roy. *The Perilous Trade: Book Publishing in Canada 1946–2006*. Toronto: McClelland & Stewart Ltd., 2007.

McDonald, Marci. *Yankee Doodle Dandy: Brian Mulroney and the American Agenda*. Toronto: Stoddart Publishing Co. Limited, 1995.

Newman, Peter C. The *Canadian Establishment: Volume Two*. Toronto: McClelland and Stewart Limited, 1981.

Newman, Peter C. *The Establishment Man: A Portrait of Power*. Toronto: McClelland and Stewart Limited, 1982.

Newman, Peter C. *Titans: How the New Canadian Establishment Seized Power*. Toronto: Penguin Books Canada Ltd., 1999.

Ross, Alexander. *The Traders: Inside Canada's Stock Markets*. Don Mills: Collins Publishers, 1984.

Sarlos, Andrew. *Fireworks: The Investment of a Lifetime.* Toronto: Key Porter Books Limited, 1993.

Smith, Cameron. *Unfinished Journey: The Lewis Family.* Toronto: Summerhill Press Ltd., 1989.

Articles, Papers, BlogPosts

Campbell, Neil, Jun Chao Meng and Francois Tougas, "Monopsony Power and the Relevance of the Sell-Side Market," Canadian Competition Law Review, Vol. 26, No.2, 2013.

Campbell, Neil, Jun Chao Meng, James Musgrove, and Francois Tougas, "Group Buying—A Canadian Case Study," The Antitrust Source, at www.antitrustsource.com, December, 2013.

Clifford, John F. and Sorcha O'Carroll, "Monopsony and Predatory Buying: The Canadian Landscape Is Wide Open." Paper presented at Competition Law Section of Canadian Bar Association Annual Conference, October 11–12, 2007, Gatineau, Quebec.

Nevlin, Shawn, Michael Kilby, Jon W. Leopold and Michel Gelinas, Stikeman Elliott LLP, "Canada: Foreign Investment in the Canadian Book Industry," last updated October 6, 2014.

Theriault, Chelsea, "First, Do No Harm; Five Years of Book-Industry Data Sharing With Booknet Canada Sales data." Project submitted in partial fulfillment of the requirements for the degree of Master of Publishing in the Faculty of Communication, Art and Technology, Simon Fraser University, Fall 2010.

Court Orders, Regulatory Decisions, Statements of Affairs, Registrations

Order of the Ontario Securities Commission: "In the matter of the Securities Act, R.S.O. 1990, c. S.5, as amended and in the matter of Chapters Inc. and Trilogy Retail Enterprises L.P." January 11, 2001.

Ruling of the Ontario Securities Commission: "In the matter of the Securities Act R.S.O. 1990. Chapter 466 and In the matter of Canwest Capital Corporation and in the matter of Onex Capital Corporation and Oncap Holding Corporation, (sections 73 and 99), March, 1986.

Ontario Superior Court of Justice Commercial List In the matter of an application under the Companies' Creditors Arrangement Act, R.S.C. 1985, c. C-43 And in the matter of a plan of compromise or Arrangement of General Publishing Co. Limited, General Distribution Services Limited, Stoddart Publishing Co. Limited, The Boston Mills Press Ltd., and House of Anansi Press Limited, The Honourable Mr. Justice Ground, Tuesday, April 30, 2002.

Statement of Affairs (Sec. 158) In the Matter of the Bankruptcy of General Distribution Services Limited, August 19, 2002.

Statement of Affairs (Sec. 158) In the Matter of the Bankruptcy of General Publishing Co. Limited, August 20, 2002.

Province of Ontario Financing Change Statement/2005/09/27 regarding McClelland & Stewart Ltd., filed by McMillan Binch Mendelsohn LLP with the Personal Property Security Registration Database under File Number FN # 619229727, expired on 2012/09/27.

Government Documents and Papers

Investing in the Future of Canadian Books: Review of the Revised Foreign Investment Policy in Book Publishing and Distribution, Discussion Paper, Department of Canadian Heritage, July, 2010.

Canadian Culture in a Global World: New Strategies for Culture and Trade, The Cultural Industries Sectoral Advisory Group on International Trade, February, 1999.

Book Publishing Industry Profile, Ontario Media Development Corporation, www.omdc.on.ca

Reports

Standing Committee on Canadian Heritage. "The Challenge of Change: A Consideration of the Canadian Book Industry," Clifford Lincoln, M.P. Chair, June, 2000.

Bennett Family Foundation. Annual reports for 2008–2013, Canada Revenue Agency, Charities Branch, CD-ROM.

Department of Canadian Heritage: Overview November 2015; Administration of the Investment Canada Act November 2015;

Cultural Industries November 2015; Cultural Affairs Sector November 2015; An Introduction to grants and contributions at Canadian Heritage, November 2015.

Evidence

Standing Committee on Access to Information, Privacy and Ethics:
Testimony of Nigel Wright, Tuesday, November 2, 2010.

Standing Committee on Canadian Heritage
Testimony on book publishing:
Tuesday, December 7, 1999.
Thursday, February 24, 2000.
Tuesday, February 29, 2000.
Thursday, March 2, 2000.
Thursday, April 13, 2000.
Tuesday, March 28, 2000.
Thursday, March 30, 2000.
Tuesday, May 9, 2000.
Tuesday, March 13, 2001.
Testimony on proposed purchase of Lions Gate:
Tuesday, June 1, 2010.
Thursday, June 3, 2010.
Testimony on newspapers and broadcasting:
Tuesday, February 23, 2016.

Access to Information and Freedom of Information and Protection of Privacy

Responses to requests under *Access to Information Act*
Request #1
Advice/Recommendation to Minister Moore, Issue-Enjeu Random House Canada Announcement regarding Its Acquisition of McClelland & Stewart, November 16, 2011.
Advice/Recommendation to Minister Moore, Issue-Random House

Canada Announcement Regarding Its Acquisition of McClelland & Stewart, January 4, 2012.

Advice/Recommendation to Minister Moore, January 4, 2012.

Advice/Recommendation to Minister Moore, Issue-Enjeu Random House of Canada Announcement Regarding Its Acquisition of McClelland & Stewart, January 20, 2012. Source: January 10, 2012 Announcement by Random House Canada.

Advice/Recommendation to Minister Moore, Issue-Enjeu Doubleday Canada and McClelland & Stewart merge into new publishing group, June 20, 2012. Source: National Post, June 20, 2012.

Untitled document labelled only Q & A.

Untitled document listing page numbers withheld under subsection 24(1) of the *Access to Information Act*.

Request #2

Untitled and unlabelled spreadsheet with headings as follows: names, category, email, table number, comments, Twitter handle, under 40, Aboriginal, Industry, Organization, Title/role as presented on CD-ROM.

Statement that pages 9–14 of an unlabelled document have been withheld pursuant to section 19(1) of the *Access to Information Act*.

Responses to requests under FIPPA

FIPPA #1

Request for Opinion Regarding First Plazas Inc. Gift of 75% of McClelland & Stewart Business to University of Toronto and Sale of Remaining 25% to Random House of Canada Ltd., June 2, 2000.

Memorandum to Members of the Business Board, University of Toronto: Agenda Item: 6. Proposed Gift, June 20, 2000.

Memorandum to President Robert Prichard Re: Transfer of a Majority Interest of McClelland & Stewart Ltd. to the University of Toronto by First Plazas Inc., June 20, 2000.

Letter from J. Robert S. Prichard, President, University of Toronto to Director of Investments, Department of Canadian Heritage, Attention Michael Wernick, re: McClelland & Stewart Ltd., June 21, 2000.

Letter from Minister of Canadian Heritage, Sheila Copps, to Mr. N. William C. Ross, Weir & Foulds, re: Request for an opinion under Section 37 of the *Investment Canada Act* regarding First Plazas Inc. gift of 75% of McClelland & Stewart Ltd. to University of Toronto and sale of remaining 25% to Random House of Canada Ltd., June 23, 2000.

University of Toronto News, "McClelland & Stewart Owner Donates Canadian Publishing House to University of Toronto," June 26, 2000. Contacts: Jane Stirling University of Toronto Public Affairs; Kelly Hechler Director of Publicity McClelland & Stewart, Kelly Duffin VP, Director of Communications, Random House of Canada.

Letter from Louis R. Charpentier, Secretary of the Governing Council, University of Toronto, to Professor J.R.S. Prichard, President, University of Toronto re: McClelland & Stewart gift to the University of Toronto, June 29, 2000.

Fax via Torys from J. Robert S. Prichard, President and Louis R. Charpentier, Secretary, Governing Council, University of Toronto to Director of Investments, Canadian Heritage, re: Opinion of the Minister Regarding the Acquisition of McClelland & Stewart Ltd. by the University of Toronto and Random House of Canada Ltd., June 30, 2000.

Agreement Between: First Plazas Inc. (the "Donor") and The Governing Council of the University of Toronto (the "University"), signed by J. Robert S. Prichard, President, University of Toronto, and Avie Bennett, First Plazas Inc., June 30, 2000.

Share Purchase Agreement between: First Plazas Inc., (the "Vendor") and Random House of Canada Ltd., (the "Purchaser") signed by First Plazas Inc., signing officer and John Neale (and one other) for Random House of Canada Ltd. 6:00 a.m. July 1, 2000.

Administrative Services and Financial Support Agreement between: McClelland & Stewart Ltd. and Random House of Canada Ltd., signed by Douglas M. Gibson, for McClelland & Stewart Ltd. and John Neale plus one other for Random House of Canada Ltd., July 1, 2000.

Unanimous Shareholder Agreement between: The Governing Council of the University of Toronto and Random House of

Canada Ltd. and McClelland & Stewart Ltd. and First Plazas Inc., signed by Wendy M. Cecil-Cockwell, Chairman, and Louis R. Charpentier, Secretary of the Governing Council, John B. Neale, Chairman and Douglas A. Foot, Chief Operating Officer Random House of Canada Ltd., Douglas M. Gibson, President McClelland & Stewart Ltd., and Avie Bennett, President First Plazas Inc., July 1, 2000.

Certificate of McClelland & Stewart Ltd. regarding transfer of 7500 common shares to University of Toronto as a deed of gift and transfer of 2500 common shares to Random House of Canada from the capital of the corporation from First Plazas Inc. has been approved, as signed by the sole shareholder of the Corporation, signed by Douglas M. Gibson, President of McClelland & Stewart Ltd., July 1, 2000.

Transitional Services Agreement between First Plazas Inc., and McClelland & Stewart Ltd. and Random House of Canada Ltd. signed by Avie J. Bennett, President First Plazas Inc., and Douglas Gibson, President, McClelland & Stewart Ltd., and by John Neale, Chairman, Random House of Canada and Douglas A. Foot, Chief Operating officer, Executive Vice-president and Secretary, Random House of Canada Ltd., July 1, 2000.

Authorization Form Number 2, Date July 10, 2000, Authorization on behalf of the Governing Council Under Summer Executive Authority, recommended by Louis B. Charpentier, approved on behalf of Governing Council, President Robert J. Birgenau, Chairman Wendy M. Cecil-Cockwell.

Interoffice Memorandum from Tad W. Brown to Donald Lindsey and copies to Robert Birgenau, Jon Dellandrea, Robert White, Louis Charpentier, re McClelland & Stewart Shart Certificate, July 11, 2000.

Letter from Neil Dobbs, Assistant Secretary of Governing Council, University of Toronto to Robert J. Birgeneau, President, University of Toronto, re McClelland & Stewart Gift, July 19, 2000.

News @U of T, "Major Canadian publishing house donated to U of T: Owner Bennett acts to ensure McClelland & Stewart's future," by Jane Stirling. June 26, 2000.

Memorandum from Ronald W. Scott, BA, CA, CBV, Ernst & Young Corporate Finance Inc. to W.G. Tad Brown, LLB., Finance and Development Counsel, University of Toronto, re: Fair Market Value of Shares of McClelland & Stewart Ltd. Donated to the University of Toronto, August 4, 2000.

Interoffice Memorandum from W. G. Tad Brown, Finance & Development Counsel, University of Toronto to Susana Gajic, copy to Rivi Frankle, re: Tax Receipt for Donation of Shares of McClelland & Stewart Ltd. September 12, 2000.

Letter from W.G. Tad Brown, Finance and Development Counsel, University of Toronto, to Avie Bennett, First Plazas Inc., copies to Jon Dellandrea and Rivi Frankle, re: chartiable tax receipt of $15,900,000, September 26, 2000.

Letter from W.G. Tad Brown, Financial and Development Counsel, University of Toronto, to Avie Bennett, First Plazas Inc., re: copy enclosed of original valuation report prepared by Ernst & Young, October 4, 2000.

Certificate issued by The University of Toronto Campaign, official receipt for income tax purposes to First Plazas Inc., for $15,900,000 for 7,500 McClelland & Stewart shares. Receipt Number 176352. Date received: July 1, 2000; date issued September 21, 2000. Appraiser: Ronald W. Scott, Ernst & Young Corporate Finance Inc.

Letter from Avie Bennett, Chairman, McClelland & Stewart Ltd., to W. G. Tad Brown, Finance and Development Counsel, University of Toronto, October 5, 2000.

Letter from Andrew Drummond, Secretary of the Executive Committee (University of Toronto) to The Honourable Frank Iacobucci, Interim President, University of Toronto, re: External Appointments: McClelland &Stewart Ltd., copies to Dr. Avie Bennett, Chair, McClelland & Stewart Ltd. and Ms. Catherin Riggall, Vice-President, Business Affairs, March 16, 2005.

Letter from Henry Mulhall, Secretary of the Executive Committee, to Professor David Naylor, President, University of Toronto, re: external appointments: McClelland & Stewart Ltd., copies to Dr.

Avie Bennett, Chair, McClelland & Stewart Ltd., Ms. Catherine Riggall, Vice-President, Business Affairs, April 28, 2006.

Memorandum from Helen Choy, Manager, Accounting Services, Office of the Vice-President, Business Affairs-Financial Services, to Pierre Piché, Controller & Director, Financial Services Department, re: Investment write-down for McClelland & Stewart Ltd., April 26, 2006.

Emails between Helen Choy, Pierre Piché and Catherine Riggall, dated October 23, 2007, October 24, 2007, May 1, 2008.

Letter from Henry Mulhall, Secretary of the Executive Committee, Governing Council, to Professor David Naylor, President, University of Toronto, re: External Appointment: McClelland & Stewart Ltd. (appointment of Ms. Trina McQueen) copies to Dr. Avie Bennett, Chair, McClelland & Stewart Ltd., and Ms. Catherine Riggall, Vice-President, Business Affairs, December 1, 2006.

Letter from Henry Mulhall, Secretary of the Executive Committee, Governing Council to Professor David Naylor, President University of Toronto, re: External Appointments: McClelland & Stewart Ltd.,copies to Dr. Avie Bennett, Chair, McClelland and Stewart Ltd., and Ms. Catherine Riggall, Vice-President, Business Affairs, March 13, 2007.

Letter from Henry Mulhall, Secretary of the Executive Committee, Governing Council to Professor David Naylor, President, University of Toronto, re: External Appointment: Directors, McClelland and Stewart Ltd., copies to Dr. Avie Bennett, Chair, McClelland & Stewart Ltd., and Ms. Catherine Riggall, Vice-President, Business Affairs, March 17, 2008.

Letter from Henry Mulhall, Secretary of the Executive Committee, Governing Council to Professor David Naylor, President University of Toronto Re: External Appointments: Directors, McClelland & Stewart Ltd., copies to Dr. Avie Bennett, Chair, McClelland & Stewart Ltd., and Ms. Catherine Riggall, Vice-President, Business Affairs, February 17, 2000.

Letter from Henry Mulhall, Secretary of the Executive Committee to Professor David Naylor, President University of Toronto re:

External Appointments: Directors, McClelland and Stewart Ltd. copies to Dr. Avie Bennett, Chair, McClelland and Stewart Ltd., Ms. Catherine Riggall, Vice-President, Business Affairs, March 3, 2010.

Letter from Henry Mulhall, Secretary of the Executive Committee Governing Council to Professor David Naylor, President University of Toronto re: External Appointments: Directors, McClelland and Stewart Ltd,. copies to Dr. Avie Bennett, Chair, McClelland and Stewart Ltd., Ms. Catherine Riggall, Vice-President, Business Affairs, March 15, 2011.

Letter from Catherine J. Riggall, Vice-President, Business Affairs, University of Toronto to Ms. Missy Marston-Shmelzer, Director Cultural Sector Investment Review, Canadian Heritage, re: Proposed Disposition of the University of Toronto's Shares in McClelland & Stewart Ltd., July 4, 2011.

Letter from Catherine J. Riggall, Vice-President, Business Affairs, University of Toronto to Ms. Missy Marston-Shmelzer, Director Cultural Sector Investment Review Canadian Heritage, re: Proposed Disposition of the University of Toronto's shares in McClelland & Stewart Ltd. July 6, 2011.

Email from David Naylor, President University of Toronto to Brad Martin, CEO, Random House of Canada, September 26, 2011.

Email from Brad Martin, CEO Random House of Canada, to David Naylor, President, University of Toronto, September 26, 2011.

Waiver from First Plazas Inc., Avie Bennett, to The Governing Council, University of Toronto, re: Deed of Gift, waiving all conditions, requirements and obligations of U of T under the Agreement of June 30, 2000, December 15, 2011.

Editorial *Toronto Star*: "Canadian writing enjoys a golden age despite takeover of McClelland & Stewart," January 13, 2012.

Letter to Editor *Toronto Star*, "Bennett's efforts deserve praise," re: Canada's golden age of literature, Editorial Jan. 14, by David Naylor, President, University of Toronto, Jan. 19, 2012.

Asset Purchase Agreement between: First Plazas Inc. and McClelland & Stewart Ltd. Signed by Avie Bennett for First Plazas Inc. and Douglas M. Gibson for McClelland & Stewart Ltd. At 12:01 a.m. July 1, 2000.

Share Purchase Agreement among: Random House of Canada Limited ("Buyer") and the Governing Council of University of Toronto ("Seller") and McClelland & Stewart Ltd. ("the Company") signed by Brad Martin, CEO and Douglas Foot, Chief Financial Officer or Random House of Canada Limited, and Catherine J. Riggall, Vice-President, Business Affairs for the Governing Council of University of Toronto and Brad Martin Director and Douglas Foot, Director of McClelland & Stewart Ltd. December 30, 2011. Attachments include: consent of Minister of Canadian Heritage signed November 14, 2011; letter of Bradley Martin, President and Chief Executive Officer Random House of Canada Limited to Ms. Missy Marston-Shmelzcr, Director Cultural Sector Investment Review re: Proposed Increase in the Random House of Canada Limited ("RHC") ownership interest in McClelland and Stewart Ltd. ("M&S") dated October 11, 2011, stating M&S business in distress for some years and no Canadians prepared to buy it, and including Schedule A "Undertakings. "

Email from David Naylor to Cathy Riggall and Judith Wolfson dated September 1, 2011.

Email from Cathy Riggall to David Naylor and Judith Wolfson dated September 6, 2011.

Email from David Naylor to Cathy Riggall and Judith Wolfson dated September 7, 2011.

Email from Cathy Riggall to David Naylor, copy to Judith Wolfson, dated September 7, 2011.

Email from David Naylor to Cathy Riggall, copy to Judith Wolfson, dated 7 September, 2011.

Email from David Naylor to Brad Martin, CEO Random House of Canada, copies to Michael Kurts, Laurie Stephens, Judith Wolfson, Cathy Riggall, dated September 26, 2011.

Email from Brad Martin to David Naylor, copies to Michael Kurts, Laurie Stephens, Judith Wolfson, Cathy Riggall.

Responses to FIPPA #2
Non-consolidated Statement of Income and Retained Earnings, McClelland & Stewart Ltd. for the period from June 8, 2000 to December 31, 2000, PriceWaterhouse Coopers.

Non-Consolidated Statement of Operations and Retained Earnings (Deficit) for the year ended December 31, 2001, with comparative figures for the period from June 8, 2000 (date of inception) to December 31, 2000, McClelland & Stewart Ltd.

Non-Consolidated Statement of Operations and Deficit Year ended December 31, 2002 with comparative figures for 2001, McClelland & Stewart Ltd.

Non-Consolidated Statement of Operations and Deficit Year ended December 31, 2003 with comparative figures for 2002, McClelland & Stewart Ltd.

Non-Consolidated Statement of Operations and Deficit Year ended December 31, 2004, with comparative figures for 2003, McClelland & Stewart Ltd.

Non-Consolidated Financial Statements of McClelland & Stewart Ltd. Year ended Dec. 31, 2005, Draft #7, April 4, 2006.

Amendment No. 1 Unanimous Shareholder Agreement Between: The Governing Council University of Toronto and Random House of Canada Ltd., and McClelland & Stewart Ltd. And First Plazas Inc. signed by Catherine Riggall for Governing Council University of Toronto, John Neale for Random House of Canada, Doug Pepper for McClelland & Stewart Ltd. and Avie Bennett for First Plazas Inc., April 1, 2004.

Interoffice Memorandum from Tad Brown, Finance & Development Counsel University of Toronto to Felix Chee re: McClelland & Stewart, November 18, 2003.

Certificate from McClelland & Stewart Ltd. directors, Brad Martin and Douglas Foot, to the Governing Council University of Toronto and to Random House of Canada Limited re: share purchase agreement between University, Random House and McClelland & Stewart, December 30, 2011 with attachments, copy of the articles of amalgamation and bylaws, including certificate of amalgamation between McClelland & Stewart Ltd. and Macfarlane, Walter & Ross, signed by Douglas Pepper, President and Publisher McClelland & Stewart and Douglas Pepper, President and Publisher Macfarlane, Walter & Ross, dated July 1, 2004; statement of Director or Officer, signed by Douglas Pepper,

June 15, 2004, for McClelland & Stewart; statement of Director or Officer, signed by Douglas Pepper, June 15, 2004 for Macfarlane, Walter & Ross; Certified copy of the Resolution of the Board of Directors of McClelland & Stewart Ltd., signed by Douglas Pepper and dated June 15, 2004; certified copy of the resolution of the board of directors of Macfarlane, Walter & Ross, signed by Douglas Pepper and dated June 15, 2004; resignation of Connie Fullerton sent to McClelland & Stewart Ltd. and to the Board of Directors and Members of the Corporation, dated May 3, 2005 and finally: Bylaw No. 1 of McClelland & Stewart Ltd. adopted on amalgamation on July 1, 2004, but enacted on June 8, 2000 and signed by Douglas Gibson, President.

Offering Memorandum and Reorganization Documents

Confidential Private Offering memorandum Onex Capital Corporation and Oncap Holding Corporation, February 3, 1986.

In the Matter of the Securities Act R.S.O 1980, Chapter 466 and In the Matter of Canwest Capital Corporation and In the Matter of Onex Captial Corporation and Oncap Holding Corporation, Ruling.

Selected Newspaper and Magazine Articles

Anderson, Scott. "Avie (Bennett)'s Master Stroke," *Quill & Quire*, August, 2000.

Bagli, Charles V. "Trump Built His Empire as King of the Tax Break," *The New York Times*, September 18, 2016.

Barber, John. "Simon & Schuster gets green light to publish Canadian books domestically," *Globe and Mail*, May 29, 2013.

Bastien, Laurent. "The developer, the fugitive and the feud," *Globe and Mail*, July 9, 2016.

Bennett, Avie. "Random Thoughts," *Toronto Life*, November, 2003.

Bethune, Brian. "Giving Away the Store: Avie Bennett's unprecedented donation of industry icon, McClelland & Stewart brings praise—and a storm of criticism," *Maclean's*, July 10, 2000.

Bland, Jared. "Why the head of mega-publisher Penguin Random House is a man with a mission," *Globe and Mail*, July 21, 2013

Bradshaw, James. "Postmedia cuts deal to reduce debt load," *Globe and Mail,* Report on Business, July 8, 2016.

Bradshaw, James. "Star crossed," *Globe and Mail* Report on Business, January 21, 2017.

Bradshaw, James, Tim Kiladze. "Top Postmedia shareholder seeks to sell," *Globe and Mail,* March 15, 2016.

Brown, Ian. "Home away from home," *Globe and Mail,* July 2, 2016.

Burton, Charles. "Visit to China is tricky for Trudeau: Ottawa wants a 'more balanced' relationship with Beijing, but is that realistic?" *Globe and Mail,* Opinion, A11, August 24, 2016.

Byers, Michael. "Is Canada's national security now for sale?" *Globe and Mail,* Opinion, A13, January 25, 2017.

Campion-Smith, Bruce. "Shrinking media a 'worrisome' trend: Business model is at risk, Torstar chair tells MPs studying state of business," *Toronto Star,* A8, September 30, 2016.

Chase, Steven. "No national reviews on foreign takeovers raise fears Liberals are loosening controls," *Globe and Mail,* A4, January 28, 2016.

Chase, Steven. "CSIS, DND warned Ottawa on China deal," *Globe and Mail,* A1, January 23, 2017.

Chase, Steven. "Chinese group buying stake in health care chain: if approved by Ottawa, purchase of B.C.-based retirement home operator would give Anbang a role in province's deliver system," *Globe and Mail,* A1, November 28, 2016.

Chown Oved, Marco. "How a Quebec firm hid millions from tax," Panama Papers, *Toronto Star,* A10, January 25, 2017.

Chown Oved, Marco. "White collar criminals find home in Canada: new report says lax corporate disclosure rules make it easy to hide ill-gotten gains," *Toronto Star,* A22, December 10, 2016.

Cryderman, Kelly. "Enbridge, Spectra reach $37-billion deal," *Globe and Mail,* Report on Business, September 7, 2016.

Dolski, Megan. "Order of Canada welcomes dozens of new members," *Toronto Star,* September 24, 2016.

Dougherty, Michael Brendan. "The telling seeds of Trump's ascent," *Globe and Mail,* Opinion, August 27, 2016.

Everett-Green, Robert. "Heritage Minister learns from Tory mistake," *Globe and Mail,* April 30, 2016.

Editorial. "Let's be clear on Can-Con," *Toronto Star*, September 7, 2016.

Doyle, John. "Rethinking Cancon: Welcome to a new nightmare," *Globe and Mail*, April 28, 2016.

Doyle, Simon. "Appointed by the PM to rein in the PM Michael Wernick, new Clerk of the Privy Council, promises to bring rigour to the way patronage appointments are handed out," *Globe and Mail*, February 13, 2016.

Faiola, Anthony and Stephanie Kirchner. "Language of Nazism revived in Germany: Long-taboo terms defended under guise of free speech as nationalist feelings surge," *The Washington Post* as carried in *Toronto Star*, World, A8, December 11, 2016.

Ferguson, Rob. "Metrolinx errors and delays cost taxpayers millions: report," *Toronto Star*, A16, December 1, 2016.

Fife, Robert, Steven Chase. "Trudeau defends fundraiser as effort to encourage investment from China," *Globe and Mail*, A1, November 23, 2016.

Fife, Robert, Laura Stone. "Duffy makes 'subdued' return to Hill," *Globe and Mail*, May 3, 2016.

Fingleton, Eamonn. "Nazi Atrocities, Modern Germany's Silence, and a Hidden Threat to American Intellectual Independence," *Forbes*, Business, June 22, 2014.

Foran, Charles. "Searching for a Canada of the soul, not the census," *Globe and Mail*, June 18, 2016.

Freeman, Sunny. "A front seat to a changing industry: Torstar president Holland to retire," July 7, 2016.

Grewal, San. "Metrolinx to fix bus station built close to homes," *Toronto Star*, March 28, 2016.

Hall, Alan. "Revealed: How the Nazis helped German companies Bosch, Mercedes, Deutsche Bank and VW get VERY rich using 300,000 concentration camp slaves," *Mail Online*, June 20, 2014.

Hardach, Sophie. "Liz Mohn, the woman behind Penguin Random House," the *Telegraph*, December 13, 2012.

Healy, Patrick. "'Brexit Revolt Cast Shadow on Clinton Caution," The *New York Times*, June 26, 2016.

Hebert, Chantal. "When do media woes become public policy?" *Toronto Star*, A8, January 21, 2016.

Hennessey, Kathleen. "Obama orders review of U.S. election hacking," Associated Press as it appeared in *Globe and Mail*, December 10, 2016.

Hodd, Thomas. "Literary award nominations point to our inferiority complex," *Globe and Mail*, October 12, 2015.

Honderich, John. "Get your facts straight, Paul," *Toronto Star*, Opinion, A13, January 27, 2016.

Houpt, Simon. "Robert Lantos, then and now," *Globe and Mail*, June 11, 2016.

Ibbitson, John. "The peaceable kingdom in an increasingly populist world," *Globe and Mail*, July 2, 2016.

Karimi, Nasser. "Former Iranian president dead at 82," *Globe and Mail*, A5, January 9, 2017.

Keohane, Joe. "Robots Wrote This Story," *Wired*, March, 2017.

Khan, Sheema. "Fifty years in Canada, and now I feel second-class," *Globe and Mail*, Opinion, A15, October 7, 2015.

Kopun, Francine. "Indigo's next chapter includes chainwide refresh," *Toronto Star*, July 7, 2016.

Lawson, Guy. "North Star: As Canada's new prime minister, Justin Trudeau looks to restore his father's legacy," *New York Times Magazine*, December 13, 2015.

Leblanc, Daniel. "Former CRTC head backs Cancon review '...we have to rethink how we foster Canadian content,' von Finkenstein says following Heritage Minister Joly's announcement," *Globe and Mail*, April 26, 2016.

Leblanc, Daniel. "Canada leads charge to force Web giants to boost local fare," *Globe and Mail*, A13, December 12, 2016

Leblanc, Daniel. "Google opposes tax change to Canadian Web advertising," *Globe and Mail*, A 4, January 26, 2017

Leblanc, Daniel. "Foreign firms seen to have unfair advantage over Cancon," *Globe and Mail*, May 7, 2016

Leblanc, Daniel. "Sweeping Cancon review in the works: changes to Canada's cultural policies would be first major overhaul in decades, reports Daniel Leblanc. "Everything is on the table,' Heritage Minister Mélanie Joly says," *Globe and Mail*, April 23, 2016.

Leblanc, Daniel, James Bradshaw, "The Challenge of Reshaping Canada's Cultural Landscape," *Globe and Mail*, May 2, 2016.

Lederman, Marsha. "Watching, and editing, the detectives: How the late, legendary editor Ellen Seligman helped novelist Steve Price shape, and reshape, his epic mystery, By Gaslight," *Globe and Mail*, R2, August 27, 2016.

Levin, Dan. "Chinese in Canada Feel the Chill of Beijing's Reach," *The New York Times*, August 28, 2016.

Lewis, Michael. "Rogers reduces production of several magazines: *Sportsnet, Maclean's, Flare* and *Chatelaine* among those hit by media overhaul," *Toronto Star*, A6, October 1, 2016.

Lewis, Michael. "Ottawa noncommittal on new digital taxes," *Toronto Star*, Business, January 11, 2017.

Lewis, Michael. "Paul Godfrey wants more foreign ownership: source," *Toronto Star*, Business, p. B1, January 30, 2016.

Lewis, Michael. "Joly declares 2017 year of CanCon exports," *Toronto Star*, Business, GT8, February 14, 2017.

Livesay, Bruce. "The man who brought Canadian newspapers to their knees...is now a member of the Canadian News Hall of Fame," *Toronto Star*, IN1, November 28, 2015.

Lu, Vanessa. "Postmedia to shed 20% of salary expenses," *Toronto Star*, A2, October 21, 2016.

MacKinnon, Mark. "The Global Reboot," *Globe and Mail*, Focus, January 21, 2017.

Martin, Lawrence. "A crisis that cries out for a public inquiry," *Globe and Mail*, February 2, 2016.

Martin, Lawrence. "NDP's Leap is the Waffle reborn," *Globe and Mail*, April 12, 2016.

McCarthy, Shawn. "OEB considers Spectra review," *Globe and Mail*, Report on Business, September 9, 2016.

McFarland, Janet. "The CEOs who cashed in as their companies cut back," *Globe and Mail*, June 4, 2016.

McFarland, Janet. "Surging pay for directors draws criticism: companies paying more to attract top talent, but scrutiny of compensation lacking," *Globe and Mail*, November 28, 2016.

McMahon, Tamsin. "Competition Bureau targets condominium renovation industry in criminal probe," *Globe and Mail*, May 26, 2016.

Medley, Mark. "Exclusive book offer awaits Canada," *Globe and Mail*, March 5, 2016.

Medley, Mark. "Celebrated editor Ellen Seligman dies," *Globe and Mail*, March 25, 2016.

Medley, Mark. "A mentor to literary stars dies," *Globe and Mail*, March 26, 2016.

Medley, Mark. "Two Canadians shortlisted for prestigious literary award," *Globe and Mail*, September 14, 2016.

Mendes, Errol. "Senate Cleansing is under way, and overdue," Opinion, *Globe and Mail*, May 3,2016.

Mullin,Joe. "Top Nazi's estate owed copyright royalties by biographer, German court rules: German court orders Random House to pay relatives of former top Nazi," *Ars Technica*, July 13, 2015.

Olive, David. "Good Reviews: Despite Putdowns and Nasty Rumours, Avie Bennett and Adrienne Clarkson may yet be the Best Thing to Happen to the Incestuous Universe of Canadian Books, An Unexpected First Reading," *Toronto Life*, June, 1988.

Olive, David. "As long as it continues to live, Postmedia is blight to readers," *Toronto Star*, Business, p. B1, January 30, 2016.

Olive, David. "There is a cancer on Canadian journalism," the *Star. com*, January 30, 2016.

Palango, Paul. "The Bull of Toro Road: Mystery developer Marco Muzzo knows how to use both wealth and clout—just ask the Premier," *Globe and Mail*, October, 1989.

Pedwell, Terry. "New report investigates Canada's media crisis," *The Canadian Press* carried in *Toronto Star*, A2, January 26, 2017.

Perreaux, Les, Tu Thanh Ha. "Charges reach Quebec's highest ranks," *Globe and Mail*, March 18, 2016.

Posner, Michael. "Mister Wright," *The Walrus*, September 12, 2012.

Ross, Alexander. "The LBO is Dead: Gerry Schwartz built Onex on LBOs—can he rise above its legacy of leverage?" *Canadian Business*, December 1989.

Sagan, Aleksandra. "Postmedia proposes debt-reduction plan," *The Canadian Press* as carried in *Toronto Star*, July 8, 2016.

Saunders, Doug. "In 1967, change could no longer be stopped," *Globe and Mail*, Folio: Canada 150, p. A6, January 2, 2017.

Schuler, Thomas. "A New Leading Lady: Bertelsmann owner Reinhard Mohn decides who is next in line," *The Atlantic Times*, October, 2008.

Semeniuk, Ivan. "Elite celebrate Maurice Strong's role at UN: ceremony pays tribute to the diplomat who melded environment with development and brought world leaders together," *Globe and Mail*, A10, January 28, 2016.

Siekierska, Alicja. "The campaign to keep Canadian content alive: Heritage Minister visits T.O. as part of mission to support homegrown art in digital age," *Toronto Star*, GT5, October 13, 2016.

Snyder, Gabriel. "Keeping Up With the Times," *Wired*, March 2017.

Spector, Norman. "The best thing you'll read today on Nigel Wright," Special to *Globe and Mail*, November 3, 2010.

Star Staff. "Torstar announces plans to lay off more than 50 staff," *Toronto Star*, A2, August 10, 2016.

Stead, Sylvia. "A Parliamentary committee to save the news? Good luck with that," *Toronto Star*, February 27, 2016.

Steward, Gillian. "Postmedia cuts more bad news for Alberta," *Toronto Star*, Opinion, A15, January 26, 2016.

Subramanian, Samanth. "Welcome to Veles, Macedonia, Fake News Factory to the World," *Wired*, March, 2017.

Tait, Carrie. "Strange bedfellows in Alberta: once bitter rivals, Postmedia's Calgary Sun-Calgary Herald merger signals more than just a media corporation's financial struggles," *Globe and Mail*, A6, January 23, 2016.

Taylor, Kate. "Broadcasting the future, one think tank at a time," *Globe and Mail*, May 28, 2016.

Taylor, Kate. "To tell, and sell, Canadian stories," *Globe and Mail*, May 7, 2016.

Taylor, Kate. "Quality isn't enough: Canadian arts content needs government support," February 24, 2017.

Taylor, Kate. "Long on good intentions and short on coherent planning." *Globe and Mail*, April 30, 2016.

Taylor, Kate. "Cows and cars, but never culture," *Globe and Mail*, October 10, 2015.

Tomlinson, Kathy. "Dozens of real estate firms run afoul of money-laundering law," *Globe and Mail*, March 18, 2016.

Toughill, Kelly. "Does democracy need newspapers? Not so much," *Toronto Star*, IN6, January 28, 2016.

Unifor, The Union/le syndicat. "Minister, it's on our watch," letter to Minister Mélanie Joly appearing as an advertisement in *Globe and Mail*, A6, October 12, 2016.

VanderKilppe, Nathan. "PM shows readiness to bolster ties by joining Chinese-led bank," *Globe and Mail*, A1, August 31, 2016.

VanderKlippe, Nathan, and Sunny Dhillon. "China charges Canadian with spying, stealing state secrets," *Globe and Mail*, 1, January 29, 2016.

VanderKlippe, Nathan. "The Global Reboot," Focus, *Globe and Mail*, January 21, 2017.

Watson, Thomas. "Interview: Prichard the Third," *Canadian Business Magazine*, April 8, 2011.

Wong, Tony. "Keeping Canadian TV Canadian: Should Shonda Rhimes or Vince Gilligan get Canadian money to make TV in this country? Critics say new CRTC rules would allow exactly that," *Toronto Star*, E1, September 4, 2016.

Wood, Allan. "Sending Quebec culture out into the world," *Toronto Star*, E4, October 15, 2016.

Word for Word. Bennett on Books, *Maclean's*, September 27, 1999.

Yardley, Jim, Alison Smale, June Perlez, Ben Hubbard. "Britain rattles postwar order," *The New York Times*, June 26, 2016.

Younglai, Rachelle. "The Canadian banker taking Alibaba to the world: former Goldman Sachs executive Michael Evans helped shepherd the first big privatization of a Chinese state company. Now, he's helping the Chinese e-commerce giant double transaction volumes to $1-trillion," *Globe and Mail*, Report on Business, B6, September 10, 2016.

Index